COYOTE STORIES

International Journal of American Linguistics

NATIVE AMERICAN TEXTS SERIES

Eric P. Hamp, Series Editor

Alma Dean Kolb, Managing Editor

The following *IJAL-NATS* monographs are available *on demand* from University Microfilms International:

No. 1. *Coyote Stories*, edited by William Bright (1978)

NATIVE AMERICAN TEXTS SERIES

COYOTE STORIES

Edited by
William Bright

IJAL-NATS Monograph No. 1, 1978

THE UNIVERSITY OF CHICAGO PRESS

Published through the Imprint Series,
Monograph Publishing on Demand.
Produced and distributed by
University Microfilms International
Ann Arbor, Michigan 48106

Library of Congress Cataloging in Publication Data

Coyote stories.

(The IJAL-NATS monographs ; no. 1) (Monograph publishing on demand : Imprint series)
At head of title: International journal of American linguistics. Native American texts series.
Includes bibliographical references.
1. Indians of North America–Legends. 2. Indians of North America–California–Legends. 3. Coyotes–Legends and stories. 4. Trickster. I. Bright, William, 1928-
II. Series.

E98.F6C83 398.2'09794 78-5927
ISBN 0-226-36713-4

The *IJAL Native American Texts Series* was established to disseminate and preserve representative segments of Amerindian language and literature. As a medium for the spoken and written voices of native Americans, the *Series* considers for publication texts in all languages indigenous to North, Middle, and South America. Selections are limited neither by form nor content and include myths, tales, rituals, and fiction, as well as personal narratives, descriptions of daily life, correspondence, and other casual texts.

Material for publication should be sent to Professor Eric P. Hamp, Department of Linguistics, University of Chicago, 5845 So. Ellis Avenue, Chicago, Illinois 60637. An *IJAL Native American Texts Series* style sheet, including detailed instructions for authors on the preparation of text materials, may be obtained from Alma Dean Kolb, University of Chicago Press, 5801 So. Ellis Avenue, Chicago, Illinois 60637. Contributors are encouraged to study this style sheet before submitting text material.

In 1978, the University of Chicago Press, in cooperation with University Microfilms International, began publishing the *IJAL Native American Texts Series* on demand as a regular series of monographs. The monographs are produced and distributed *on demand* by University Microfilms on an individual order rather than a subscription basis (with a 10% discount on standing orders). For order information and price schedules, please write University Microfilms International, 300 No. Zeeb Road, Ann Arbor, Michigan 48106.

CONTENTS

Coyote Stories

Monograph No. 1, 1978

The cover design for this monograph was drawn by Leanne Hinton, University of Texas, Dallas.

INTRODUCTION

"The sheepmen complain, it is true, that the coyotes eat some of their lambs. This is true, but do they eat enough? I mean, enough lambs to keep the coyotes sleek, healthy and well fed. That is my concern." (Abbey 1968:31)

The biological coyote, Canis latrans, is native to Western North America and Meso-America, ranging from the Pacific Northwest to Mexico. The mythic Coyote, often known as "Old Man Coyote", is perhaps the most conspicuous figure in the oral literatures of the Native American peoples in the same area. This collection will illustrate the facets of Old Man Coyote's personality: divinity, creator, lawgiver, trickster, buffoon, and victim.

Why are the Coyote stories of the Native American peoples so popular, not only among those peoples themselves, but also among whites who have had the chance to hear them? It seems to me that the oral literature about Coyote brings together two irresistible sets of forces, one from biology and one from human culture. On the biological side, it is clear that Canis latrans is an exceptionally gifted and fascinating animal; his intelligence and ingenuity have made him legendary even among the Anglo-American and Spanish-American newcomers on this continent, and have in fact made him the subject of several popular books (Barclay 1938, Dobie 1949, Van Wormer 1964, Ryden 1975, Leydet 1977). Furthermore, his adaptability has enabled him to prosper following white settlement, in an ever-broader geographical domain--Alaska, the eastern United States, and Central America--and in urban areas as well (Gill 1970). Simultaneously, on the cultural side, we can recognize the world-wide popularity and importance in myth of the Trickster personage (Radin 1956): the supernatural figure who creates and is destroyed, who cheats and is ultimately cheated--who surpasses all others in intelligence, but finally "outsmarts himself". In parts of Native North America, the mythic Trickster role is played by Raven, by Hare, by Spider, or by other characters; but in those areas where Canis latrans thrives--and perhaps in Native California above all--the role of trickster par excellence has been neatly filled by Old Man Coyote.

My own feelings, in undertaking to edit a collection of Coyote stories, are of great personal satisfaction. I was first introduced to Old Man Coyote in 1949, by the Karok Indians of northwestern California; and some of my Karok friends did me the ambiguous honor of naming me Pihnê·fič--"Coyote", in their language. I became a fan, and was glad to find several subsequent opportunities to get Karok Coyote stories into print (Bright 1954, 1957, 1972, 1978). But starting around the same time, Old Man Coyote was also beginning to make his appearance in original poetry and prose by Anglo-American authors, especially Gary Snyder. A journal of new writing, published since 1970, is called Coyote's Journal. The present collection will, I hope, make Coyote even better known to readers, whether they are Native or transplanted Americans, who are interested in American Indian language, culture, and literature.

The stories published here are arranged from north to south; they come from the Plateau, California, Southwestern, and Meso-American culture areas, in that order. No claim can be made that this collection is fully representative: because of various accidents, I was unable to obtain texts from the Northwest Coast, from the Great Basin, or from the Plains--and Meso-America is only sparsely represented here. Yet I may not be completely biased, as a Californian and a Californianist, in believing that we see Coyote at his most complex and most interesting in texts from the Plateau and from Native California. In these stories we meet Coyote in his role as one of the First People--the primeval inhabitants of the earth, somehow human yet non-human in form, who bore names like Bear and Deer and Crane. Among these, Coyote above all foresaw the Great Change, when Humankind would spring into existence and the First People would be transformed into the animals we know today. It is Coyote above all who is responsible for how things are to be in the new age: animals will have their present form; human beings will have to work for a living; when people die, they will not return to life. At the same time, Coyote provides a "horrible example" of how people should NOT behave; he breaks every taboo, and frequently "dies" as a result--but regularly re-appears for new escapades.

A legitimate question which can be raised about this collection is: do "Coyote stories" really constitute a distinctive, unified class? It is true that the same adventures which are here ascribed to Coyote are sometimes attributed to other tricksters, even in California; and it is true that as one moves toward Meso-America, one finds Coyote less often as the trickster-creator, and more often as the trickster-dupe, in stories that echo Old World themes blended with those of Native America. Yet there seems to me something distinctive, over a wide area, about the fusion of the universal Trickster personality with that of <u>Canis latrans</u>. From the range of behavior displayed in the stories below, readers can begin to decide, for themselves, what Coyote means to them.

I hope that readers will in fact find this collection of value not only as data for linguistic, anthropological, and literary research. I hope they will laugh when Coyote plays the fool; and be shocked when Coyote commits incest, murder, or cannibalism; and be morally edified when Coyote gets his comeuppance. He shows us some parts of ourselves--parts which we need to see more clearly.

> "Coyote never dies, he gets killed plenty of times, but he always comes back to life again, and then he goes right on traveling." (Snyder 1977:71)

* * *

I am grateful to Leanne Hinton for the illustration which appears on our cover. The collection is dedicated, with admiration and gratitude, to Gary Snyder.

WILLIAM BRIGHT
University of California,
Los Angeles

COYOTE AND GOPHER

(Spokane)

Barry F. Carlson

University of Victoria

The Spokane language of eastern Washington belongs to the Interior Division of the Salishan family. Spokane is very similar to neighboring Kalispel, and also to Flathead, spoken in Montana. All three may be considered mutually intelligible dialects of a single language.

Before the arrival of the white man people from these tribal/linguistic groups occupied territory along the area's major river courses. They fished for salmon in the then free flowing waters, gathered a wide variety of plant foods and medicines, and hunted game in the forests and on the prairies.

Today the Indian people live on reservations and in the nearby cities. The Spokanes have a large, efficiently managed reservation touching the shores of the Columbia and Spokane rivers, some 50 miles northwest of Spokane, Washington.

The Spokane language is now used only by adults. The few remaining traditional narrators are all past 80 years of age. Since 1969 the author has been studying the structure of this language, and attempting to record and transcribe the oral literature and traditions of the people. This work has been supported most generously by the National Science Foundation, through a grant held by Dr. Laurence C. Thompson; the Canada Council; the University of Victoria; the American Philosophical Society; and the Alex Sherwood - Mary Owhi Moses Language Fund.

The story of Coyote and Gopher presented here was related by Lucy Peuse, a revered story teller whose wit and style bring the characters in the Coyote tales to life. Margaret Sherwood, a lady in her early 70's, worked with the author on the translation of this and countless other Spokane stories. Her enthusiasm, perseverance, and unique linguistic intuition, have made it possible for the author to learn the structure of this language and to know the literature which it most richly preserves.

The story is written in broad phonetics, with an interlinear translation and a morpheme-by-morpheme analysis given for each word. This analysis of underlying forms follows the author's grammatical sketch of Spokane (Carlson 1972). Kalispel has been described by Hans Vogt (1940).

Abbreviations

Reduplication

[R_1]	distributive plural	C_1VC_2-
[R_2]	diminutive	C_1V-
[R_3]	inceptive aspect	-VC_2
[R_4]	repetitive aspect	C_1e-

Affixes

cause	causative	form	formative/stem derivative
class	classifier	imper	imperative
coll	collective plural	instr	instrumental
cont	continuative aspect	intr	intransitive
contr	control	mid	middle voice

nom	nominal
obj	object
pass	passive
pers class	person classifier
pl	plural
poss	possessive
prog	progressive/imperfective aspect
red	redirective
sg	singular
stat	stative
subj	subject
tr	transitive
unreal	unrealized mode
3,2,1	third person, second person, first person

Common syntactic particles

conj	hoy	sentence conjunction 'then/ then finally'
conj	kʷent	sentence conjunction 'then/ and then'
adj	ɬuʔ	adjunct marker (also ɬiʔe 'this')
fut	m	future 'will'
dep	ne	dependent clause marker
obl	t	oblique marker
conj	u	conjunction

COYOTE AND GOPHER

by Lucy Peuse, K̓ʷimpé

(1)	ʔepsxʷsíʔxʷəlts	ʔuɬspílyeʔ	n	puliyahá,
	they had children	Coyote	and	Gopher
	ʔepɬ-si(-ʔ-)xʷlt-s	ʔuɬ-spílyeʔ	n	
	have-child[R_1](-pl-)3 poss	coll-Coyote	conj	

čəmúsəməs.	(2)	kʷent	xʷəʔéʔneʔ	ɬu	t	səʔíɬən
four		then	they had a lot			food
č-mus		kʷent	xʷʔi-e(-ʔ-)neʔ	ɬuʔ	t	s-ʔiɬn
pers class-four[R_1]		conj	many-surface(-pl-)	adj	obl	nom-eat

ɬu	t	sx̣écts	ɬuʔ	puliyahá.	(3) hoy	kʷent
		her digging		Gopher	finally	then
		s-x̣ect-s			hoy	
		nom-dig roots/camas-3 poss			conj	

esčɬíp,	hesčɬíp,	hesčɬíp	ɬuʔ	spílyeʔ.	(4)	ho·y
he hunted	he hunted	he hunted		Coyote		finally
hec-č-ɬip						
prog-toward/after-hunt/pursue						

čənək̓ʷéɬc̓eʔ	ʔeɬlémt	puliyahá.	(5)	kʷent
[he killed] one	she was happy	Gopher		then
č-nk̓ʷuʔ-eɬc̓eʔ	ʔeɬ-lem-t			
class-one-animal	back/again-glad/happy-stat			

xʷcəntéʔs	kʷent	čəńəšíš	puliyahá.	(6)	hey,
they butchered it	and then	she helped	Gopher		hey
xʷic-n-t-e(-ʔ-)s		čń-šiš			
cut off-contr-tr-3 subj(-pl-)		hold-red intr			

ʔeɬəʔácx̣is	spílyeʔ,	"hoy,	qəʔenc̓ixʷcíɬəls."
he glanced at her	Coyote	oh	she's going to eat our food
ʔeɬ-ʔacx̣-n-t-es			qeʔ-hec-n-c̓eyxʷ-cin-ɬul-l-es
back/again-look at-contr-tr-3 subj			1 pl obj-prog-in/at-remove/consume-mouth-tr-1 pl obj-3 subj

(7)	ʔeɬəménsəm	puliyahá	u	esc̓éńəm	ɬiʔe	t
	she looked away again	Gopher	and	he got some		
	ʔeɬ-mens-m			hec-c̓eń-m		
	back/again-turn away from-mid			prog-which-mid		

nsənuxʷúls	c̓əʔúlixʷ	u	məńɬəlɬílis,
blood	deer	and	he sprinkled it between her legs
n-s-n-xʷul-s			mń-ɬil-n-t-es
in/at-nom-in/at-bore through-3 poss			between the legs-sprinkle[R_1] contr-tr-3 subj

hoy	məńƛ̓əməƛ̓úḿ.	(8)	"ʔácx̣ənt!	kʷecčícənəms
then	she was just bloody between the legs		look	you are getting
	mń-ƛ̓uḿ		ʔácx̣-n-t	kʷ-hec-čic-n-m-s
	between the legs-bloody[R_1]		look at-contr-tr	2 sg subj-prog-arrive-contr-mid-3 poss

t	asəwéyt."	(9)	"ta,	ta	ƛ̓e	xʷučɬəwéys."
	your sickness		no	no	already	it's left me
	han-s-weyt					xʷu-č-ɬwen-n-t-es
	2 sg poss-nom-sick					1 sg obj-after/toward-leave-contr-tr-3 subj

(10)	"ʔunéxʷ,	xʷúyš	ƛ̓ékʷš!"	(11)	hoy,
	oh yes	go	away		well then
		xʷuy-š	ƛ̓ekʷ-š		
		go-imper intr	leave-imper intr		

meʔmíntəm	puliyahá	hoy	xʷúy	ʔócqeʔ	c̓qʷáqʷ.
she was told to leave	Gopher	then	she went	she went out	she cried
meʔ-min-n-t-em					c̓aqʷ
inappropriate/out of place-instr-contr-tr-pass					cry[R_3]

(12)	c̓qʷáqʷ	u	nx̣ssəméls	u	čłx̣ʷəntés
	she cried	and	got over her crying	and then	she bored
			n-x̣es-m-els		č-łox̣ʷ-n-t-es
			in/at-good[R_3]-form-feelings		after-opening/hole-contr-tr-3 subj

łu	č̓	cíʔtxʷs.	(13)	čłx̣ʷəntés	u	číčš.
	to	their house		she bored	and	she got there
	č̓	ci(-ʔ-)txʷ-s				
	to	house(-pl-)3 poss				

(14)	w̓eʔúkʷiʔs	łiʔe	səʔíłis	u	c̓síp.
	she kept packing		her food	and	all were gone
	ʔukʷ-n-t-es		s-ʔiłn-s		c̓s-p
	pack[R_4]-contr-tr-3 subj		nom-eat-3 poss		consumed-lack of control

(15)	npxʷpéxʷis	təmált	u	q̓ʷcq̓ʷéct	čłpkʷpkʷúsis
	she dug and piled	dirt	and	filled up the containers	she put camas on top
	n-pexʷ-n-t-es			q̓ʷec-t	čł-pukʷ-us-n-t-es
	in/at-dig and pile[R_1]-contr-tr-3 subj			full[R_1]-stat	on-pile-berry/bulb-contr-tr-3 subj

hoy	nqəmpéls.	(16)	hoy	c̓spənúʔis	hoy
	she rested and relaxed		then	they ate it up	then
	n-qm-p-els			c̓s-p-nu-ʔ-n-t-es	
	in/at-stop/rest-lack of control-feelings			consumed-lack of control-success -pl- contr-tr-3 subj	

č̓sq̓əméltən,	č̓sq̓əméʔltən.	(17)	hesṫúk̓ʷ	spílyeʔ
he got hungry	they all got hungry		he was lying there	Coyote
č̓es-qm-eltn			hec-ṫuk̓ʷ	
bad-swallow-throat/stomach			prog-long object lies	

u	cúis	łiʔe	šəʔíti,	"hackʷənə́m̓	t	yúlt."
and	he told		oldest	go get		big [stick]
	cuw-n-t-es		šʔit-i	han-hec-kʷen-m		yul-t
	say-contr-tr-3 subj		first-?	2 sg poss-prog-take-mid		big-stat

(18)	nxʷƛ̓xʷƛ̓áqsis.	(x̣ʷa	kʷent	qłtə́m̓tis.)
	he whittled it to make it sharp on both ends	possibly	then	what is he going to use
	n-xʷiƛ̓-aqs-n-t-es			qł-tem̓-tn-s
	in/at-whittle-nose-contr-tr-3 subj			unreal-what-instr-3 poss

(19)	"hoy,	kʷpúxʷ,	i	kʷpúxʷ."	(20)	"xʷacqʷən̓cínəmstxʷ
	so	you stink	really	you stink		you're just accusing me for nothing
		kʷ-puxʷ				xʷu-hec-qʷin̓-cin-m-s-t-exʷ
		2 sg-stink				1 sg obj-prog-mean/ugly-mouth/speech-form-cause-tr-2 sg subj

kʷent	stə́m̓	m	čənecəʔíłənʔ	čənecəʔócqeʔ."	(21)	"ʔunéxʷ
so then	what	will	I eat	I'm empty		oh yes
	s-tem̓		čn-hec-ʔiłn	čn-hec-ʔocqeʔ		
	nom-what		1 sg-prog-eat	1 sg-prog-go out		

i	kʷpúxʷ,	cxʷúyš	kʷisəʔácx̣łtəm."
really	you stink	come over here	I look at it for you
		c-xʷúy-š	kʷ-hin-s-ʔacx̣-ł-t-m
		toward speaker/referent-go-imper intr	2 sg subj-1 sg poss-nom-look-red-tr-mid

(22)	hoy	xʷúy	čsčən̓úpsis	hesčésc	u
	then	he went	held his tail up	fooled with it	and
			č-s-čn̓-ups-n-t-es	hec-čes-s-t-es	
			after/toward-nom-hold-tail-contr-tr-3 subj	prog-put down-cause-tr-3 subj	

q̓ʷələntés.	(23)	ho·y	p̓iy̓áq.	(24)	ʔíʔłis
he cooked him		then	it got cooked/ripe		they ate it
q̓ʷl-n-t-es					ʔi(-ʔ-)łn-n-t-es
roast-contr-tr-3 subj					eat(-pl-)contr-tr-3 subj

u	č̓síp	hoy	łiʔe	č̓	čečeʔłés	hecəyáʕ	ʔíʔłis.
	all gone	then		to	three	all	they ate it
	č̓s-p				čeʔłés	hec-yaʕ	
	consumed-lack of control				three [R_1]	prog-all	

(25)	hoy	pupuʔsénč	spílyeʔ	hoy	c̓e	c̓aˤcín̓š̓ən
	then	he mourned	Coyote	finally then	still	Skinny Legs
		pʔus-enč				c̓aˤ-cin̓š̓n̓
		heart-[R_1]-stomach				thin-leg

hoy	xʷúy	q̓ʷéłtəmis	u	tkʷəʔúʔt.	(26)	tkʷəʔúʔt	u
then	he went	put him on his back	and	they walked		they walked	
		q̓ʷełt-m-n-t-es		tkʷʔu(-ʔ-)t			
		carry on back-form-contr-tr-3 subj		walk pl (-pl-)			

wíc̓is	łiʔe	čłq̓əlíʔ.	(27)	hayó	čłʔayuʔtétkʷ	łuʔ	k̓ʷəsíxʷ.
saw		lake		oh	they were sitting on the lake		Geese
wič-n-t-es					čł-ʔay̓ew̓t-etkʷ		
see-contr-tr-3 subj					on-sit pl-water		

(28)	cúis	łuʔ	qʷqʷsəʔéłts,	"hoy	qeʔtixʷscəʔíłən."
	he said to him		his little boy		we've got something to eat
	cuw-n-t-es		qʷseʔ-elt-s		qeʔ-tixʷ-s-s-ʔiłn
	say-contr-tr-3 subj		?[R_2]-child-3 poss		1 pl-get-nom-nom-eat

(29)	xʷúy,	cúti	łiʔe	ʔuł̓kʷəsíxʷ	"ʔexʷ	i	pƛ̓íl,
	meanwhile	said	the	Geese	suppose	really	you keep still
	xʷuy	cuw-t-i		ʔuł-k̓ʷsixʷ			p-ƛ̓il
	go/went	say-stat-cont		coll-goose			2 pl-still/dead

ta	pqsxʷəʔéʔ,	ʔexʷ	ne	m	spílyeʔ	ʔexʷ	ne
not	you fly	suppose	that	will	Coyote	suppose	that
	p-qł-s-xʷʔéʔ						
	2 pl-unreal-nom-fly pl						

leʔčén̓	m	ʔax̣íləm."	(30)	hoy	i	ƛ̓íʔl.	(31)	xʷúy
somehow	will	he do		then	really	they kept still		he went
l-ʔe-čen̓		ʔax̣il-m				ƛ̓i(-ʔ-)l		
at-this-how		do-mid				still/dead(-pl-)		

t̓kʷəntés	łiʔe	sqʷqʷsəʔéłts	u	cənəʔúst,
he put down		his little boy	and then	he dove
tuk̓ʷ-n-t-es		s-qʷseʔ-elt-s		c-n-ʔust
long object lies-contr-tr-3 subj		nom-?[R_2]-child-3 poss		toward referent-in-dive

xʷúy	ɬiʔe	č̓uč̓uʔšíʔs	u	čɬq̓ʷəm̓q̓ʷúm̓šis	ʔesél
he got to		their feet	and	pulled them under	two
		č̓uʔ-ši(-ʔ-)n-s		čɬ-q̓ʷum̓-šin-s	
		?[R_1]-foot(-pl-)3 poss		underneath-take pl[R_1] foot-3 poss	

ta	st̓úxʷt.	(32)	hoy	u	q̓ʷəm̓m̓él.	(33)	"m̓a,
not	fly		then		he got some		see
	s-t̓úxʷ-t				q̓ʷum̓-el		
	nom-fly-stat				take pl[R_3]-accidentally		

cúncən	ne	m	qeʔíɬən."	(34)	hoy	xʷú·y	ɬuʔ
I told you	that	will	we eat		then	he went	
cuw-n-t-si-en			qeʔ-ʔiɬn				
say-contr-tr-2 sg obj-1 sg subj			we-eat				

necšít̓.	(35)	t̓k̓ʷəntés	(36)	"xʷúy	neščstéxʷ,
tree		he put down		go	you take care of this
n-hec-šít̓		t̓uk̓ʷ-n-t-es			n-ʔeš-čt̓-s-t-exʷ
in/at-prog-one object standing		one long object lies-contr-tr-3 subj			in/at-be-care for-cause-tr-2 sg subj

hesčɬtqéʔneɬtxʷ	ɬuʔ	č̓uč̓uʔšíʔs,	čiqsčíwəlši."
put your [hands] over		their feet	I'm going to climb the tree
hec-čɬ-taq-e(-ʔ-)neʔ-ɬ-t-exʷ		č̓uʔ-ší(-ʔ-)n-s	čn-qɬ-s-číw-lš-i
prog-on-touch-surface (-pl-)red-tr-2 sg subj		?[R_1]-foot(-pl-) 3 poss	1 sg-unreal-nom-climb-get to a position-cont

(37)	hoy	číwəlš.	(38)	put	tx̣ʷx̣ʷéw̓əs	ɬuʔ
	so then	he climbed		just	half-way [up]	
		číw-lš			tox̣ʷ-éw̓s	
		climb-get to a position			straight[R_3]-middle	

sccíwəlšs	u	cúntəm	ɬuʔ	t
tree/the thing he was climbing	and	he was told		
s-s-číw-lš-s		cuw-n-t-em		
nom-nom-climb-get in a position-3 poss		tell/say-contr-tr-pass		

sqʷqʷsəʔélts,	"ƛ̓e	yúʔn̓əm̓ist,	ƛ̓e	yúʔn̓əm̓ist."
his boy	now	they're moving	now	they're moving
s-qʷseʔ-elt-s		yu(-ʔ-)n̓-m̓ist		
nom-?[R_2]-child-3 poss		move(-pl-)refl		

(39) "čɬtqéʔnəʔent! čɬtqéʔnəʔent!" (40) "ta ƛ̓e təl̓əšéʔ
hold them down / no already from then
čɬ-taq-eneʔ-n-t / tl̓-šeʔ
on-touch-surface-contr-tr / from-that/then

yúʔn̓əm̓ist." (41) nəwísšəlštəm čaʔcín̓šən̓. (42) tən̓nəwíst
they're moving / they went up with / Skinny Legs / they went up
yu(-ʔ-)n̓-m̓ist / n-wis-šlš-t-em / tn̓-n-wis-t
move(-pl-)refl / in/at-standing/high/long-get in a position-tr-pass / from-in/at-standing/high/long-stat

u cpƛ̓éčstəməntəm. (43) ʔe· cəwéɬkʷp
and / let go of him / oh / he came down
c-pƛ̓-ečst-m-n-t-em / c-weɬkʷ-p
toward a referent-let go-hand/limb-form-contr-tr-pass / toward a referent-go down-lack of contr

spílyeʔ. (44) ɬuʔ sčt̓ɬ̓áɬqis ɬiʔe nsčlčlšəméčst
Coyote / his hair / on the limbs
s-č-t̓eɬ-qin-s / n-s-člš-m-ečst
nom-toward/after-stick[R_1]-head-3 poss / in/at-nom-turn/twist[R_1]-form-hand/limb

u čir̓ir̓ír̓ hoy ntteʔúleʔxʷ
and / got caught / then / he hit the ground
č-yir̓ / n-teʔ-uleʔxʷ
toward/after-round/around[R_1][R_3] / in/at-hit/pound[R_2]-ground

čaʕcín̓šən̓. (45) ƛ̓líl ʔeɬkʷéys hoy
Skinny Legs / he died / he took him / then
ƛ̓il / ʔeɬ-kʷen-n-t-es
still/dead[R_3] / back-take-contr-tr-3 subj

nššt̓úsis hoy ʔíɬis u čspənúis.
put him on a stick by the fire / then / he ate him / all up
n-šit̓-us-n-t-es / ʔiɬn-n-t-es / čs-p-nu-n-t-es
in/at-stand sg[R_2]-fire-contr-tr-3 subj / eat-contr-tr-3 subj / consumed-lack of contr-success-contr-tr-3 subj

(46) hoy čɬtər̓əntés ɬuʔ sɬ̓ɬ̓áɬqis
then / he foresaw / his hair
čɬ-tr̓-n-t-es / s-t̓eɬ-qin-s
underneath-predict/foresee-contr-tr-3 subj / nom-sticky[R_1]-head-3 poss

ɬu	ne	xʷúy	ɬu	tixʷstə̓lsqélixʷ	ne	qɬkʷúkʷtis
	if	it happens		there are people	then	going to save a lot of
		xʷuy		tixʷ-s-t̓l-s-qelixʷ		qɬ-kʷukʷ-tn-s
		go/went		get-nom-tear open-nom-person/Indian		unreal-save/help-instr-3 poss

ɬu	t	sqélixʷ.	(47)	hoy	tə̓lə̓šéʔ	xʷíst	xʷí·st	ɬiʔe
		people		then	from there	he walked	walked	
					t̓l-šeʔ	xʷis-t		
					from-that	walk-stat		

nesčɬlóʕʷtəm.	(48)	čɬʔečsušé·w̓əs	ɬiʔe	səməʔém
in valley		he saw standing		woman
n-hec-čɬ-loʕʷ-t-m		čɬ-ʔeč-s-wiš-ew̓s		
in/at-prog-on-fit together-stat-mid		on-be-nom-standing-mid		

hecx̣écti	i	kʷíl̓l̓qs.	(49)	hoy	č̓ečí·tšəlš
digging roots	really	dressed in red		then	he started to sneak around
hec-x̣ec-t-i		kʷil-al̓qs			č̓it-šlš
prog-dig roots-stat-cont		red-dress			get close[R_4]-get in a position

u	č̓ítəmis.	(50)	"hayó	k̓ʷ	inpuliyahá."	(51)	hoy
and	he got close to her		oh		my Gopher		then
	č̓it-m-n-t-es			k̓ʷ	hin-puliyahá		
	get-close-form-cont-tr-3 subj			evidently	1 sg poss-Gopher		

čxʷúyəmis	u	ɬiʔe	nsčɬčəmélsc	u
he went	and		got in front of her	and
č-xʷuy-m-n-t-es			n-s-čɬ-čm-el-s-t-es	
toward/after-go-form contr-tr-3 subj			in/at-nom-under-body-front-cause-tr-3 subj	

t̓kʷəncút	u	cacalqépəm,	"hoy	nc̓spúleʔxʷ
laid down	and	cried aloud		they're all gone
t̓ukʷ-n-t-sut		calq-ep-m		n-c̓s-p-uleʔxʷ
long object lies-contr-tr-refl		cry[R_4]-foot/below-mid		in/at-consumed-lack of control-ground/earth

ɬuʔ	qeʔsxʷsíxʷəlt	sq̓əméltən."	(nc̓ípc̓psəm
	our children	starvation	he had his eyes closed
	qeʔ-sixʷəlt	s-q̓m-elt-tn	n-c̓ip-us-m
	1 pl poss-child[R_2]	nom-swallow-stomach-instr	in/at-pinched[R_1]-eye-mid

kʷent	hesc̓qʷáqʷi.)	(52)	xʷíst	puliyahá	yeč̓əʔé.
and	he was crying		she left	Gopher	somewhere
	hec-c̓aqʷ-i		xʷis-t		i-ʔé-č̓-ʔe
	prog-cry[R_3]-cont		walk-stat		really-this-to-this

(53)	c̓qʷáqʷ	u	ʔeɬčxʷpxʷpəmúsəm,	č̓ú.	(54) šé	təl̓šeʔ
	he cried	and	opened his eyes	she was gone		
	c̓aqʷ		ʔeɬ-č-xʷp-m-us-m	č̓uw	šeʔ	tl̓-šeʔ
	cry[R_3]		back-after/toward-open[R_1]-form-eye-mid	gone	that	from-that

čxʷúyəmis.	(55)	hoy	nəʔayx̣ʷténeʔməntəm	t puliyahá.
he went [on] to her		then	got tired hearing him	Gopher
č-xʷuy-m-n-t-es			n-ʔayx̣ʷ-t-eneʔ-m-n-t-em	
toward-go-form-contr-tr-3 subj			in/at-tired-stat-ear/hearing-form-contr-tr-pass	

(56)	cúntəm,	"ʔa	xʷúyš	cič̓šéʔ	u
	she said	oh	you go	over there	
	cuw-n-t-em		xʷuy-š	ci-č̓-šeʔ	
	say/tell-contr-tr-pass		go-imper sg intr	toward a referent-to-that	

ləšéʔ	ɬu	qeʔsxʷsíxʷəlt."	(57)	"č̓čén̓?"	(58)	"cič̓šeʔ."
that's where are		our children		where		over there
l-šeʔ		qeʔ-sixʷlt		č̓-čen̓		ci-č̓-šeʔ
at-that		1 pl-child[R_1]		to-how		near a referent-to-that

(59)	hoy	xʷúy	nəʔúɬxʷ.	(60)	ye	nč̓ɬənč̓č̓əmép
	then	he went	went in		right	by the door
			n-ʔuɬxʷ		hi-ʔe	n-č̓ɬ-n-č̓im-ep
			in/at-go		really-this	in/at-under-in/at-body[R_2]-foot/bottom

u	č̓ɬənʔemətép	caʕcínšən.	(61)	put	u
	he was sitting by the door	Skinny Legs		just exactly	
	č̓ɬ-n-ʔemut-ep				
	under-in/at-sit[R_2]-foot/bottom of				

sč̓itš	ye	čečeʔɬés.	(62)	č̓əʔe	u	ʔay̓éw̓ət.
he got there		were three		over there		they were sitting
s-č̓it-š	hi-ʔe	čeʔɬes		č̓-ʔe		ʔay̓éw̓t
nom-get close-get in a position	really-this	three[R_1]		to-this		sit pl

(63)	ta	sčq̓əʔélsəməntəm	spílye.	(64)	"he,	čiesčsq̓əméltəni."
	not	pay attention to him	Coyote		say	I'm hungry
		s-č-q̓eʔ-els-m-n-t-em				čn-hec-č-s-q̓m-elt-tn-i
		nom-toward/after-pinch-feelings-form-contr-tr-pass				1 sg-prog-after/toward-nom-swallow-stomach-instr-cont

(65)	ta	sčq̓əʔélsəməntəm	hoy	ʔeɬəyaʕʕmíl̓š,	hecəyáʕ	ɬuʔ
	not	pay attention to him	then	they all got together	all	
				ʔeɬ-yaʕ-m-il̓š	hec-yaʕ	
				back-gather[R_3]-mid-get in a position	prog-gather	

sxʷsíxʷəlts	ʔeɬxʷlxʷílt.	(66)	kʷent	šéy̓	ɬiʔe	sɬ̓ɬ̓áɬqis
his children	came alive again		and then	that's it		his hair
sixʷlt-s	ʔeɬ-xʷil-t			šeʔ-i		s-ɬ̓eɬ-qin-s
child[R_1]- 3 poss	back-alive-stat			that-cont		nom-sticky[R_1]-top-3 poss

ɬiʔe	sšáw̓ətəmqən	ɬiʔe	kʷent	heck̓ʷúləmsc	sqélixʷ
	tree moss		then	they use it	people
				hec-k̓ʷúl-m-s-t-es	
				prog-do-form-cause-tr-3 subj	

hecəʔíɬisc	sɬ̓ɬ̓áɬqis	spílyeʔ.
they eat it	his hair	Coyote
hec-ʔiɬn-s-t-es	s-ɬ̓eɬ-qin-s	
prog-eat-cause-tr-3 subj	nom-sticky[R_1]-top-3 poss	

šéy̓	u	hóy
that's		all

Free Translation

(1) Coyote and Gopher had four children. (2) They had a lot to eat, the things Gopher dug. (3) Coyote hunted and hunted and hunted. (4) Finally he killed one animal and Gopher was happy. (5) Then they butchered it and Gopher helped. (6) Hey, Coyote glanced at her, "Oh, she's going to eat some of our food." (7) Gopher looked away and he got some deer blood and sprinkled it between her legs so she was bloody between her legs. (8) "Look! You are getting your sickness [menstrual period]." (9) "No, no, it's gone, I just had it." (10) "Oh yes [you do], go away, leave!" (11) Well then, Gopher was told to leave, so she went out and cried. (12) She cried

and got over her crying and then she started to bore [tunnel] towards their house. (13) She bored and got there. (14) She kept packing away her roots until they were all gone. (15) She dug and piled dirt and filled up the containers, putting camas on top, then she rested. (16) Then they [Coyote and the sons] ate everything up, and then he got hungry, they all got hungry. (17) Coyote was lying there and he told his oldest son, "Go get a big stick". (18) He whittled it to make it sharp on both ends. ("I wonder what he's going to use that stick for?"). (19) "So [Coyote says], you stink, you really stink!" (20) [His son says] "You're just accusing me for nothing, what could I have eaten? I'm empty." (21) "Oh yes, you stink, come over here and I'll look at it [his rear end]." (22) Then he held his tail up, fooled with it and cooked him [on the sharp stick]. (23) Then he got cooked. (24) They [Coyote and the sons] ate him all up; three [sons] were eaten the same way. (25) Coyote mourned, then Skinny Legs was still left and he put him on his back and they walked. (26) They walked and saw a lake. (27) Oh, Geese were sitting on the lake. (28) He said to his little boy, "Now we've got something to eat." (29) Meanwhile, the Geese said to each other, "Now keep really still, don't fly, Coyote will probably try something." (30) They kept still. (31) [Coyote] put down his little boy, dove, got to the Geese, and pulled two of them under by their feet, they didn't fly. (32) So, he got some. (33) "See, I told you we'd eat." (34) Then he [Coyote] went to a tree. (35) He put [the Geese] down. (36) [He told his son] "Go, take care of these [Geese], put your hands over their feet, I'm going to climb the tree." (37) So he climbed. (38) He had just gotten halfway up the tree and he was told by his son, "They're moving, they're moving." (39) [Coyote told him] "Hold them down, hold them down!" (40) "No, they're already moving." (41) They flew up with Skinny Legs. (42) They went up and let go of him. (43) Oh, Coyote came down. (44) His [Coyote's] hair got caught on the limbs, then Skinny Legs hit the ground. (45) He [the son] died, then [Coyote] took him, put him on a stick by the fire, then ate him all up. (46) Then he foresaw about his hair that if it happens that people come [to the world], then [the hair] is going to save a lot of people. (47) From there [Coyote] walked and walked until he got to the valley. (48) He saw a woman standing there digging roots, in a bright red dress. (49) Then he started to sneak around and got close to her. (50) "Oh, my Gopher." (51) Then he went and got in front of her, lied down and cried aloud, "Our children are all gone from starvation." (He had his eyes closed and was crying.) (52) Gopher left and went somewhere. (53) [Coyote] cried, then opened his eyes and she was gone. (54) He went on to her. (55) Then Gopher got tired of hearing him. (56) She said, "Oh, you go over there and that's where our children are." (57) "Where?" (58) "Over there." (59) Then he went there and went in. (60) Sitting right by the door was Skinny Legs. (61) He had just gotten close and here were the three of them [the other sons]. (62) They were sitting over there. (63) They didn't pay attention to Coyote. (64) "Say, I'm hungry" [says Coyote]. (65) They didn't pay attention to him, then they all got together, all his children came alive again. (66) Then that's his hair, the tree moss [Alectoria fremontii] that the people used to eat, Coyote's hair.

COYOTE AND ROCK

(Columbian Salish)

M. Dale Kinkade

University of British Columbia

The Columbian language was spoken aboriginally along the Columbia River and its tributaries from about Priest Rapids north to the mouth of the Methow River. The language has been called Columbia or Columbian by linguists and anthropologists since Boas, but the official name for its speakers is Moses Columbian, and most speakers simply call the language Moses. No published grammar of this language yet exists, and only a few articles pertaining to it have ever appeared in publications. Teit described the culture of the southernmost group of Columbians (Teit 1928), and Ray includes a considerable amount of information about other groups in his treatments of Plateau culture (Ray 1939, 1942). The Columbian language is part of the southeastern division of Interior Salish, and its grammar is in most respects similar to neighboring Okanagan and Kalispel (for grammars of these languages, see Mattina 1973, Carlson 1972, Vogt 1940). No texts have ever been published in Columbian; in 1930 the Washington Farmer printed twelve folktales written down by Emily M. Phillips, a granddaughter of Chief Moses (a well-known leader of the Moses-Columbia band), and these are said to be Columbian tales (Phillips 1930).[1]

The following story was told to me in 1964 by Moyise Simon, who died some ten years ago. He knew a number of stories, and relished telling them, especially to his daughter, who made it possible for me to make this recording. Style in Columbian tales varies considerably from speaker to speaker, and this one has some rough edges, which I have not attempted to edit out. The transcription and translation were made with the assistance of Mary Marchand in 1969.

In Columbian folktales, Coyote is both trickster and transformer, although not always both in all tales. In the following tale, he is trickster only; in this role he provides great entertainment for all Plateau Indians.

An important narrative feature in Columbian (and other Interior Salish) tales is the use of rhetorical lengthening for emphasis and other special effects. I have marked this lengthening in the following text with raised dots, using series of dots to indicate relative length; length is not otherwise distinctive in Columbian. Actually, this particular narration has relatively little of this lengthening compared to many other recordings I have made. Sometimes this lengthening is accompanied by a switch to falsetto voice or a sharp raising of pitch. Another rhetorical feature noted here is extra-strong stress; this is marked with a double acute accent (˝). Less apparent features of style involve word order and the use of particles. Particles are extremely important in Columbian syntax in any case, and indicate all sorts of nuances of meaning, sometimes only implied, and are often difficult to translate. Normal word order puts the main predicate (with satellite particles) first in a clause, but other main sentence parts often precede it for emphasis; this is particularly common in tales, where whole sentences are occasionally inverted in repetitions. Deictic usage is particularly complex and elaborate, and no attempt is made here to explain it.[2]

(1) ʔani s-ki̋nt xƛ̓űt ʔac-x̣a̋q̓-s-t-m,[3] kʷaʔ hűy s-ta̋m̓, kʷaʔ x
Those Indians Rock he had to be paid, and then something, and they

yaʕ̓-tű s-ki̋nt s-ta̋m̓ kʷaʔ x̣a̋q̓-nt-m. (2) s-ta̋m̓ s-ɬxʷ-lʔ-a̋··kst,[4]
all (the) Indians something and he got paid. Something gloves,

s-tám̓ kɬ-yər̓-cín,[5] s-n-ttám̓tam̓-tn,[6] yaʕ-tú s-tám̓ ʔac-x̣áq̓-s-c. (3) ʔá···y
something neckerchiefs, beaded bags, all things they paid him. And so

kʷaʔ n-iʕ-ápʔ[7] ci kʷ núx̣ʷ-t kʷaʔ x̣áq̓-nt-xʷ ʔani xƛ̓út. (4) hú··y smiyáw̓,
and every time there you go and you pay it that rock. So Coyote

"ʔa·· laʔká xƛ̓út kʷaʔ ʔac-x̣áq̓-s-t-m." (5) húy kʷaʔ
(thought), "Oh, where (since when) Rock and we have to pay him?" And so

núx̣ʷ-t p̓əç̓-ṣ, tkay̓-áʔst-s,[8] k-mənak-áʔst-s.[8] (6) "k-ƛ̓ə́m̓-n
he went defecated on it, urinated on the rock, defecated on the rock. "I'm going

a··, lút na-x̣áq̓-n, xƛ̓út nəm̓nəm̓-ús,[9] kam̓ xƛ̓út
to pass it, oh, not I pay it, that Rock it's nothing, when did we have to Rock

kʷaʔ ʔac-x̣áq̓ ?" (7) ʔi kʷaʔ nú·x̣ʷ-t, cí cq-ánaʔ-am-s[10] t-ʔas-tíy̓iʔ[11] xƛ̓út.
and pay?" And then he went, there he heard rolling Rock.

(8) ʔácx̣-s -- "tíl kxáp-n-c[12] xƛ̓út, húy x̣əlq̓-n-cá-s."[12] (9) ʔí·
He looked -- "Oh, he's chasing me Rock, and he'll clobber me." So

n-tər̓q-p-n-cút[13] smiyáw̓; k-ƛ̓ílx[14] xər̓xər̓-úləxʷ[15] cí ciʔ-áɬ, xƛ̓út,
really took off running Coyote; he ran up a rocky hill up through there, Rock,

kxáp-nt-m, húy kas-x̣ə́lq̓-nt-m. (10) hú··y kʷaʔ
was being chased right behind, and was going to get clobbered. And then

ʔáyəx̣ʷ-t tíʔ,[16] ham-p-mn-cút smiyáw̓. (11) hú·y cmál xƛ̓út ƛ̓ə́x̣-t
he got tired very, he dropped over Coyote. And so just now Rock (ran) fast

cí ciʔ-áɬ xƛ̓út, húy ka-na-kíc-kn̓-t-m,[17] ʔí· na-k̓ə́r-m. (12) lút
up through there, Rock, and now going to catch up with him, so he swam. Not

tiʔ cní, xƛ̓út, cí num̓ na-k̓ə́r-m. (13) tíy̓iʔ kʷaʔ
indeed (that) he, Rock, (could swim, but) there also he swam. Rolled and

n-tiyy-átkʷ[18] kʷaʔ kxáp-s waʔ[19] smiyáw̓. (14) kat-ʔílx,
rolled into the water and it chased him that Coyote. He went ashore,

n-tər̓q-p-n-cút smiyáw̓, ʔani xƛ̓út cí ciʔ-áɬ. (15) hú··y kʷaʔ ʔáyəx̣ʷ-t
he really ran Coyote, that Rock right behind him. Then and really tired

smiyáw̓ : "tíʔ ka-na-kíc-kn-c, húy kn túx̣ʷux̣ʷ." (16) náw̓-lx,
Coyote: "Oh, he's going to catch me, and then I (will) die." He ran,

wík-ɬ-c waʔ yəx̣ʷyx̣ʷút-xn[20] s-txʷúl-s, l-cí n-qən-m-úləxʷ.[21]
he saw it that Badger his house, right there he dove into the ground.

(17) na-kíc-kn̓-tus[22] waʔ xƛ̓út, kɬ-n-tp-áp-nt-m.[23] (18) hú···y
(Then) he caught up to him that Rock, he blocked the entrance. And then

smiyáw̓ kʷaʔ lup-cín,[24] t-qənxʷ-áyn.[25] (19) "tíʔ kn túx̣ʷux̣ʷ.
Coyote and (began to get) dry, hungry. "Oh, I (will) die.

(20) hu̓y kn t-qənxʷ-áyn." (21) ʔi·· k̓k̓al̓á···· l-cí xƛ̓út
And I (will) starve to death." And so real slowly . . . (but) there Rock

c-kɬ-n-tp-áp. (22) "tíl̓ kn kas-tux̣ʷux̣ʷ-míx." (23) hú··y sáw-nt-m,
blocked the door. "Oh my, I am going to die." And then it was asked,

cút, "ʔà tíl̓ nasù[26] kʷ kaɬ-yil-mix̣ʷ-m,[27] smiyáw, ʔi kʷaʔ nasu
he told (himself), "Oh indeed will you will be chief, Coyote, and will

kʷ wáh-m kʷaʔ naʔ[26] kʷ waʔ wáh-m kʷaʔ p̓əlk̓-mn-cút." (24) kʷaʔ p̓əlk̓-mn-cút
you bark and will you that bark and roll over." And so he rolled over

ciʔ ç̓óṣ ç̓óṣ ç̓óṣ[28] ʔá·, ʔí· smiyá··w cút, "hú··y tí··l̓
there, he made a lot of clattering noise, and then Coyote said, "Well, indeed

ʔay̓kʷ-á·ṣt cíʔ kt ʔí··m̓x yaʕyaʕ-tú. (25) p̓əƛ̓-nt-m[29] ʔani t̓əxʷ
tomorrow there we move all of us. We'll break up camp those ?

s-txʷúl-t, kas-ʔím̓x-əxʷ." (26) ʔí smiyáw t̓əq̓ʷ-cín . . . p̓əlk̓-mn-cút,
our houses, going to move." And so Coyote hollered . . . he rolled over,

ç̓óṣ, ʔí·· núm̓as l-p̓əlk̓-mn-cút, ç̓óṣ. (27) ʔí··· p̓əlk̓-mn-cút
clattered, and any more again rolled over, clattered. And he rolled over

ç̓oṣç̓ó·ṣ-lx kʷaʔ k̓ə́w-p.[30] (28) ʔí kʷaʔ ḥáw̓wi[31] t x̣x̣ƛ̓-cín[32]
(with) a lot of rattling and then stopped. And then made like a dog

waḥwaḥ-í··lx, kʷaʔ k̓ə́w-p. (29) tíl̓ tí lx ʔím̓x. (30) xƛ̓út
roaring, and then he was quiet. Well indeed they moved. (But) Rock

l-cí··· kʷaʔ lút s-cq-ánaʔ núm̓-x, lút húy kʷaʔ k̓ə́w-p. (31) "k̓ú··w
still there and not he heard anything, not so and it was quiet. "Gone

tíl̓ maxʷ ʔím̓x smiyáw, lút kʷən̓ na . . . xʷiʔít kʷən̓ waʔ
indeed, I guess he moved Coyote, not evidently will . . . many evidently that

s-nək̓ʷ-p-ɬ-mʔúmt-s[33] kɬ-wán-t l mʔúmt." (32) hú···y ci xƛ̓út ci
in-laws down under in the ground." And so then Rock then

s-ʔal-núx̣ʷ-t-s, tíl̓ l-kʷílx xƛ̓út. (33) q̓əw-t-ú··· smiyáw : "cí
his going back, indeed got away from there Rock. Crawled over Coyote: "There

k̓ə́w xƛ̓út. (34) hú··y x̣ə́lu tíl̓ tx̣ʷ-ús-t-m-s[34]. . . ." (35) hú··y
gone Rock. So just indeed he's gone and left me . . . ." And so

q̓əw̓-t-ú t-qənxʷ-áyn cí c-təptúpaʔ ʔí··ɬn, kʷaʔ x̣əl-alwís[35]
he crawled over real hungry, there left-over scraps he ate, and so after scheming

kʷaʔ ʔicá s-xʷə́lxʷəl-t-s smiyáw. (36) lút s-túx̣ʷux̣ʷ-s, ƛ̓xʷúp-s[36]
and there stayed alive Coyote. Not his dying, he won out against him

waʔ ʔani xƛ̓út.
that that Rock.

Free Translation

(1) Indians had to pay this Rock, and all Indians paid him something, and he got paid. (2) Something like gloves, something like neckerchiefs, beaded bags, they paid him all sorts of things. (3) And so every time you go by there, you pay that Rock. (4) But Coyote thought, "Oh, since when do we have to pay Rock?" (5) And so he went and defecated on it, urinated on Rock, and crapped on it. (6) "I'm going to pass it and not pay it, that Rock is nothing; since when do we have to pay Rock?" (7) So then he went on, and heard Rock rolling. (8) He looked -- "Oh, Rock is chasing me and he'll clobber me!" (9) So Coyote really took off running; he ran up a rocky hill, up through there, but Rock was right behind chasing him, and he was going to get clobbered. (10) Then Coyote got tired, and he dropped over. (11) Then Rock ran fast right through the same place, and was about to catch up with him (Coyote), so he swam (the river). (12) (Coyote thought) that Rock couldn't swim, of course, but it did swim. (13) It rolled on and right into the water, and kept on chasing Coyote. (14) Coyote went ashore, and he really ran, with Rock right behind him. (15) Then Coyote was really tired: "Oh, he's going to catch me, and then I'll die." (16) He ran on and saw Badger's house, and right there he dived into the ground. (17) Then Rock caught up to him, and blocked the entrance. (18) Coyote (soon) began to get dry (thirsty) and hungry. (19) "Oh, I'll die. (20) I'll starve to death." (21) So very slowly (he moved toward the entrance), but there was Rock blocking the door. (22) "Oh my, I'm going to die!" (23) Then he asked (himself), told (himself, as if someone else in the hole were talking to him), "Oh, you will indeed be (our) chief, Coyote, and you will bark and then bark again and roll over." (24) So he rolled over there and made a lot of clattering noise, and then Coyote said, "Well, tomorrow we will all move. (25) We will break up camp, and we are going to move our houses." (26) So Coyote hollered; he rolled over clattering, and rolled over again clattering. (27) He rolled over with a lot of rattling, and then stopped. (28) Then he made like a dog roaring, and then he was quiet. (29) Well, they did (apparently) move. (30) But Rock was still there, but didn't hear anything at all; it was quiet. (31) "I guess Coyote really is gone, and has moved; I guess they won't . . . I guess he has a lot of in-laws down under the ground." (32) So Rock went back, and left there. (33) Coyote crawled over (to the door): "Rock is gone. (34) So it seems that he's gone and left me." (35) So he crawled over very hungry, and ate some left-over scraps of food; and so, after scheming there, Coyote stayed alive. (36) He didn't die, and he won out against Rock.

Footnotes

[1]However, Miss Phillips was raised on the Spokane Reservation, and was also part Spokane, so the stories may better be classified as Plateau, rather than attributing them to any specific society; she calls the hero of several of these tales Speelya, the name used by Spokanes for Coyote in folktales; this name is a borrowing from Northern Sahaptin, and Spokane uses a different word for coyote outside folktales, one with cognates in other Salishan languages. The other languages of the area use a single word for Coyote in all contexts.

[2]Morpheme divisions are indicated by hyphens, except that transitive **-t-** and a following object marker beginning with **s** are written together as **c** (they merge morphophonemically, whereas some other sequences of **t** and **s** do not). In order not to make the interlinear translation so complex that it is unreadable, I list here the grammatical morphemes that occur in the text, and will not indicate them separately in the translation other than to provide continuity. The principal variation within suffixes is stress; those vowels marked with ^ have the vowel present when stressed, but the vowel is deleted when unstressed. PREFIXES Aspect: **ʔac-/ʔas-/c-** 'stative' (variation determined by initial consonant and stress), **s-** 'continuative, absolutive', **kas-/kaɬ-** 'unrealized'; Direction: **c-** 'cislocative', **ʔal-/l-** 'translocative, again'; Position: **k-** 'on or against something vertical', **kat-/ka-** 'on a flat surface', **kɬ-** 'under', **k̓ɬ-** 'away from, at a distance', **n-** 'in, inside, general locative', **na-** 'in; water', **t-** 'on, against, attached to'. SUFFIXES **-t** 'immediate', **-p** 'non-control', **-îlx** 'autonomous', **-m** 'middle' (**-am** after ʔ), **-mîn-** 'relational', **-stû-** 'causative', **-ɬ-** 'redirective', **-nt-/-t-** 'transitive', **-míx** 'middle continuative', **-əxʷ** 'continuative', **-tn**

'instrumental', -cût 'reflexive', -ú 'durative', -alwís 'randomizer', -áyn 'extreme'. There are four sets of pronominal markers, given here in the order 1st sg., 2nd sg., 3rd, 1st pl., 2nd pl. (all are listed, even though some do not occur in the text). Object: -sâ-, -sî-, ∅, -âl-, -ûlm-; transitive subject: -n, -xʷ, -s/-c, -t, -p; intransitive subject clitics: kn, kʷ, ∅, kt, kʷp; possessive: ʔin-, ʔin-, -s, -t, -p (ʔin- becomes ʔi- before s). Subject clitics may be either preposed or postposed. Third plural is optional, but is often marked in this text by the clitic lx/x; it marks either subject or object. Three reduplications occur: C_1(V)- 'diminutive', C_1(V)C_2- 'collective', -C_2 'inchoative'. Lexical suffixes will be noted as they occur.

The transcription used will be familiar to American Indianists, with the following special usages: ʕ and ḥ are pharyngeals; c̣, ṣ, and ḷ are retracted, i.e., the back of the tongue is retracted, pulling back the tip of the tongue, but maintaining the point of articulation (otherwise these are articulated with the blade of the tongue); ạ and ə̣ are similarly retracted, and o is a retracted u. A stop or affricate prefix merges with an initial glottal stop to a glottalized stop or affricate.

[3]The suffixes are causative-transitive-passive. The morphophonemics of the transitive suffix are complex, but most variants occur here in the various forms of 'pay' and 'chase'. The full form is -nt-, as in sentences (1) and (3). After causative -s-, only -t- occurs (sentence 1); before a first singular subject -n, the sequence reduces to -n (sentence 6). Before a third person subject -s, the transitive suffix is lost entirely (as in kxáps, sentence 13); hence it is absent in sentence (2), where the final -c is not from -t-s, but is due to another morphophonemic rule that changes any sequence of s-s to s-c (the first -s in 2 is causative).

[4]Lexical suffix -âkst 'hand'; the root apparently has to do with ɬəxʷ- 'sew'.

[5]Lexical suffix -cîn 'mouth, edge'; root yər- 'round'.

[6]Formally a diminutive collective, but semantically a single unit; the root may be related to s-tám̓ 'what, thing'.

[7]Lexical suffix -áp 'base'; root yaʕ̓- 'gather, assemble, all'.

[8]Lexical suffix -âʔst 'rock'; roots takâý- 'urinate' and mnâk- 'defecate (firm excrement)'. Interior Salishan languages distinguish soft, runny excrement (here p̓ə̣́c̓-) from firm excrement.

[9]Lexical suffix -ûs 'face, eye, surface'; root nəm̓- 'nothing'.

[10]Lexical suffix -ânaʔ 'ear'; root cq- 'hear' (?); -am 'middle'.

[11]tíy̓iʔ from tíy̓y̓ (inchoative reduplication). y and w become i and u between consonants or finally after a consonant; y̓ and w̓ become iʔ and uʔ in these same environments.

[12]When stressed, first singular object is -(t)sá-, but only -(t)s- when unstressed; third person subject is lost in the latter instance.

[13]Root tər̓q- 'kick', -cût 'reflexive'.

[14]Root ƛ̓ílx 'climb a hill'; this may include -îlx 'autonomous'.

[15]Lexical suffix -ûl̓əxʷ 'earth, ground'; root xər- 'steep'.

[16]t̓iʔ and t̓il̓ (as in sentence 8) are variants of the same emphatic particle.

[17]Lexical suffix -îkn 'back'; root kíc- 'arrive'; kas- 'unrealized' is reduced to ka- before alveolars.

[18]Lexical suffix -âtkʷ 'water'; root tiy- 'roll'.

[19]waʔ seems to give specific designation that what follows is the object of the preceding predicate.

[20]Lexical suffix -xn 'foot, leg'; root unidentified.

[21]Lexical suffix -ûl̓əxʷ 'earth, ground'; stem n-qin- 'go into'.

[22]-tu- 'obviative', -s 'third person subject'.

[23]Lexical suffix -áp 'base'; root təp- 'cover'. The prefixes kɬ-n- with the suffix -áp always refer to a door.

[24]Lexical suffix -cîn 'mouth, edge'; root lup- 'dry'.

[25]-ə́yn 'extreme'; tqənúxʷ 'hungry', from a root qənúxʷ 'throat'.

[26]Both nasu and naʔ indicate future, but I have been unable to determine the difference between them.

[27]Lexical suffix -mîxʷ 'people'; root yəl- unidentified.

[28]c̣óṣ is onomatopoeic for banging, rattling, or clattering noises.

[29]p̓ə́ƛ̓- 'collapse, cave in'.

[30]k̓ə́w- 'silent, gone, absent'.

[31]*ḥaw̓y- 'work, fix, make', with inchoative reduplication.

[32]Lexical suffix -cîn 'mouth, edge'; root x̣ƛ̓- (uncertain meaning) with diminutive reduplication. x̣ƛ̓cîn is 'horse'.

[33]A compound of nk̓ʷ- 'one' (?) and mʔúmt 'earth, ground'.

[34]Lexical suffix -ûs 'face, eye, surface'; root tx̣ʷ- 'leave, abandon', -s 'third person possessive'.

[35]-alwís 'random activity', root possibly x̣al- 'turn'.

[36]-s 'third person possessive'. A negative is often followed by possessives; however, see sentence (6) where a regular indicative predicate follows.

COYOTE AND THE DOGS

(Sahaptin)

Bruce Rigsby

University of Queensland

Sahaptin is a native language that is spoken by several hundred Indian people who live in eastern Oregon and eastern Washington. It and Nez Perce, its close sister language, make up the Sahaptian language family, which occupied most of the Southern Plateau culture area during aboriginal times. The Sahaptian family is a subgrouping of the Penutian stock, which is widely distributed throughout the California, Plateau, and Northwest Coast culture areas.

A systematic, comprehensive Sahaptin ethnography remains to be published, but a number of shorter pieces on aspects of Sahaptin culture and society have appeared over the years. The interested reader should check the latest edition of George P. Murdock, Ethnographic Bibliography of North America, for specific references. And several modern ethnographic sketches of Sahaptin-speaking groups will appear in the Plateau volume of the new Handbook of North American Indians.

The late Melville Jacobs published a grammar of Sahaptin (1931) and two collections of oral literature (1929, 1934, 1937). These contain excellent materials and should be consulted. A modern grammatical sketch of Sahaptin (Rigsby 1975) is scheduled for publication in the Languages volume of the new Handbook.

The narrator of the present text was Mrs. Minnie Wesley Showaway. Mrs. Showaway was originally from tináynu or Tenino, the westernmost Sahaptin village on the Oregon side of the Columbia River, and she spent many years living at wayám or Celilo. She used little English, preferring to speak her own language, although she was also familiar with kikšt, the Upper Chinookan language, and Nez Perce. We worked together for several days in late January, 1964, when she visited her relation, Mrs. Vera Jones, who was my main Sahaptin teacher on the Umatilla Rservation.

The text is a shortened version of a walcácas or myth that is set in the pre-cultural era when creatures had human-like personality and could take on either animal or human appearance. The main character in the myths is spilyáy, Coyote, who is both trickster and creator. The myths often tell how Coyote ordained that the various creatures would assume their current characteristics and forms. He also instituted many features of culture for the human species, whose entrance onto the scene brought the present era into being.

The text was recorded on tape, and I transcribed and translated it later with Mrs. Jones' assistance. My knowledge of the language was weak then, and I have since rechecked and corrected the transcription from the tape and have reconsidered points of translation. In retrospect, I realize that Mrs. Showaway shortened the story and introduced some explanatory material for my benefit. She had a problem with sequencing early in the text, while other passages display the crisp set form of mythic narration that presumes the knowledgeable cultural background of an audience. That Mrs. Showaway was an excellent raconteur is not clear from this particular text, but limitations of space forced its choice over a longer, richer one. This publication of "Coyote and the Dogs" is dedicated to her memory.[1]

(1)	aw=tya[2]	míimi	i-wa-č̓á	čaw-tanán[3]	áẋʷay.	(2)	ana=kúš	ƛ̓áaẋʷ	č̓í
	now	long ago	was	no-people	yet		just like	all	this

kákya-tun.[4]	(3)	tunẋtúnẋ.[5]	(4)	č̓áw	áẋʷay	tanán	i-wa-č̓á.	(5)	ana=kú
creature-kinds		different		not	yet	people	was		when

pá-tamanwi-ya[6]	čaaná[7]	tiič̓ám-na[8]	ku	pá-tamanwi-ya	k̓usik̓úsi-na.	(6)	ku	náẋš
created	this	earth	and	created	dog		and	one

áyat	ku	náẋš	wínš.	(7)	ku	pa-q̓ínun-ẋa-na[9]	pa-nišáy-ša-na	waƛ̓amałaní...
woman	and	one	man		and	they would see	they were dwelling	Watłamałani

pa-nišáy-ša-na kúsikúsi-yáy-ma[10] kʷiiní.[11] (8) ku pa-qínun-x̣a-na
they were dwelling Dogs those two and they would see

ku tanán=tya aw-kú míimi pa-wa-čá ana=kúš čí i-wá ƛ́aaxʷ-tún[12]
and people and then long ago they were just like this is all-kinds

kákya či-kúuk. (9) pa-qínun-x̣a-na pa-kʸíyan-ɨm-š. (10) ku
creature presently they would see they are coming and

pamá-palata-x̣a-na kúnki[13] kúsikúsi-nmí-ki[14] wapáwat-ki. (11) ƛ́aax-míš[15]
they would put on that dog's costume all-sorts

wapáwat. (12) patá-wiyanawi-yawa-na.[16] (13) "aw kúsikúsi-ma=tya-x̣aš
costume they would come to his place now just dogs

čí pa-wá". (14) patá-wilaalakʷɨn-x̣a-na. (15) ana=tun-yáy=tya áw
this they are they would leave him Anything now

i-wína-x̣a-m-a ƛ́aaxʷ čí wí-wanič-i kákya. (16) i-wyánawi-ya spilyáy íkʷɨn.
he would come all this named creature he came Coyote there

(17) pá-qinu-na. (18) i-pxʷí-na "míš či-kúš pa-wá"? (19) pamá-ptpalata-na.
he saw him he thought how this-way they are they put theirs on

(20) pa-yaqáynač-a níit-yaw.[17] (21) pamá-wina-ptpalata-na kúsikúsi-nmí-ki.
they ran inside house-to they put theirs on fast dog's

(22) kúsikú::si[18] pa-qá-wa". (23) pá-'aštwana-na. (24) pa-qá-la-ku-ša[19]
dog they become he followed them in they are gathering together

kúsikúsi-ma. (25) pá-sạmxna-na húuy. (26) aw-kú i-pxʷí-na spilyáy
dogs he talked to him in vain and then he thought Coyote

"íi ka-'aw-kú kúsikúsi-ma pa-wá ku tanán pa-tx̣ána-x̣a.
yes although dogs they are and people they turn into

(27) ku čaw-šín[20] pá-qinun-x̣a íkʷɨn.[21] (28) ku táay[22] k'ʷay-kúš[23]
and no-one sees him do that and for what that

pa-wá-ta aw-kú? (29) aw=tya anáw[24] pa-wá-ta kúsikúsi.
they will be and then now ? they will be dog

(30) čaw=tya-mún[25] pa-čá-kʷck-ta k'ʷáy ana=kúš tun-táatpas.[26] (31) aw=tya
never they will take off that just like clothing now

tɨ́minwa=tya á-wa-ta kúsikusi-nmí pɨnmín wáwnakšaš-pa".[27] (32) ku=tya
forever he will have dog's his body-on and

pa-sɨ́nwi-x̣a-na=tya kúsikúsi-ma. (33) ku pá-tamanwi-ya aw-kú "čaw=pam-ún[28]
they used to talk dogs and he ordained it and then you never

íkuš wá-ta. (34) aw=tya-pam wá-ta kúsikúsi ana=kú tanán i-wyánawi-ta.
thus will be now you will be dog when people will come

(35) ku=pam pa-'aní-ta kúsikúsi-yawticáwas=tya".[29] (36) pá-wilaalakʷ-a
and-you they will make dog-companion he left him

aw-kú spilyáy-n.[30] (37) ƛ́áax̣ʷ-na pá-tamanwi-ya ana=kúɬ čí i-wá
and then Coyote all he ordained it just like this is

kákya ƛ́aax̣ʷ-tún.[31] (38) pá-wi-waničá-a. (39) i-winá-na aw-kú. (40) kʷa=ku[32]
creature all-kinds he named them he went and then and

máal aw-kú i-winá-na. (41) kʷyáam aw-kú kúsikúsi pa-tx̣ána-na
how far and then he went truly and then dog they turned into

aw-kú. (42) "tanán á-wi-wa-m-š cáa-pa-ká. (43) ku=pam pa-q́ínu-ta
and then people many are coming close-by and-you they will see

"ée[33] ḱʷáy i-wá amú'amu kúsikúsi". (44) ku=pam pa-wɨ́np-ta.
yes that is cute dog and-you they will pick up

(45) ḱʷáy=pam aw-kú iyawticáwas pa-'aní-ta. (46) tanán i-wá-m-ta ku
that-you and then companion they will make people will come and

i-wahwák-ta. (47) á-taax̣ʷa-ta-nam[34] tanán-a. (48) íkuš=pam wá-ta". (49) ḱʷáy
he will bark you will warn people thus-you will be that

aw kʷáal.
now thus far

Free Translation

(1) Long ago there were no people yet. (2) There were all kinds of birds and animals like there are now. (3) There were different kinds. (4) There were no people yet. (5) When this earth was created, the dogs were created too. (6) A female one and a male one. (7) They would see... Watɬamaɬaní and... were dwelling... Those two Dogs were dwelling there. (8) They would see... The people long ago were just like all the birds and animals there are now. (9) The two dogs would see people coming. (10) And they would put on those dog costumes. (11) All sorts of them. (12) The people then would come to the dogs' place. (13) And they would say, "Oh, there's just dogs here". (14) And then they would leave them. (15) Just any of the birds and animals would come to the dogs' place. (16) Coyote came there. (17) He saw them. (18) He thought to himself, "What kind of animals are these? (19) They put on their dog costumes. (20) They ran inside their house. (21) They put their dog costumes on quickly. (22) And they've become dogs". (23) He followed them inside. (24) The dogs gather together now. (25) He tried in vain to talk to them. (26) And then Coyote thought to himself, "Yes, although they are dogs, they turn into people. (27) Nobody sees them do that. (28) What will they be good for like that? (29) Let them just be dogs! (30) They will never take off those dog costumes. (31) They will wear those dog costumes on their bodies for all time". (32) The dogs used to be able to talk. (33) But Coyote ordained, "You will no longer be like that. (34) You will just be dogs when the people come. (35) They will make companions of you". (36) And then Coyote left them. (37) He ordained that all the birds and animals would be as they are now. (38) He gave them their names. (39) And then he went. (40) I wonder just how far he did go. (41) And then they truly had become real dogs. (42) Coyote said, "Lots of people are coming soon. (43) They will see you and say, "That's a cute little dog". (44) And they'll pick you up. (45) Then they'll have you be their companion. (46) There'll be people coming then and he'll bark. (47) You'll warn people that someone is coming. (48) That's the way you'll be". (49) That's all.

Footnotes

[1] The orthography and orthographic conventions used here are as in Rigsby (1975). I have indicated most, but not all, morpheme boundaries in the Sahaptin forms. The hyphen marks a simple morpheme boundary, the equals sign marks a clitic boundary, and a space marks a word boundary. Interlinear translations that contain hyphens parallel the Sahaptin constituents, while those that lack hyphens do not. Interlinear translations are not provided for all constituents. The serious linguistic reader should consult Jacobs (1931) and Rigsby (1975) to parse and gloss the forms with more delicacy.

[2] =tya is the contrastive enclitic.

[3] čaw-tanán is a compound of two free forms. tanán 'Indian person, people' is morphologically singular. There is no overt distinction between the singular and the collective plural (as opposed to the distributive plural) in nouns and verbs. Collective plurals are given singular interlinear translations here.

[4] kákya-tun is a compound.

[5] The reduplication of tunx̣túnx̣ marks distributive plurality.

[6] The pá- verb prefix cross-references a third singular subject on third singular object, but in this case where the subject has been zeroed and lacks an overt antecedent, the verb is best translated as a passive.

[7] čaaná is the objective singular case-form of 'this'.

[8] -na is the objective singular case-ending.

[9] Mrs. Showaway had difficulty with sequencing in (7) and (8). She first started to refer to the two dogs by name, then simply referred to them as k̓usik̓usi-yáy-ma, using the personified form of 'dog'.

[10] -yay is the personifying suffix and -ma is the productive distributive plural suffix.

[11] kʷiiní is apparently a dual nominative case-form of 'that'. The same form generally functions as the nominative obviative case-form of the paradigm.

[12] ƛ̓aaxʷ-tun is a compound.

[13] kúnk̇i is the instrumental case-form of 'that'.

[14] -nmí is the possessive singular and -ki the instrumental case-ending.

[15] ƛ̓aax̣-míš is a compound.

[16] -yawa- is the directive verb derivational suffix.

[17] -yaw is the allative case-ending.

[18] The two colons mark rhetorical lengthening.

[19] The verb is inflected for present imperfective here.

[20] čaw-šín is a compound.

[21] íkʷɨn is the allative case-form of 'that'. The verb q̓ínu- 'see' commonly takes sentential complements in the allative. The antecedent of íkʷɨn is the tanán pa-txána-xa 'they turn into people' of the previous sentence.

[22] ṫáaẏ 'for what' is a marginal case-form of the tún 'what' paradigm.

[23] k̓ʷay-kúš is a compound.

[24] I cannot identify or gloss the anáw here.

[25] čaw=tya-mún is a compound with =tya enclitic to its first member.

[26] tun-táatpas is a compound.

[27] -pa is the locative case-ending.

[28] čaw=pam-ún is a compound with =pam 'second person plural' enclitic to its first member. -ún is reduced from mún 'indefinite-interrogative time pronoun' due to the preceding identical final consonant of =pam.

[29] kúsikusi-yawticáwas=tya is a compound with the =tya contrastive enclitic on the second member. The initial i- of iyawticáwas 'companion' has been deleted.

[30] -n is an allomorph of the obviative nominative case-ending.

[31] ƛ'áaxʷ-tún is a compound.

[32] kʷa- is a modal proclitic that indexes the speaker's lack of knowledge of some matter and a mild curiosity about it.

[33] ée is presumably a lowered form of íi 'yes'.

[34] =nam is the second person singular enclitic. I would have expected =pam, the second person plural form, here.

COYOTE AND FOX

(Nez Perce)

Haruo Aoki

University of California, Berkeley

The Nez Perce language, together with the Sahaptin language, constitutes the Sahaptian linguistic family, and was spoken aboriginally in north central Idaho, southeastern Washington and northeastern Oregon. There are an ethnographic study by Spinden (1908a), a collection of folktales in Nez Perce by Phinney (1934) and a study of acculturation by Walker (1968). Two Nez Perce grammars (Morvillo 1891, Aoki 1970) and an English-Nez Perce dictionary (Morvillo 1895) have been published, and a collection of texts (Aoki 1978) is scheduled for publication.

The Nez Perce Tribe recently published Nu Mee Poom Tit Wah Tit (Nez Perce Legends)(1972) and Noon Nee Me Poo (We, The Nez Perces)(1973), strengthening the hope that pride in the Nez Perce tradition will grow.

The present text has not been previously published, and was tape-recorded by Mrs. Elizabeth P. Wilson in 1962 at her home in Kamiah, Idaho. The recording was made at natural storytelling speed, and later transcribed by playing the tape back sentence by sentence. Her call of "whoa", as though to stop a horse, marked the end of each sentence. "Coyote and Fox" is a translation of ?iceyé·ye tilípe?ni·n, and is identified as a myth by the fact that the scene is set before humans came, and when only titwatityá·ya or 'myth people' lived. There are many stories which belong to the Coyote and Fox group, which is characterized by having two parts: the first part, in which Fox obtains food miraculously, and the second part, in which Coyote imitates Fox and fails miserably.[1]

Mrs. Elizabeth P. Wilson was born in 1882 in the middle fork area of the Clearwater River in Idaho. The place is a few miles east of Kooskia. Except for her years at Carlisle between 1902 and 1909 she lived on the Nez Perce reservation. Besides being knowledgeable in the baking of camas roots, the tanning of hides, the smoking of meat, and in beadwork, she was a fine storyteller and a kind and patient teacher of the language. She died three days after her ninety-first birthday in 1973. This publication of "Coyote and Fox" is gratefully dedicated to her memory.[2]

(1)	?iceyé·ye	tilípe?ni·n	hitéw̓yecine.	(2)	kawó?	yú?cme
	Coyote	with Fox	was living		then	poor (pl)

he·yé·qcix.[3]	(3)	kawó?	?iceyé.ye	hiq̓oyímnaqana[4]	?ipnalaqá·ciqana.	
be hungry		then	Coyote	went up hill	looked for mice	

(4)	kawó?	kú?mac	hi?náhpayxqana	koná	ka·	wiwá·q̓ic	payax̣wayikó·qana
	then	some	he brought	there	and	alive	tossed across to him

tilípe?ne	yû?sne.	(5)	ka·	kál̓a	hipewí·wu·yn	lá·qac.	(6)	kí·
to Fox	poor		and	just	scattered	mice		this

k̓álawnik̓aẏ tilípe? hiné·ke, "wá·qo? ?é·te·x toláyca pí·k̓un má·t̓atx."
finally Fox thought now surely go upstream river upstream

(7) kawó? hitoláynikika koná hinaspaynó·ya ?isí·met[5] qí·wn
then he went on upstream there he came to them there old man

ha·ní·sa wistitámo ka· há·cwal hix̣e·lé·wise wé·?iktki ?ipnacawlatayíca
was making sweatbath and boy was playing with fat was kidding around

koná. (8) konó? papaynó·ya. (9) "?e·hé ?itú·pke·tem tilípe? kú·me."
there there he came to him yes why you Fox came

(10) "k̓álo? kí· ku?ús ?ipsqilá·nx̣ ka· ?é·tx kí· paynó·s."
just this like this walking around and you (pl) this came upon

(11) "kúy q̓uyím ka· yóx̣ koná hí·wes ?iní·t. (12) tax̣c̓e· koná t̓awa[6]
go go up and that there is house soon you there that

hipú? hipst̓ú·ẏ. (13) hipst̓ú·ẏ núkt hí·wes ?iléx̣ni. (14) k̓ála
will eat enough enough meat is much just

kem?itú·ne tax̣caw̓yá·x̣no? qó?c k̓ála ?í·n hí·tem̓yekse ka· qó?c
whatever you soon will find later just I am sweatbathing and later

tax̣c̓e· paynó·tano?." (15) "?e·hé" pé·ne (16) kawó? hiq̓uyímne
soon to you will come yes he said to him then he went up

ha?áca ?í··· ?isí·met núkt hitehémce hicapá·?laqẏawisa. (17) ka·
he went in there meat it was dark was drying and

hiwse?íce wá·qo? ?ilaqyá·wiǹ ka· sisílq̓is hite?épetu. (18) konó? ka·
it lay already dried and fresh (pl) was there there and

hihípe hipst̓ú·ẏ· kawó? koná pá·?yax̣o?ya capá·ypa hipapá·yna há·cwal
he ate his fill then there he waited after a while they came boy

qí·wni·n. (19) konó? ka· ?ipná?pipc̓anaq̓is hú·sus siléq̓is
with old man then and he just finished washing hair head wet

qó?c ka· hicapá·?laqẏawisa konmá t̓awa ?alá·px pé·ne "?e·hé
still and he was drying that way that against the fire said yes

wá·qo? ?é·tem hípe." (20) "?e·hé qe?ciỷé·ẁyeẁ wá·qo? hipsťú·ỷ hípe."
already you ate yes than you already enough ate

(21) kawó? ?aẁlaqỷa·wya hú·kux ka· núkt pé·?nike?nye koná q̓o? káľo?
then his dried hair and meat he put for him there quite just

ćiníňis ?isé·ps "kí· ?e· ?inéhnece" pé·ne. (22) "?e·hé qe?ciỷé·ẁyeẁ"
heavy bundle this you (sg) carry he said yes thank you

tilípe?nim pé·ne. (23) kawó? hi?sé·pe ka· hickilí·ne koná láwtiwa·
Fox said then he packed on back and went home there friend

?iceyé·ye hipaynó·ya. (24) "kíyex ?ináhpayksa núkt kí·." (25) "?o·
Coyote came to for us I brought meat this oh

qe?ciỷé·ẁyeẁ" ?iceyé·ye hihíne. (26) kawó? tató?s pe?énye ka·
thank you Coyote said then some gave him and

hipetéẁyenike káľa hipa·yáwya núkt ?iléx̣ni hipt. (27) wá·qo? ka·
they lived just they relaxed meat much food now and

?o·yalá?amktacix. (28) ka· wá·qi koná ?iceyé·yenm pé·ne "míne ka· kínye
it was running out and now there Coyote told him where and this

?eẁnípe. (29) wá·qo? ?i·ňke kú·se. (30) qecem?í·m." (31) kawó? pé·ne
get now I also go if you can I can then said

"lawwí·ťo ?e· kiyú? (32) ?e· we wé·ťu lawwí·t. (33) qí·wn hitó·ẁyece
right you will do you are not right old man lives

má·ťa. (34) koná ?e· paynó·tano?. (35) wé·tmet ?imá·?nahciẁatko?.
upriver there you will go do not get yourself in trouble

(36) ?e· wé·s wé·ťu ća?a ?iceyé·ye." (37) "?e·hé ka· ?itú·px kex
you are not correct Coyote yes and why should I

?iná·?nahciẁatko?qa." (38) kawó? hitoláyna hi··· hinaspaynó·ya
get myself into trouble then he went upriver (far) he came to them

(39) ?isí·met wistitámo ha·ní·sa qí·wn ka· há·cwal hix̣e·lé·wise
there sweatbath was making old man and boy was playing

wé·?iktki ka· pá·tqa?npa?niqana ka· pá·pa?niqana. (40) ka· qí·wnim pé·ne
with fat and he grabbed his and ate it and old man said

"?ú·s kál̓a t̓awa ł̓í·k̓is ?itqí·n. (41) kúy koná ciklí·n. (42) ?iléx̣ni
is just that dirty with soil go there turn much

koná núkt kem hipít̓e." (43) wé·t̓u q̓o? pé·msteqe?npe kál̓a qiyé̓·s
there meat you eat not quite he answered just sullen

?iceyé·ye. (44) kawó? hiq̓uyímne ka· koná pé·xne nukúne. (45) kál̓a
Coyote then he went up and there he saw meat just

hiwí·sapc̓a?ksa hicapá·?laqy̓awisa ?óykaslix núkt. (46) ka· konó?
was hanging was drying all over meat and there

hitqé·pe ka· hiwx̣si?lí·ke konó? pá·?yax̣o?ya. (47) wá·qo? ka·
he quickly ate and he sat down there he waited now and

qí·wn hipá·yn ku?stí·t. (48) "?e·hé we·t qetu hipsá·qa
old man came in the same way yes did you some ate

hipst̓ú·y̓. (49) yóq̓o? ku?ús hí·wes núkt." (50) ka· wé·t̓umi?s
enough that thus is meat and not at all

pé·msteqe?npe kál̓a sáw̓is ?iceyé·ye. (51) kawó? koná hicapá·?laqy̓awya
he answered just ignored Coyote then there he dried

hú·kux qí·wn qó?c hicapá·?laqy̓awisa hú·kux ka· wá·qi ?iceyé·ye hi?né·pte
hair old man still he was drying hair and now Coyote held

wec̓ílli·ke?s kiné·px pá·wawya?nya hú·sus. (52) ?i··· la?ám̓ yox̣ kakalá
club to here hit his head oh all that as much as

núkt hisá·pc̓a?ksa wax̣ ?óykaslix hite?épetu hitqehúx̣eleke?yke ?ímes
meat was hanging and all over lying suddenly stood up deer

hipewc̓é·ye qí·wn ka· há·cwal la?ám̓ ?iní·t sáw hikúye.[7] (53)
they became old man and boy all house disappeared did

kál̓a pú·yetkuyten̓ixne kípk̓iceyé·yene hi?lwá·pa?yika ?inekí·k̓u kál̓a. (54)
just shoved him around this way Coyote dodged around though just

"námax kú·se. (55) sá...w. (56) wé·t̓u ?itú· míne hitqé·wse.
what happened gone not anything where is it

(57) cá?ya ?itú· núkt, ?itú· ?iní·t" (58) kawó? hi?psqíwewitiye
absent any meat any house then he walked downstream

k̓iyú·pc ?í··· papaynó·ya tilípe?ne. (59) "wá·qo? ?e·
with nothing (long distance) he came to Fox now you

?imá·?nahciw̓atka ?iceyé·ye. (60) yóx̣ kex kíne waqa wéwcetespe
got yourself into trouble Coyote that which here was at pillow

núkt la?ám̓ hipeté·lehte[8] kínix kál̓a hipú·yetkuyteye. (61) ?e· kál̓o?
meat all ran out from here just ran over me you just

kiyex wé·t̓u tá?c. (62) wá·qo? ?e· hicá·qa 'lawwí·t ?e· tá?c
for us not good already you I told right you good

timí·p̓niyu? ?iceyé·ye, wé·tmet ?imá·?nahciw̓atko?.' (63) wá·qo? ka·
will think Coyote do not get yourself into trouble now and

kíye hé·n̓eke heyé·qcix, ?e·he." (64) kál̓o? hitqetemé·yex̣six yú?cme
we again are hungry yes just they sat down poor ones

cá?ya ?itú· míne hípt. (65) yóx̣ ná·qc titwá·tit.
not anything anywhere food that one story

Free Translation

(1) Coyote and Fox were living. (2) The poor ones were hungry. (3) Coyote used to go uphill looking for mice. (4) Then he would bring some and would throw live ones across to the poor Fox. (5) Then the mice would run in different directions. (6) Finally Fox thought, 'Now I am going up the river.' (7) Then he went upstream, there he came to an old man making sweatbath and a boy playing with (a ball of) fat and just kidding around. (8) He came to them. (9) 'Yes, why did you come, Fox?' (asked the old man). (10) (Fox answered) 'I was just walking around like this and I came upon you here.' (11) (The old man said) 'Go up, then there is a house. (12) You will eat enough there. (13) There is plenty of meat. (14) (Help yourself to) whatever you will find, I have to take sweatbath yet and later I will come to you.' (15) 'Yes,' he (Fox) said to him (the old man).

(16) Then Fox went up, and went in (to the house), and oh! meat was drying (there was so much that) it was dark. (17) Some lay already dried and some was lying there fresh. (18) After he had his fill, he waited for him (the old man), and after a while the boy and the old man came. (19) He (the old man) had just finished washing his hair and his head was still wet, and was drying it against the fire and said, 'Yes, already you ate.' (20) (Fox said) 'Yes, thank you, I already ate my fill.' (21) Then his hair was dried and he put some meat for him (Fox) in quite a heavy bundle, and 'You take this' he said. (22) Fox said, 'Yes, thank you.' (23) Then he carried it on his back and went home to his friend Coyote. (24) (Fox said) 'I brought this meat for us.' (25) 'Oh, thank you,' said Coyote.

(26) Then he gave him some meat and they lived in comfort with much meat and food. (27) Now it was running short.

(28) At this time Coyote said to him (Fox), 'Where did you get this? (29) I am going also. (30) If you can, I can.' (31) Then he (Fox) said to him (Coyote), 'you do it right. (32) You do not behave right. (33) An old man lives upriver. (34) You go there. (35) Do not get yourself into trouble. (36) You do not know how to behave correctly, Coyote.' (37) (Coyote said) 'Oh yeah, why should I get into trouble?'

(38) Then he went way upriver, and he got there. (39) There the old man was making sweatbath and the boy was playing with (a ball) of fat, then he (Coyote) grabbed it (fat) and ate it. (40) Then the old man said, 'That is dirty, it is with dirt. (41) Go around there. (42) There is much meat which you can eat.' (43) Coyote would not even answer and was sullen. (44) Then he went up and saw meat there. (45) The meat was hanging to be dried all over. (46) He quickly ate and sat down and waited. (47) The old man came as before. (48) (The old man asked) 'Yes, did you have enough to eat? (49) That is the way meat is.' (50) But Coyote did not answer, he ignored him. (51) Then the old man dried his hair, he was still drying his hair and Coyote took a club and hit his head.

(52) Then all that meat that was hanging and lying all over suddenly stood up and became deer. The old man, the boy and the house all disappeared. (53) They (deer) shoved Coyote around even though he tried to dodge. (54) 'What happened? (55) Gone! (56) Not a thing (is left), where did it go? (57) No meat, no house.'

(58) Then he (Coyote) walked downstream empty-handed, and came to Fox. (59) (Fox said) 'Now you got yourself into trouble, Coyote. (60) The meat that was at my pillow all ran out from here running over me. (61) You are just no good. (62) I told you to think right and be good and not to get into trouble, Coyote. (63) Now we are going to be hungry again, yes.' (64) The poor ones just sat without any food anywhere. (65) That is one story.

Footnotes

[1] Besides Phinney's version (1934:285-301), which is in the original Nez Perce, Coyote and Fox stories were published in English by Spinden (1908b: 23), Farrand (1917:169-70), and the Nez Perce Tribe (1972:163-169).

[2] The transcription is the same as that used in Aoki 1970; note that /e/ is [æ]. In the grammatical notes, references of the type 'G112' refer to page numbers in my Nez Perce grammar.

[3] cix is a plural present tense ending (G112-120). This is a case of historical present.

[4] qana is a frequentative remote past ending (G115-124). Two or more verbs with the same ending show that a single action is described as a complex of two actions. Here 'Coyote went uphill looking for mice.'

[5] ?isí·met indicates that what follows is new information.

[6] ˀtawa is used when the speaker cannot recall the right word: 'Whatchamacallit.'

[7] This verb is in the singular form and is used to indicate collective action.

[8] té·l is a prefix meaning that the subject of 'run' is a hoofed animal. Without the word ?ímes'deer' (in sentence (52)) a listener can guess that the subject is deer.

SQUIRREL AND ACORN-WOMAN

(Wintu)

Harvey Pitkin

Columbia University, New York

This characteristic text was tape recorded as it was told to me on July 19, 1957, during my second summer of field work, by Carrie B. Dixon, in Redding, California. It was transcribed, emended and translated by her immediately afterward. The late Mrs. Dixon (née Radcliffe), the granddaughter of Chief Qolčulu·li of the McCloud River Wintu, was then 68 years old, a fluent bilingual speaker of Wintu and English, who had lived all her life in northern California, most of it in Redding. She was a very patient, intelligent, generous and gracious lady whose kindness to me made possible the success of my fieldwork, and to whose memory this publication is gratefully dedicated.

This traditional myth (bo·las) was told with evident pleasure and amusement, the only long text she ever volunteered. It resembles a shorter published text, "Coyote Eats Grasshoppers", collected in English by Cora du Bois (du Bois and Demetracopoulou 1931) from Jo Bender of the Upper Sacramento Wintu, with which it shares a central motif, although this version is otherwise rather different. It may also be compared with "Coyote and Bullhead", a Wintu myth appearing in Northern California Texts in this NATS series (Golla and Silver editors, vol. 2, 1978), since various information concerning the language and many of the forms which appear in this text are already described there and will not be repeated below. The abbreviations and other conventions used are the same.

(1) tepca[2]-kilake·[1]	lendada[2]	k̓aysas[3]	ʔuna·[26]	ƛ̓iƛep̓o·qtam[4]	p̓uqanit.[5]
emerge-conditional-hearsay	long ago	fast walker	then	acorn-female-human-object case	wife-particular

(2) ʔuna·[26]	pe·l[1]	bo·s[6]	pur[7]	bo·sin[8]	pe·l[1]	bo·s[6]	ʔuna·.[26]	(3)	ʔuna·[26]
then	they-two	site/stay	3rd-possess.	site-locative	they-two	site/stay	then		then

buha-harat[9]	pule·n[10]	tu·na[37]	henpaq[13]	pule·t[11]	sedet.[7]	(4)	ʔuna·[26]
stay-progressive-partic.	their-dual	ahead	arrive-benefactive	them-dual	coyote-particular		then

ʔel-q̓ayas[12]	pule·t[11]	bira·s,[13]	"yencay[14]	q̓aya·[15]	ʔibi·da,"[32]	ʔuni.[33]	(5)	ʔut,[6]
in-walk	them-dual	hungry	nephew	walk	be-imperfect-I	quote		then

"peh-ma·[16]	ʔelewda[17]	ba·s[18]	beme·mina,"[19]	ʔuni[33]	pi[3]	k̓aysas-to·t.[20]	(6)	ʔut,[6]
what-concessive	negative-I	food	possess-not	quote	that	fast walker-agent		then

"peh[16]	ʔilay-ma·[21]	ba·mah[22]	ʔewet,"[23]	ʔuni[33]	pi[3]	k̓aysas-to·t[20]
what	little-concessive	eat-causative	this-particular	quote	that	fast walker-agent

λ̓iλeṗo·qtam[4]	pur[7]	p̓u·qat.[24]	(7) ʔut[6]	pi[3]	λ̓iλep̓o·qta-to·t[25]	pulu·q[26]
acorn-female-human-object	3rd possess.	wife-particular	then	that	acorn-female-human-agent	basket

xun-tune-buha,[27]	xun-tune-buha[27]	ken-λincuma·[28]	ko·m[25]	paruma·[29]
toward-haul-durative	toward-haul-durative	down-snot-transitive-reflexive	all	fill

ken-λincuna·r[30]	paruma·[29]	λ̓iλe[30]	yiwit.[31]	(8) ʔut[6]	ʔuna·[26]	ba·mah[22]
down-snot-transitive-reflexive-subord.	fill	acorn	stirred-particular	then	then	eat-causative

dawina[32]	ʔuhet̓an[33]	we·quna·[34]	pi[3]	sedet-to·t[35]	we·quna·[34]	ʔelew[48]
serve	even so	nausea-reflexive	that	coyote-particular-agent	nausea-reflexive	negative

λupus-koyumina.[35]	(9) "ken-λincuna·[28]	pur[7]	ʔelewda[17]	ba·s-koyumina,"[36]
acorn soup-desiderative-not	down-snot-transitive-reflexive	3rd possess.	negative-I	food-deserative-not

ʔuni.[33]	(10) ʔut[6]	pi[3]	λipalar[37]	put[81]	hiwalna·r,[38]
quote	then	that	teased-subordinate	3rd-object	insulted-reflexive-subordinate

"ʔelew[48]-wirabi·da[39]	ʔewin[40]	sukmina,"[41]	ʔuni[33]	pi[3]	λiλep̓o·qta-to·t[25]	pur[7]
negative-future-imperfect-I	this-locative	stand-not	quote	that	acorn-female-human-agent	3rd-possess.

wiyit.[42]	(11) ʔuna·[26]	pur[7]	wiyi-to·t[43]	ʔelew[48]	peh[16]	ti·nmina[50]	ʔut̓an.[44]
male-particular	then	3rd-possess.	male-agent	negative	what	speak-not	then-contrary

(12) "hara·[36]-wirabi·da,"[39]	ʔuni[33]	pur[7]	p̓uqan-to·t.[45]	(13) "nompom[46]	net[47]
go-future-imperfect-I	quote	3rd-possess.	wife-agent	west-land	1st-possess.

bo·spom[48]	hara·[36]-wirabi·da,[39]	nompom[46]	λiλepom-to·n[49]	hara·[36]-wirabi·da."[39]
dwell-land	go-future-imperfect-I	west-land	acorn-land-agent-location	go-future-imperfect-I

(14) ʔunibuha[77]	"ke·namahle-ba·da[50]	yo·la[51]
thus-durative	deep-causative-inevitable-durative-I	snow

dilmahle-ba·da."[52]	(15) "ʔelew-weret[53]	ʔewer[54]	maya·mina,[55]	ʔut[6]
drop-causative-inevitable-durative-I	negative-future-particular	this-instrum.	follow-not	then

ʔol-t̓epum-to·nin[56]	qati·[57]	po·m[58]	calamahle-ba·da[59]	mat[60]	wira-weres;[61]
up-spring-agent-location-locative	equivocal-reference	land	good-causative-inevitable-durative-I	2nd-possess.	come-future

(16) ʔunir[62]	ʔeh[123]	ba·s[18]	ʔilay[163]	mis[63]	yalupaqta,"[64]	ʔuni.[33]	(17)
thus-because subordinate	this	food	little	2nd-object	leave-benefactive-subord.	quote	

ʔunibuna[77]	po·qat[65]	hiwalna·r[66]	hara·[36]	pi[3]	nompom[46]	pur[7]	bo·spom[48]
thus-durative	now-reference	insulted-subordinate	go	that	west-land	3rd-possess.	dwell-land

nompom[46]	ƛ̓iλepom.[49]	(18) ʔut[6]	pi[3]	k̓aysas-to·t[20]	ʔunibuha[77]	sedet-to·t[35]
west-land	acorn-land	then	that	fast walker-agent	thus-durative	coyote-particular-agent

buha[9]	ʔuna·[26]	pʰo·h[67]	c̓an-to·nin[68]	pi[3]	loni[69]	lonimina[70]	k̓aysas-to·t[20]
stay	then	fire	side/half-agent-locative	that	bark(tree)	bark-not	fast walker-agent

ba·-biya[71]	k̓aca·-biya[72]	pur[7]	horuma·paqas[73]	ʔuna·[26]	ba·s[18]
eat-imperfect	chew-imperfect	3rd-possess.	remain-gener.-com-benefact.-generic	then	food

yalupaqas.[74]	(19) ʔuna·[26]	pi[3]	sedeto·t[75]	k̓etem[76]	pʰo·h[67]	c̓anin[77]	biya,[80]
leave-benefactive-generic	then	that	coyote-agent	one/other	fire	side/half-locative	lie

"peh[16]	yencay[14]	k̓acar[78]	ʔiye[31]	ʔibiyam,"[19]	ʔuni.[33]	(20) ʔut,[6]	"ʔuwe[79]
what	nephew	chew-subord.	copula	imperfect-2nd interrog.	quote	then	anyway

loni-ma·n[80]	k̓acar[78]	ʔiye[31]	ʔibi·da,[32]	peh-p̓eni[81]	ʔuwe[79]	loni,"[69]	ʔuni.[33]	(21)
bark-concessive	chew-subord.	copula	imperfect-I	what-without	anyway	bark	quote	

ʔut[6]	po·qat,[65]	"ʔelew[48]	piyo[82]	bintʰe·[83]	peh[16]	calumina[84]	net[85]
then	now-reference	negative	3rd-emphat.	imperfect non-visual sensory evidential	what	good-not	1st-possess.

ba·s,[18]	ʔelew-bintʰe·[86]	lelna·[87]	ʔisto·mina,"[88]	ʔuni[33]	pi[3]
food	negative-imperfect-sensory evid.	transform	some kind-not	quote	that

sedeto·t.[75]	(22)	ʔut,[6]	"ʔuna·[26]	hima·[89]	ʔukin-ma·[90]	hara·-wira[91]	ʔibi·da[32]
coyote-agent		then	then	morrow	that-locative-concessive	go-future	copula-imperfect-I

net[47]	p̓uqar[92]	su·s-to·n[93]	nom-λ̓iλepom[94]	hara·-wirabi·da,"[39]	ʔuni[33]	pi[3]
1st-possess.	wife-possess.	tribe-agent-location	west-acorn-land	go-future-imperfect-I	quote	that

k̓aysas-to·t.[20]	(23)	ʔut,[6]	"haras-kuda[95]	yo,"[96]	ʔuni[33]	pi[3]	sedet-to·t.[35]
fast walker-agent		then	going-desiderative-I	emphatic	quote	that	coyote-particular-agent

(24)	"ʔuhet̓an[189]	ʔele·les[297]	mi·[188]	yo·la[51]	ke·nas[97]	cupmina,"[98]	ʔuni[33]
	nevertheless	negative-inevitable-future	you	snow	deep-generic	wade-not	quote

pi[3]	k̓aysas-to·t.[20]	(25)	niqati·[99]	mi·[100]	wanwan-to·n[101]	hale-ba·da,"[102]
that	fast walker-agent		I-reference	trees	top-top-agent-location	go-inevitable-durative-I

ʔuni.[33]	(26)	ʔut[6]	ʔuna·[26]	hima·[89]	ʔukin[138]	hara·[36]	pi[3]	k̓aysas-to·t.[20]	(27)
quote		then	then	morrow	that-locative	go	that	fast-walker-agent	

pur[7]	p̓uqar[92]	bo·spom-to·n[103]	nompom[46]	hara·.[36]	(28)	ʔut[6]	henus[104]
3rd-possess.	wife-possess.	dwell-land-agent-location	west-land	go		then	how

ʔiwiyana·r[105]	sedeto·t[75]	ba·s[18]	ʔelewar[106]	beme·mina.[19]	(29)	peh[16]
not know-reflexive-subord.	coyote-agent	food	negative-subordinate	possess-not		what

ba·sleli[107]	ʔele·t[108]	be·mina.[109]	(30)	maya·.[110]	(31)	ʔut̓an[111]	yo·la[51]
food-transformed	negative-particular	be-not		follow		then-contrary	snow

ke·namat[112]	pur[7]	λ̓iλep̓o·qtan-to·t.[113]	(32)	ʔelew[48]	lelna·[114]
deep-causative-particular	3rd-possess.	acorn-female-human-instrumental-agent		negative	transform

ʔisto·mina,[115]	ʔelew[48]	he·[44]	q̓a·q[116]	x̣an-t̓ira,[117]	q̓aya·[15]	yo·la[51]
somekind-not	negative	exclamation	crazy	away-move	walk	snow

se-cupe-biya,[118]	ʔuni[33]	harat[119]	po·qat[65]	nomti[120]	nomc̓araw.[121]	(33)	pi[3]
distributive-wade-imperfect	thus	going-particular	now-reference	west-side	west-valley		that

qati·[122]	k̓aysas-to·t[20]	hinar[123]	ho·n[124]	buha[125]	pur[7]	p̓u·qat[24]
reference	fast walker-agent	arrive-subordinate	already	stay	3rd-possess.	wife-particular

ʔelwine.[126]	(34) ʔuna·[26]	pi[3]	sedet-to·t[35]	q̓aya·-hara·[127]	yo·la[51]
accompany	then	that	coyote-particular-agent	walk-progressive	snow

cupe-hara·[128]	po·qat[65]	nom-ke·n[129]	nompomin[130]	nompat-k̓uda.[131]	(35) ʔuna·[26]
wade-progressive	now-reference	west-deep	west-land-locative	west-out-step	then

tu-winit[132]	pur[7]	tu·na[37]	puba·np̓urun[133]	nepum[134]	yewci[135]	buya·[136]
ahead-seen-particular	3rd-possess.	ahead	them-reciprocal-instrumental	grasshoppers-object	gathered	many

pi[3]	bayi-to·n[137]	ko·m[25]	holholoq-to·n[138]	ko·m[25]	nu·q[139]	ʔilay[163]	biya.[80]
that	do by fire-agent-location	all	holes-agent-location	all	smoke	little	lie

(36) ʔunibuha[77]	pʰo·[140]	ʔilay[163]	biya.[80]	(37) ʔuna·[26]	tu·na[37]	pur[7]
thus-durative	fire	little	lie	then	ahead	3rd-possessive

xunpat-k̓odut[141]	holholq-to·nin[142]	pi[3]	nep[143]	q̓an[144]	biya[80]	nep[143]
toward-out-step-particular	holes-agent-location-locative	that	grasshopper	wings	lie	grasshopper

tole[145]	biya[80]	nep[143]	pʰoyoq[146]	biya.[80]	(38) ʔut̓a[236]	peh[16]	ʔel-p̓imana·[147]
legs	lie	grasshopper	heads	lie	then-after	what	in-peck at-reflexive

ʔel-p̓imana·[147]	bira·s[13]	po·[272]	be·sile·s.[148]	(39) ʔuna·[26]	ʔel-p̓imana·-hara·.[149]
in-peck at-reflexive	hungry	now	imperfect-visual-evidence (copula)	then	in-peck at-reflexive-progressive

(40) ʔut̓an[44]	ʔelew[48]	peh[16]	q̓omihna·[150]	ʔisto·nmina.[151]	(41) ʔuna·[26]	ba·-hara·[152]
then-contrary	negative	what	full-reflexive	some kind-not	then	eat-progressive

ba·-hara·[152]	po·qat[65]	yel-wine.[153]	(42) ʔuna·[26]	pur[7]	yel-wine[153]	tu·na[37]
eat-progressive	now-reference	back-see	then	3rd-possess.	back-see	ahead

pe·h[154]	kele·l[155]	supcu·t[156]	ʔule·s[157]	ʔuni[33]	pi[3]	nep[143]	q̓an.[144]	(43)
what	long	string-particular	just like	thus	that	grasshopper	wings	

ʔunibuha[77]	nep[143]	pʰoyoq[146]	nep[143]	tole[145]	pur[7]	ba·s.[18]	(44)
thus-durative	grasshopper	heads	grasshopper	legs	3rd-possess.	food	

ʔut̓an[44]	ʔelew[48]	teƛi[328]	ʔel-be·mina[158]	ʔuwe[79]	weremt̓ah-to·n[159]	pat-hara·ra.[160]
then-contrary	negative	belly	in-lie-not	anyway	buttocks-agent-location	out-go-iterative

(45) ʔuna·[26]	po·qat,[65]	"peh[16]	hen[161]	yo[96]	ʔel-t̓uyemena·-wirabi·da."[162]
then	now-reference	what	wonder how	emphatic	in-plug-causative-reflexive-future-imperfect-I

(46) "peh[16]	niqa·-kila,"[163]	ʔuni[33]	ʔuna·[26]	hudes[164]	poʔilay[165]	niqa·.[166]
what	find-conditional	quote	then	pitch	just-little	find

(47) ʔuna·[26]	hudesana·[167]	ʔuku[284]	ʔel-t̓uycuna·[162]	hudes.[164]	(48) ʔuna·[26]	po·qat[65]
then	pitch-reflexive	yonder	in-plug-transitive-reflex.	pitch	then	now-reference

se-p̓uyuy-hara·[168]	se-p̓uyuy-hara·[168]	po·qat[65]	hire·.[169]	(49) ʔuna·[26]	pi[3]
distributive-thrust-progressive	distributive-thrust-progressive	now-reference	burn up	then	that

hire·[169]	ƛ̓aqal[170]	pi[3]	sedet-to·t.[35]	(50) ʔuna·.[26]
burn up	obsidian-stative	that	coyote-particular-agent	then

Free Translation

[The following translation does not capture the casual and colloquial style used in the telling, but has a stilted tone which accommodates the repetitions and certain glosses, e.g. 'lo and behold', which I found difficult to render in a comparable English style.]

(No Wintu title was offered by C.D.)

(1) It appears that a long time ago a grey squirrel had an acorn-woman for a wife. (2) And they lived at his house, so did the two of them live. (3) And after they had been at home for a time thus, the two beheld Coyote arrive where they were. (4) And he visited them and being hungry he said, "Nephew, thus have I come here to you."

(5) But, "I don't really have anything at all to eat," said that Grey Squirrel.

(6) Then, "Feed this one a little something," said the Grey Squirrel to the Acorn Woman, his wife.

(7) Then the Acorn Woman gathered her container baskets together, she collected them, and blowing as though snot out of herself she filled them all up, from blowing out of her nose, she filled the baskets all with acorn soup.

(8) Then in that fashion did she feed him, dishing out the food, even though it nauseated him and the Coyote felt like vomiting and didn't want to eat the acorn soup. (9) "Because she blew snot out of herself, I don't want to eat it," he said.

(10) Then she got insulted (by Coyote's remark), her feelings got hurt, "I am not going to remain here," said the Acorn Woman to her husband. (11) And her husband never said anything even so. (12) "I'm going to go away," said his wife. (13) "I'm going

over to Trinity Valley where I come from, to Trinity Valley to the acorn country will I go." (14) And continuing she said, "Then will I make the snow fall very deep, very deep will I make it." (15) "In that way he (Coyote) will not be able to follow me, and then in the Spring I will make the land beautiful so that you can come to me." (16) "And so I'm leaving this little bit of food for you," she said. (17) And continuing in the same way just then did she go away to the land of her people to Trinity Valley, to the land of acorns, because of feeling herself insulted.

(18) So then the Grey Squirrel and the Coyote remained there, on opposite sides of the fire, but it was not tree bark that the Grey Squirrel was eating, he was eating and cracking and chewing the bones of the food that she had left for him, it was the food that had been left for him that he was eating. (19) And that Coyote was lying on the other side of the fire and said, "What, oh nephew, are you chewing on?"

(20) Then the other answered saying, "I'm just chewing on some tree bark or other, just nothing much, just some bark."

(21) So right then in answer, that Coyote replied saying, "This stuff that I'm eating for my food is no good, it isn't exactly food, it doesn't seem to have anything to it."

(22) So then that Grey Squirrel said, "Tomorrow then I guess I'll be going where my wife is, west to the acorn country I'll go."

(23) So then that Coyote said, "I do want to go too."

(24) "But you can't wade in the deep snow anyhow," said that Grey Squirrel. (25) "As for me, though, I will be going over the tree tops," he said.

(26) And so then on the next morning the Grey Squirrel left. (27) He went to Trinity Valley, his wife's people's country.

(28) But then Coyote didn't know what to do with himself because he didn't have anything to eat. (29) There was no food for him. (30) Coyote followed Grey Squirrel.

(31) After that the Acorn Woman made the snowfall deep. (32) Coyote got lost in this unreal place, while never losing consciousness, still he strayed as he walked, wading around in the snow drifts, he went on in that fashion as far as the western valley which was beyond him to the west. (33) As for the other one, the Grey Squirrel, he had arrived there already and was residing with his wife. (34) Eventually Coyote, traveling along, continuing to wade in the snow, finally then, he arrived there at Trinity Valley way out in the west. (35) And up ahead of him Coyote saw where a group were together collectively gathering grasshoppers, driving them out of cover by means of many little fires all around, at all the holes there were all the little puffs of smoke where they were. (36) And there was still a little fire burning around. (37) Thus when he arrived there at the place ahead with the holes all around, he beheld there grasshopper wings, grasshopper legs, and grasshopper heads.

(38) After that he was so hungry that he immediately fell to grazing on anything that was there, and he picked up all those small scraps, pecking like a bird at crumbs, feeding on whatever was left of the grasshoppers there. (39) And thus did he continue to feed himself up.

(40) But even so he never was able to get full and appease his hunger with any of that stuff he had been eating. (41) And in that way he kept on eating and kept on eating, until at one point he looked back. (42) Then after he looked back, lo and behold, he saw a long procession just like a string of those grasshopper wings. (43) And continuing in addition there were the grasshopper heads and grasshopper legs which he had eaten.

(44) After all that (eating) nothing remained in his belly, somehow they kept on passing though, exiting from his rectum. (45) Well, so then Coyote said, "I wonder whatever am I going to be able to plug it up with?" (46) "If something could only be found," he said, and "if I could only find a little bit of pitch." (47) So then he put pitch up himself there, with that pitch he plugged himself all up there. (48) And then instantly he began to stick his behind in every which direction, hopping around and thrusting out his buttocks every which way until right then he just burned up altogether. (49) And then that Coyote, he was all burned up to a crisp. (50) Thus it was.

Footnotes

All footnote numbers refer to the footnotes of "Coyote and Bullhead" in Northern California Texts, edited by Golla and Silver, NATS Vol. 2, unless they are underlined, in which case they are given below.

[1]kil conditional attributive auxiliary + a indicative stem formant + kele hearsay evidential suffix (262.22, 221, 243.12).

[2]le·n 'old, past, ancient, ago' + da intensifier (243.21) repeated.

[3]k̓ay 'walk fast, hurry' (cf. q̓ay 'walk') + s intensive (242.2) + a indicative (221) + s generic aspect (320.2); kenning for grey squirrel.

[4]λ̓iλ 'acorns' + a indic. + p̓Ok 'female, marry' + ta human classifier + um object case (325.1).

[5]p̓Ok cf. FN 4 + u imperative stem formant (222) + n reflexive (241.2) + i nominal stem formant (223) + t particular aspect (320.1).

[6]bOh 'sit, stay, dwell' + s generic (320.2).

[7]pi cf. FN 3 + t possessive case (325.5).

[8]Cf. FN 6 + in locative case (325.3).

[9]bOh cf. FN 6 + a indic. + har progressive aspectual attributive auxiliary (262.142) + i nominal (223) + t particular (320.1).

[10]pi cf. FN 3 + ·l dual (350.1) + e non-singular pronominal stem formant (350.4) + un genitive case (325.2).

[11]pi cf. FN 3, FN 10 + t particular (320.1).

[12]ʔel cf. FN 105 (231) + q̓ay 'walk' + a indic. + s generic (320.2).

[13]bir 'crave, hunger' (from *bEr 'starve', from b 'eat') + i nominal (223) + s generic (320.2).

[14]ye vocative prefix + nica 'nephew' cf. FN 14.

[15]q̓ay 'walk' + a indic., cf. FN 12.

[16]pe· interrogative root + s generic, cf. FN 24, + ma· concessive suffix, hesitation (probably from m dubitative + a indicative).

[17]Cf. FN 48, + da first person subject ('selfness') (243.21).

[18]b 'eat' + i nominal, cf. FN 76, + s generic.

[19]bEm 'own, possess, have, belong' + u imperative (222) + mina negative suffix (241.71).

[20]Cf. FN 3, to· postclitic, topicalizer (331.1) + t particular.

[21]Cf. FN 163 and FN 16.

[22]Cf. FN 18, + u imperative + m causative (241.3) + a indicative + h (in other ideolects this is realized as vowel length, the appropriate variant shape of the indicative a in this environment, C.D. preferred /ah/ to the /a·/ of other speakers).

[23]Cf. FN 64 + t particular.

[24]Cf. FN 5.

[25]Cf. FN 4 and FN 20.

[26]pulu·q 'container, basket'.

[27]xun 'toward' verb radical directional prefix (231) + tun 'put in the indicated direction' (from tu·n 'ahead, haul', from tu 'ahead, front'), cf. FN 37, + a indicative + bOh + a cf. FN 58.

[28]ken 'down' verb radical directional prefix (231) + λin 'snot, blow the nose' + c transitive (233.5) + u imperative + n reflexive + a indicative.

[29]par 'full, filled' + u imperative + m causative + a indicative.

[30]Cf. FN 28, r subordinating causal anteriority (243.15).

[31]yiw 'stir, mix, acorn mush' + i nominal + t particular.

[32]daw 'round and flat' + in locative case (325.3) + a indicative.

[33]Cf. FN 189.

[34] we·q 'nausea, distaste, regurgitate' + u imperative + n reflexive + a indicative.

[35] sedet cf. FN 7, to·t cf. FN 20.

[36] ba·s cf. FN 18, kOy desiderative modal attributive auxiliary (262.21) + u imperative + mina negative (241.71).

[37] ƛEp 'tease, insult, wither' + el stative suffix (?) (233.6) + a indicative + r subordinating causal anteriority (243.15).

[38] hEw 'bent, sag' + el stative suffix (?) (233.6) + n reflexive + a indicative + r subordinating (243.15).

[39] wEr future intentional attributive auxiliary (262.141) + a indic. + allegro elision of ʔibi·da, from ʔiy proximal copula (261.1) + bEy imperfective aspect attributive auxiliary (262.11) + da first person subject (selfness) suffix (243.21).

[40] Cf. FN 64.

[41] suk 'stand'/perfective aspect attributive auxiliary (262.13) + mina negative suffix (241.71), cf. FN 23.

[42] wiy 'husband' + i nominal + t particular.

[43] Cf. FN 42, + to·t cf. FN 20.

[44] ʔuw cf. FN 6, + t̓an cf. FN 189; cf. also FN 236.

[45] p̓uqan cf. FN 5, + to·t cf. FN 20.

[46] nom 'west' + pom 'earth, land'.

[47] net 'my', from ni 'I' + t possessive case (325.5).

[48] Cf. FN 6 and FN 46.

[49] Cf. FN 4 and FN 46.

[50] ke·n 'deep' (from ken 'down') + a indic. + m causative, cf. FN 22 + le inevitable future (241.61) + bOh durative attributive auxiliary (262.12) + da cf. FN 39.

[51] yo·l 'snow, frost' + a indicative.

[52] dil 'drop, fall, alight' + m caus., cf. FN 22, cf. FN 50.

[53] ʔelew cf. FN 48, + wEr cf. FN 39 + i nominal + t particular.

[54] ʔe cf. FN 64, + r instrumental case (325.4).

[55] may 'follow, track' + a indic. + mina cf. FN 41 and FN 110.

[56] ʔol 'up, above' cf. FN 22, t̓Ep 'spring (season)' (from tEp 'emerge, sprout' ?) + um object case (325.1) + to· cf. FN 20 + in locative case (325.3) repeated ('at that location').

[57] qati· cf. FN 254.

[58] po·m 'earth, land' cf. FN 46.

[59] cal 'good, beautiful, correct, ideal', cf. FN 50 and 75.

[60] mat 'your' from mi 'you' + t possessive case, cf. FN 47.

[61] wEr 'come, approach', cf. FN 53 + s generic aspect.

[62] ʔunir, from ʔuni cf. FN 33, + r subordinating (243.15).

[63] mis cf. FN 100.

[64] yal 'leave, desist' + u imperative + paq benefactive (241.42) + ta subordinating (temporal) suffix (241.76), cf. FN 106.

[65] po· 'now' cf. FN 272, qat referential 'as regards' cf. FN 254.

[66] Cf. FN 38.

[67] pʰo· cf. FN 57.

[68] c̓an cf. FN 109, FN 56.

[69] lon 'tree bark' + i nominal.

70 Cf. FN 69, FN 55.

71 ba· cf. FN 18 and 76, biya from bEy imperfective + a indicative.

72 k̓ac 'chew something dry and crunchy, grind, chew bones' + a indicative + bEy + a cf. FN 71.

73 nOr 'be left, remain' + u imperative + m generic comitative suffix (241.13) + u imperative + paq benefactive + a indicative + s generic ('that generic aspect noun object remaining for your sake', i.e. ba·s cf. FN 18).

74 Cf. FN 64 and 73.

75 Allegro speed version of 35.

76 Cf. FN 68, + um object case.

77 Cf. FN 68, + in locative, cf. FN 223.

78 Cf. FN 72, + r subordinating.

79 Cf. FN 156.

80 Cf. FN 69 and 160.

81 Cf. FN 16, + p̓eni generic aspect of the privative p̓e 'without', from *p̓En 'unable, lack' (cf. p̓in auxiliary of inability (262.411)) with i nominal.

82 pi cf. FN 3, + o emphatic pronominal suffix (350.3), cf. FN 196.

83 bEy imperfective (262.11) + $nt^{h}ere$ non-visual sensory evidential (243.11).

84 cal cf. FN 50, + u imperative + mina negative cf. FN 41.

85 Cf. FN 47.

86 Cf. FN 48 and FN 83.

87 lEl 'transform, make, manufacture, become' + u imperative + n reflexive + a indicative (i.e., 'to put self in a position to be transformed, for one to be like the other, to imitate, to change, etc.').

88 ʔisto· cf. FN 281, + mina cf. FN 41.

89 him 'morrow' + a indicative.

90 ʔukin cf. FN 138, ma· cf. FN 127 and 21.

91 Cf. FN 36 and 39.

92 p̓Ok cf. FN 5, + i nominal + t possessive case (325.5).

93 su·s from suk cf. FN 41, + s generic + to·n FN 20 + in locative, cf. FN 56.

94 nom cf. FN 46, ƛ̓iƛ cf. FN 4, a indicative + pom cf. FN 46.

95 haras cf. FN 36, + s generic + kOy desiderative + da 1st person (243.21).

96 yo emphatic/vocative cf. FN 45 and 159.

97 ke·n cf. FN 50 + a indicative + s generic.

98 cup 'wade' cf. FN 105 ('stuck') + mina negative.

99 ni cf. FN 47, qati· cf. FN 57.

100 mi· 'trees' generic aspect.

101 wan 'tip, end, top', to·n cf. FN 20 and 93.

102 har 'go' + le inevitable future, cf. FN 50.

103 bo·s cf. FN 6, pom cf. FN 46, to·n cf. FN 93.

104 hen 'how' + u imperative + s generic, cf. FN 309.

105 ʔiwiya 'to be unable, to not know (how)' from ʔiw 'unable, not know' + n reflexive + a indicative + r subordinate.

106 ʔelew cf. FN 48, + a indicative + r subordinating.

[107]ba·s cf. FN 18, lEl 'transform, make' + i nominal.
[108]ʔelew cf. FN 48, + t particular.
[109]bEy imperfective + mina negative.
[110]may 'follow, track' + a indicative.
[111]Cf. FN 44.
[112]Cf. FN 97, + m causative + a indicative + t particular.
[113]Cf. FN 4, + un instrumental use of genitive case (325.2), cf. FN 20, 25.
[114]Cf. FN 87.
[115]Cf. FN 281, + mina negative.
[116]q̓a·q 'crazy', cf. FN 280.
[117]xan 'away' directional prefix (231), + t̓Er 'move, act, tend' + a indicative.
[118]ṡe distributive directional prefix (231) + cup 'wade' + a indicative + bEy imperfective + a indicative.
[119]Cf. FN 95.
[120]nom 'west' + ti locative directional suffix 'toward' ('westward').
[121]nom 'west' + c̓araw 'valley, flat' (from c̓ar 'green').
[122]Cf. FN 57 and 254.
[123]hEn 'arrive' + a indicative + r subordinate.
[124]ho·n 'already'.
[125]bOh cf. FN 6, + a indicative.
[126]ʔelwine 'with' (from ʔel 'in, intensively' + wine 'seeing' or win 'human' ?).
[127]q̓aya· cf. FN 15, + har progressive aspectual attributive auxiliary (262.142) + a indicative.
[128]cupe cf. FN 98 and FN 127.
[129]Cf. FN 46 and FN 50.
[130]Cf. FN 46, + in locative.
[131]Cf. FN 46, + pat 'outside, out, away' directional prefix (231) + k̓Od 'move, step' + a indicative.
[132]tu 'ahead, apex' directional prefix (231) + win 'see, look' + i nominal + t particular.
[133]Cf. FN 67, + un instrumental use of genitive case (325.2).
[134]nep 'grasshoppers' + um object case.
[135]yew 'gather, collect food' + c transitive + i nominal.
[136]bO 'many' cf. FN 5, + s generic + a indicative.
[137]bay 'cauterize, do by fire' + i nominal + to·n cf. FN 93.
[138]holoq 'hole(s)', cf. FN 93.
[139]nu·q 'smoke' generic aspect.
[140]Cf. FN 67 (variously recorded as p^ho· and p^ho·h).
[141]xun 'toward' + pat 'out' + k̓Od cf. FN 131, + u imperative + t particular.
[142]Cf. FN 138 and FN 56.
[143]Cf. FN 134.
[144]q̓an 'wing(s)' generic aspect.
[145]tole 'leg(s)' generic aspect (perhaps from to·l 'grow').
[146]p^hoyoq 'head(s)' generic aspect (from p^hOy 'protrude').

147 ʔel 'in, intensively' directional prefix (231) + p̓im 'peck at, pick at' + u imperative + n reflexive + a indicative.

148 bEy imperfective + s generic + ʔel dependent copula (visual evidential) auxiliary (261.3) + s generic.

149 Cf. FN 147, cf. FN 127.

150 q̓om 'fill, answer, believe, agree, conclude' + i nominal + h stative derivational suffix (242.1) + n reflexive + a indicative.

151 Cf. FN 88, + un genitive + mina negative.

152 Cf. FN 76, and FN 127.

153 yel 'back, behind' directional prefix (231) + win 'see, look glance' + a indicative.

154 Cf. FN 16 and 24 (perhaps vowel length affective).

155 kel 'long, far, forest' + V·l pluralizer, extender derivative suffix (233.2).

156 sup 'unravel' (perhaps from sOp 'undress', cf. sub 'unravel string') + c transitive u imperative + t particular.

157 Cf. FN 305.

158 ʔel 'in' + bEy 'be in a lying position' + mina 'negative'.

159 werem 'rectum' (cf. wenem 'middle', wan 'tip, end') + t̓ah 'nearby' (from t̓a· 'bottom'), to·n cf. FN 93.

160 pat 'out' + har 'go' + V·r repetitive time-space extender (233.3) + a indicative.

161 hen 'wonder, how', cf. FN 104.

162 ʔel 'in' + t̓uy 'plug/stop/fill up, seal' + u imperative + m causative + u imperative + n reflexive + a indicative + wEr future auxiliary + bEy imperfective + da first person (self) suffix.

163 nEq 'find, acquire' + a indicative + kil conditional attributive auxiliary (262.22) + a indicative.

164 hu·d 'pine pitch' + i nominal + s generic.

165 po 'just' from po· 'now, new, young' cf. FN 272, ʔilay 'little' cf. FN 21.

166 Cf. FN 163.

167 Cf. FN 164, + u imperative + n reflexive + a indicative.

168 se distributive prefix (231) + p̓uy 'to have one's bare ass raised up' (possibly from po·y 'be hunched over', from pOy 'be bent over') + V·y iterative (probably, despite vowel length recorded) of plural locations (233.4) + hara· cf. FN 127.

169 hir 'fire, burn, conflagration' + a indicative.

170 ƛ̓aq 'obsidian, chip' + el stative suffix (233.6).

Note: ʔut[6] 'then' seems to be used as a marker of paragraph divisions in this text, although in "Coyote and Bullhead" J.C. uses ʔuna·[26] 'then' for the same function.

This text, like "Coyote and Bullhead", has both humorous and very serious elements. In both instances Coyote acts foolishly, without the normal common sense and propriety of the other myth characters, and in ways that explicitly break the rules of appropriate behavior. Moreover, he uses cunning and trickery, and tries to acquire food in ways that are culturally inappropriate. In both cases he is punished or suffers, even to the point of death. The theme of hunger and the attention to the question of how hunger may be satisfied, while not transgressing rules of behavior, is presented so as to inspire laughter, thus co-opting an audience into the, at least tacit, recognition and acceptance of the culturally appropriate rules: when the audience laughs at his antics they thereby acknowledge those antics as rule-breaking and inappropriate (Toelken 1969). This function of reiterating a code of correct behavior, specifying appropriate relations between individuals, and indicating how satisfaction of an important biological need may be achieved, also regulates how individuals are to interact with nature in their attempts at survival. It specifies retribution for those who are predators lacking restraint in their exploitation of their prey. The issue of acquiring enough food to satisfy hunger without breaking sociological and ecological restraints is a crucial underlying theme of these texts (McLendon 1977).

COYOTE AND BADGER

(Wintu)

Alice Schlichter

University of California, Berkeley

Wintu, the northernmost of the Wintun family of languages, was spoken originally in Shasta, Trinity, and Siskiyou counties of northern California. The territory extended approximately from Mount Shasta in the north to Cottonwood Creek in the south. Part of the southwestern boundary was the South Fork of the Trinity River, and the northwestern limit was close to the Trinity Alps. The eastern boundary ran close to Cow Creek in the south, and farther north extended east almost as far as the present town of Big Bend.

The present text was obtained in 1977 from Mrs. Grace MacKibben of Hayfork, California, one of the five or six Wintu remembering their language today. The fieldwork was supported by the Survey of California and Other Indian Languages, Department of Linguistics, University of California, Berkeley. The analysis of the text is based on Pitkin (1963) and Schlichter (1977).

Demetracopoulou and Du Bois (1932: 380) note that Wintu myths are "often told without the naming of the chief characters." In this text, Coyote's gambling partner who was identified as Badger by my informant is only referred to as "a person" (winthu·h) or "the other one" (k'ete·tto·t). Our story, which at first glance may seem to go nowhere, is held together by having an ending opposite to its beginning. Coyote is initially portrayed as a hardworking, lucky man; he sets his traps every day and catches many gophers. He catches every time he sets his traps. By night he sleeps, and by day he traps. Then, temptation in the form of Badger comes to him. When Coyote asks him what he is up to, Badger sounds as if he either has a guilty conscience or knows what will happen. First he says that he is going north, to watch the gambling, to watch a big time, but finally comes to the point: "I am going to gamble." He does not like the idea of taking Coyote along but has no luck trying to make him stay trapping for gophers.

At the gambling, Coyote, convinced from the first moment that he will win, bets everything he has and, even as he is already losing, continues to sing his pretentious song: "I alone will win." He only lets Badger guess once, and Badger wins a counter, but then Coyote guesses again and again, until they lose everything. In short, Coyote starts out as a lucky trapper and ends up as an unlucky gambler. Note, however, that Coyote is considered the patron of gamblers (Du Bois 1935: 43). My informant commented that it seems as if people followed Coyote's example even though the story was told to keep them from doing so. The moral is: work hard, don't gamble.

The game described here is the grassgame. There are two teams of two players facing each other, each pair sitting side by side. One team gets two bones or sticks, one marked, the other unmarked, wrapped in grass or straw to conceal the mark. In our story, sticks are used, but in the free translation they will be referred to as "bones" in order to be able to tell them apart from the ten sticks placed in the middle between the teams as counters. The team that has the two bones moves them back and forth, in front, and behind their backs, from one person to the other, throws them up in the air and catches them again; and finally they stretch out their hands in front of them and one person on the other team has to guess where the marked bone has ended up. He can make one of four possible guesses: (1) kenti, lit. "down inside", the marked bone is in the middle, i.e., in either one of the two inside hands of the two players sitting side by side; (2) čoki, lit. "near", the bone is in one of the outside hands; (3) puy, lit. "east", the bone is in one of the left hands of the players; and (4) nom, lit. "west", it is in either one of the right hands of the two players. The two latter options are called "betting in a straight row", i.e., from left to right, rather than from inside to outside. If a team guesses correctly, they win a counter and it is their turn to handle the two bones. While moving the bones back and forth, one or both of the men in the team sing. In our story only Coyote sings. If Badger sang, his song is not reported, and the other team and their song remain unidentified.

Wintu songs are divided into several types: handgame songs, war songs, bear dance songs, deer songs, puberty songs, etc. They consist either of nothing but nonsense syllables, or of a text and nonsense syllables as a refrain beginning and interrupting the text. The nonsense syllables used are practically identical within each type of song. The nonsense syllables of Coyote's handgame song, sowe·ni, are interesting in that they are remarkably reminiscient of the Yuki word sąwe--the nasalization of the ą becoming n in Wintu--, which denotes the unmarked bone. It appears that even though war between the Wintu and the Yuki was common, they also played the handgame with each other. Since sowe·ni is a sequence of nonsense syllables for the Wintu whereas sąwe has a meaning in Yuki, we must conclude that the song originated with the latter. This looks like an intertribal joke played on the Wintu. The Yuki taught them to sing a song about sąwe, the unmarked bone, dooming them to lose. Coyote added to this the words "I alone will win" not realizing that what he was saying was: "The unmarked bone I alone will win." Remember that Badger is not singing and when it is his turn to guess, he wins.

This story differs from the usual Wintu story. The commonest plot has a beginning, then builds up to a climax, and ends with a conclusion that gathers the themes together, summarizes them, or otherwise closes the story in such a way that the listener is returned peacefully to reality. This story of Coyote and Badger has only two parts, the beginning and the exposition with the climax, ending abruptly when Coyote finally loses. The abrupt ending must have had the same shock value to the Wintu listener that we feel today when a song stops abruptly or a play ends without a complete unravelling of all the problems that have been presented.

The device that is exploited repetitively in this text is that of contrast: the lucky hunter against the unlucky gambler; the red bone against the losing white; the lucky Badger losing with the unlucky Coyote; the winning song which actually invokes losing. And behind it all the moral: hunting and hard work are good, gambling may be bad.

Abbreviations used are: CAUS causative, DEM demonstrative, DIS distributive prefix, DP disjunctive postclitic, DUA dual, DUB dubitative, DUR durative aspect auxiliary, EMP emphatic, FUT future auxiliary, G generic aspect, GO generic object, GS generic subject, IMPF imperfect aspect auxiliary, LOC locative, O object, P particular aspect, PO particular object, PRO progressive aspect auxiliary, PS particular subject, QUOT quotative, REC reciprocal, REF reflexive, S subject, SUB subordinator.

(1) waytay čʼarawah puqe. (2) puqebiya,
north-a short distance from here one in the field-PS[1] trap trap-IMPF

čʼarawin puqebiya. (3) yi·lalam qʼapma·, qʼapma·, pat-ʔiłe
field-G-LOC trap-IMPF gopher-GO get caught-CAUS[2] catch out-take

hiʔuni, xi·na. (4) hiʔan, yi·lalam hiʔan qʼapma·. (5) ken-pana
again sleep again gopher-GO again catch down in-change posit-

hiʔan pat-ʔiłe, hiʔan puqe, hiʔan qʼapma·. (6) hiʔan puqe, ʔuna·
ion again out-take again trap again catch again trap and

hiʔan xi·na, pomin-pana xi·na, hiʔan ken-pana,
again sleep down-change position sleep again down in-change position

hiʔan yi·lalam puqe. (7) qʼapma·. (8) hiʔan puqe, hiʔan qʼapma·.
again gopher-GO trap catch again trap again catch

(9) ʔuna· serpanułum ƛʼo·ma, čʼansem serpanułum ƛʼo·ma.
and twice-three-O kill one side-hand twice-three-O kill

(10) ʔuka· wint^{h}u·h wira. (11) "pe·h wikčam?" čʼarawayumto·n,
then person-PS come what-G do-DUB Coyote-PO-DP-O

"pe·h   wikčam?"   (12) "puqehara·r   ?iyebida.   (13) ču·dičada,   serpanułum
what-G   do-DUB   trap-PRO-SUB do-IMPF-I   lucky-I   twice-three-O

ho·nhom   q'apma·da,"   ?uni.   (14) "?ut   mi   heke   hara·m?"
already-only-G catch-I   QUOT   and   you where   go-DUB

č'arawah   k'ete·m   wint^hu·numto·n.   (15) k'ete·tto·t,   "?o·,   waypom
Coyote-PS   one-PO   person-PO-DP-PO   one-PS-DP-PS   oh   north-ground

hara·da,   č'uhus   ?ałma   hara·da,   winyupus   harma,   winyupus
go-I   gambling-G watch   go-I   people-gathering-G   go to   people-gather-

        ?ałma.   (16) č'uhus   č'uhe   hara·."   (17)"?o·,   nihot,   nihot
ing-G   watch   gambling-G   gamble   go   oh   I-only-PS I-only-PS

č'uher,   nihot   č'uhepuke·r   ?iyebida.   (18) ni   hara·skuda   mis
gamble-SUB   I-only-PS   gamble-might-SUB do-IMPF-I   I   going-want-I you-O

maqaya.   (19) hare·   ma·n,   mis   maqaya."   (20) "miya   war   ?uwe-?ewina,
follow   go-let's then   you-O   follow   you   come-IMP right-here

puqebe,   ?ewetam,   yi·lalam   puqebe."   (21) "hesti·n   puqeleba·da,
trap-IMPF IMP   this-GO   gopher-GO   trap-IMPF IMP   INT-LOC   trap-can-DUR-I

mis   maqaya   han,   hare·."   (22) "hare·   ma·n,"   k'ete·tto·t,
you-O   follow   go-let me   go-let's   go-let's   then   one-PS-DP-PS

"hare·   ma·n,"   ?uni.
 go-let's   then   QUOT

        (23) hara·   pe·l,   way-hara·   pe·l.   (24) č'uhus,   hina   pe·l
             go   they-DUA   north-go   they-DUA   gambling-G   arrive   they-DUA

?ukin.   (25) hinabohan   pe·l,   kalay-?iłna,   dama·.   (26) č'arawah
DEM-LOC   arrive-DUR-SUB   they-DUA   among-get-REF   bet   Coyote-PS

puris   t'ałas   dama·,   ko·m   dama·.   (27) pe·l   č'uhe,   pe·l
his-G   clothes-G bet   all-GO   bet   they-DUA   gamble   they-DUA

?el-č'uqp'ure,   pa·lel   hara·sto·t.   (28) ?el-č'uqp'ure   pe·l
in-help-REC   two-G   the ones that go-DP-PS   in-help-REC   they-DUA

č'uhe.   (29) č'a·wa   č'arawahto·t.   (30) "mi   č'a·wu   mihot   č'a·wu.
gamble   sing   Coyote-PS-DP-PS   you   sing-IMP you-only-PS sing-IMP

(31) mihot   č'uhuskoyit   biya,   mihot   č'a·wu."
     you-only-PS   gamble-want-PS be   you-only-PS sing-IMP

        (32) "sowe·ni,   sowe·ni,   sowe·ni,   sowe·n.
              sowe·ni   sowe·ni   sowe·ni   sowe·n

              sowe·ni,   sowe·ni,   sowe·ni   sowe·n
              sowe·ni   sowe·ni   sowe·ni   sowe·n

              niyoken,   niyoken,   toku·m   p'ur,   toku·m   p'ur.
              I-EMP   I-EMP   stick-GO you all stick-GO you all

toku·m p'ur, ɬučuwen, niyoken, niyoken,
stick-GO you all pierce-I'll I-EMP I-EMP

toku·m p'ur, ɬučuwen, niyoken, niyoken."[3]
stick-GO you all pierce-I'll I-EMP I-EMP

(33) t^{h}aka·r k'ete·t. (34) "wilesbo· čepet." (35) č'arawahto·t
hit-SUB one-PS try-GS-DUR guess-PS Coyote-PS-DP-PS

čipakila mana·. (36) "hiʔan nito·t hiʔan ʔol-ɬiya, ni hiʔuni,
guess-when miss again I-DP-PS again up-throw I again

hiʔuni", k'ete·tto·t. (37) hiʔuni č'arawah, "ni hiʔan čepen."
again one-PS-DP-PS again Coyote-PS I again guess-I'll

(38) čipakila mana· hiʔan. (39) hiʔan ʔol-ɬiya, hiʔuni se-hilayuna.
guess-when miss again again up-throw again DIS-spread

(40) čipakila hiʔan mana· č'arawahto·t. (41) "ni po·hom ma·n
guess-when again miss Coyote-PS-DP-PS I now-only then

ʔiyebida ma·n čipawira ma·n ʔiyebida." (42) čipa, hiʔan mana·,
do-IMPF-I then guess-FUT then do-IMPF-I guess again miss

ƛ'a·wi, hiʔan. (43) hiʔan ʔol-ɬiya, hiʔan č'a·wa, hiʔan čipakila,
four again again up-throw again sing again guess-when

hiʔan mana·, č'ansem. (44) ʔuna· k'ete·tto·t, "were ni čepen,
again miss one side-hand and one-PS-DP-PS come IMP I guess-I'll

hida mana·sken." (45) čipa, mana·. (46) hiʔan čipa k'ete·tto·t.
too miss-you guess miss again guess one-PS-DP-PS

(47) t'opma·. (48) hiʔuni č'arawayumto·n, "ʔol-ɬeyʔ." (49) "ho·.
hit again Coyote-PO-DP-PO up-throw-IMP yes

(50) niyoken, niyoken, tokumar, tokumar.
I-EMP I-EMP put out sticks-SUB put out sticks-SUB

niyoken, niyoken, tokumar, tokumar."
I-EMP I-EMP put out sticks-SUB put out sticks-SUB

(51) č'ansem ho·nhom č'ansem ɬuča. (52) se-hilayuna,
one side-hand already-only-G one side-hand pierce DIS-spread

čipa, čipa č'arawah. (53) ʔelew k'ete·mto·n čepmaskoyumina.
guess guess Coyote-PS not one-PO-DP-PO let guess-want-did (not)

(54) čipa, mana·. (55) hiʔan ʔol-ɬiya, hiʔuni č'u·s, čipa, hiʔan mana·,
guess miss again up-throw again stick guess again miss

hiʔan ʔol-ɬiya, se-hilayuna. (56) č'arawahto·t čipa hiʔan mana·.
again up-throw DIS-spread Coyote-PS-DP-PS guess again miss

(57) hiʔan se-hilayuna, ʔol-ɬiya, ʔuna· se-hilayuna, čipa č'arawah,
again DIS-spread up-throw and DIS-spread guess Coyote-PS

mana·. (58) hiʔan ʔol-ɬiyakila, hiʔan se-hilayuna, hiʔan č'arawahto·t
miss again up-throw-when again DIS-spread again Coyote-PS-DP-PS

čipa hiʔan mana·, č'ansem. (59) lapal, tu·n-dami lapal.
guess again miss one side-hand lose first-bet lose

(60) hiʔan, x̣a·l hiʔan dama·, x̣a·l dama·.
again other again bet other bet

(61) "sowe·ni, sowe·ni, sowe·ni, sowe·n.
sowe·ni sowe·ni sowe·ni sowe·n

sowe·ni, sowe·ni, sowe·ni, sowe·n."
sowe·ni sowe·ni sowe·ni sowe·n

(62) čipa, t'opma·. (63) piletam t'opma·. (64) ʔuna· č'anto·n
guess hit both-O hit and one side-DP-LOC

hiʔan, ʔol-ɬiya, se-hilayuna. (65) č'arawahto·t čipa, mana·.
again up-throw DIS-spread Coyote-PS-DP-PS guess miss

(66) se-hilayuna hiʔan. (67) č'arawahto·t hiʔan čipa, hiʔan mana·.
DIS-spread again Coyote-PS-DP-PS again guess again miss

(68) se-hilayuna hiʔan, ʔol-ɬiya. (69) č'arawahto·t čipa hiʔan mana·.
DIS-spread again up-throw Coyote-PS-DP-PS guess again miss

(70) hiʔan se-hilayuna, ʔol-ɬiya. (71) ʔuna· hiʔuni se-tuqčuna·,
again DIS-spread up-throw and again DIS-hold arms out

č'arawah čipa, hiʔan mana·. (72) se-hilayuna, hiʔan se-hilayuna.
Coyote-PS guess again miss DIS-spread again DIS-spread

(73) hiʔan č'arawahto·t hiʔan čipa, hiʔan mana·.
again Coyote-PS-DP-PS again guess again miss

Free Translation

(1) Coyote trapped to the north. (2) He was trapping, trapping in the fields. (3) He caught gophers. He caught them, took them out of the traps and went to sleep. (4) Again he caught gophers, again he caught. (5) He got up again, took them out of the traps, set the traps again, and caught again. (6) Again he set the traps and again he slept; he lay down and slept; again he got up, and again he trapped for gophers. (7) He caught. (8) He set the traps again, and caught again. (9) And he killed six, five or six he killed.

(10) Then someone came up to him. (11) "What are you doing?" he asked Coyote, "what are you doing?" (12) "I am trapping. (13) I am lucky, I already caught six," Coyote answered. (14) "And where are you going?" Coyote asked the other one. (15) The other one said: "Oh, I'm going north. I'm going to watch people gamble, I'm going to a big time, to watch the big time. (16) I am going to gamble." (17) "Oh, I, I gamble too, I might gamble, too. (18) I want to come with you. (19) Let's go, I come with you." (20) "You stay right here trapping these, trapping these gophers." (21) "I can always trap some other time; let me go with you; let's go." (22) "Let's go then," said the other one, "let's go."

(23) They went; north they went. (24) They got to where the gambling was. (25) They arrived, got into the game and bet. (26) Coyote bet his clothes, he bet everything he had. (27) The two of them gambled. The two that had come together helped each other gamble. (28) They helped each other gamble. (29) Coyote sang. (30) They had said to him: "You sing, it's up to you to sing. (31) You want to be a gambler, so you sing!" (32) Coyote sang:

"Sowe·ni, sowe·ni, sowe·ni, sowe·n.
Sowe·ni, sowe·ni, sowe·ni, sowe·n.
I alone, I alone will win. You all give me your sticks!
I'll win all your sticks, I alone, I alone.
I'll win all your sticks, I alone, I alone."

(33) The other side guessed him. (34) "Let's see you guess us now," the other team said. (35) Coyote guessed and missed. (36) "Now let us throw the bones again," said someone on the other side. (37) And Coyote said: "I'll guess again." (38) When he guessed he missed again. (39) Again the other team threw the bones up, moved them back and forth. (40) Coyote guessed and missed again. (41) "But now I will guess you, now I will!" (42) He guessed, and again he missed; again; the fourth stick was lost. (43) Again the other side threw the bones up, again they sang. And when Coyote guessed he missed again. They lost their fifth stick. (44) And now the other one, Coyote's partner, said: "Let me guess, you miss too often." (45) He guessed and missed. (46) Again Coyote's partner guessed. (47) He hit the other side. (48) And he said to Coyote: "Throw up the bones!" (49) Coyote said: "Yes." (50) And he sang;

"I alone, I alone will win. Put out your sticks!
I alone, I alone will win. Put out your sticks!"

(51) The other side had already won five sticks. (52) They moved the bones back and forth, and he guessed. Coyote guessed. (53) He didn't want his partner to guess. (54) He guessed, he missed. (55) Again the other side threw the bones up, and Coyote guessed and missed. Again they threw them up, moved them back and forth. (56) Coyote guessed again and missed. (57) Again the other side moved the bones back and forth, threw them up, and moved them back and forth. Coyote guessed and missed. (58) Again they threw up the bones and again they moved them back and forth, and again Coyote guessed and again he missed. They had lost the other five sticks. (59) They lost, lost their first bet.

(60) They bet again, made another bet. (61) Coyote sang:

"Sowe·ni, sowe·ni, sowe·ni, sowe·n.
Sowe·ni, sowe·ni, sowe·ni, sowe·ni."

(62) The other side guessed and hit them. (63) Both were hit. (64) And again the men on the other side threw up the bones, moved them back and forth. (65) Coyote guessed and missed. (66) Again they moved the bones back and forth. (67) Coyote guessed again, and again he missed. (68) The other side moved the bones back and forth, threw them up. (69) Coyote guessed and missed again. (70) Again the other team moved the bones back and forth, threw them up. (71) And again they held their hands out. Coyote guessed and missed. (72) They moved the bones back and forth, back and forth. (73) Again Coyote guessed. Again he missed.

Footnotes

[1] One in the field will henceforth be simply Coyote.

[2] Henceforth simply catch.

[3] The song consists of five lines, each containing four phrases. Lines one and two, the refrain, contain eleven syllables stressed on the second, fifth, and eighth syllables. Lines three to five, the song proper, contain four stresses each on the second, fifth, eighth and eleventh syllables. In all lines the fifth syllable is on a higher pitch than the other syllables, and all syllables at the ends of lines have a short fall in pitch. All the phrases are trisyllabic except the last one in lines one and two.

Lines one and two: ˘ ´ ˘ + ˘ H́ ˘ + ˘ ´ ˘ + ˘ ˘ ↓
Lines three, four, and five: ˘ ´ ˘ + ˘ H́ ˘ + ˘ ´ ˘ + ˘ ´˘ ↓

(I am grateful to Jesse Sawyer for helping me analyze this song.)

MINK, BULLETHAWK AND COYOTE

(Patwin)

Kenneth W. Whistler

University of California, Berkeley

Patwin is a group of languages formerly spoken by a people living in the southwestern portion of the Sacramento Valley of California. It is closely related to Nomlaki and Wintu, which were located to the immediate north of Patwin. Today Patwin is spoken by about ten people, mostly quite elderly, with only one or two speakers of each former dialect.

The Patwin Coyote story I have chosen was originally told by Mrs. Nora Lowell of Brooks, in Yolo County, California, to Mrs. Elizabeth Bright of the Survey of California Indian Languages in 1951. The text was dictated, not taped. In order to prepare the text for publication, I have reconstructed it from Mrs. Bright's notes during my fieldwork with Rev. Harry Lorenzo, also of Brooks, in August and September, 1977.

Mrs. Lowell was a speaker of the Cortina subdialect of Hill Patwin. Rev. Lorenzo speaks a slightly different subdialect, which I refer to as Cache Creek Hill Patwin. In the course of the reconstruction, I followed the original narrative structure and diction of Mrs. Lowell's telling, but resolved phonological and grammatical problems in favor of Rev. Lorenzo's interpretations, which I could then check and recheck with him. The result is not a "pristine" Patwin text, but is very close to the original performance. And with the exception of two or three instances remarked on in the footnotes, the text can be considered grammatically reliable.

Another telling of the same myth has survived in the manuscript Patwin texts recorded by Paul Radin from Mr. Anderson Lowell[1] in 1932. Mr. Lowell's version of the Mink, Bullethawk and Coyote myth is told in the Tebti subdialect of Hill Patwin and differs in a number of structural details from Nora Lowell's version. In the footnotes I have occasionally referred to the Radin text in order to clarify the significance of details in Mrs. Lowell's telling.

The Patwin Coyote stories are in one sense just clever tales that the Patwin used to tell for enjoyment's sake during evenings and at social gatherings. But they are also myths with deeper social functions. "Mink, Bullethawk, and Coyote" is a good example of the Coyote story as a kind of morality play with the effective function of demonstrating in exaggerated form the consequences of unacceptable social behavior and of providing a model of approved behavior. In this tale Bullethawk Chief gets into some hair-raising situations and causes a worldwide devastation because he steals someone else's property. Coyote Old Man may or may not be a party to the crime--we're never quite sure--but he does take the socially more responsible stance of trying to negotiate a way out of the conflict.

The following abbreviations are used in the interlinear glosses to the text. See the grammatical notes following the translation of the text for more grammatical detail. OBJ - objective case; GEN - genitive case; LOC - locative case; VOC - vocative case; MOD - modal suffix; PART - modal particle; EVID - evidential suffix; NEG - negative suffix or auxiliary; COP - copula.

(1)	sedew-č̓iyak	t̓okhi·li	hara-s.	(2)	t̓okhi·l-taro[2]	hene-s.
	Coyote-Old Man	to gather wood	went		gathered wood and	came

(3)	"he·-tuka	har-mu-ʔa[3]	ka	thay-ču?"	(4)	kathit-se·ktu	sinpe	pan-ti
	whither?	go-EVID	PART	grandson-my		Bullethawk-Chief	doorway	on top of

ham-taro	bo·s.	(5)	t̓okhi·l-ka	wini-s	ʔut.	(6)	thasi:	"po	hene-s	na·no
sitting	was		gather wood-but	saw	him		Mink	who?	came	my

di·-ła." (7) č́o·wi-ła[4] ʔuy, ʔele·-s, thasi-no č́o·wi-ła. (8) kathit-se·ktu
home-LOC look-when he not there Mink-by look-when Bullethawk-Chief

ʔel-hara-s ʔu·no kewe-ła. (9) har-me-s[5] hiłi·. (10) thasi were-s. (11) hen-taro
in-went his house-LOC took beads Mink coming came and

ho·le sata-s. (12) hiłi· ʔele·-s. (13) "po-ka na·no hiłi· har-me-m-ʔa."
sack grope in beads not there someone my beads took-EVID

(14) kathit-se·ktu hene-s pi-na-ʔu di·-ła. (15) sedew-č́iyak: "he·-ti mi
Bullethawk-Chief came back home-LOC Coyote-Old Man where-from you

hene-say?" (16) "čel-taro ču hene-s." (17) thasi hene-s sedew-č́iyak-matin.[6]
coming? travelling I came Mink came Coyote-Old Man-LOC

(18) "hiłi· na·no were-ʔ!" (19) "ʔele·-s ču were·-m-ʔu." (20) "ʔele·-m-ʔu.
beads my bring! NEG I took-NEG no

(21) nat ma-thay ʔe·če-sa. (22) pi-na-ʔu were-ʔ!" (23) thasi: "ʔe·t-taro-bo
me your-grandson stole back bring! Mink is stolen

nat ʔi-s. (24) thič́a-s ču ʔupeley har-me.[7] (25) depi č́o·-m ha-le." (26)
me COP know I their (2) take again to see I'll go

hene-s sedew-č́iyak-matin. (27) "piʔu-m-ʔu![8] (28) nat yuduk-ni,[9] doyu-pa-thi!"
came Coyote-Old Man-LOC do that-NEG! me pity and (pl.) give back to!

(29) "ʔele·-s po were·-m-ʔu. (30) ʔe·, har-me-n[9] na·no." (31) "ʔele·-s ču
NEG anyone took-NEG here! take and... mine NEG I

pi-ma ḱayu-m-ʔu. (32) na·no-wol[10] ču ḱayi-s." (33) thasi pi-na-ʔu were-s. (34)
those want-NEG mine-only I want Mink back coming

ʔu·no di·-ła hene-s. (35) "čeme-s-ʔu[11] pipel." (36) sedew-č́iyak: "doyu-pa-le
his home-LOC arrived have-EVID they (2) Coyote-Old Man I'll give

were-ʔ!" (37) "ʔele·-s ču ʔe·t-mu-ʔu." (38) "ʔele·-m,[12] mi pi-ła hen-taro
back bring! NEG I steal-NEG no you there went and

bo·-s. (39) win-taro bo·-s thasi. (40) ʔe·če-ma[13] mit win-taro bo·-s."
were saw and was Mink steal-OBJ you (OBJ) saw and was

(41) kathit-se·ktu: "ʔele·-s ču hen-mu-ʔu pi-ła. (42) bal-ʔa-ro ʔi-s
Bullethawk-Chief NEG I go-NEG there lying COP

thasi-č́iyak." (43) "na·me pa ču hara·-t́i. (44) č́o·wi pi ču hara·-t́i."
Mink-Old Man last time PART I will go to see PART I will go

(45) sedew-č́iyak hiłi· du·-taro were·-s, ʔaba·-ła paro·-ma-ro. (46)
Coyote-Old Man beads packed and took packbasket-LOC make full and

"ʔe·, ʔiwe ʔe·! (47) ʔe·t-ma ʔele·-ʔunana-boti[14] mit." (48) "ʔele·-m-ʔu,
here! take! these steal-OBJ NEG-EVID-EVID you (OBJ) no

nat ʔe·če-sa pi. (49) wini-sa ču ʔut. (50) pi-na-ʔu har-me. (51) na·no-wol
me stole he saw I him back take! mine-only

ču k̓ayi-s." (52) pi-na-ʔu were·-s sedew-č̓iyak. (53) hen-taro, "mi ʔupu
I want back brought Coyote-Old Man came and you I hear

were·-m. (54) wini-ʔunana-s mit pi. (55) he·-na mat ɬomu·-ro-be[15]
took saw-EVID you (OBJ) he where-at your hidden away

were-ʔ! (56) har-me-le. (57) saltu[28] ʔi-s č̓iyak, pi ma-tapan. (58)
bring! I'll take (back) saltu COP old man that your-grandpa

pe· mi t̓othu·-ro ʔe·t-ta, yay-ɬa paro·-ro be·-ɬa?" (59) "bal-ʔa-ro ʔi-s
what? you lacking and steal back-LOC full and is-when lying COP

pi č̓iyak. (60) pe· ču pi-na har-mu ʔele·-s." (61) thasi-č̓iyak: "na·me
that old man never I there go-NEG NEG Mink-Old Man last time

ha-le, doyu-m ʔele·-ɬa-ʔu. (62) mo·n-mu ha-le." [arrives] (63) "hiɬi· nat
I'll go give-NEG NEG-although to recover I'll go beads me

were·-thi!" (64) sedew-č̓iyak: "ʔele·-ʔunana-s pi hen-mu-ʔu, nay t̓ihi·tu-t."[16]
(pl.) bring! Coyote-Old Man NEG-EVID he come-NEG my ask (him)

(65) "ʔele·-m-ʔu, hene-sa pi-ɬa. (66) piʔu-ro nay na·me hene· ʔi-s." (67)
no came there and my last time come COP

"were-ʔ, thay. (68) were-ʔ he·-na mat ɬomi. (69) saltu ʔi-s
bring! grandson (VOC) bring! where-at your hid away saltu COP

č̓iyak. (70) t̓uke-ʔa-ro-bo! (71) pe·-t̓o mat ʔe·če? (72) pe· t̓othu·-ro?"
old man be brave! what-for? your steal what? lacking

(73) thasi: "ʔole·l-ʔa-ma-ro, ʔew wilak-no me·m-na lib-thi-ɬa ʔepaypi.[17]
Mink make high and this world-GEN water-in sink-when may it be!

(74) ču-wol hori-t̓i-bo. (75) muhu·-ro pi nay ʔemus ɬeye·-ɬa, lib-thi-t̓i-be
I-only shall be saved sing and PART my four times shall sink

wilak." (76) [song] "thasi wo·ʔina;[32] win-ma yalu-sa." (77) sedew-č̓iyak:
world Mink ? people-OBJ left Coyote-Old Man

"pi! pi! pi! me·m were·-be-s. (78) were-ʔ, were-ʔ! (79) mat ɬomi
look! look! look! water is coming bring! bring! your hid away

doyu-pa-se." (80) t̓ati-ɬa me·m-na wilak lib-thi-s. (81) sedew-č̓iyak
let's 2 give back dawn-when water-in world sink Coyote-Old Man

loko·ya-no č̓ili koru·-ro, pi-na ʔel-hara-s. (82) kathit-se·ktu tho·k-ɬa
elk-GEN antler grind and there-in in-went Bullethawk-Chief tree-LOC

hama·-ɬa, pi lib-thi-s. (83) piʔu-t ʔonolay-tho·ɬ-tuka hara-s. (84) ƛ̓ap-thu-ro
sit-when that sink so Sutter Buttes-to went wet

thu·n. (85) hama-s tho·ɬ-ɬa. (86) tho·ɬ-pili-men:[34] "po pa depi
body sat mountain-LOC Snake someone PART again

yiɬ-ma-t pa po hama·-bo?"[18] (87) "ču ʔi-s, ʔa·pa-khe·." (88) "he·-ɬa
heavy PART someone sit-MOD I COP grandpa-VOC where?

sun bo-say ma-tapan?" (89) č̓o·wi-ɬa ʔuy, peri-t̓o ʔut. (90) wa·wu-ro
here is? your-grandpa look-when he about to swallow him gaping

were-s tho·ɬ-pili-men-saltu. (91) piʔu-t winit-taro hara-s
open and coming Snake-saltu so took off and went

ben-tho·ɬ-tuka. (92) ben-tho·ɬ-ɬa hama-s. (93) ka·k: "po pa depi
big-mountain-to big-mountain-LOC sat Raven someone PART again

thu·n-ɬa nat hama·-bo?" (94) hupu-s-men: "t̓ew-mu-ʔu! (95) č̓o·w har-taro. (96)
body-LOC me sit-MOD Grebe talk-NEG! look go and

he·-ti win hene·-boti." (97) "ʔa·pa-khe·, ču ʔi-s. (98) ʔa·pa-ču
where-from person come-EVID grandpa-VOC I COP grandpa-my

he·-ɬa lu·mu-s. (99) me·m lib-thi-s wilak. (100) he·y." [falls over] (101)
somewhere died water sink world he·y

"ʔow, thay. (102) ʔel-wer! (103) po pi ʔele·-be[19] č̓iyak-ma ʔut
o.k. grandson in-come! no one PART NEG-MOD old man-OBJ that

ʔe·t-mu-ʔu. (104) ʔe·t-taro mipel, wilak yoha·-ma-s." (105) hupu-s-men-k̓ay me·m
steal-NEG steal and you 2 world ruined Grebe-Old Lady water

k̓ak-ma-s, kowu-ma-ro ʔut. (106) p̓era·-ro ɬima-ho-ma winit-ma-ro ʔut. (107)
heated bathed and him cold and faint made get up him

thi·r-ma ba·-ma-s, t̓ipa-da-ʔu. (108) beh-na-ʔu me·m khon-taro be·-s. (109)
fish-OBJ made eat bread-and next morning water dry was

t̓ipa kholčhis-na ƛ̓op-taro, du·-taro were-s. (110) "ʔa·pa-čut ha-le
bread bag-into put and packed and came grandpa-my (OBJ) I'll go

č̓o·-m he·-ɬa bo·-ma, bo·-ma pe·-ma."[20] (111) hene-s sedew-č̓iyak-matin. (112)
to see where lives living or what... came Coyote-Old Man-LOC

"ʔa·pa-khe·, he·-ɬa mi bo-say?" (113) kapi-s ʔel-be. (114) sedew-č̓iyak-no
grandpa-VOC where? you are? dug in Coyote-Old Man-GEN

may hen-pa-s. (115) ƛ̓er-ta-ʔa-s: "ʔa·pa-ču wayi·!" (116) sedew-č̓iyak: "pe·
foot discovered cried out grandpa-my poor! Coyote-Old Man what?

he·-ɬa po lu·mu-say -- ma-tapan? (117) wiči·su nat may-ti!" (118) wiči·su-ro,
where? who? is dead? your-grandpa pull! me foot-by pulled and

pat-ɬeye-s ʔut. (119) "hali·hali-ʔele-s. (120) č̓o·w wilak-no yoha·! (121)
out-got him [you] are rash look at world-GEN ruin

depi pi ʔu-m ʔiwe-ʔ!"[21] (122) "ʔe· ba-ʔ, ʔa·pa-khe·." (123) "ʔow, ʔow,
again do that-NEG do! here! eat! grandpa-VOC yes yes

ʔow, were-ʔ! (124) ba·-le. (125) were-ʔ!" (126) sedew-č̓iyak: "he·-ɬa mi
yes bring! I'll eat bring! Coyote-Old Man where? you

horu-ta·, thay?" (127) "nome·l, ben-tho·ɬ-ɬa. (128) pi-ɬa bo-sa
were saved? grandson far to west big-mountain-LOC there was

ka·k-č̓iyak." (129) "pi-ɬa pi bo·-bo ma-tapan."
Raven-Old Man there PART stay-MOD your-grandpa

Characters Appearing in the Text:

COM	Coyote Old Man	(sedew-č̓iyak)	
BHC	Bullethawk Chief	(khathit-se·ktu)	[prairie falcon]
	Mink (Old Man)	(thasi-č̓iyak)	
	Snake[34]	(tho·ɬ-pili-men)	
	Raven (Old Man)	(ka·k-č̓iyak)	
	Grebe (Old Lady)[36]	(hupu-s-men-k̓ay)	[Raven's wife]

Translation of the Text:

(1) Coyote Old Man went to get wood. (2) He gathered wood and came back. (3) COM: "I wonder where my grandson could be." (4) Bullethawk Chief was sitting above [Mink's] doorway. (5) He [COM] was gathering wood but saw him.

(6) Mink: "Someone has come to my house." (7) When he looked, there was no one, ...when Mink looked. (8) Bullethawk Chief went inside his [Mink's] house. (9) He took the beads [that were there].

(10) Mink was coming. (11) He got back and searched inside [his] sack. (12) The beads were gone. (13) Mink: "Someone must have taken my beads!"

(14) Bullethawk Chief came back home. (15) COM: "Where have you been?"[22] (16) BHC: "Just around."[23]

(17) Mink came to Coyote Old Man's place. (18) Mink: "Bring me my beads!" (19) COM: "I didn't take them." (20) Mink: "No.[24] (21) Your grandson stole them from me. (22) Bring them back!" [Mink returns home.]

(23) Mink: "He did too steal from me! (24) I know those two took them. (25) I'll go back and see again." (26) He came to Coyote Old Man's place. (27) Mink: "Don't be that way! (28) Take pity on me and give them back." (29) COM: "No one took them. (30) Here, take mine." (31) Mink: "I don't want those. (32) It's my own I want." (33) Mink came back. (34) He came to his house. (35) Mink: "Those two do have them."

(36) COM to BHC: "Bring me those so I can give them back to him."[25] (37) BHC: "I didn't steal them." (38) COM: "No, you were there. (39) Mink saw you. (40) He saw you stealing." (41) BHC: "I never went there. (42) Mink Old Man is a liar."[26]

(43) COM: "Shall I go for the last time?[27] (44) I'll go see." (45) Coyote Old Man brought beads, packing them, having filled a packbasket full. (46) COM to Mink: "Here, take this! (47) He himself said he didn't steal from you." (48) Mink: "No, he stole them from me. (49) I saw him. (50) Take yours back. (51) It's my own I want."

(52) Coyote Old Man brought them back. (53) He got there [and said] "I hear you took them. (54) He himself said he saw you. (55) Wherever you have them hidden, bring them! (56) I'll take them [back]. (57) The old man is a saltu,[28] that grandfather of yours. (58) What did you need to steal, when it's full in back?[29]" (59) BHC: "That old man is a liar. (60) I never went by that place."

(61) Mink: "I'll go for the last time, even though they won't give them [to me]. (62) I'll go to recover them." [arrives] (63) Mink to COM: "Bring back the beads to me!" (64) COM: "He himself said he'd never been there, when I asked him." (65) Mink: "No, he went there. (66) And this is the last time I'm coming here."

(67) COM to BHC: "Bring them, grandson! (68) Bring them, wherever you hid them. (69) The old man is a saltu. (70) Be brave![30] (71) What did you steal for? (72) What

do you lack?"

(73) Mink: "May it be made high when this world[31] sinks under the water! (74) Let me alone be saved! (75) When I have sung four times, let the world sink under! (76) [sings] Mink wo·ˀina; [he] left the people."[32]

(77) COM: "Look! look! look! the water is coming. (78) Bring it! Bring it! (79) Let's give back what you've hidden away."

(80) At the break of day, the world was under water. (81) Coyote Old Man ground a hole in an elk antler and went inside. (82) The place where Bullethawk Chief was sitting on a tree went under water.

(83) So he went to Sutter Buttes.[33] (84) His body was all wet. (85) He sat down on the mountain. (86) Snake:[34] "Who could that heavy one be who's sitting on me again?" (87) BHC: "It's me, grandpa." (88) Snake: "Does your grandpa live somewhere here?" (89) When he [BHC] looked, he [Snake] was about to swallow him. (90) The Snake-saltu was coming with his mouth gaping open.

(91) So he took off and went to Mt. Konocti.[35] (92) He sat down on Mt. Konocti. (93) Raven: "Who could that be sitting on my body again?" (94) Grebe:[36] "Don't talk! (95) Go and see! (96) Someone has come here from someplace." (97) BHC: "Grandpa, it's me. (98) My grandpa has died somewhere. (99) The world is under water. (100) he·y!" [He falls over from the cold.] (101) Raven: "All right, grandson. (102) Come in! (103) Nobody can steal from that old man. (104) By stealing, you two ruined the world."[37]

(105) Grebe Old Lady heated water and bathed him. (106) She revived him, who had fainted from cold.[38] (107) She fed him fish and acorn bread.

(108) Next morning the water was dried up. (109) He [BHC] put acorn bread in a sack and came packing it. (110) BHC: "I'll go look for my grandfather, wherever he is, whether he's alive or not."

(111) He got to Coyote Old Man's place. (112) BHC: "Grandpa, where are you?" (113) He dug in [the ground]. (114) He found Coyote Old Man's foot. (115) He cried out, "Oh, my poor grandpa!" (116) COM: "Who has died here anyway--your grandpa??[39] (117) Pull me by my foot!" (118) He [BHC] pulled and got him out. (119) COM: "You've been rash.[40] (120) Look at the world's ruination! (121) Don't do that again!"

(122) BHC: "Here, eat [this], grandpa."[41] (123) COM: "Yes, yes, yes, bring it! (124) I'll eat. (125) Give it to me!"

(126) COM: "Where were you saved, grandson?" (127) BHC: "Far to the west, on Mt. Konocti. (128) Raven Old Man was there." (129) COM: "Your grandpa does live there."[42]

Grammatical Notes

1. Orthography: Patwin /r/ is an alveolar tap intervocalically and a voiceless alveolar trill syllable-finally. /λ̓/ is an ejective lateral affricate. /ɬ/ is a voiceless lateral fricative. /s/ is a "California s", variable but generally backed further than a dental [s]. Aspiration is indicated by an h in line. Other symbols follow current, standard North American orthography.

2. For further general notes on stem structure, aspect, pronouns, etc., see Whistler (n.d.).

3. Morphological elements (Cache Creek Hill Patwin): The following list of grammatical suffixes, particles and auxiliaries is intended as a minimal guide to the grammatical phenomena manifested in the text. Items are listed alphabetically to facilitate lookup of morphemes isolated with dashes in the text but not glossed there. Only those suffixes, particles and auxiliaries which actually appear in the text are listed here. See Whistler (n.d.) for others. N.B.: In a few cases (starred in this list) the analysis here differs from that for the same items in Whistler (n.d.). In such cases, the current analysis represents a refinement and should supplant the earlier analysis. For items of especial interest, line references are also included here.

A) Suffixes and clitic auxiliaries

* -bo/-be (animate/inanimate form)
- a. general modal: should, shall; could, can; etc. usually cooccurs with pi or pa modal particle in the clause. See lines 74,75,86,93,103,129.
- b. attributive or headless relativizer ('who/which is...'). See lines 55,113.
- c. auxiliary 'to be' following -ro; not clearly distinct from bo(·)/be(·) auxiliary. See below and lines 23,70.

-boti evidential (animate form). See footnote 14.

	-ču	suffix of personal relation (suffixed to kin-terms)
	-čut	objective form of -ču. See line 110.
	-da	comitative case ('with'). See line 107.
	-ho	verb-deriving suffix. See line 106.
	-khe·	vocative case
	-le	first person exclusive hortatory, 'I'll...'
	-ƚa	inanimate locative case; also marks if/when clauses.
*	-m/-mu	(follows vowels/follows consonants) This is the general subjunctive mood marker. It has a number of special uses: a. negative. See lines 38,60,61,121. b. purposive. See lines 25,62,110. c. other. See line 53.
	-mˀa/-muˀa	evidential, 'must be that...' See lines 3,13.
	-mˀu/-muˀu	negative
	-ma	valence-changing (i.e. voice) suffix: CAUSATIVE
	-ma	objective case (animate); also marks some object clauses. See -t.
*	-matin	animate locative case. See lines 17,26,111 and footnote 6.
	-me	valence-changing suffix: 'with' (e.g. 'come' > 'bring')
	-men	noun-deriving suffix. See lines 86,90,94,105.
	-n/-ni	(follows vowels/follows consonants) participle B. See lines 28,30 and footnote 9.
	-na	postposition, 'along, at, into'
	-no	inanimate genitive case; the genitive case also marks subordinate subjects and demoted agents. See lines 7,73,81,114,120.
	-pa	valence-changing suffix: 'for, back'; BENEFACTIVE
	-ro	participle A (vowel stems). See -taro.
*	-s	neutral, unmarked-tense suffix. This marks a verb as sentence-completing (i.e. not participial) but does not explicitly indicate tense.
	-sa	past tense
	-say	present tense interrogative
	-se	dual inclusive hortatory, 'let's two...'
*	-t	verb suffix of uncertain function, but possibly related to the archaic nominal aspect marker -t and/or to the participle in -ta. See lines 64,83,86,91.
	-ta	participle A (consonant stems) This form is rare in Cache Creek, though standard in Kabalmem Hill Patwin. See -taro and line 58.
	-ta·	past tense interrogative. See line 126.
	-taro	participle A (consonant stems) This is the usual form of participle A in Cache Creek Hill Patwin. Marks a verb in a clause as not completing a sentence. See also -ro.
	-ti	directional suffix, 'from, by'
	-tuka	directional suffix, 'towards'
	-thi	dual/plural imperative
	-thu/i	stem-derivational suffix

-tí future tense

* -tó a. inceptive, 'about to...'. See line 89.
b. 'to what end, with what goal'. See line 71.

-wol contrastive, 'the only, the very...'. See lines 32,51,74.

-Vt objective case (archaic); <u>V</u> stands for zero or a copy of the preceding vowel.

-Vy genitive case (archaic and mostly restricted to pronouns)

-ʔ emphatic (a prosodic element)

-ʔa auxiliary 'to have'. See lines 42,59,70,73,115.

-ʔele negative auxiliary; contrasts with <u>-ʔa</u>. See line 119.

* -ʔu auxiliary 'to do; to say'

-ʔunan evidential, 'x said himself that...'. See lines 47,54,64 and footnote 14.

ʔupu 'hear that...' (evidential?). See line 53.

* -ʔu post-case (often functions as conjunction)

-daʔu 'and...' (a conjunction). See line 107.

-ɬaʔu 'even though...'. See line 61.

-naʔu marks some adverbs. See lines 14,22,33,50,52,108.

-sʔu evidential, '<u>did</u> do...'; definite evidence that... See line 35.

B) <u>Modal particles</u> (often are postclitic)

* ka "subjunctive" mode particle, often indicating incompleted action, unattained goal, or results counter to expectation--hence often translated "but"; also commonly occurs with interrogative pronouns to indicate indefiniteness of reference. See lines 3,5,13.

* pa interrogative mode particle; most commonly used in the future tense.

* pi declarative mode particle; commonly used in the future tense.

C) <u>Interrogative roots</u>

he· 'where?'

pe· 'what?' This is the most general interrogative root, and is often extended to express 'how?', etc.

po 'who?'

D) <u>Full auxiliaries</u>

be(·) inanimate auxiliary 'to be' (existential/locative). See lines 58,77,108.

bo(·) animate auxiliary 'to be' (existential/locative); full verb 'to stay; to live at.' See lines 38-40,128,129.

ʔele· negative auxiliary; full verb 'to be absent, gone'

ʔi auxiliary 'to be' (copula); full verb 'to do; to use'

ʔiwe irregular imperative of <u>ʔi</u> 'to do', used to form periphrastic negative imperatives. See lines 46,121.

Footnotes

[1]In Whistler (n.d.) I mistakenly identified Mr. Anderson Lowell as Mr. Lowell Anderson, on the basis of a reference in Radin's Patwin manuscripts. Mr. Lowell's real name was Anson Lowell, but he was generally known as Anderson. He was, in fact, Mrs. Lowell's brother-in-law. I am endebted to Mrs. Jennie Regalado of Colusa for pointing out this error to me.

[2]Participle A (-ro on vowel-final stems, -taro on consonant-final stems) marks a verb in a non-final clause; i.e. there is almost always another clause (or clauses) continuing the sentence. The verb in a sentence-completing clause, which may follow or precede a participial clause, is marked with -s or any of several tense-marking suffixes. I generally translate the participle as 'did ... and ...' Cf. footnote 9.

[3]The -mʔa/-muʔa evidential in the interrogative conveys 'I wonder...' and in the declarative, 'It must be that...' It seems to denote inferences, often paralleling English must. See also line 13.

[4]When- or if-clauses in Hill Patwin are formed by adding the locative case to the nominal stem of the verb and placing its subject in the genitive case. ʔuy is the genitive form of pi 'he'. The third clause in this sentence is an afterthought which here expresses the subject as a full noun in the genitive case: thasi-no 'Mink's...' See also lines 73,75,89 for similar constructions.

[5]harme is one of a series of derived forms for 'to take', 'to bring' etc. in Patwin. Since these derived verbs are well-represented in the text, I include a chart of the various forms:

	I	II	III	IV
to go	har	harme	hari·	harpa
to arrive at (coming or going)	hen	henme	heni·	henpa
to come	wer	were·	weri·	[werpa-]

The forms under I are the basic verbs of coming and going. The forms under II mean 'to go with an inanimate object,' i.e. 'to take' etc. The forms under III mean 'to go, taking along an animate being,' i.e. 'to take along' etc. The forms under IV are marked for BENEFACTIVE and are more idiosyncratic in meaning. harpa means 'to go for or after something', henpa is 'to come upon, to discover', and werpa appears only in werpap̓ir 'to answer'.

[6]-matin as a unit marks animate locative case, although it can be further analyzed into three pieces: -ma (animate object), -t (archaic nominal aspect or object marker), -in (archaic locative case marker).

[7]This is an example of an object complement. The embedded verb is a zero-marked nominal form, and its subject is in the genitive case. See also lines 66,71,79 for analogous treatment of nominalized clauses functioning as arguments (other than object) in a main clause.

[8]piʔu is a complex stem: literally 'that-do', which results in a meaning of 'to do that' or 'to do like that'. However, it often takes on specialized conjunctional functions. See lines 66,83,91.

[9]-n/-ni The use of participle B forms is not yet well-understood. They are relatively infrequent. It may be that they are used for prospective actions rather than for completed actions. The usage in line 30 is opaque to me. Perhaps the expression is elliptic there. harmen is definitely not a normal imperative form.

[10]-wol might be thought of as functioning like a cleft in English to focus a given NP: "It's mine I want". It also resembles the Japanese particle sae .

[11]-sʔu functions here like an evidential, in that it emphasizes speaker certainty regarding an event: "They do in fact [I know it] have them."

[12]This is the short form of ʔele·mʔu. See line 20.

[13]The object complements of certain verbs (here a sensory perception verb) have the verb marked with the objective case suffix -ma, rather than zero. See also line 106, where the object clause is functioning like a headless relative.

[14]-ʔunan is an evidential which emphasizes that what you are reporting was indeed said by another party. (The speaker can thereby disclaim responsibility for the statement, whatever it is.) It is composed of -ʔu 'to say' + nan REFLEXIVE. See also lines 54 and 64. -boti is another evidential of broad application, including probably sensory evidence, inference based on sensory evidence, and hearsay. See also line 96.

[15]The use of be(·) or bo(·) 'to be' following a form in -ro generally indicates an ongoing state. See also lines 58,108.

[16]The structure of this clause is not clear, since I cannot account for the -t suffixed

to the verb. One possibility is that the object pronoun ʔut 'him' has been incorporated onto the verb, but such processes do not seem to occur elsewhere in Patwin.

[17] ʔepaypi is a noun meaning 'curse' which is used verbally to introduce actual curses.

[18] The internal structure of this sentence is opaque. It may be that tho·łpilimen just talks strangely.

[19] ʔele·be here can be understood as a compound modal verb meaning 'cannot'.

[20] bo·ma pe·ma is a collocation meaning 'alive or not', 'dead or alive', etc.

[21] An example of a periphrastic negative imperative formed with the negative/subjunctive suffix (-m) added to the verb, followed by the imperative of 'to do'.

[22] Literally, "Where are you coming from?"

[23] Literally, "I arrived [back from] travelling around [nowhere in particular]."

[24] ʔele·mʔu might best be translated, 'On the contrary...' It implies a disagreement with a prior assertion. It also appears in shortened form as ʔele·m. See line 38.

[25] A somewhat free rendering of the Patwin.

[26] balʔaro, which should mean 'is lying', appears to be lexicalized here to mean 'a liar'. A few other verbal formations in -ʔaro in Patwin also show this nominalization of a participial form. bal is almost certainly related to River Patwin balu 'to tell, to relate s.t.' Cf. the English usage "to tell a story" meaning 'to lie'.

[27] The text is somewhat murky here. I interpret this sentence as a rhetorical question by Coyote as he is making up his mind what to do. However, why he should say "for the last time" remains obscure.

[28] saltu means variously 'a spirit; a supernatural being; a dangerous person; a bad man', etc. I view 'being endowed with or with expert access to Power' as approximating its meaning closely, but choose not to translate the word in the text, since there is no simple English equivalent without erroneous connotations. Cf. Whistler (n.d.) for more examples of the use of saltu.

[29] Coyote means here that since he had plenty of beads himself (baskets or sacks full in the back of his house), there was no need for Bullethawk to go steal someone else's.

[30] ťukeʔarobo is always translated 'be brave', both by Rev. Lorenzo and by Nora Lowell in Mrs. Bright's notes. I suspect, however, that understood within the cultural context, the term probably means 'face up to your responsibilities' or something similar. The basic meaning of ťukeʔaro is 'to be strong'.

[31] The text is unclear here. Anderson Lowell's version includes the invocation of the flood of the world, but does not include anything about "making it high". "Making it high" may refer either to the depth of the floodwaters to come or to the stormclouds building up. The appearance of the stormclouds is mentioned in Anderson's version of the tale. Note also that wilak means both 'valley' and 'world', which for at least the River Patwins were pretty much coextensive. Large floods on the Sacramento River would spread out over hundreds of square miles of floodplains in the Sacramento Valley.

[32] Mink's song is compact and formulaic. I have no good translation for wo·ʔina. However, the sense of the song seems to be "Woe is me! (or Angry am I! ?)--I'm abandoning the people of the world."

[33] Sutter Buttes, also known as Marysville Buttes, are the eroded remains of a large extinct volcano in the center of the Sacramento Valley, in Butte County just east of the major River Patwin settlements. It was a well-known "spirit mountain", reserved for hunting and power seeking by men. It figures importantly in the Patwin creation myth, which also tells of a world flood.

[34] tho·łpilimen (literally 'mountain-wrap around-thing') is a mythic snake of enormous size. It is often described as a python or boa-like snake which hangs in trees and squeezes its victims. It is also known as tho·łpolokomen, which may mean 'mountain-round-thing'.

[35] Mt. Konocti is a relatively young volcanic cone on the south shore of Clear Lake, in Lake County. It dominates the lake, hence the Patwin name "big-mountain". It is well outside Patwin territory, but the Hill Patwin had extensive trade and cultural contact with the Clear Lake Pomo and Miwok groups and can be expected to have been familiar

with the mountain. Nora Lowell called it "Uncle Sam Mountain".

[36]The little pied-billed grebe is locally known as "helldiver". The Patwin name is literally "diver". In Nora Lowell's version of the myth, Grebe Old Lady is married to Raven, whereas in Anderson Lowell's version, Bullethawk meets a Grebe family, man and wife.

[37]Literally, "You two stole and [thereby] ruined the world."

[38]Literally, "He who was cold and fainted, him she made get up."

[39]This line is clearly intended ironically, to make fun of Bullethawk.

[40]hali·haliʔa apparently means 'to have thoughts about, to consider'. Cf. halu 'to think'. Thus hali·haliʔele would mean 'not to have thoughts about', i.e. 'rash, foolhardy, impetuous.'

[41]The significance of this line is lost in this version of the story. Bullethawk is offering his grandfather, Coyote, food to eat from that which he packed with him. In Anderson Lowell's version the significance is clearer, since the theme of generosity is further developed. In Mr. Lowell's telling, Coyote suggests first that Bullethawk get some gophers (to eat) for him from Mink, who at the time was out hunting gophers. Bullethawk instead takes advantage of Mink's absence to steal a sack of his best beads. During the subsequent negotiations about the stolen beads, Mink does offer Coyote a gopher to eat, even though he refuses Coyote's offer to substitute other beads for the stolen ones. Coyote accepts the food. After the flood, in Anderson's version, Bullethawk brings fish which he gives Coyote to eat. And then after Coyote's exhumation, Coyote returns Mink's beads and is again given a gopher to eat. Thus, in Anderson Lowell's telling of the myth, the theme of the moral commendability of generosity is developed as a counterpoint to the condemnation of stealing.

[42]It may seem that Bullethawk has too many "grandpas". However, the Patwin stems for "grandfather"-- ʔa·p-, -tapan --also refer to one's mother's brother and his direct male descendants, to male ancestors of grandparents, and probably to one's grandmothers' brothers, while thay is the reciprocal kinterm for all these relations. In current Patwin usage, the details of kinship structure have become somewhat unclear. Rev. Lorenzo translated each occurrence of ʔa·p-, etc. as "grandpa" and was no more specific about the kin relations implied in the text. For more detailed analysis of Patwin kinship see Gifford (1922), pp. 94-97. Also see Kroeber (1917) and Lounsbury (1964), p. 377. Lounsbury identifies the Patwin kinship system as an example of his Type IV Omaha system, with generation skewing for both the mother's brother class and the father's sister class. Note that in such a system it is perfectly possible for some of one's "grandfathers" to be younger than oneself. Also see McKern (1922) for a discussion of Patwin family structure and Goldschmidt (1951), p. 321 for a kinship analysis of the closely-related Nomlaki.

Fire, Flood, and Creation
(Lake Miwok)

Catherine A. Callaghan

The Ohio State University

Lake Miwok is a California Indian language formerly spoken south of Clear Lake in Long Valley and the surrounding foothills, about 100 miles north of San Francisco. It is closely related to Coast Miwok, spoken on the Marin Peninsula, and more distantly related to Eastern Miwok, spoken on the western slopes of the Sierra Nevada Mountains and the northern San Joaquin Valley. The Miwok family is in turn related to the Costanoan languages spoken from San Francisco South to Monterey.

No detailed ethnographic work was done on the Lake Miwok, but their culture was apparently very similar to that of the surrounding Pomo Indians as described by Kroeber in his Handbook of the Indians of California (1925). A Lake Miwok dictionary has been published (Callaghan 1965). There is also a grammatical sketch of Lake Miwok with texts (Freeland 1947) and an unpublished Lake Miwok grammar available on microfilm (Callaghan 1963). C. Hart Merriam (1910) published an interesting collection of Miwok tales in English translation.

The language today is remembered by about five people on the Middletown Rancheria who may still use it when conversing among themselves. At the time of my principal field trips in the summers of 1956, 1957, and 1958, the culture was a memory, often secondhand, of the oldest informants. Dances were no longer held in the local roundhouse, although some of the Indians still participated in ceremonies on other reservations. Shamanism was and still is practiced in the area. In recent years, an Indian cultural center has been established at Lower Lake, and there is some hope that local identity will survive.

"Fire, Flood, and Creation" was recorded by James Knight during the summer of 1958, and his brother, the late John Knight, provided a sentence-by-sentence translation with slight corrections in the text. To some extent, sentence divisions are arbitrary, since phonological, morphological, and syntactic criteria do not coincide.

Events concern the end of the pre-human epoch and the beginning of the current one. Although they encompass the world, they are set primarily in Long Valley, the aboriginal homeland of the Lake Miwok Indians. The characters are animal personages with both human and animal attributes, and some of them also have supernatural powers.

Chief among them is Old Man Coyote, a projection of man in all his sublime and ridiculous apsects. In this story, he is alternately an old man, a loving grandfather, Trickster, magician, and wielder of creative power. After the earth is destroyed by fire and flood, he must repopulate it with the plants, animals, and human beings of today. Superimposed on these events is the coming of age of Bullet Hawk within his tribal domain.

An earlier version of this tale appeared in the Merrian collection. James Knight owned a copy and used it for reference, although his version differs in several places. I will indicate significant differences in footnotes.

James Knight is a natural story teller, and his style has added considerable drama to this creation story. I dedicate the text to him and his brother in deepest gratitude.[1]

(1)	kilá·	kó·can[2]	hú·ni	lí·lawhintec[3]	kaʔáp·in	kaʔúnun
	old-time	person SUBJ	story	tell REL OBJ	my father SUBJ	my mother SUBJ

kaṭu	kani[4]	liláwne.	(2)	kaʔát·a[5]	he	kawé·ʔamakon
that-way	me	tell BEN		my older-siblings	and	my relative PLURAL POSS

hú·kewa[6] hú·ni né.[7] (3) né· hú·nin weno[8] kilá·yomit[9] hóyot.[10]
before LOCAT story here this story SUBJ it-is-said Old Place ALL begins.

(4) ʔolé·nawani[11] wékwek hóypuni hanacác·oni[12] nít
Coyote Old-Man COM Bullet-Hawk Chief COM his grandchild COM here ALL

kocṣúkuh.[13] (5) ní·t kocyómik.[14] (6) ni hín·at wékwek
they-two stay here ALL they-two home HAVE here spot ALL Bullet-Hawk

mélih hanapá·pani.
grows-up his grandfather COM

(7) mákṣat kén·ehi weno ʔiʔóp·oyu[15] ʔé·ya. (8) kal ne
that-time ALL one day it-is-said he go OBJ wants they this

lóklon nákac ʔiṭi ʔóp·oynuka -- ʔekal ma· ʔóp·oyạ.[16]
valley POSS end OBJ him travel CAUS then there he-goes-around.

(9) ká·l dó·mpat[17] ʔíṣ·a wé·ṭa ʔé·ya páwih ʔúṭe. (10) lóklo
then there toward ALL still go wants mountain he-sees valley

ʔúṭe. (11) wúw·e ʔúṭe. (12) pólpolu ʔúṭe hoká·pawih he
he-sees creek he-sees. lake OBJ he-sees Rocky Mountain and

lupíkpawih ʔúṭe. (13) má· numán·inuka, wékweknu,[18] wéno
Pointed Hill he-sees that wonder CAUS Bullet-Hawk SUBJ it-is-said

mákṣat milé·ko halí·hali mákṣan pál·a. (14) huyú·ma
that-way ALL bird PLURAL all-kinds that-kind SUBJ fill-it-up meadowlark

ʔúṭe mákṣamele[19] cokó·ko. (15) halí·hali ʔúṭe.
he-sees that-kind birds quail everything he-sees

(16) makṣaṭu wé·ṭaṭu wé·ṭa[20] kal ʔíṣ·a dó·kaniṭu wé·ṭa.
that-way INSTR he-goes INSTR go then still move-away INSTR he-goes

(17) mákṣan nakáhto ʔó·ni wénok pólpolu ʔuṭé· weno.
that-much POSS far ALL he-comes Guenoc Lake OBJ he-sees it-is-said

(18) kal papá·[21] nit pólpol ṣukúh wace mú·.
then grandfather VOC here ALL lake is-situated must

(19) ʔú· kaṣa[22] weno. (20) nit ṣúkuh pólpolnu. (21) ma
yes he-said it-is-said here ALL is-situated lake SUBJ that

pólpoluc[23] wenókṭu konlakát weno; mama pólpolun ʔúṭe.[24] (22) ma
lake OBJ Guenoc INSTR they call it-is-said that's lake OBJ you see there

dó·ṣam ʔóṭ·apawin ʔúṭe? (23) mám ʔúʔkaṣapawikoc ṣe
other side LOC two mountain you see that-is great mountain DUAL also

kaṣa weno.
he-said it-is-said

(24) lupíkpawih kénne -- miṭi kén·eʔayen ṣe lá·kte mákṣa ʔunu
Pointed Hill one and another one SUBJ also has-name that-way but

má· kahólṭi. (25) ʔolé·nanan keláckelacmu[25] halí·hali né·nut;
it I don't-know Coyote Old-Man SUBJ old-times ABL everything knows

ʔiʔúd·i.
he great.

(26) mákṣat caṭín ṣe ʔóp·oy weno; mákṣat
that-time ALL Weasel SUBJ also is-around it-is-said that-way ALL

ʔiṭín ṣe ʔúʔkaṣa makṣa hél·a ne ʔolé·nawanṣaka ʔúʔkaṣa
he SUBJ also great but not this Coyote Old-Man POSS like great

má·ʔayen. (27) kal má·hintet ʔadé· ʔálwan taláh weno.
that one SUBJ. then there somewhere ALL big tree SUBJ stands it-is-said

(28) má·n hé·lay ʔak hélak. (29) men yomún·aka mélen
it POSS limb moreover not PASS just pretty bird POSS

tuyén·iʔalanṣakah[26] mac tuyé·ṭu wé·ṭa ʔáw·eni.
rest IMP tree POSS like there OBJ he-rests INSTR go morning IMP

(30) né· wénok pólpolto ká·c[27] ʔóp·oy. (31) kiláckilac kó·cakon
this Guenoc Lake ALL fish is there long-ago person PLURAL

né· yólum. (32) má· ká·c lákten pilí·t. (33) ʔúmcuṣ, káṣ·i,
SUBJ this eat. that fish name SUBJ pilí·t. suckers salmon

hú·l, c̓í·kut mát ṣúkuh. (34) má·n tóp·at[28] ʔaye
trout little-chubs there ALL are-situated that POSS after ALL however

numá· ká·c mát ʔukán ṣe. (35) konsémla. (36) ʔúṭuk ká·c
different fish there ALL comes-in also they plant-it beard HAVE fish

he cáne ká·c maṣáw.uṭehinte konsémlahintec níh. (37) mapólpolto
and many fish we have REL they plant REL OBJ now that lake ALL

ṣúkuh níh.
is-situated now.

(38) ʔaká·l kén·ehi ʔi· ʔadét·uma[29] muhínti mélih. (39) miṭi papá·
then one day he big INCHO you-know grows-up then grandfather

kaṣa weno.
VOC he-said it-is-said

(40) há·y ? kaṣa weno.
what he-said it-is-said

(41) híntiṭu hél·a[30] né· kakát·en tém·a né· melé·konuc,
what INSTR not these I kill can these bird PLURAL OBJ.

lákac? (42) tóhlok mákṣan ma pál·a muhínti wénok pólpoluc
geese OBJ mudhens that-kind SUBJ it OBJ fills you-know Guenoc Lake OBJ

he huyú·man.[31] (43) kal ʔiʔánwaṭi.
and meadowlark SUBJ then he goes-back.

(44) ʔó·w; kawilík ʔina[32] má· kó·nuc kaṣa weno. (45) hintí·l
well I get FUT that gun OBJ he-said it-is-said . olt-time

kó·nuc[33] ʔeká·l.
bow-and-arrow now

(46) má·wilik hú·kewa lám·at ʔukán weno.
that getting before LOCAT sweathouse ALL he-goes-in it-is-said

(47) má·wilik hú·kewa nóc·a wél·ak miṭi hák·oyṭu ṣút·u wén·a
that getting before LOCAT cry he-pretends and spit INSTR eye OBJ smears

miṭi nóc·a wél·ak.[34]
and cry he-pretends

(48) híntiwelakun nóc·a papá·? kaṣa weno.
what sake OBJ you cry grandfather VOC he-said it-is-said

(49) ʔá·y ném kaʔáp·i he kaʔáp·in ʔáp·in kíw·ac mi
well this-is my father and my father POSS father POSS arrow OBJ you

kawayán ʔina miṭi henán kani ʔobú·t[35] kanóc·a kaṣa weno.
I give SUBJ FUT and spirit SUBJ me bad ALL I cry he-said it-is-said

(50) ʔolé·nawan mákṣat ʔó·w. (51) mam híntin ma·
Coyote Old-Man SUBJ that-way ALL all-right that-is what SUBJ that

pólpol, wénok pólpol yolé·wa ṣiwí·ṣiwi ʔiṭi tú·lyaṭi kaṣa weno.
lake Guenoc Lake near LOCAT green-stuff it circles he-said it-is-said

(52) ʔáy mam kó·l; mákṣa mayolúmṭu mawé·ṭa ṣe kaṣa weno.
well, that's tule that-kind we eat INSTR we go also he-said it-is-said

(53) kál ma yolú·mu mená·wu ʔé·ya ṣe hél·a kí·kto ʔúkan
then that eat OBJ try OBJ he-wants also not water ALL he-goes-in SUBJ

tém·a.
can

(54) miṭi ne pólpoluc do ká·wimun welé·ṭet yomún·aka.
when this lake OBJ there down ABL you look ALL pretty

(55) ʔóṭ·apawikoc ʔóṭ·a lám·anṣakaṭu ṣúkuh. (56) miṭi
two mountain DUAL two sweathouses POSS like INSTR are-situated and

má·n ká·win ʔamlákte?aye[36] ṣálṣal. (57) má·ʔaye cáṭin yomí· weno
that POSS down POSS its name one ṣálṣal that one Weasel POSS home it-is-said

máh. (58) mat lám·an mát ˀeket şúkuh.
emphatic there ALL sweathouse SUBJ there ALL somewhere ALL is-situated

(59) ˀiṭilám·an.
his sweathouse SUBJ

(60) kal wékwek ne ˀálwa tuyé· miṭi ˀuṭé·ṭu wé·ṭa ma
then Bullet-Hawk this tree rests and he-sees INSTR go that

ˀélu.[37] (61) delé·ka ˀoṭóṭ·ahi mat tuyé· miṭi cácih.
he-looks-at three four days there ALL he-perches and he-watches

(62) ˀáw·eni kela také·ṭu wé·ṭa weno. (63) ˀekémpat
morning IMP at-that-time he-goes-out INSTR go it-is-said somwhere

wé·ṭaṭu wé·ṭa. (64) yolúmni welíkşipoṭu[38] wé·ṭa.
DIR ALL he-goes INSTR go eat IMP he-gets AND REFL INSTR go

(65) kal kén·ehi ni kíw·ac ˀiṭi wáyan tóp·at weno
then one day this arrow OBJ him give POSS after ALL it-is-said

ˀiˀokénṭu wé·ṭa halí·halic tóhlokuc. (66) mákşa ˀóken.
he catches INSTR go all-kinds OBJ mudhens OBJ that-kind he-catches

(67) kal hél·a ma yólum ṭé·le ˀaye yolúmṭu wé·ṭa weno.
then not that he-eats breast just he-eats INSTR go it-is-said.

(68) miṭi ˀiṭipapá·ˀayen má·c kíc·awˀaye halí·hali mákşan
and his grandfather one SUBJ that OBJ bloody one everything that-way SUBJ

yolúmṭu wé·ṭa men -- kúč·işa wikít tolá· miṭi ma yolúmṭu
he-eats INSTR go just little while fire ALL he-throws and it he-eats

wé·ṭa, kíc·awˀayec. (69) mákşan lá·walit şá·hit weno.
INSTR go bloody one OBJ that-way POSS then ALL long-time ALL it-is-said

(70) ˀeka·l má·tayh kaˀemá·ṭin ˀina má· kaşa weno.
then that man I visit AND SUBJ FUT emphatic he-said it-is-said

(71) ma cáṭin lám·antulet ˀukán ˀina ˀeká·l.
that Weasel POSS sweathouse POSS inside ALL he-goes-in SUBJ FUT now

(72) kal má· cáṭin wé·yi ˀukán weno ˀeká·l -- ˀáw·eni[39]
then that Weasel POSS house goes-in it-is-said then morning IMP

wé·ṭa man tóp·ato. (73) halí·hali ˀuṭé· weno má·hinteto.
he-goes that POSS after ALL everything he-sees it-is-said right-there ALL

(74) ˀóṭ·atumaywali[40] miṭi má·hintet ˀúkan, ma lám·at.
two stick years when right-there ALL he-goes-in that sweathouse ALL

(75) kal halí·hali yolúmnin şúkuh mát·o. (76) ˀúşkun, cíp·a--
then all-kinds eat IMP SUBJ are-situated there ALL pinole bread

wayá· cíp·a. (77) cámih, ṣúk·i, k̓učúy[41] ká·c -- mákṣan ʔemé·ne
acorn bread rabbit deer little fish that-kind SUBJ good

yolúmnin mát ṣúkuh. (78) ká·l kustá·lat ṣúkuh weno.
eat IMP SUBJ there ALL is-situated then sack ALL it-is-situated it-is-said

(79) ṣúk·in kuwé·lu kustá·la konʔokáyṭu wé·ṭa, ʔekal mat ʔú·neṭu
deer POSS hide sack they make INSTR go then there ALL puts-in

wé·ṭa, halí·halic -- wáyac. (80) ʔekal ma kén·e kustá·lantulet
INSTR go everything OBJ acorns OBJ then that one sack POSS inside ALL

hú·yan ṣúkuh. (81) halí·halin yolúmnin cáṭin lám·a
beads SUBJ are-situated all-kinds SUBJ eat IMP SUBJ Weasel POSS sweathouse

pál·a.
fill-up

(82) ká·l ʔihólṭi ʔeká·l ma ménaw. (83) ʔekal hanaʔúkuc[42] ma·
then he not-knows then it tries then his hand OBJ that

ʔúlkintulet ʔú·ne. (84) miṭi má· ʔálu. (85) kawá·cun
acorn-much POSS inside ALL he-puts-in then it he-tastes sugar SUBJ

halí·halin ṣúkuh. (86) yólum tóp·at k̓úc·i melén miṭi
everything SUBJ is-situated eat after ALL little-bit he-finishes when

má·hintet weno ṣiwá·ku ʔú·neṭu wé·ṭa púṭac. (87) púṭa
right there ALL it-is-said green-grass OBJ he-puts-in go straw OBJ straw

ʔú·h, hél·a ṣíwak, púṭa. (88) ma pál·anuka miṭi ʔeká·l má· caníhṭu
yeah not green-grass straw it fill-up CAUS and then it he-ties INSTR

wé·ṭa ṣe he hínti kí·kuc mát molé·ṭiṭu wé·ṭa.
go also and some-kind water OBJ there ALL he-pours INSTR go

(89) hintí·l ʔú·nu ṣáw·uṭe mát·o ṣe -- ṣá·l halí·halic kilá·
old-time fruit he-has there ALL also clover all-kinds OBJ old-time

kóc·an yolúmnic. (90) mákṣa ṣáw·uṭe má·hintet.
people POSS eat IMP OBJ that-kind he-has right there ALL

(91) ká·l ne hú·ya ʔúṭe; hú·ya kustá·lat ʔekal ma wúla.[43]
then these beads he-sees bead sack ALL then it he-steals.

(92) wulá· men té·men. (93) má·n ʔobú·t ʔiṭi tóla.
steal just he-things-about that SUBJ wrong ALL him throws

(94) kal má·c kówun nákah ʔá·wi weno. (95) miṭi wénok
then that OBJ half POSS so-much he-packs it-is-said and Guenoc

pólpol lí·lewa má·hintet sá·hat má· ṣólak. (96) hanapápan
Lake above LOCAT right there ALL ditch ALL it he-hides his grandfather

yómin yolé· ʔiná·ya miṭi.
POSS home POSS near he-approaches and

(97) mákṣaṭu delé.ka ʔoṭóṭ·ahin wé·ṭa weno. (98) ʔekál ne
that-way INSTR three four days SUBJ go it-is-said then this

caṭí·nawan henán ʔiṭi ʔobú·ṭu wé·ṭa. (99) né·ne kahíntikaṣa?
Weasel Old-Man POSS spirit SUBJ him is-bad go this-is my what kind

kaṣa. (100) híntin ʔeket ʔobú· wace mú· ní· yowá·to kaṣa.
he-said something SUBJ somewhere ALL wrong must be this earth ALL he-said

(101) kaṣukún ʔina ma ní·hi yomí·to kaṣa weno.
I stay SUBJ FUT emph this day home ALL he-said it-is-said

(102) ʔeka·l ʔiṣúkuh. (103) hanawé·yi wálil. (104) yolúmnic muʔé·
then he stays his house he-sweeps eat IMP OBJ all

ʔélu. (105) ʔawé·cu ʔiʔalíwnukahinten weno ma hú·ya ʔáliw.
he-looks-at all he-misses CAUS REL SUBJ it-is-said those beads he-misses

(106) púṭan mat ṣúkun kówun nákah.
straw SUBJ there ALL is SUBJ half POSS that-much

(107) káṣ·a kahólṭi ʔak kaṣa weno caṭí·nawan.
it-seems I not-understand but he-said it-is-said Weasel Old-Man SUBJ

(108) ʔemé·neṭu ʔanṣúkun wace ʔóbu. (109) yomún·akaṭu ʔanṣukúhto
good INSTR someone lives SUBJ must bad fine INSTR someone lives

ʔobú· wace kaṣa weno.
ALL bad must he-said it-is-said

(110) ʔiʔáṣkay ʔeká·l. (111) ʔó·w! mi kané·nut má·h!
he gets-angry then Oh yeah! you I know emphatic

(112) mántic mi kané·nut mákṣat mi kalimán ʔina níh kaṣa
who OBJ you I know that-way ALL you I look-for SUBJ FUT now he-said

weno.
it-is-said

(113) ka·l helókpat weno wé·ṭa miṭi mát hanahóc·i
then behind DIR ALL it-is-said he-goes and there ALL his spear

wilík[44] weno, wikí· hóc·ic.[45] (114) weyá·walimpat kí·wi.
he-gets it-is-said fire spear OBJ Lower World DIR ALL he-points

(115) lí·lewalimpat kí·wi· ʔoló·mwalimpat kí·wi. ʔá·lawalimpat
Upper World DIR ALL he-points west world DIR ALL he-points east world DIR

kí·wi. mákṣa ʔak hél·a mánti ʔúṭe. (116) tamálpat
ALL he-points that-way but not anybody he-sees north DIR ALL

kí·wi; mámpat kí·wi. (117) hél·a hínti mánti ʔúṭe. (118) mákṣa
he-points there DIR ALL he-points not any someone he-sees that-way

ʔunu ʔolómwalimpat kí·wi.[46] (119) miṭi ʔiʔúṭe.
but southwest world DIR ALL he-points then he sees-him

(120) ʔó·w mi kahólṭi ʔak kaṣa weno. kahólṭi ʔayen
all-right you I not-know but he-said it-is-said I not-know however

hú·ni [47] máh.
you-think emphatic

(121) kal mákṣat né· hóc·i kí·wit kó·cakon men
then that-way ALL this spear he-points ALL person PLURAL SUBJ just

yó·kṭu wé·ṭa. (122) cú·p --wíkin muʔé·wa cókte.
die INSTR go burned-up fire SUBJ all LOCAT comes

(123) kal wékwek papá· kaṣa weno.
then Bullet-Hawk grandfather VOC he-said it-is-said

(124) há·y? kaṣa.
what he-said

(125) yolé·wac muʔec halí·halin cú·p ma! kaṣa.
near LOCAT OBJ all OBJ everything SUBJ burns-up emphatic he-said

(126) ʔay ʔú· ṣe mákṣa má· các.o kaṣa weno.
oh yeah also that-way that grandchild he-said it-is-said

(127) káṣ·awalit kó·ca kó·l konyuléntu konwé·ṭa. (128) makṣat
this-kind season ALL people tules they burn-off INSTR they go that-

ṣowá·n sélpi, (129) ʔíṣ·a mákṣaṭu konwé·ṭa máh kaṣa.
way ALL don't you be-scared always that-way INSTR they go emphatic he-said

(130) delé·ka he ʔoṭóṭ·aṣe mákṣaṭu ʔiṭi henúh weno.
three or four times that-way INSTR him he-asks it-is-said

(131) ʔakál ne ʔolé·nawaʔayen né·nut kela ne hú·ya
then this Coyote Old-Man one SUBJ knows already these beads

wulá·hintec ʔiṭicác·on. (132) mákṣa ʔunu hél·a hínti ʔá·ṭaw.
steals REL OBJ his grandchild SUBJ that-way but not anything he-says

(133) ʔó·w papá· nec muʔén·ukan! (134) ká· cú·p
all-right grandfather VOC this OBJ stop CAUS IMV I burn-up

ʔinaj ma kaṣa. (135) hél·a kaʔé·ya né·c, wíkin ʔé·tawhintec.
FUT emphatic he-said not I like this OBJ fire SUBJ hot REL OBJ

(136) miṭi hanapápa cémay.
and his grandfather he-tells

(137) ká·l ʔiṭi pápan ʔów kaṣa, (138) kamuʔén·ukan
then his grandafther SUBJ all-right he-said I stop CAUS SUBJ

ʔina né·wikic.
FUT this fire OBJ

(139) kál hóypu tiyámpat weno ʔadé· kíl·i caníh weno.
then chief pole DIR ALL it-is-said big horn he-ties it-it-said.

(140) ká·l má· cánih ʔemé·neṭu.[48] (141) miṭi má·ntulet
then that he-ties good INSTR and there POSS inside ALL

kíl·intulet ʔukán weno.
horn POSS inside ALL he-goes-in it-is-said

(142) miṭi ʔeká·l múṣmuṣuṣi ʔú·pa.[49] (143) múṣmuṣuṣi ʔú.paṭu múla. (144)
and then drizzling rain drizzling rain INSTR he-beats

kustá·laṭu sáw.uṭe múla. (145) mícpa ʔú·pa múla. (146) ṣití·tiṣi
sack INSTR he-has he-beats fog rain he-beats sprinkling

ʔú·paṭu múla. hójpu tí·ya ʔú·pa múla. (147) tána múla. (148) má·
rain INSTR he-beats chief pole rain he-beats snow he-beats it

mulá· weno ʔekál miṭi ma tú·let hínti.
beat it-is-said then then that inside ALL he-does-it

(149) ʔekal kí·k lí·lekaniṭu cókte. (150) kal lám·an pukú·ya
then water rise INSTR comes then sweathouse POSS top

ʔiná·yan ʔina. (151) hín·at ʔiʔá·ṭaw weno ʔiṭipápan.
it-approaches SUBJ FUT that-time ALL he says it-is-said his grandfather

(152) hanacác·o ʔí·lip.
SUBJ his grandson he-teases

(153) ʔó·w ʔunú· kanic wáyan ma ʔúṣkunuc ma ṣúk·ic
all-right mother VOC me OBJ give IMV that pinole OBJ that meat OBJ

ma· ʔató·luc. (154) halí·hali máksa yolúmni lákat. (155) ʔakál
that starch OBJ everything that-kind eat IMP he-names then

má·ʔaye hanacać·o ʔí.lip. (156) hél·a hínti yólum ʔunu men má·
that one his grandchild he-teases not anything he-eats but just that

ʔá·ṭaw muhínti ʔekal ʔiṭicác·on ma ʔálu.
he-says you-know then his grandchild SUBJ it hears

(157) ka·l má· lulú·ṭin[50] ʔina[51] ʔiná·ya. (158) mákṣan
then he fly-away SUBJ FUT it-approaches that-way POSS

lá·wit[52] ma lám.an pukú·yat weno kí·k ʔó·nit. (159) ʔaká·l
until ALL that sweathouse POSS top ALL it-is-said water comes ALL then

lulú·ṭi. (160) wékwék wékwék wékwék wékwék kaṣa weno.
he-flies-away he-said it-is-said

(161) ma wé·ṭ·a.
he's gone

(162) ʔekémpat wé.ṭa hólṭi. (163) kí·k muʔen ṣúkuh.
where DIR ALL go he-not-know water all SUBJ is-situated

(164) ká·l weno ʔidí·pawin[53] pukú·ya k̓úč·in ṣúkuh.
then it-is-said highest mountain POSS peak a-little SUBJ is-there

(165) má·mpat lulú·ṭi ʔak má·n ṣe hél·ak. (166) kí·k má·c
there DIR ALL he-flies but that SUBJ also not PASS water that OBJ

muʔe hínti cácih.
all something he-watches

(167) ʔeké·kahi lulú·ṭi. (168) miṭi ʔekál weno ne ʔupúṣminkoc
how-many days he-flies and then it-is-said these helldiver

ʔiʔúṭe. (169) mé.j miṭi táwlik kí·klilet łápłapaṣi.
DUAL he sees he's-tired and wings water above ALL flapping

(170) mákṣaṭu ʔóp·oy lá·walit ne ʔupúṣminkocto ʔó·ni.
that-way INSTR he-goes-around until ALL those helldiver DUAL ALL he-comes

(171) kanic welénc oc! kaṣa weno.
me OBJ help IMV DUAL he-said it-is-said

(172) ʔó·w các·o kaṣa weno. (173) kalú.mat túyen
all-right grandchild he-said it-is-said my back ALL light IMV

ṣolánṣakaṭu. (174) má·hintet kapá·ṭal ṣukú·hinten
slow POSS like INSTR right there ALL my scabs are-situated REL

kołá·ṭiwelak kaṣa weno. (175) pó·ti láktek. (176) kapó·tin
you break-off might they-said it-is-said heat-sores name PASS my heat-

yedá·ṭiwelak kaṣa weno.
sores you break might they-said it-is-said

(177) kal kén·en ʔiṭi ʔá·wiṭi; kén·en ṣe ʔá·wiṭi. (178) wé·ṭa
then one SUBJ him packs one SUBJ also packs it-goes

mákṣaṭu. (179) mákṣan lá·walit ʔoṭóṭ·atumaykawul ʔú·pa.[54]
that-way INSTR that-way SUBJ for ALL four stick nights it-rains

(180) ʔoṭóṭ·atumayhi ʔú·pat yowán muʔen pólṭeṭi weno.
four stick days it-rains ALL earth SUBJ all SUBJ is-flooded it-is-said

(181) mákṣan nákat ʔawé·cu ʔoṭóṭ·an ʔáyuh. (182) ʔóṭ·a ʔupúṣmim
that-much POSS so-far ALL only four SUBJ are-left two helldivers

wékwek he ʔolé·nawani. (183) ne halí·hali locókhinten hanacác·owelaku
Bullet-Hawk and Coyote Old-Man COM this everything he-does REL SUBJ his grandchild

ʔaye lócok. (184) ʔiṭicác·on hínti ʔé·yat ma·
sake OBJ however he-does his grandchild SUBJ something wants ALL it

ʔokáyṭu wé·ṭa.
he-makes INSTR go

(185) ká·l ne ʔóṭ·a ʔupúṣminkoc túmay polé·yahinte welík miṭi
then these two helldiver DUAL sticks floating REL gather and

máṣ·u ṣunúc ʔiṭi kocʔokáyne weno kí·klileto.
that INSTR bird-nest OBJ him they DUAL make BEN it-is-said water above ALL

(186) kí·k ká·wit cókteṭu wé·ṭa ʔeká·l níh. (187) kal mákṣan
water down ALL comes INSTR go then now then that-way POSS

lá·walit hínti ʔiṭi kocyóp·u-- ká·c. (188) híntic kocʔuṭé·hintec
then ALL something him they DUAL feed fish what OBJ they DUAL see REL OBJ

má·c ʔiṭi kocyóp·ut mát súkuh.
that OBJ him they DUAL feed ALL there ALL is-situated.

(189) ṣá·hit weno ʔeká·l kí·k muʔen ká·y. (190) kal
long-while ALL it-is-said then water all SUBJ dries-up then

mat ʔé·c.[55] (191) delé·kahi ʔoṭóṭ·ahi túye. (192) ʔupúṣminkoc
there ALL he-sleeps three days four days he-rests helldiver DUAL

ʔiṭi háypa. (193) mákṣaṭu súkuh.
him watch that-way INSTR he-stays

(194) kal kén·ehi weno papá· kewé·ṭan ʔina ma.[56]
then one day it-it-said grandfather VOC I go SUBJ FUT emphatic

(195) ka·l ká·wimpat kawicáy ʔina miṭi kaʔó·nin ʔina ṣe kaṣa.
then down DIR ALL I walk FUT and I come SUBJ FUT again he-said

(196) ká·l ma ká·yhinten wuwec ká·wimpat wé·ṭa weno.
then it dries-up REL SUBJ creek OBJ down DIR ALL he-goes it-is-said

(197) ʔak dó·ṣam kén·e kilá·nawa ʔúṭe.
then other side LOC another old man he-sees

(198) kilá·nawa! kaṣa weno.
old man he-said it-is-said

(199) hé·y? (200) híntin láktek?
what what-is you name PASS

(201) mí· ʔaye, híntin láktek? kaṣa weno.
you however what-is you name PASS he-said it-is-said

(202) ʔinlákte kané·nut kaʔé·ya kaní· ṣe, mákṣat kanic
your name I know I want me also that-way ALL me OBJ

lilá̂wnen kaṣa weno.
tell BEN IMV he-said it-is-said.

(203) ʔá·y ném kán·i wékwek kaṣa weno.
oh-yeah this-is me Bullet-Hawk he-said it-is-said

(204) ká·l ʔihúyka. (205) lí·let tikú·ṭi miṭi cacó· cacó·
then he glad up ALL he-jumps and grandchild VOC grand-

cacó· cacó· cacó· cacó·[57]! kaṣa
child VOC grandchild VOC grandchild VOC grandchild VOC grandchild VOC he-said

weno.
it-is-said

(206) kal helókwampat wé·ṭa miṭi má·hintem híc·uw
then back LOCAT DIR ALL he-goes and right there ABL he-runs

weno kó·l kól kól kól. (207) wúw·en dó·ṣam tikú·ṭi
it-is-said creek POSS other side ABL he-jumps

weno. (208) kal các·o lú·tituma.
it-is-said. then grandchild he-hugs

(209) ʔuyé· kaní·ni ʔuyé·.[58] (210) yomímpat ʔicʔánwaṭi. (211) mi
come-on me COM come-on home DIR ALL we DUAL go-back you

kalíma máh; mi kayó·ne kaṣa weno.
I look-for emphatic you I not-find he-said it-is-said

(212) ʔó· hanáh ʔaye. (213) dot kén·e kilá·hukuyni
all-right wait just over-there ALL one old lady COM

kén·e kilá·nawani.[59] (214) kani kocháypa. (215) hínti kalilá̂wneṭiwelak.
one old man COM me they DUAL wait something I tell BEN AND let

(216) ʔáw·et ṣe nít kaʔó·nin ʔinaj kaṣa. (217) ʔolé·nawa
tomorrow ALL again here ALL I come SUBJ FUT he-said Coyote

lilá̂wne wékweknu.
Old-Man tells BEN Bullet Hawk SUBJ

(218) ʔó·w -- ʔáw·et kaṣ̂·at ṣe ʔinʔuṭé·welak kaṣa
all-right tomorrow ALL this-time ALL again you see I-hope he-said

weno.
it-is-said

(219) ká·l ʔiʔánwaṭi miṭi ʔupúṣmin·awa he ʔupúṣminhukuy lilá̂wne --
then he-goes-back and Diver Old-Man and Diver Old-Lady he-tells BEN

kén·e kilá·nawak[60] ʔuṭé·hinten kapápa hú·nin dót
one old man I see REL SUBJ my grandfather he-claims SUBJ over-there ALL

ˀiṭi kaˀúṭe. (220) makṣat ˀáw·et kani yáy·u mákṣat.
him I saw that-way ALL tomorrow ALL me he-wants that-way ALL

(221) ˀáw·et ˀiṭí·ni kawé·ṭan ˀina kaṣa weno.
tomorrow ALL him COM I go SUBJ FUT he-said it-is-said

(222) ˀay ˀú·, ˀiṭi ˀicné·nut máh. (223) ˀó·w ˀiṭí·ni wé·ṭan
oh yeah him we DUAL know emphatic all-right him COM go IMV

ˀekal. (224) huná· mi háypa. (225) ˀúˀkaṣanawa mamá·n ṣe
then so-that you he-takes-care great old-man that-one SUBJ also

kaṣa weno.
he-said it-is-said

(226) ma ˀáw·entala wé·ṭ·a.[61] (227) wú·wenyole wé·ṭa miṭi
that morning POSS stand he-goes. creek POSS near he-goes and

hanapápa ˀúṭe. (228) kal dó·ṣampat lulú·ṭi; ˀiṭí·t ˀó·ni
his grandfather he-sees then other side DIR ALL he-flies him ALL he-comes

ˀekal lám·ampat kocwé·ṭa. (229) má·hintet kocˀó·ni.
then sweathouse DIR ALL they DUAL go right there ALL they DUAL come

(230) kal né·yowan weno híntin helak men
then this earth SUBJ it-is-said anything SUBJ not PASS just

yólcinakaṭu ṣúkuh.
barren INSTR it-stays

(231) papá· kaṣa weno. (232) mat ˀeké·kahi
grandfather VOC he-said it-is-said three ALL how-many days

ṭí·[62]ni ṣukú· miṭi henán ˀiṭi ˀóbu.
he here stays and spirit SUBJ him bad

(233) ne ní·hintet hél·a mántin hél·ak? kaṣa weno.
now this place ALL not anyone SUBJ not PASS he-said it-is-said

(234) méle halí·hali mákṣan hél·ak? kaṣa weno.
birds everything like-that SUBJ not PASS he-said it-is-said

(235) ˀú·h cáne. (236) halí·halimelen cáne. (237) ˀáw·et
yeah lots every-kind birds SUBJ numerous tomorrow ALL

konˀó·nin ˀáw·eto. (238) kal má·hintet ˀilakát wayíkwamelec.
they come FUT tomorrow ALL then right there ALL he names some LOCAT birds

(239) láka lákat. (240) wátmayu lákat, tóhlokuc, paná·k,
OBJ geese he-names ducks OBJ he-names midhens OBJ woodpeckers

púl·u, cokó·ko, ciyá·k, ká·kali, ˀé·c pác·a, wíṣ·ap, téktek, mákṣa
doves quails yellow-hammers crows sapsuckers robins chicken-hawks that-kind

méle kó·cakon kelac nít ṣáw·uṭehinte. (241) mú'en láktek
birds Indian PLURAL SUBJ used-to here ALL have REL all SUBJ name HAVE

-- lóklomele, c̓iṭú·ke, cilá·t, p̓úyp̓uymele, wá·k, tiwí·cik, cokó·ko,
valley birds, grey-birds, brown-birds, creek-birds cranes killdeer quail

wéṣweṣ cilá·t, ʔoyé·n, ṣú·n, c̓uyú·luk; melé·kon
crested-bluejays brown-birds spotted-towhee eagles hummingbirds bird PLURAL SUBJ

ní·yowat ṣukú·hintec; kó·cakon lákte wáyṭeṭahinte weno
this earth ALL stay REL OBJ Indian PLURAL SUBJ name give REL it-is-said

wóṭe, ṣí.t wá·li, túk·uli, potí·k; mákṣa nít
billy-owls night-birds bats owls Oregon woodpeckers that-kind here ALL

ṣukúh kelac.
lives long-ago OBJ

(242) kal má· lá·katuc hínte. konʔó·nina[63] kaṣa weno.
then that name OBJ he-does they PLURAL POSS FUT he-said it-it-said

(243) kal mán ʔáw·entala weno né·melekon weno
then that POSS morning POSS stand it-is-said these bird PLURAL it-is-said

ʔáw·eni ʔaṭá·waṣi. (244) wuṭé. tóhlok he láka mák·on weno
morning IMP talking wild midhens and geese that PLURAL it-is-said

ʔá·ṭaw yomún·aka ʔá·ṭawuc.
say pretty speech OBJ

(245) ʔemé·ne má· papá· mákṣak ʔalú· kaʔé·ya ma.
good that grandpa VOC that-kind I hear I like emphatic

(246) hél·a men nít huná· kaṣukúh kaʔé·ya. (247) hél·a ṣáʔṣato
not just here ALL alone I live I want not quiet-place ALL

kaṣú·kuh kaʔé·ya kaṣa weno wékweknu.
I stay I like he-said it-is-said Bullet-Hawk

(248) ʔó·w kaṣa weno. (249) katíṣwaṭu kawé·ṭa ṣe
all-right he-said it-is-said I cold INSTR I go also

ʔáw·eni mákṣat. (250) wikí· maʔé·ya ma níh kaṣa weno.
morning IMP that-time ALL fire we need emphatic now he-said it-is-said

(251) ʔó·w các·o má· mawelík ʔina máh. (252) ne
all-right grandchild that we get FUT emphatic these

wikí·wulakoc kayáy·un ʔina huná· má· kocwelíkṣe má·c kaṣa weno.
fire steal DUAL I CALL SUBJ FUT so that DUAL get AND that OBJ he-said it-is-said

(253) ká·l wikí·wula[64] yáy·u-- mán ʔó·ni. (254) miṭi ʔeká·l
so fire steal he-calls they SUBJ comes and then

wá·k weno háypa né·c lám·at ʔekét·o. (255) ká·l
crane it-is-said watches this OBJ sweathouse ALL somewhere ALL then

máṣ·u hínti cowá·ṭi miṭi kaṭu wá·k·on wá·k wá·k, mákṣaṭu
that INSTR something scared-of when that-way crane PLURAL wá·k wá·k that-way

wé·ṭa. (256) ma mákṣahinteṭu weno.
INSTR they-go that that-way REL INSTR it-is-said

(257) ne hú·nin mákṣaṭu lí·lawṭu ṣúkuh muhínti kiláckilacnu.
this story SUBJ that-way INSTR tell INSTR stays you-know long-time-ago

(258) kal né· wikí· konwúla.[65]
SUBJ then this fire they steal

(259) miṭi ne wikí·wula konʔuṭé· konʔé·ya weno ʔkúč·i
and these fire steal they find they want it-is-said small

láktek.[66] (260) ṣá·nim túmay he hokán hél·at ʔukán miṭi. (261) mát
too-much leaves brush and rock POSS under ALL they-go-in and there

kocṣolí·pa. (262) ʔiṭi kontuná·ṭi weno hél·a ʔiṭi konʔúṭen
ALL they DUAL hide him they kick it-is-said not him they find SUBJ

tém·a né·c wikí·wulac. (263) máṣ·u ní·yowat wikí· konṣáw·uṭe
can this OBJ fire steal OBJ that INSTR this earth ALL fire they have

weno wékwek né·wiki ʔé·yahinteṭu.
it-is-said Bullet-Hawk this fire wants REL INSTR

(264) kál mán tóp·at ʔaye hí· ʔé·ya weno ṣewi.
then that POSS after ALL however sun he-wants it-is-said also

(265) papá· né·n cáket káṣ·a káwul? (266) hél·a né·
grandfather VOC this POSS like ALL this-way dark not this

kaʔé·ya; hí· kaʔé·ya kaṣa weno.
I like sun I want he-said it-is-said

(267) ʔó·w má· ʔicwelíkwelak kaṣa.
all-right that we DUAL get let he-said

(268) ká·l púl·ukoc ʔiyáy·u weno ʔóṭ·ac, ʔelám·ukṣu
then dove DUAL he calls it-is-said two OBJ younger-sibling CONT

miṭi ʔát·akṣu miṭi kocpúl·uc. (269) makṣat miṭi ʔedá·k
and older-brother CONT and they DUAL doves OBJ that-way ALL and long

cikó·tenṣaka ʔóṭ·a konṣáw·uṭe. (270) má·c koncán·anlile kocwí·pa
rope POSS like two they have that OBJ their heads POSS above they DUAL

miṭi má· koctolá·ṭu kocwé·ṭa; mákṣaṭu weno
swing and that they DUAL throw INSTR they DUAL go that-way INSTR it-is-said

ne hí· kocwilík weno.
this sun they DUAL get it-is-said

(271) mí· tólan hú·kec. ˀelám·u; mí·ˀayen kíwa.
you throw IMV first OBJ younger-sibling you one SUBJ strong.

(272) mí·ˀayen ˀemé·nen táwlik ˀak kalí·lewac kaṣa weno.
you are SUBJ good SUBJ arms HAVE so my above LOCAT OBJ he-said it-is-said

(273) hanak̓úč·i ˀelám·u henám·ak, ˀudí·ˀoni púl·u.
his little younger-sibling he-brags-about older one dove

(274) ˀó·w ˀekal kamenáw·elak kaṣa weno. (275) kal ma·
all-right then I try let he-said it-is-said then that

tóla. (276) ma wí·pa wí·pan lá·walit weno tóla ˀak
he-throws that he-swings swing POSS until ALL it-is-said he-throws but

weno má· k̓uṣá·ṭi ˀekal ne hí·n weno k̓úč·i táke.
it-is-said that it-glances-off then this sun SUBJ it-is-said a-little comes-out

ˀém ˀém ˀém ˀém kaṣa weno ˀolé·nawan.
he-said it-is-said Coyote Old-Man SUBJ

(277) ˀó·w ˀów ˀó·w ˀów kaṣa weno.
all-right all-right all-right all-right he-said it-is-said.

(278) kal ma· k̓úč·iˀonin tóla. (279) kal ma hí·c k̓úč·i
then that smaller one SUBJ throws than that sun OBJ a-little

k̓uṣá·ṭit ˀém ˀém ˀém kaṣa weno ˀolé·nawan.[67]
he-grazes ALL he-said it-is-said Coyote Old-Man SUBJ

(280) mí· mená·min ˀatá· kaṣa weno k̓úč·iˀó·nin
you try IMV older-brother VOC he-said it-is-said smaller one SUBJ

(281) ˀekal má·c weno wí·pa wí·pan lá·walit tóla.
than that OBJ it-is-said he-swings swing POSS until ALL he-throws

(282) hí·n kówun hín·a mená·ṭi weno, ˀekal hí·n také·
sun POSS center POSS right-there he-hits it-is-said then sun comes-out

weno. (283) dót wé·ṭa miṭi takáh miṭi ˀúteh
it-is-said over-there ALL he-goes and he-goes-backward and he-falls

weno mákṣat ˀaye ˀolé·nawan.
it-is-said that-time ALL however Coyote Old-Man SUBJ

(284) ˀuṭé·, mi kahenám·ak kaṭi; hukéc kela ˀatá· mí·
look you I proud just-like first OBJ already older brother VOC you

ˀinmenáw he. (285) ˀíṣ·iṣa ˀicwilíkˀuṭa kaṣa weno. (286) mákṣan
you try should sooner we DUAL get would he-said it-is-said that-way

tém·a ˀicwílik níh ˀaye kaṣa weno.
SUBJ can we DUAL get now however he-said it-is-said

(287) ʔó·w, papá·. (288) ʔálwan ṣiwí·ṣiwi kaʔé·ya ma ṣe,
all-right grandfather VOC trees SUBJ green I want emphatic also

yomún·akac kaṣa weno wékweknu.
pretty OBJ he-said it-it-said Bullet-Hawk SUBJ

(289) ʔó·w. (290) má· mawelík ʔina muhínti kaṣa weno
all-right that we get FUT you-know he-said it-is-said

ʔolé·nawan. (291) kamenáw welak kaṣa.
Coyote Old-Man SUBJ I try let he-said

(292) kal mákṣat ní·yowat híntin hél·ak ní·yowat
then that-time ALL this earth ALL anything SUBJ not PASS this earth ALL

kelac. (293) halí·halin muʔen hél·ak -- ʔá·lwa[68] ṣíwak pawín
long-ago everything SUBJ all SUBJ not PASS trees green-grass mountains

muʔen weno kilac hél·ak.
SUBJ all SUBJ it-is-said long-ago not PASS

(294) ni ʔolé·nawan kó·cakon lí·lewali kó·canṣaka.
this Coyote Old-Man Indian PLURAL POSS upper world person POSS like

(295) katu konhú·ni ne· hú·nic. (296) halí·hali ʔókay.
that's-the-way they tell this story OBJ everything he-makes

(297) halí·hali camánka. (298) mákṣaṭu né·yowa híc·uwnuka.
everything die CAUS that-way INSTR this earth run CAUS

(299) mákṣat né· hú·nin ʔolé·nawan kó·caʔaṭawyomin
that-time ALL this think POSS Coyote Old-Man SUBJ Indian language group SUBJ

lí·lewali ʔuṭélṣaka ʔúʔkaṣa.
upper world magician like powerful.

(300) né· ní·yowat mákṣaṭu nehú·nin lí·lawku.
now this earth ALL that-way INSTR this story SUBJ tell PASS

(301) katé·menhinten he muʔé· kó·can té·menhinten ne kilá·
I think REL SUBJ maybe all old-timers SUBJ think REL SUBJ these old

hú·nin wayíkwan henú·. (302) ʔúʔkaṣa mélekon, ʔuʔkaṣa
stories SUBJ some LOCAT SUBJ true wonderful bird PLURAL great

p̓ódwayko ʔúʔkaṣa wá·wmele ʔúʔkṣan halí·halin kelac
snake PLURAL wonderful freak birds wonderful things SUBJ all SUBJ long-ago

ní·yowa pál·a.
this earth fill-up

(303) níh ʔaye halí·halin muʔen ʔemé·netuma. (304) ʔuṭélkon
now but everything SUBJ all SUBJ good INCHO white-man PLURAL

má·nsinuka né·yowac̓. (305) keláckelac ʔaye hél·a káṣ·aṭu
SUBJ tame CAUS this earth OBJ long-ago but not this-way INSTR

hú·ni konlí·law. (306) ˀú·pat ˀaye konlí·lawṭu konwé·ṭa né·c,
stories they tell it-rains ALL but they tell INSTR they go this OBJ

he kawú·luč; hél·a hí·t káṣ·aṭu kalí·lawṣakaṭu.
or night-time OBJ not day-time ALL this-way INSTR I tell like INSTR

(307) ˀaká·l ma wayík ˀálwa kané·nuthinteˀayen -- hákyaˀala,
then that some plants I know REL ones SUBJ mush-oak trees

pátpatˀala, ṣú·kˀala, kiṭénˀala, potó·potokaye he káye, céčiṣ
flat-tule plants young oak elderberry trees grey willow and willow, tanoak

lumé·ˀala -- halí·haliˀala nít ṣukú·hinten láktek mákṣa
yellow-pine trees all-kinds trees here ALL living REL SUBJ name HAVE that-way

ˀunu wayíkwa ˀaye kahólṭi.
but some LOCAT however I forget

(308) kané·nuthintec kahiyán ˀina ne ˀá·ṭaw má·kinampat.
I know REL OBJ I send FUT this talking machine DIR ALL

(309) čiwílˀala, ṣanákˀala, kiṭénˀala, lumé·ˀala -- mákṣaˀalakon
coyote-brush plant pine trees elderberry trees yellow-pine trees that-many tree

kané·nut ˀawé·cu kalakáthinte.
PLURAL SUBJ I know that's-all I name REL

(310) mákṣaˀalac nít ˀokáyhintet ˀakál wékwek húyka
that-many trees OBJ here ALL he-makes REL ALL and Bullet-Hawk glad

weno. (311) ma· lákat. (312) miṭi· ní·yowat kó·cakon
it-is-said. them he-names and this earth ALL person PLURAL

ˀokáyhinte; níh ná·mit ˀokáyhinteˀayen. (313) tumáyṭu kon
he-makes REL now last ALL he-makes REL ones SUBJ sticks INSTR them

ˀokáy weno halí·hali tumáyṭu.[69] (314) máṣ·u ní·yowat
he-makes it-is-said all-kinds sticks INSTR that INSTR this earth ALL

kó·cakon ṣúkuh níh. (315) ˀuṭélko pólpol dó·ṣam
person PLURAL SUBJ are-here now white-man PLURAL lake other side LOC

kon ṣe cané· ˀuṭélkon ṣe ṣúkuh. (316) mákṣaṭu ma
they also many white-man PLURAL SUBJ also live that-way INSTR us

ˀokáy miṭi ní·yowat maṣúkuh níh.
he-makes and this earth ALL we are-situated now

(317) mákṣat nem ˀawé·cu kané·nuthinten nakáh kalí·law.
that-way ALL this-is all I know REL POSS the end I tell

(318) ˀó·w· (319) ˀawé·cu.
all-right that's all

Free Translation

(1) My father and my mother told this story to me the way the old timers used to tell it. (2) The story was here before my brothers and sisters, before my relatives. (3) It began in the Old Rancheria. (4) Old Man Coyote stayed there with his grandson, Chief Bullet Hawk. (5) They had a home there. (6) Right there is where Bullet Hawk grew up with his grandfather.

(7) Then one day he wanted to go around. (8) He [Old Man Coyote] let him travel to the end of the valley, so he went over that way. (9) He wanted to go farther up and saw the mountains. (10) He looked over the valley. (11) He saw the creek. (12) He saw the lake, Rocky Mountain, and Pointed Hill. (13) He was contemplating everything, Bullet Hawk that is, and the valley was filled with all kinds of birds. (14) He saw the meadowlark and the quail. (15) He examined everything.

(16) He went around like that and kept going further. (17) He went far enough to see Guenoc Lake. (18) Then he said, "Grandpa, there must be a lake there."

(19) "Yes," he said. (20) "There's a lake there. (21) They call that lake Guenoc; that's the lake you saw. (22) Did you see two mountains on the other side of it? (23) Those are great mountains, too", he said.

(24) One is Pointed Hill and the other one has a name too, but I don't know it. (25) Old Man Coyote knew everything in olden times; he was the greatest.

(26) Weasel was around there too, and he was also powerful, but not as great as Old Man Coyote. (27) And there was a big tree standing right there. (28) It didn't have any limbs. (29) Just like a pretty bird's resting place where it can perch in the morning.

(30) There was [a type of] fish in Guenoc Lake. (31) Long ago, the people used to eat it. (32) The name of that fish was pilí·t. (33) Suckers, salmon, trout, little chubs were there. (34) But later, a different [kind of] fish came in there too. (35) They planted it. (36) Catfish, and a lot of fish we have now were planted there. (37) They're all in that lake now.

(38) Then one day he [Bullet Hawk] was getting big, you know; growing up. (39) "Grandpa!" he said.

(40) "What?"

(41) "What can I kill these with, these birds and geese?" (42) Mudhens, meadowlark--Guenoc Lake was full of them, you know. (43) So he went back.

(44) "Well, I'm going to get a gun," he [Old Man Coyote] said. (45) "A bow and arrow, that is."

(46) Before getting it, he went into the sweathouse. (47) He smeared his eyes with spit and pretended to cry.

(48) "What are you crying for, Grandpa?"

(49) "Well, this arrow I'm giving you belonged to my father and my father's father. I feel sad, so I'm crying." he said.

(50) Then Old Man Coyote said. "All right. (51) What is that green stuff growing around Guenoc Lake? (52) Well, that's tule. We eat that too." (53) He wanted to eat it too, but he couldn't get in the water.

(54) When you look at the lake from down below, it's pretty. (55) There are two mountains standing just like a sweathouse. (56) And the name of the one below is ṣálṣal. (57) That's Weasel's home. (58) There's a sweathouse there somewhere. (59) It's his sweathouse.

(60) So Bullet Hawk rested in the tree and kept on looking at it. (61) He perched there and watched it for three or four days. (62) He would go out early in the morning. (63) He would go around. (64) He went to get food for himself.

(65) One day after they gave him the arrow, he started catching all kinds of things, mudhens. (66) He caught them. (67) But he didn't eat them all; he just ate the breasts. (68) And his grandafther ate everything bloody--he just threw them in the fire a little while and ate them with the blood dripping. (69) That went on for a long time.

(70) Then he [Bullet Hawk] said, "I'm going to visit that man." (71) He was going to go inside Weasel's sweathouse. (72) So he left early and went to Weasel's house. (73) He found lots of things there.

(74) He was twenty years old when he went in that sweathouse. (75) All kinds of food were there. (76) Pinole, bread--acorn bread. (77) Rabbit, dear, little fish --there was all that good food there. (78) It was in sacks. (79) They used to make deerhide sacks to store everything in--acorns. (80) There were beads in one of the sacks. (81) Weasel's sweathouse was filled with all kinds of food.

(82) He didn't know if he [Bullet Hawk] was going to try it. (83) So he stuck his hand in the acorn mush. (84) And he tasted it. (85) There was sugar and everything. (86) After eating a little bit, he put grass in there, straw. (87) Straw, yeah, not grass, straw. (88) He filled it up and then he tied it again and poured water on it. (89) He [Weasel] had buckeye there too--clover and all kinds of old-timers' food. (90) He had it all right there.

(91) Then he [Bullet Hawk] saw beads in the sack, and he took it. (92) He thought about stealing it. (93) It might put him in the wrong. (94) Then he packed half of it. (95) And he hid it in a ditch right there above Guenoc Lake. (96) He got pretty close to his grandfather's home.

(97) Three or four days passed. (98) Then Old Man Weasel started feeling bad. (99) "What's the matter with me?" he said. (100) "Something must be wrong somewhere around here. (101) I'm going to stay home today."

(102) So he stayed home. (103) He swept his house. (104) He looked at all his food. (105) They say all he missed was those beads. (106) Half [the sack] was straw.

(107) I don't know what's going on," said Old Man Weasel. (108) "It's a bad thing if someone's living well [off of this]. (109) If they're living high, something's wrong."

(110) Then he got angry. (111) "Oh yeah! I know you! (112) I know who you are, and I'm going to look for you now," he said.

(113) Then he went behind [the sweathouse] and got his spear there, his fire spear. (114) He pointed it at the Lower World. (115) He pointed it at the Upper World. He pointed it west. He pointed it east. But he didn't see anybody. (116) He pointed it over toward the north. (117) He didn't see anyone at all. (118) Then he pointed it southwest. (119) And he saw him.

(120) "So, I don't know you!" he said. "You really think I don't know."

(121) Wherever he pointed his spear, people kept dying. (122) Burned up--the fire spread all over.

(123) So Bullet Hawk said "Grandpa!"

(124) "What?"

(125) "Everything is burning up all around us."

(126) "Oh yeah, it's always that way, Grandson. (127) People burn off the tules this time of year. (128) So don't be scared. (129) They always do it," he said.

(130) He [Bullet Hawk] asked him about it three or four times. (131) Old Man Coyote already knew his grandson had stolen the beads. (132) But he didn't say anything.

(133) "All right, Grandpa, stop this! (134) I'm going to burn up. (135) I don't like this--the fire is too hot." (136) He said all this to his grandfather.

(137) Then his grandfather said "All right. (138) I'll stop this fire."

(139) So he tied a big horn to the center pole. (140) He tied it securely. (141) And he crawled inside the horn.

(142) Then [there was] a drizzling rain. (143) He hit it [the center pole] with drizzling rain. (144) He used a sack he had. (145) He tried foggy rain. (146) He beat the center pole with heavier rain. (147) He used snow. (148) After all this, he crawled inside [the horn].

(149) And the water kept rising. (150) It came to the top of the sweathouse. (151) Just then, his grandfather said something. (152) He was teasing his grandson.

(153) "All right, Mother. Give me that pinole, that meat, that starch." (154) He named all the different kinds of food. (155) He was just teasing his grandson. (156) He wasn't eating anything, but he said all that anyway, and his grandson heard it.

(157) It was almost time for him [Bullet Hawk] to fly away. (158) Then the water came right up to the top of the sweathouse. (159) So he flew away. (160) He went "Wékwék wékwék wékwék wékwék." (161) Then he was gone.

(162) He didn't know where to go. (163) The water was everywhere. (164) The highest mountain peak showed just a little bit. (165) He flew over that way, but it disappeared too. (166) The water covered everything he saw.

(167) He flew for several days. (168) Then he saw two helldivers. (169) He was tired, and his wings were flapping just above the water. (170) He had been going that way until he came to the helldivers.

(171) "Help me!" he said.

(172) "All right, Grandson." they said. (173) "But light on my back gently.

(174) You might knock off the scabs there." (175) They're called heat sores. (176) "You might break my heat sores."

(177) First one of them carried him, then the other. (178) It went on that way. (179) It went on until it had rained for forty nights.

(180) After it rained forty days, the whole earth was flooded. (181) By that time, only four people were left. (182) The two helldivers, Bullet Hawk, and Old Man Coyote. (183) He [Old Man Coyote] did it all for his grandson. (184) Whenever his grandson wanted something, he made it for him.

(185) Then these two helldivers gathered the sticks that were floating around and made a nest for him [Bullet Hawk] on top of the water. (186) The water was going down now. (187) Meanwhile, they fed him something--fish. (188) They fed him whatever they saw, whatever was there.

(189) After a long time, the water all dried up. (190) Then he slept there. (191) He rested three or four days. (192) The helldivers were watching him. (193) He kept on resting.

(194) Then one day, he said "Grandpa, I'm leaving. (195) I'm going to walk down and then come back again."

(196) So after it was dry, he went down the creek. (197) And he saw another old man on the other side.

(198) "Old Man!" he said.

(199) "What? (200) What's your name?"

(201) "How about you? What's your name?"

(202) "I want to know your name too, so you better tell me."

(203) "Oh yeah,it's me, Bullet Hawk."

(204) Then he was glad. (205) He jumped up and said "Grandson, Grandson, Grandson, Grandson, Grandson, Grandson!"

(206) He backed up and came on down running--kó·l kól kól kól. (207) He jumped over the creek. (208) Then he hugged his grandson.

(209) "Come on with me, come on! (210) Let's go back home. (211) I've been looking for you and I couldn't find you," he said.

(212) "All right, but wait a minute. (213) There's an old lady and an old man over there. (214) They're waiting for me. (215) Let me go and tell them. (216) I'll come back here again tomorrow," he said. (217) Bullet Hawk was telling this to Old Man Coyote.

(218) "All right--I expect to see you again this time tomorrow," he said.

(219) Then he want back and told Old Man Diver and Old Lady Diver, "I saw an old man over there who said he was my grandfather. (220) He wanted me [to come] tomorrow. (221) So I'm going to go with him tomorrow."

(222) "Oh yeah, we know him. (223) Go with him then. (224) Let him take care of you. (225) He's a great old man, that one," they said.

(226) He left the next morning. (227) He went by the creek and saw his grandfather. (228) He flew to the other side and came up to him, then they went to the sweathouse. (229) They came right up there.

(230) But the earth was empty and barren.

(231) "Grandpa!" he said. (232) He had been there several days, and he was sad.

(233) "Is there no one around here? (234) Aren't there any birds or things like that?"

(235) "Yeah, lots. (236) All kinds of birds. (237) They're going to come tomorrow morning," he said. (238) Right then, he named some of the birds.

(239) He named the geese. (240) He named the ducks, mudhens, woodpeckers, doves, quail, yellowhammers, crows, sapsuckers, robins, chicken hawks; all the different kinds of birds the Indians used to have around here. (241) They all have a name--valley birds, grey birds, brown birds, creek birds, cranes, killdeer, quail, bluejays, brown birds, towhees, eagles, hummingbirds; all the birds on this earth that the Indians named-billy owls, night birds, bats, owls, Oregon woodpeckers; all the birds that were around here in olden times.

(242) He named them all and said "They're going to come." (243) And the next morning, all these birds were talking. (244) Wild mudhens and geese were singing pretty songs.

(245) "That's good, Grandpa, I like to hear all that. (246) I don't want to live here alone. (247) I don't enjoy staying in a quite place," Bullet Hawk said.

(248) "All right," he went on. (249) "I feel cold in the morning. (250) We need fire now."

(251) "All right, Grandson, we'll get it! (252) I'll call the Fire Stealers

to fetch it," he said.

(253) So he called the Fire Stealers, and they came. (254) There was a crane watching in a sweathouse somewhere. (255) When cranes get scared of something, they go wá·k wá·k! (256) That's why they do it [because of their name].

(257) The story has been told like this since olden times. (268) They stole the fire.

(259) They [the pursuers] tried to find the Fire Stealers, [but they were] too small. (260) They went into leaves, brush, and under the rock. (261) They hid there. (262) They kicked him, but they couldn't find him, this Fire Stealer. (263) That's why there's fire on this earth, because Bullet Hawk wanted it.

(264) But later on, he wanted a sun too. (265) "Grandfather, is it going to be dark like this? (266) I don't like it, I want a sun", he said.

(267) "All right, let's get one." he said.

(268) So he called two doves, younger and older brothers. (269) They had two long ropes. (270) They weung it [presumably a missile] above their heads and hurled it; that's how they got the sun.

(271) "You throw first; you're my younger brother and you're strong. (272) You have better arms than I do," he said. (273) He was bragging about his little brother, the older dove.

(274) "All right, let me try it," he said. (275) Then he threw it. (276) He swung it and then hurled it, but it glanced off, and the cun only came out a little. "ʔém ʔém ʔém ʔém," said Old Man Coyote [from fright].

(277) "All right, all right," he said. (278) So the smaller one threw it. (279) When he grazed the sun a little, Old Man Coyote said, "ʔém, ʔém, ʔém."

(280) "You try now, Brother," the smaller one said.

(281) So he swung it and then hurled it. (282) He hit the sun right in the center, and it came out. (283) That time, Old Man Coyote went over there and fell over backwards.

(284) "Look, I'm proud of you; you should have tried first. (285) We would have gotten it sooner. (286) But that's all right, we got it anyway," he said.

(287) "All right, Grandpa. (288) I want the trees to be green and pretty too," said Bullet Hawk.

(289) "All right. (290) We'll have it," Old Man Coyote said. (291) "Let me try."

(292) At that time, there was nothing on this earth. (293) Nothing existed--there were no trees, green grass, or hills.

(294) Old Man Coyote is just like an Indian god. (295) That's the way they tell this story. (296) He makes everything. (297) He destroys everything. (298) That's the way he runs this earth. (299) That's how the Lake Miwok Indians think of Old Man Coyote, like a powerful god from above.

(300) Around here, the story is told that way now. (301) I think all the old-timers believe that some of these old stories are true. (302) Wonderful birds, great snakes, freak birds--the earth was full of all sorts of wonderful things a long time ago.

(303) But now, everything is being improved. (304) The white people have tamed the earth. (305) A long time ago, they didn't tell stories like this. (306) They used to tell them when it was raining or at night time, not in the day time the way I'm doing.

(307) And I know some plants--mush oak, flat tule, young oak, elderberry, grey willow and willow, tanoak, yellow pine--all the trees here have a name, but I forget some of them.

(308) I will dictate whatever I know into the tape recorder. (309) Coyote brush, pine, elderberry, yellow pine--I have named all the trees I know.

(310) When he [Old Man Coyote] made all those trees here, Bullet Hawk was glad. (311) He named them. (312) Then he put people on the earth last of all. (313) He made them from sticks, all kinds of sticks. (314) That's why people are here now. (315) There are a lot of white people living on the other side of the lake too. (316) That's the way he made the earth we're in now.

(317) I'm coming to the end of what I know. (318) All right. (319) That's all.

Footnotes

[1]The transcription is the same as that used in Callaghan 1965 except that a raised dot indicates length and y is used for the palatal glide. c is [ts]. t is often inter-dental or slightly post dental. ṭ is post alveolar.

In the interlinear translation, multiple English sequences corresponding to single Lake Miwok elements are connected by hyphens. English sequences corresponding multiple Lake Miwok elements are separated by spaces. Glosses of certain grammatical categories are written in capitals, e.g. FUT "future." REL is used for the relative clause marker -hinte. Case markers are indicated as follows: SUBJ "subjective," POSS "possessive," OBJ "objective," ABL "ablative," ALL "allative," LOC "locative," INSTR "instrumental," COM "comitative," and VOC "vocative." The subjective-possessive is actually a single case.

Other abbreviations are BEN "benefactive," LOCAT "locational," CAUS "causative," IMP "impersonal agentive," INCHO "inchoative," AND "andative," REFL "reflexive," IMV "imperative," PASS "passive," CONT "continuative," C "any consonant," and V "any vowel."

CV́CV(C) → CVCV́(·)(C) obligatorily before suffixes and optionally before words in the same sentence.

[2]kó·ca can be translated as either "person" or "people," since plural markers are optional. -n is the post-vocalic allomorph of the subjective case.

[3]-c is the common post vocalic allomorph of the objective case. Consequently -hintec indicates a relative clause in the objective case.

[4]The objective case marker is zero after a vowel stem immediately preceding a verb not in the imperative.

[5]ʔát·a means "older brother." It is here used in the sex indefinite sense of "brothers and sisters".

[6]There are no Lake Miwok prepositions. Prepositional relationships are expressed by suffixes or possessed nouns. konhú·kewa "their beforehand" translates "before them" (before their time).

[7]There is no Lake Miwok copula except for ṣúkuh "to live, be situated (physically)."

[8]weno is the common narrative particle indicating an event not witnessed by the narrator.

[9]"Old Place" indicates the Old Rancheria in Long Valley.

[10]Verbs are tenseless except for a periphrastic future formation.

[11]Proper names illustrate a head-attribute construction.

[12]hana- "his, her, its" refers to the subject of the sentence. Otherwise, the third person singular possessive is ʔiṭi-. Note that ʔolé·nawani "Old Man Coyote", wékwek hóypuni "Chief Bullet Hawk", and các·oni are all in the comitative case.

[13]Lake Miwok has a fully developed dual in the pronominal system.

[14]{-k/V_ ~ -ak/C_} indicates intimate possession.

[15]-u "objective case" is the post consonantal allomorph immediately preceding a verb.

[16]A third person singular subject or object need not be indicated.

[17]"toward" is -npa ~ -mpa/V_ and -pa/C_.

[18]-nu is the post consonantal subjective case allomorph of stems following verbs. The usual order is subject-object-verb. A post-verbal noun or phrase indicates emphasis or an afterthought.

[19]"bird" is míle ~ méle.

[20]Continuous action is indicated by a verb stem in the instrumental case plus wé·ṭa "go."

[21]The vocative is formed by lengthening the final vowel, sometimes with stem reduction.

[22]kaṣa is a direct quotative particle.

[23] -uc "objective case" is the post-consonantal allomorph before verbs in the imperative or when the object does not immediately precede the verbal unit.

[24] -n "you singular subject" attaches to a preceeding word ending in a vowel.

[25] kelac is a frozen objective case of kela ~ kila "ago." Often it is reduplicated into keláckelac- a particle meaning "long ago". The longer particle has been reinterpreted as a new noun stem.

[26] -ʔala "tree" is a weak combining form.

[27] The post-consonantal allomorph of the subjective-possessive case is zero.

[28] The allative case also has a temporal function.

[29] -tuma is a non-productive inchoative suffix.

[30] The presence of the negative particle is unexplained.

[31] The repetition of plant, animal, and bird names served an educational function for the young.

[32] Verb stems take the subjective case before the future marker.

[33] ko·no ~ ko·nu now means only "gun," although it originally meant "bow" or "bow and arrow." The latter is now designated by hintí·l kó·no from Spanish gentil "pagan."

[34] In the Merriam version, Coyote gave Bullet Hawk a sling and shot instead of a bow and arrow, and he did not pretend to cry.

[35] The allative case has a temporal meaning following a verbal clause.

[36] ʔam- ~ ʔan- is a third person indefinite pronominal prefix.

[37] In the Merriam version, Bullet Hawk watched Weasel's house from the top of a round house.

[38] The common andative suffix is -ṭi meaning "to go and do something." -ṣi ~ -ṣe is an old allomorph that once followed certain obstruents.

[39] ʔáw·eni here means "early."

[40] ʔóṭ·atumay "twenty" literally means "two sticks." Sticks were used as counters in gambling games.

[41] This is the distributive form of k̓úc·i ~ k̓úč·i "small."

[42] "Hand" is usually ʔúk·u.

[43] Bullet Hawk took only beads in the Merriam version.

[44] "Get" is wélik ~ wilik.

[45] In the Merriam version Weasel used his yác·i as a fire wand. yác.i was a stick used to hold a bun in place.

[46] The order of directions in the Merriam version is north, west, east, up, down, and finally south toward tú·leyome, Old Man Coyote's home. He did not know in advance who the thief was.

[47] hú·ni means "to think something is so" when it is false or doubtful.

[48] The instrumental case of an adjective functions as an adverb.

[49] Coyote did not put out the fire in the Merriam version until Bullet Hawk had confessed his guilt.

[50] lulú·ṭi is a variant of lilú·ṭi "to fly away" used by James Knight.

[51] The future particle indicates action posterior to the time of discourse.

[52] lá·wit is a reduced form of lá·walit "until then."

[53] ʔidí· is a variant of ʔudí· "superior", used by James Knight. Merriam identifies ʔudí·pawih as Mt. Konokti and had Bullet Hawk resting on its peak until the flood was over.

[54] This is syncretism. It only rained ten days and nights in the Merriam version.

[55]In the Merriam version, Bullet Hawk stayed in the helldivers' round house after the flood.

[56]pápa "grandfather" and cấc·o "grandchild" have a wider semantic range than in English.

[57]James Knight sometimes uses this vocative form.

[58]"Come," "go", "look" and "wait" have special imperative forms.

[59]James Knight says that even today bullet hawks will not kill helldivers becuase they once saved Bullet Hawk's life.

[60]-k is a reduced form of ka- "I" which is attached to the previous word.

[61]wế·ṭ·a is prolonged form.

[62]ṭí· is reduced form of ʔíṭi "he."

[63]The future has many allomorphs, one of which is -a.

[64]wïkí·wula is a type of mouse. Merriam identified it as a shrew mouse.

[65]The mice stole fire from Crow in the Merriam version.

[66]"They" here refers to northern people who owned the fire. The Fire Stealers were given a stick which they put in the fire until it blazed up. They ran away with it and hid in a tree.

In the Merriam version, the Fire Stealers used a piece of dead wood to catch the fire and touched the back of a firefly with it. They hid from their pursuers under the bank of a dry creek.

[67]I had to turn the tape over at this point. James Knight retold the last paragraph for continuity.

[68]This is a prolonged form.

[69]In the Merriam version, Old Man Coyote made people from the feathers of the geese Bullet Hawk had killed at Guenoc Lake.

COYOTE AND THE GROUND SQUIRRELS

(Eastern Pomo)

Sally McLendon

Hunter College and the Graduate Center
of the City University of New York

The Eastern Pomo language, one of seven Pomoan languages within the Hokan stock, was formerly spoken around the northwestern half of Clear Lake, about 100 miles north of San Francisco. No detailed Eastern Pomo ethnography has been published, although a sketch of some aspects of Eastern Pomo society has appeared (McLendon 1977b) and a shorter summary of the ethnography and relevant ethnographic sources is in press (McLendon and Lowy 1978). A grammar has been published (McLendon 1975) and a dictionary is in preparation.

Coyote and the Ground Squirrels was told in both Eastern Pomo and English on March 21, 1975, by Mr. Ralph Holder of Upper Lake, California, who was then in his seventies. It belongs to a genre of narrative called ma·rú· 'myth,' of which another exemplar (also told by Mr. Holder on March 21, 1975), "Bear Kills Her Own Daughter-in-Law, Deer," has been published in an earlier volume of NATS (McLendon 1977c). (Details concerning the performance and transmission of ma·rú· as well as the contemporary Eastern Pomo speech community are given in the introduction to this text.) Mr. Holder has told me a remarkable total of 14 ma·rú· since we began work in 1973 (several of even greater length and elaboration), all of which he learned from his terminological grandfather, Jim Bateman, ši·yé·, with whom Mr. Holder lived from the age of approximately 6 to 15 (roughly between 1907/1908 and 1916 when Jim Bateman died). Additional biographical details concerning Jim Bateman are given in "Bear Kills Her Own Daughter-in-Law, Deer" (McLendon 1977c).

Many of these ma·rú· Mr. Holder volunteered. Coyote and the Ground Squirrels was not volunteered, however. Mr. Holder recalled having heard it when I checked through the titles and plots of ma·rú· collected around the turn of the century by Barrett (1933), but was at first reluctant to provide a performance as he felt he did not remember it well, and only did so after much urging. All locational details characteristic of the fullest well-formed performances of ma·rú· (McLendon 1977a) are missing. When queried about where this ma·rú· began, Mr. Holder commented, "They used to tell where it happened, but this one I don't know." The extensive use of direct quotations, however, is a mark of a well-formed performance, and Mr. Holder was able to recall not only the words but the music of the Ground Squirrel's teasing song, as well as including the humorous detail of Coyote's penis slipping and giving him away. Mr. Holder volunteered in transcribing this text that of course Coyote's penis was 4 feet long and so it splattered a lot of coals when it slipped out--an aspect of Coyote and of this text which apparently was not conveyed to Barrett earlier. It is thus extremely fortunate that Mr. Holder overcame his reluctance and allowed this quite rich version of Coyote and Ground Squirrels to be preserved.

Two other performances of this ma·rú· were collected from Eastern Pomo speakers around the turn of the century by S. A. Barrett. One was told by Tom Mitchell in English, December 19, 1902 (verbatim transcript in McLendon 1977a, edited version in Barrett 1933:251-254). The other, an extremely elaborate version, was told in English by Dave Thompson on May 30, 1904 (verbatim transcript in McLendon 1977a, edited version in Barrett 1933:246-250). Both Tom Mitchell and Dave Thompson's wife were relatives of Ralph Holder's terminological grandfather, Jim Bateman. According to Barrett

---

*Various parts of this research were supported by NIMH Grant R01 MH22887, a Guggenheim Fellowship, and a grant from the Faculty Research Award Program of the City University of New York.

(1952:17) Tom Mitchell was born circa 1870, while the 1900 census gives Dave Thompson's birth as circa 1840 (although the 1880 census estimated his age at 30). Dave Thompson was thus a near contemporary of Jim Bateman, and would have grown up, learned ma·rú·, been initiated and participated in ceremonials at a period when Eastern Pomo society was possibly as yet largely unaffected by contact with White society.

Tom Mitchell's version is very similar to the one given here, which may reflect the fact that Tom Mitchell's maternal grandfather from whom he is most likely to have learned this ma·rú· was Jim Burris, ṭa·ta, who like Jim Bateman originated in Big Valley. Dave Thompson's version is much more elaborate, which might reflect the fact that he was not from Big Valley, but could also represent a symbolically elaborated version more appropriate to adults than to a child such as Mr. Holder was when he learned this ma·rú·--particularly a child growing up in a changing society in which the old ceremonials were no longer performed.

Eastern Pomo ma·rú· (as well as analogous narratives from Northern Pomo and Central Pomo) have been characterized by Barrett as frequently consisting of a loose stringing together of unrelated episodes which may be related by a single protagonist such as Coyote, but need not be. Dave Thompson's version seems at first a good example of this type. It consists of four episodes, only two of which have any apparent relation to each other. Barrett titles these four epidoes: I Coyote rescues Duck (a species of), II Coyote catches Ground Squirrels by magic, III Coyote regulates death, IV Coyote builds Kelsey Creek and establishes fishing customs. (The versions of Tom Mitchell and Ralph Holder cover the material involved in Dave Thompson's episode II.)

When viewed from the perspective of the dominant ecological concerns of the Eastern Pomo (discussed in McLendon 1977a) the apparently randomly connected episodes included in Dave Thompson's version seem not to be entirely unrelated. For example: presumably fish-eating water-dwelling protagonists in Dave Thompson's first episode (a species of duck and his abductor, another species of waterfowl) are replaced by land-dwelling protagonists (ground squirrels and Coyote) in his second episode (also given by Tom Mitchell and Ralph Holder), one of whom is fish eating (Coyote), while the other, the ground squirrels, are treated like fish (i.e., Coyote gets materials to build a storage cache actually only used for fish, ground squirrels not being stored, according to both Dave Thompson and Tom Mitchell). The fourth episode of Dave Thompson's version concerns the origins of one of the most important creeks for Eastern Pomo subsistence--Kelsey Creek--which is named in Eastern Pomo "híč^h-creek" after the species of fish, híč^h, which ran up that creek in prodigious numbers to spawn in the spring. híč^h are a species of fish that could be caught in such quantity that, in dried form, they not only constitutes the protein staple of the diet throughout the year, but usually provided a surplus which could be exchanged with the Northern Pomo and central Pomo neighbors referred to in Thompson's text.

The ground squirrels are caught by Coyote sticking his attractively decorated hand into their burrow in all three versions (although the Eastern Pomo actually caught ground squirrels in traps and snares) while the subsequent fourth episode of Dave Thompson's version describes Coyote manufacturing a special conical shaped fish trap basket, ša-mi·čè, with a small opening at the top and a larger open bottom, used at night or when the waters were very muddy to catch, not híč^h (the fish being caught in the myth), but the ša·mól or suckerfish that went up the creek to spawn before the híč^h.

These šá-mi·čè were used by men wading several abreast up the creek, who suddenly thrust the whole trap down to the bottom of the creek, and then while holding the trap firmly in contact with the bottom reached in through the narrow opening at the top and felt around the space enclosed by the trap for fish--just as Coyote feels inside the squirrels' burrows for squirrels which he will later attempt to dry and store like fish. Since it is híč^h that were caught in sufficient quantities to be exchanged in trade with neighboring groups, and híč^h were caught with a different technology, it seems clear that šá-mi·čè were mentioned to strengthen the symbolic associations between the ground squirrel episode and Dave Thompson's last episode, specifically with respect to the similar shape of šá-mi·čè 'fish traps,' ground squirrel burrows, and underground ceremonial houses, such as the one Coyote builds for the ground squirrels to dance in. The fish-eating protagonist in Dave Thompson's first episode steals a valuable from nó-na·phòti and is killed for it, being burned up (in fact, roasted or baked) in an underground ceremonial house. The ground squirrels who steal Coyote's arm in his second episode are punished in the same way, being burned up (i.e., roasted or baked) in an underground ceremonial house. While in Dave Thompson's fourth episode fish, which are appropriately baked in underground ovens, are given to potential opponents (the Northern Pomo) who pay for them appropriately rather than steal them and are therefore allowed to depart in peace and not killed, but specifically told that there will be another gathering together for exchange the following year. (Cf. FN 102 for another parallel between ceremonials and trade feasts.)

The most awesome of pre-contact Eastern Pomo ceremonials involved the return of the dead--qa·lúy-kà·wk^h 'ghosts' who had been cremated and reappeared at certain points during this ceremonial, flaming. (See McLendon 1977c for a description and FN 108.) The qa·lúy-kà·wk^h had a special relationship to fire--one of the important events during the ritual was a sweating contest between the 'ghosts' and the initiated men of the village-community and neighboring groups--and some of the 'ghosts' had the ability to handle and 'eat' fire without being burned. During the course of this ceremonial, which lasted four days and took place in the underground ceremonial house of the sort Coyote builds for the Ground Squirrels to dance in in this myth, boys were initiated into the secret society. During the course of the ceremonial and initiation the boy initiates were referred to as mu·líy 'young ground squirrel(s).' Thus fire, ground squirrels (who eat acorns and live in underground burrows, in which they hibernate during the winter as Eastern Pomo men who ate acorns spent the winter 'hibernating' in the underground ceremonial house which functioned, at least at that season, as a men's house), underground ceremonial houses, and ceremonial activities of the most central sort, i.e., concerning death and initiation, were associated. "Coyote and the Ground Squirrels" would appear to have communicated, then, simultaneously at several levels on ecological, social and religious concerns.

No detailed comparative study of this myth is known to me (it is not discussed by Lévi-Strauss 1971) and none has been attempted, but I have accidentally come across two different but clearly related versions of Tom Mitchell's and Ralph Holder's performance of this myth: one in Maidu entitled "Coyote and the Ground Squirrel Women" (Shipley 1963:32-33); the other in Navajo but given only in an English translation (Toelken 1969) in which ground squirrels are replaced by prairie dogs. It seems likely that it is a widely distributed theme.

The presentational format employed here is the same as that used in "Bear Kills Her Own Daughter-in-Law, Deer" (McLendon 1977c) with two exceptions. (1) Two types of footnotes are used. Underlined numbers refer to notes at the end of this article. Non-underlined numbers refer to notes in "Bear Kills Her Own Daughter-in-Law, Deer," published earlier in this series (McLendon 1977c). (2) Primarily verbs are footnoted in this article, the class membership of non-verbs being signaled in the inter-linear translation by the abbreviations listed below. Interested readers will find relevant grammatical information about such forms in the appropriate section of *A Grammar of Eastern Pomo* (McLendon 1975) listed after each abbreviation. N: Noun (Section 740); PN: Personal Noun (Section 720); Adj: Adjective (730); Pro: Pronoun (Section 610); KT: Kinship Term (Section 650); D: Demonstrative (Section 750); Num: Numeral (Section 760).

Reference in Eastern Pomo is handled very differently from that in English--a combination of verbal (switch reference) suffixes as well as pronouns, kinship terms, personal nouns and number-concord with the verb being used to keep track of who is doing what to whom. For greater ease in tracking, each of the characters has been assigned a subscript number, in order of appearance. This number occurs at the end of the English gloss of each Eastern Pomo form referring to a character: Old Man Coyote$_1$; Buteo-Chief$_2$; Boys playing at Buteo-Chief's village$_3$; Buteo-Chief's mother$_4$; Ground Squirrels$_5$; Blind Ground Squirrel Old Woman$_6$; Skunk Girls$_7$.

(1)	yu[1]	xa[2]	ku·nú·la-bù·c̓ike	má·l·le[1] .
	perfective	they say	Coyote(N)-Old Man$_1$(PN)	went around-they say

(2)	mí·n[11]	má·liday[2]	xa[2]	mí·p[19]	š̓ó·k^h·le[3] ;
	like that	go around-then (switch reference)	they say	he$_1$(Pro)	heard-they say

k̓i·yá·-kà·xalik^h	ma·ʔáy-bi·Yà	ʔí·[4] ,	q̓ômc^{h}a	ma·ʔáy ,	ma·ʔáy
Buteo(N)-Chief$_2$(PN)	food(N)-hands(N)	had	lots of	food(N)	food(N)

du·ṭélkʰ[5] .	(3) mí·n[11]	šó·kʰiy[202]	xa[2]	kʰi[13] . . .	báy[147]
kill many	like that	hear-then (co-reference)	they say	he$_1$	over there (D)

lîl-uhùba[6]	dá	dú·yeqal·le[7] ,	dá·yawal	ná·ṭ̓a·naw.
away-go-in order to	woman$_1$(PN)	made-they say	young woman$_1$(PN)	nice(Adj)

(4) dá·yawal	yó·qay[8]	xa[2]	kʰi[13]	báy[147]	lîl-uhò·le[9] .
young woman$_1$(PN)	become-then (co-reference)	they say	he$_1$	over there(D)	away-they say

(5) mí·n[11]	ʔí·day[12]	xa[2]	. . . kʰi[13]	mí·pix	na·pʰóNa
like that	was-then (switch reference)	they say	he$_1$	his(Pro)$_2$	village(N)-at/to

xól-uhù·[10] . . .	bá·[10]	xa[2]	kʰi[13]	qa·wíkʰla·l	ni·nêx·le[11] ;
approach a goal-came	then	they say	he$_1$	boys(PN)-collective agentive-patient$_3$	asked-they say

xów	qa·wíkʰ	ṭʰáyk̓·le[12] .
outside	boys$_3$(PN)	played-dist. pl.-they say

(6) "čʰé·ṭ̓a	ba·[24]	k̓i·yá·,	k̓i·yá·-kà·xalikʰ	ká·[13]?"
where(D)-interrog(1052)	that(D)	Buteo$_2$(N)	Buteo(N)-Chief$_2$(PN)	one to dwell

(7) ní·n[45]	Néqan[14]	xa[2]	kʰi[13]	ba·qóyake·le[15] .
like that	say-when (switch reference)	they say	they$_3$	revealed-they say [the location]

(8) ʔíqan[84]	xa[2]	kʰi[13]	báy[147]	xól-uhò·le[16] ,	dáq̓a·ra̓[118]
then (switch reference)	they say	he$_1$	there(D)-loc.	towards-went-they say	old lady$_4$(PN)

ká·day[17]	šá·ri	kʰi·bún[18] . . . [problem with tape recorder]
sit-ing (switch reference)	basket(N)	coil-ing (co-reference)

dáq̓a·rà[118]	ká·le[19] ,	šá·ri	kʰi·bún[18] .
old lady$_4$(PN)	sat-they say	basket	coil-ing (co-reference)

(9) ʔíqan[84]	xa[2]	kʰi[13] . . .	ni·néx·le[20] ,	dáq̓a·rà-mì·ral[162] ,
then (switch reference)	they say	he$_1$	asked-they say	old lady(PN)-her$_4$(Pro) (patient)

čʰé·[21]	ba[124]	k̓i·yá·kà·xalikʰ	ʔí·[4] .
where(DLoc)	that (particular)(D)	buteo(N)-chief$_2$(PN)	is

(10) "káw	kʰúya[22]	ká·kʰkìl[23] ,	(11) ʔá·m[61]	ma·ʔáy
home(N)-loc.	don't	sit-habitually	thing(N)	food(N)

ba·bílkìla[24] ,	mí·p̓[19]	má·lkìlin[25] ."
gather (i.e. hunt)	he	go out-habitual-while (co-reference)

ní·n[45]	xa[2]	Né·le[46] ,	dáq̓a·ràheʔmì·ṭ̓ .
that	they say	said-they say	old lady(PN)-agent$_4$

(11) "baya[138]	ka·kíme[26]	šówmicʰeʔèkʰ[77] ,	báya[138]	ka·kíme[26] !
there (DLoc)	sit down-pl. imp.	daughter-in-law$_1$(KT)	there (D)	sit down-pl. imp.

(12) šé·[97]	kál-uhùba[27]	ʔinčʰa[241]	baʔè[28] "
soon	homewards-go-to	nevertheless	that is

mí·n[11]	xa[2]	kʰi[13]	Né·le[46] .	(13) dáyawal[85]	ná·ṭa·na·w
like that	they say	she$_4$	said-they said	young lady$_1$(PN)	pretty(Adj)

du·bákʰ-k̓ìy[29]	xa[2]	kʰi[13]	xól-uhò·le[16] .
made-extentive reflexive-then (co-reference)	they say	she$_1$	towards-went-they say

(14) bá·[10]	mí·n[11]	du·wékʰqan[30]	xa[2]	k̓i·yá·heʔ
then	like that	evening began-then (switch reference)	they say	Buteo(N)-specifier$_2$

kál-uhò·le[31] ,	qu·már	q̓ómcʰa	kʰi·dí·l[32] .	(15) báya[138]
home-came-they say	ground squirrel (N)	lots	carry on back	there(D)

qó-kʰi·dè·le[33] ,	báya[138] . . .	qa·wélipal	ṭ́é·ṭe·lin[34] :
down-locate-they say	there(D)	son(KT)-patient$_2$	told

"méqa[35]	kʰi[13]	méya[128]	xôl-uhùya[36] ,	mí·Nal[37] ."
	she$_1$	here(D)	towards-come	you$_2$(Pro)-towards

mí·n[11]	xa[2]	kʰi[13]	Né·le[46] .
like that	they say	she$_4$	said-they say

(16)	ba·[10]	xa[2]	kʰi[13]	mí·n[11]	qu·marhe?	qa·wáyk̓[38] ,
	then	they say	they$_{1,2,4}$	like that	ground squirrels(N)	eat-distributive pl. continuative

qa·wáyk̓iy[39]	ká·ya[75]	kʰi[13]	ku·ṭ́ép̓kiya[40] ,	ku·ṭ́ép̓ke·le[40] .
eat-distributive pl. continuative-then(co-reference)	afterwards	they$_{1,2,4}$	go to bed	went to bed-they say

(17)	bá·[10]	mí·n[11]	ku·ṭ́émiday[41]	xa[2]	kʰi[13] . . .	dáhe?
	then	like that	laying down(pl.)-then (switch reference)	they say	he$_2$	woman(PN)-specifier$_1$

. . . ?í[42] ,	ma·rá·-k̓i·yà·l?e[43]	?íqan[84]	dáhe?mì·ṭ	c̓á·l-k̓i·yà·l·le[44] ,
have	wanted-transitive-stative	then (switch reference)	woman(PN)-agent$_1$	refused-transitive-they say

mí·n[11]	?á·m[61]	me·?éla-kʰùy[191]	ší·kin[45] .
like that	thing(N)	know-negative	said-then (co-reference)

(18)	?íqan[84]	xa[2]		kʰúy·le[242]	qa·dál-du·bà·l[46] .
	then (switch reference)	they say	[he$_2$]	did not-they say	bother, tease [her$_1$]

(19)	bá·[10]	xa[2]	mí·n[11]	ku·ṭ́émiday[41]	xa[2]	. . .
	then	they say	like that	laying down (pl.)-then (switch reference)	they say	[she$_1$]

xów-aqà·le[47] ,	xa·?á·	da·?él[48] .	(20)	báywa[49]	kʰi[13]	káw-uhùday[50]
outside-go-they say	dawn	[to] examine [i.e., to urinate]		from there	she$_1$	inside-come-then (switch reference)

xa[2]	. . . ˀá·m[61]	. . . há·yišè·[51]	kʰi[13]	ˀá·m[61]	kʰi·kʰóyk̓heˀè[52]
they say	thing(N)	grape(N)-vine(N)	she/he$_1$	thing(N)	tied-reflexive-specifier

ˀíy[92]	xa[2]	kʰi[13]	xa·má·l	mu·pʰúc̓ke·le[53] .	(21) mu·c̓ápʰkiy[54]
then (co-reference)	they say	it	back	slip-semelfactive-they say	spring back-semelfactive-then (co-reference)

xa[2]	dáq̓a·rà[118]	míl-wi·nà·[55]	ma·síkʰheˀè	ku·mú	kʰi·bólˀwa·le[56] .
they say	old lady$_4$(PN)	that-on top of	coals(N)-specifier	all	splash-on-they say

(22) ˀiqan[84]	xa[2]	ku·nú·la-bù·c̓ike	pʰu·díkʰ·le[57] .
then	they say	Coyote(N)-Old Man$_1$(PN)	ran out-they say

(23) pʰu·díkiy[58]	xa[2]	kʰi[13]	cʰá·-kà·le[59] ;	kal-akà·le[60] .
ran out-then (co-reference)	they say	he$_1$	away-ran-they say	homewards-ran-they say

(24) xa·ˀá·qan[61]	xa[2]	kʰi[13]	yák̓aMi	Wílheˀ
dawn-then (switch-reference)	they say	he$_1$	right away	abalone shell(N)-specifier

ma·káy[62]	xa[2]	kʰi[13]	dúyeqal·le[63] .	(25) dúyeqaliy[64]	xa[2]
looked for-then (co-reference)	they say	he$_1$	made [some]-they say	made [some]-then (co-reference)	they say

kʰi[13]	bi·YáNa	sémk̓iy[65]	ká·ya[75]	xa[2]	kʰi[13]	qa·qó·kàx·le[66] ;
he$_1$	hand(N)-on	put on-then (co-reference)	afterwards	they say	he$_1$	fields-went out-they say

mí·n[11]	kʰi[13]	wá·l-du·lè·le[67] ;	kʰi[13]	wá·l-du·lìy[68]	qu·már
like that	he$_1$	walked around-continuously-they say	he$_1$	walked around-continuously-then (co-reference)	ground squirrel(s)$_5$(N)

ma·ká·le[69] .	(26) q̓óm:cʰa	xa[2]	qu·márheˀè	k̓áli	móday
looking for-they say	lots of	they say	ground squirrel(N)-specifier$_5$	one(Num)	hole(N)-in

káw-bi·là·le[70] .	(27) ba·[24]	ká·rkiy[71]	. . . báy[147]	xa[2]	kʰi[13]
inside-flock-they say	that	saw-then (co-reference)	there(D)-in	they say	he$_1$

yu[1] bi·Yá bi·da·-dòx·le[72] . (28) báy[147] xa[2] bi·YáNa

perfective hand(N) downwards-reach-they say there-in they say hand(N)-on

xól-ki·yàkinke·le[73] bi·ṭemk^hmanke·le[74] ʔínč^ha[241] xa[2]

approach-do-plural agents-personal perception-they say many to cling-extentive plural agents-personal perception-they say exist-while (co-reference)-nevertheless they say

k^húy·le[242] wálay ʔí·[4] .

not-they say fast(Adj) do

(29) bá· xa[2] k^hi[13] . . . qu·márheʔbè·k^h bi·Yá k^hú·y[119]

then they say $they_5$ ground-squirrels(N)-agents hand(N) another

du·báyk·le[75] , bi·Yáheʔ ʔík^hki·màba[76] ʔi·k^hùy[77] . (30) ʔíy[92]

struggle-distributive plural continuative-they say hand(N)-specific do-habitually plural agents-purposive exist-negative was-then (co-reference)

xa[2] k^hi[13] dáqa·ra [xa[2] k^hi[13]] xa·díyake·le[78] , báy[147]

they say they old $lady(PN)_6$ they say $they_5$ went and got-plural agents-they say there(D)-in

ká·w mérkil[79] námk , xówaqak^hkil-k^huy[80] , ʔúy-na·sày . (31) mí·ral[162]

inside lies-habitually always outside-walk-habitually-never blind(Adj) her(Pro)-$patient_6$

k^hi[13] xa·díyakiqan[81] mí·ṭ[90] xa[2] ʔé·le[82] , k^ha·Núk^h·le[83] :

$they_5$ went and got-plural agents-then (switch reference) $she(Pro)_6$ they say did-they say said-they say

(32) "ku·nú·la - bù·čike bi·Yá[84] . (33) ʔá·m[104] yúbiya

Coyote(N) - Old $Man(PN)_1$['s] hand(N) [is] thing(s)(N) always

do·k^hótkikìla[85] ; ʔá·m[61] ba·[24] dû·riqalkila[86] ."

trick/fool-semelfactive-habitual indicative thing(s)(N) that mislead/deceive-habitual-indicative

mí·n[11] xa[2] k^hi[13] Né·le[46] .

like that they say she_6 said

(34) "šu·múkakibaʔ[87] ,	ku·mûla·	šu·mûkakibaʔ[87] !"
pull-plural agents-jussive	everybody	pull-plural agents-jussive

(35) ʔíy[92]	xa[2]	ku·múla·	bi·ṭ̓émakiy[88] ,	šu·múkakiy[89]
was-then (co-reference)	they say	everybody	many to cling-plural agents-then (co-reference)	pull-plural agents-then (co-reference)

šu·músu·muyk̓iy[90]	xa[2]	k^hi^{13}	c̓u·wá·heʔ	šu·qúp^hkiyake·le[91] ,
pull-distributively-distributive plural continuative-then (co-reference)	they say	$they_{5+6}$	arm-specific$_1$	pulled-off-semelfactive-plural agents-they say

(36) ba·[10]	xa[2]	ku·nú·la - bù·c̓ike	qa·líy-akàkiy[92]
then	they say	Coyote(N) - Old Man(PN)$_1$	up-ran-semelfactive-then (co-reference)

bay[147]	xa·lé·yowiday	ki·máliy[93] ,	yi·bû ,	xáy	p^hu·c̓á·[94]
there(D)-in	trees(N)-under-in	running around-then (co-reference)	limb(N)	stick(N)	blown off

mér[95]	ʔį·[53]	xa[2]	k^hi^{13}	c̓u·wâ·day	kók^hkiy[96]	bá·Mak̓
lying (there)	was	they say	he$_1$	arm(N)-in	long object to be perpendicular-then (co-reference)	that(D)-with

kál-uhò·le[97] .
home-went-they say

(37) mí·n[11]	má·lkil[98]	k̓émiday[99]	xa[2]	. . . qu·már
like that	go around-habitually	maintain in a state-when (switch reference)	they say	ground squirrel(N)$_5$

k̓ali	qó·y-uhu·le[100] ,	ṭ̓é·ṭe·k̓·le[101] :
one(Num)	appeared-they say	told [him]-they say

(38) "mí·Nal[37] ,	wa·[78]	xáy	kál-ak̓èqà·[102] ,	xê	k̓i·yáyk̓ba[103]
you(Pro)-to	we$_5$(Pro)	stick(N)	home-carry long object-causative	dance (N)	do-distritubive plural-to

xáy	kál-ak̓eqa[102] ,	xé	k̓i·yáyk̓ba[103] ,"
stick(N)	home-carry long object-causative	dance(N)	do-distributive plural-to

ní·n[45]	xa[2]	kʰi[13]	Né·le[46] .
that	they say	he$_1$	said

(39) "ʔó·w,	ba·[24]	q̓o·díyʔè[28] ."	
	O.k.	that	good-is

(40) ʔín[298]	xa[2]	ku·nú·la - bù·čikeheʔmì·p̓	Márakʰ
then (co-reference)	they say	Coyote(N) - Old Man(PN)-agent$_1$	ceremonial house(N)

de·hél-du·kè·le[104] .	(41) de·héliy[105]	de·héliy[105] ,	xa[2]	kʰi[13]
dig-inceptive-they say	dig-then (co-reference)	dig-then (co-reference)	they say	he$_1$

yu[1]	ṭé·lqa·le[106] .
perfective	finish-causative-they say

(42) mí·n[11]	ʔí·day[12]	xa[2]	yu[1]	qu·márheʔbè·kʰ
like that	was-then (switch-reference)	they say	perfective	ground squirrels-agent$_5$

yu[1]	xé	k̓é·lake·le[107] .
perfective	dance(N)	do-continuously-plural agents-they say

(43) bá·[10]	xa[2]	kʰi[13]	yu[1]	xe	lóm-du·lè·le[108] :
then	they say	they$_5$	perfective	song(N)	several to sing-continuously-they say

(44) "mi·	Yá	mi·	Yá	ti·lí·min[109]
[it is] your	bone(s)(N)	your	bone(s)(N)	are jingling-which (co-reference)

ti·lí·min[109] "
are jingling-which (co-reference)

"mi·	Yá	mi·	Yá	ti·só·min[110]
[it is] your	bone(s)(N)	your	bone(s)(N)	are jangling-which (co-reference)

ti·só·min[110] "	
are jangling-which (co-reference)	

ní·n[45]	xa[2]	k^hi[13]	lóyk̓-du·lè·le[111] ,	xéheʔ	k̓é·lakin[112] .
that	they say	they$_5$	several to sing-distributive plural continuative-continuously-they say	dance(N)	do-continuously-plural agents-while (co-reference)

(45) ba·[10]	yu[1]	Márakay	káw-ake·lè[113] ,	káw-p^hi·lè·le[114] ,
then	perfective	ceremonial house(N)-into	inside-go dancing-they say	inside-several to walk in-they say

ku·mú .	(46) báy[147]	k^hi[13]	mí·n[11]	k̓i·yáyk̓[115] ,	mí·n[11]	k^hi[13]
all [of them]	there(D)-in	they$_5$	like that	do-distributive plural	like that	they$_5$

k̓i·yáyk̓[115] ,	yu[1]	xa·ʔá·yaqaday[116]	xa[2]	k^hi[13]	ba·qó·le[117]
do-distributive plural	perfective	dawn-future-when (switch reference)	they say	he$_1$	find out [what they re singing about]-they say

(47) "wi[57]	k^hi[13]	p^hi·ráy-k̓i·yàyk̓[118] ,	wi[57]	k^hi[13]	c̓óqaxàyk̓[119] ."
me$_1$ (Pro)	they$_5$	laughing-do-distributive plural	me$_1$ (Pro)	they$_5$	teasing-distributive plural

xa[2]	k^hi	ba·qó·le[120] .	(48) ʔíy[92]	nu·p^hér - q̓a·rà·ya	xa[2]
they say	he$_1$	he found out-they say	was-then (co-reference)	skunk(N) - girls(PN)$_7$	they say

mí·pal	ma·c^hé·xmaqa·le[121] ,	xóc^h .	(49) bé·kal[186]	xa[2]	k^hi[13]
his(Pro)-patient$_1$	his own-mother's brother-reflexive-plural-they say	two(Num)	them(Pro)-patient	they say	he$_1$

dúyk^h·le	kál-p^hi·lèxba[122] ;	ʔá·m	Marák^hheʔ	ša·ṭ̓ó·ba[123] .
ordered-they say	home-several to go-to	thing(N)	ceremonial house(N)-specific	burn-in order to

(50) ʔíy[92]	xa[2]	yu[1]	q̓a·rá·yaheʔ	xów-p^hi·lèx·le[124] .
was-then (co-reference)	they say	perfective	girls(PN)-specific	out-several to leave-they say

(51) bá·[10]	kʰi[13]	mí·n[11]	k̓i·yayk̓iday[125]	yu[1]	xa[2]
then	they	like that	doing-distributive plural-while (switch reference)	perfective	they say

bú·c̓ikeheʔ	ki·má-du·kè·le[126] .
old man(PN)-specific₁	run around-inceptive-they say

(52) "qa·wík̓u·la· ,	c̓ʰíʔ-k̓i·yà·nke[127] ,	kâ·y	bi·t̓á·kin[128]
boys(PN)-agent₅	something-is going to happen-personal perception	feeling good-because (co-reference)	

kʰúyink̓e[129] ,	ká·y	lé·m-akʰùy[130]	yóx-du·link̓e[131] ,
not-personal perception	perception-without		become-continuously-personal perception

qa·wíku·la·ya ,"
boys(PN)-agents-plural₅

ní·n[45]	xa[2]	kʰi[13]	ka·Núl·le[132] ,	ki·má·lin[133]	bá·Mak̓ .
that	they say	he₁	spoke	running around-while (co-reference)	that-with

(53) mí·n[11]	kʰi[13]	má·liy[134]	xa[2]	kʰi[13]	Wá-ka·tè·
like that	he₁	ran around-then (co-reference)	they say	he₁	door(N)-beside

xól-akay[135]	ša·ṭó·le[136] ,	ʔá·mheʔè ,	Márakʰheʔè .	(54) bá·Mak̓
towards-ran-then (co-reference)	burn-they say	thing(N)-specific	ceremonial house(N)-specific	that-with

xa[2]	pʰu·díkʰ·le[137] .	(55) báy[147]	xa[2]	ba·[24]
they say	ran away-they say	there(D)-in	they say	that(D)

si·q̓á·lmank̓e·le[138] ,	qu·márheʔ	si·q̓álma·[139] .	(56) xa·ʔáqan[61]
screaming-extentive plural agents-personal perception-they say	ground squirrel(s)(PN)-specific₅	screaming-extentive plural agents	dawn-then (switch-reference)

xa[2]	ku·mú	c̓ó·m·le[140] .
they say	all	gone-they say

(57)	ʔíqan[84]	xa[2]	k^{h}i[13]	bó·xaNal	ku·sí	xáy
	then (switch-reference)	they say	he$_1$	coast-towards	nest(N) [i.e., storage container]	pole(s)(N)

hí·p̓·le[141] ;	ba·[24]	qu·márheʔ	qa·qába[142]	báy[147] .
collect-they say	those(D)	ground squirrels(PN)-specific$_5$	place in a container-to	there(D)-in

(58)	ba·[10]	k^{h}i[13]	mí·n[11]	xáy	kál-k^{h}i·dìy[143]	k^{h}i[13]	ba·[24]
	then	he$_1$	like that	poles(N)	home-brought-then (co-reference)	he$_1$	that(D)

Márak^h	Wámo	qól-anèqan[144]	xa[2]	ba·[24]	ʔa·m[61]	mí·p̓[19]
ceremonial house's(N)	door(N)	threw down-then (switch-reference)	they say	that(D)	thing(N)	he(Pro)$_1$

k^{h}i·dílheʔ[145]	káyNa	ba·kú·qan[146]	xa[2]	qu·márheʔ
carrying-specific	on the ground	dropped-when (switch-reference)	they say	ground squirrel(s)(PN)-specific$_5$

ku·mú	ma·k^{h}ú·lk^{h}le[147] .
all	escaped/ran away-they say

(59)	bá·[10]	xa[2]	k^{h}i[13]	du·bé·du·bè·le[148] ,	k̓álik̓a
	then	they say	he$_1$	chased several things around-distributively-they say	one(Num)-only

k^{h}i[13]	da·k^{h}ó·le[149] .
he$_1$	caught-they say

["That's all."]

Free Translation

(1) Old Man Coyote had been going around.

(2) He'd been going around like that and he heard the news: that Buteo-Chief was a wonderful hunter, always killing a lot of food. (3) When he heard that he made himself a young woman in order to go over there, a pretty young woman. (4) Having become a young woman he left for over there [for Buteo-Chief's village].

(5) After awhile, coming to the village . . . he asked the children playing outside there:

(6) "Where does Buteo-Chief live?"

(7) When he asked, they told him.

(8) Then he went over there to the place where the old lady was sitting, weaving a basket [problem with tape recorder]; an old lady sat weaving a basket.

(9) Then he asked her, the old lady, where the Buteo-Chief was.

(10) "He don't stay home. He goes out looking for food all the time."
That's what the old lady said.
(11) "Sit down here, my daughter-in-law, sit down here!"
(12) "He'll come home soon."
That's what she said. ((13) He [Coyote] had made himself a pretty young woman before he came.)

(14) When it was evening, Buteo-Chief came home, carrying a lot of ground squirrels. (15) He put them down there [on the ground] as [she] told her son:
"She came here just to you."
that's what she said.

(16) Then they ate the ground squirrels, and after eating they went to bed.

(17) After awhile, they were lying there, and he wanted to make love to the woman, but the woman refused, saying she didn't know about things like that.

(18) Then he stopped bothering [her].

(19) They were laying there and after awhile [she, i.e., Coyote] went outside to look for the dawn [i.e., to urinate]. (20) Coming back inside, on his way to lie down, the grapevine he had tied himself with slipped and it [his penis] slipped off. (21) When it slipped it splashed coals all over the old lady [who was lying on the opposite side of the fire from her son and new daughter-in-law].

(22) Old Man Coyote ran out. (23) He ran out and ran away; ran home. (24) Next morning, first thing, he looked for that abalone shell and made some [shell pendants]. (25) Making [them], he put [them] on his hand and then went out in the fields; he walked around and around; walking around and around he looked for ground squirrels. (26) Lots of ground squirrels were flocking into one hold. (27) Seeing that he reached down in there with his hand [as far as it could reach, up to the shoulder]. (28) He could feel them approaching his hand; he could feel many getting on his hand, but it felt like they were coming slowly.

(29) The squirrels felt his hand, but it didn't seem to be the hand they were used to struggling with. (30) So they went out and got an old lady who stayed inside there all the time, who never went out anymore, being blind. (31) When they went and got her she said:
(32) "This is Old Man Coyote's hand. (33) He's always tricking [people]; he's always deceiving [people]."
That's what she said.
(34) "Let's all pull, everybody, Let's all pull it!"
(35) So everybody got on his hand and they all pulled and each one pulled and pulled continuously and pretty soon they pulled his arm off.

(36) Then Old Man Coyote jumped up and ran around in there under the [oak] trees, and found a tree limb that had been blown off lying there, and stuck that in where his arm was and went home with that.

(37) Then he was living around there and after awhile a ground squirrel came there and told him:
(38) "We're going to carry the stick [announcing a dance] to you, in order to dance; we're going to carry the stick to you, in order to dance,"
that's what he said.
(39) "Alright, That's good."
(40) So Old Man Coyote began to dig [the foundations for] a Márak^{h} or ceremonial house. (41) He dug and dug and dug and finally he finished.

(42) After awhile the ground squirrels came along dancing.

(43) They sang continuously:
(44) "It's your bone, your bone, that's jingling, that's jingling"
"It's your bone, your bone, that's jangling, that's jangling"
that's what they were each singing continuously while they were dancing along.

(45) They went dancing into the Márak^{h}, all of them. (46) In there they kept doing like that and doing like that and doing like that, and finally towards morning he found out [what it's all about].
(47) "They're laughing at me, They're making fun of me."
he found out. (48) So two skunk young ladies were his sister's children. (49) He told them to go home; in order to burn the Márak^{h} down. (50) So the young ladies left.

(51) After awhile, while the ground squirrels were dancing, the old man started running around.
(52) "Boys, I can feel that something is going to happen to me, I'm not feeling good, I'm getting numb, Boys,"
that's what he said while he was running around. (53) Then he ran around like that and

ran towards the door and set fire to the Márak^{h} [right at the door, so they couldn't come out]. (54) He ran out with that. (55) They were screaming inside, the ground squirrels were screaming, next morning they were all gone [i.e., dead].

(56) Then he went to the coast to get some poles to build a storage place to store the squirrels in.

(57) Then he brought the poles home and threw them down at the door of the Márak^{h}, and when he dropped the poles he was carrying on the ground, the ground squirrels ran away [raising lots of dust].

(58) He chased them around and around here and there, but he only caught one.

["That's all."]

Footnotes

[1]má·l Cf. FN 76 with ·le hearsay evidential, independent-verb-forming suffix (573.9). In myths, the independent verb head of the independent (or matrix) clause in each sentence is suffixed with ·le, except in sentences which are direct quotes (500, 570, 573). In Eastern Pomo the verb is the last constituent in a clause (although not necessarily in the sentence).

[2]má·l Cf. FN 76 + iday switch reference sentence connective (indicating that action of main verb continues over the same period or begins at the time indicated by the suffixed verb), dependent-verb-forming suffix (571.8).

Dependent-verb forming suffixes (571), like iday, indicate the suffixed verb is syntactically subordinated to another verb in the same sentence. Unless otherwise specified in the following footnotes, such suffixed verbs are heads of dependent clauses of which they are the last constituent.

[3]šó· 'hear' with k^{h} punctual aspect (536) + ·le hearsay evidential (cf. FN 1) head of independent clause which together with the preceding dependent clause and following two juxtaposed clauses constitutes an independent sentence.

[4]ʔi· (<ʔí verb root of doing, existing, locating, having, acquiring) + · stative mode, independent-verb-forming suffix (573.3), head of juxtaposed clause. Cf. FN 52.

Juxtaposed clauses are similar in structure to embedded clauses, both being characterized by verb heads which are bare stems (which seem frequently best translated by English present participles) and within which the hearsay evidential particle xa has not been found to occur. They are distinguished from embedded clauses, however, on the basis of their position of occurrence in a sentence. Juxtaposed clauses follow the independent verb, while embedded clauses precede it.

[5]du·ṭélk^{h} (<du· 'with or affecting the fingers' instrumental prefix [416] + ṭé 'finish, complete' + l durative manner suffix [474] [characterizing an action or state as having duration or permanence, which may, in combination with certain roots, result in termination or destruction]) with k^{h} punctual aspect (536). Head of juxtaposed clause. Cf. FN 4, 2nd para.

[6]líl 'at a distance,' directional (835) + epenthetic vowel, harmonic with root vowel: u/_ Back Vowel, a/_/ non-Back Vowel, + hú 'general verb of motion (in direction specified by preverb or directional) with ba purposive, dependent-verb-forming suffix (572.3). Cf. FN 2.

[7]dúyeqal 'make, manufacture, do' with ·le hearsay evidential. Cf. FN 1. Head of independent clause containing a dependent clause.

[8]yó·x 'become' with ay allomorph (occurring after post-velar) of iy co-reference sentence connective (indicating action of suffixed verb precedes in time that of main verb), dependent-verb-forming suffix (571.1). (This allomorph had not been identified when McLendon 1975 was written.) Cf. FN 2, 2nd para.

[9]Cf. FN 6 with ·le hearsay evidential. Cf. FN 1.

[10]xól 'approach a goal,' directional preverb (840) + cf. FN 6 with · stative mode suffix (573.3). Head of verbal phrase. Cf. FN 52.

[11]ni·néx 'ask' with ·le hearsay evidential cf. FN 1. Head of independent clause which together with the preceding dependent clause and verbal phrase and following juxtaposed independent clause constitutes an independent sentence.

[12]t^háyk̓ (< t^há 'open, undo, release' + yk̓ distributive plural continuative manner suffix [491]) with ·le hearsay evidential. Cf. FN 1. Head of juxtaposed independent clause. In transcribing, Mr. Holder corrected the taped utterance:

mí·n	ʔix	mí·pix	na·p^hô·na·p^hôNa	xôl-uhù·
like that	do	his	dwelling-at	arrive

to that printed here, perhaps in order to mark the narrative/presentational unit boundary better.

[13]ká· 'something round to be located,' by extension, 'one to dwell' with · stative mode (573.3), · + · → · . Head of independent clause which is itself an independent interrogative sentence. (Cf. McLendon in press, Sec. 10.1-2.)

[14]Né 'say' + qan switch reference sentence connective (indicating temporal anteriority of suffixed verb), dependent-verb-forming suffix (571.2). Cf. FN 2, 2nd para.

[15]ba·qó 'reveal, recognize (< ba· 'with or affecting the top and by extension, with speech,' instrumental prefix [411] + qô 'recognize, identify, perceive through one of senses') with yaki 'plural agents' (561) + ·le hearsay evidential (cf. FN 1); i → e/__·le. Head of independent clause which together with the preceding dependent clause constitutes an independent sentence.

[16]Cf. FN 10 with ·le hearsay evidential (cf. FN 1); u → o/__·le. (Because of the problem with the tape recorder which necessitated interrupting the telling of the text briefly in the middle of the sentence of which this is the main verb of the main clause, and then resuming, this sentence is atypical in structure. Mr. Holder apparently changed his strategy while the recorder was turned off.)

[17]ká· cf. FN 13 with day allomorph of iday switch reference sentence connective. Cf. FN 2.

[18]k^hi·bú 'weave with coiling technique' (< k^hi· 'with a long, thing, generally flexible agent such as needle, awl, rope or paintbrush,' instrumental prefix [411] + bú 'rounded, encircle') with n allomorph of in co-reference sentence connective (indicating temporal simultaneity and/or motivation for the action of the main verb), dependent-verb-forming suffix (571.3).

[19]Cf. FN 13 with ·le hearsay evidential. Cf. FN 1. Head of juxtaposed independent clause.

[20]Cf. FN 11. Head of independent clause which together with the preceding dependent clause and following juxtaposed clause constitutes an independent sentence.

[21]Interrogative locative demonstrative (McLendon 1975:126-127). The absence of the interrogative particle t̓a (1052) or subjunctive particle ti (1051) which are predictably present in interrogative sentences (McLendon in press, Sec. 10) marks this clause as not direct speech.

[22]k^húy negative verb with a allomorph of ya indicative mode (573.1). Independent negative verb head of independent clause.

[23]Cf. FN 13 with k^h punctual aspect (535) + kìl habitual (562). Lexical main verb of clause negated by k^húya.

[24]ba·bíl 'gather (clover, wood, acorns),' cf. FN 21 with kìl habitual (562) + a allomorph of ya indicative mode (573.1). Head of independent clause which together with the following dependent clause constitutes an independent sentence.

[25]Cf. FN 76 with kìl habitual (562) + in co-reference sentence connective. Cf. FN 18.

[26]ka·kí (<ka· 'with or affecting a blob-shaped ovoid mass, generally in movement, such as a flint knife, the buttocks, or torso,' instrumental prefix (418) + kí 'collect, group into rounded shape' with me plural imperative, independent-verb-forming suffix (500, 573, 573.11). Head of independent clause and the following juxtaposed independent clause which together with the intervening vocative constitute an independent sentence.

In Eastern Pomo parents-in-law and children-in-law use plural forms in addressing each other as a mark of respect. Buteo-Chief's mother therefore addresses the disguised Old Man Coyote in the plural when she calls him daughter-in-law.

[27]kál 'goal is human habitation' + cf. FN 6.

[28]Copula sentence in which ʔè the copula enclitic occurs instead of a finite verb (1060).

[29]du·bákʰ-ḳ̀i 'made herself' (<du· cf. FN 5 + bâ with k^h punctual aspect [536] and compounding of secondary stem ḳ̀i extentive reflexive [595] with y allomorph of iy co-reference sentence connective). Cf. FN 8.

In transcribing, Mr. Holder corrected the taped utterance:

dáyawal ná·ṭa·a·w du·bákḳ̀iy ḳ̂in xôl-uhùqan

to that printed here.

[30]du·wé 'be evening' with k^h punctual aspect (which has inceptive force with stems which refer to actions or states with extent) (536) + qan switch reference sentence connective, cf. FN 14.

[31]kál Cf. FN 27 + FN 16. Head of independent clause which with preceding dependent clause and following juxtaposed clause constitutes an independent sentence.

[32]k^hi·dí·l 'transport in a container, usually on back or shoulder' (cf. FN 23). Head of juxtaposed clause; cf. FN 4, 2nd para.

[33]qó- 'locate down,' directional preverb (840) + k^hi·dî cf. FN 23 with ·le hearsay evidential, cf. FN 1; i → e/__·le. Head of independent clause which together with the following dependent clause and, quoted independent clause and quotative independent clause constitutes an independent sentence.

[34]ṭ́e·ṭe·l cf. 253 with in co-reference sentence connective. Cf. FN 18.

[35]méqa had not been collected before Mr. Holder told this text. Mr. Holder defines it as "come purposely to see you." Its initial position in the sentence and translation suggest that it is probably a syntactic particle (1073).

[36]Cf. FN 10 with ya indicative mode, independent-verb-forming suffix (500, 570, 573.1). Head of quoted independent clause.

[37]mí· 'second person singular patient' [Chart of Pronouns, Table 3, McLendon 1975:111 has a typographical error: the oblique second person singular stem is mî·, not mî as given] + Nàl allomorph of yiNàl 'towards,' directional (960). [McLendon 1975:157 erroneously glossed this suffix as an indirect object suffix occurring only with kinship terms. Further research has revealed that the suffix is only used when movement towards the form suffixed is involved, and that the suffix also occurs with pronouns. When occurring with pronouns, however, the suffix has the allomorph given above. yiNàl thus demonstrates a variation in shape conditioned by the class of stem it is suffixed to, analogous in both type of variation and conditioning environment to that shown by the genitive suffix bax (956), the comitative-reciprocal suffix Maḱ (956) and the purposive ba (962).]

[38]qa·wáyḳ (cf. FN 55 + yḳ distributive plural continuative [indicating that plural individuals individually continue an action or state], manner suffix [491]).

[39] Cf. FN 38 + iy co-reference sentence connective, cf. FN 8.

[40] ku·ṭ̓ép̓ 'many (more than 2) to lie down' (< ku· '[1] with a flat surface, such as the palm, an iron, the buttocks, [2] achieve an optimal state/goal/arrangement/relationship,' instrumental prefix [420]) + ṭé 'establish contact' + p segmentative manner suffix (generally indicating a change in state and frequently indicating that the state or condition specified is entered into or initiated [480]) with ki semelfactive (indicating an action happening all at once; frequently conceived of as having extent or being a single instance of a general type of action [550]) + ya indicative, cf. FN 36. The use of the indicative here instead of the expected hearsay evidential is probably a slip, repaired in the next form--a repeat of the same verb with the expected ·le hearsay evidential. Eastern Pomo dwellings were usually large multi-family dwellings with each family unit sleeping around a different fire within, but could be occupied by a single family sleeping around a single fire as seems to be the case with Buteo-Chief and his mother. A typical ground plan of a traditional Eastern Pomo tule-thatched house is given below.

A Buteo-Chief and new wife

B Buteo-Chief's mother

ᨓ Fire

[41] ku·ṭ̓ém (cf. FN 40 + m arrested development [remaining constantly in state specified, and by extension, stationary or down], manner suffix [477]) with iday switch reference sentence connective, cf. FN 2.

[42] ʔí· (cf. FN 4). Head of clause complement of ma·râ·-ḱi·yà·lʔe.

[43] Cf. FN 393 with ʔè copula enclitic (used with verb stems to form statives. McLendon 1975:173 erroneously described these constructions as passives, which in fact do not exist in Eastern Pomo. Thus 'He's tired' can be either:

mí·p̓	pʰu·dálʔè	or	mí·pal	pʰu·dâla
he	tired is		he (patient)	tired
(if he's sitting down, tired)			(if he's running or working and visibly getting tired)	

[44] Cf. FN 238. Head of independent clause which together with the preceding dependent clause and stative (with clause complement) and following dependent clause constitutes an independent sentence.

[45] šʔí· 'name, call, tell, say' with kʰ punctual aspect (536) + in co-reference sentence connective, cf. FN 18.

[46] qa·dál 'bite to death, hate' (< qa· 'with jaws and teeth, with jaw-like action,' instrumental prefix [430] + dâ 'force open, expose, generally by interrupting the enclosing surface' + l durative cf. FN 5, manner suffix [474]) compounded with secondary stem du·bá·l (cf. FN 29 + ·l continuative manner suffix [475]). Lexical main verb of clause negated by kʰúy·le.

[47] xów 'out from an enclosure,' directional preverb (840) + epenthetic vowel harmonic with root vowel + qâ 'to walk in direction specified by directional or preverb' with ·le hearsay evidential, cf. FN 1.

[48] da·ʔél 'examine, scan, look over, view.' Head of juxtaposed clause. Cf. FN 4.

[49] Cf. FN 147 with wa 'motion away from,' directional (937).

[50] káw 'towards/in enclosure,' directional preverb (840) + cf. FN 6 with day allomorph of iday switch reference sentence connective, cf. FN 2.

[51] Compound: hâ·y 'wild grape' + i derivational suffix linking two members of a compound (indicating that the second member is possessed by or a part of the first) (1031) + šè· 'vine.'

[52]k^hi·k^hó 'tie up something with rope' (<k^hi· cf. FN 18 + k^hó 'with short, thrusting motion of a long object which generally contacts violently or attaches itself to another material' + yk̓ distributive plural continuative, cf. FN 38 with heˀè specifying suffix (indicating that a particular, specific variety of the form suffixed is being referred to) (965). Head of relative clause. Relative clauses are not explicitly marked, but may have a nominal affix attached to the right-most constituent (e.g., ˀba· deictic of specifying emphasis (950), a suffixal compound (970), or heˀè as here). Relative clauses are headless (cf. FN 49). Here, for example, '(the) grapevine' is modified by the relative clause, 'he tied thing [i.e., penis] up with.'

[53]mu·p^húc̓ (<mu· 'from internal energy or motivation,' instrumental prefix [426] + p^hú separate?, + c 'with/from pressure, applied to or affecting an extent of surface, manner suffix [471]) with ki semelfactive, cf. FN 40 + ·le hearsay evidential, cf. FN 1. Head of independent clause which with preceding dependent clause and noun phrase (including a relative clause) constitutes an independent sentence.

[54]mu·c̓ap^h (<mu· cf. FN 53 + c̓á 'squeeze by wringing, twisting' + p^h 'with/from pressure resulting from kinetic energy, the pressure of impact,' manner suffix [479]) with ki semelfactive, cf. FN 40 + y allomorph of iy co-reference sentence connective. Cf. FN 8.

[55]míl 'that previously verbally identified object, action, or place,' adverbial indefinite anaphoric referential locative (812) with juxtaposition of wi·nâ 'on top of.'

[56]k^hi·ból 'pour, spill' (<k^hi· cf. FN 18 + bó 'to move outwards, away, frequently against some resistance' + l durative cf. FN 5, manner suffix [474]) with ˀwa· locative of attachment (542) + ·le hearsay evidential, cf. FN 1. Head of independent clause which with preceding dependent clause constitutes an independent sentence.

[57]p^hu·dí 'fly, fly away, steal, float, long object to be extended perpendicular' (<p^hu· 'with energy of a moving current of air as a medium or locus, particularly from the plosive force resulting from the sudden release of air, or other medium which behaves similarly, such as spurting liquids,' instrumental prefix [429] + dí 'place or maintain in a specific appropriate position or state') with k^h punctual + ·le hearsay evidential, cf. FN 1.

[58]Cf. FN 57 with -iy co-reference sentence connective, cf. FN 8.

[59]c^há· 'away with no intention of returning,' directional preverb (840) + ká 'to run in direction specified by preverb' with ·le hearsay evidential, cf. FN 1. Head of independent clause, which with preceding dependent clause and following juxtaposed independent clause constitutes an independent sentence.

[60]kál cf. FN 27 + FN 59. Head of juxtaposed independent clause.

[61]xa·ˀá· 'be dawn' + qan switch reference sentence connective, cf. FN 14.

[62]ma·ká 'look for' (<ma· cf. McLendon 1975:48-49 + ká 'move with energy, intensity, rapidity, frequently against resistance') with y allomorph of iy co-reference sentence connective, cf. FN 8.

[63]Cf. FN 7. Head of independent clause which together with two preceding dependent clauses constitutes an independent sentence.

[64]Cf. FN 7 with iy co-reference sentence connective, cf. FN 8.

[65]sém 'put on' (<sé 'place, locate' + m cf. FN 41) with k̓ reflexive (537) + iy co-reference sentence connective, cf. FN 8.

[66]qa·qó· 'fields, wilderness (as opposed to village, cf. McLendon 1975:138), Directional Preverb + ká cf. FN 59 + x locative, 'on,' manner suffix (489) with ·le hearsay evidential, cf. FN 1.

[67]wá·l 'go away, with no necessary goal' (<wá 'iterative movement, generally repetition

of same sequence of movement' + ·l continuative, manner suffix (475) with compounding of secondary stem du·lí- constantive (593) with ·le hearsay evidential, cf. FN 1; i → e/__·le. Head of juxtaposed independent clause.

[68]Cf. FN 67 with y allomorph of iy co-reference sentence connective, cf. FN 8.

[69]Cf. FN 62 with ·le hearsay evidential, cf. FN 1. Head of independent juxtaposed clause.

[70]kâw cf. FN 50 + bi·lá 'for many to be together' (<bi· 'draw together, group, collect' instrumental prefix [412] + lá 'extended, spread out in a continuum') with ·le hearsay evidential, cf. FN 1.

[71]ká·r 'see' with k^h punctual (536) + iy co-reference sentence connective, cf. FN 8.

[72]bi·dá· 'downwards,' directional preverb (840) + dô 'circular motion with small circumference, generally described in a vertical plane' + cf. FN 66 with ·le hearsay evidential, cf. FN 1. Head of independent clause which together with the preceding depending clause constitutes an independent sentence.

[73]xól 'approach a goal,' directional preverb (840) + k̓í 'general root of doing, particularly linearly' + yaki plural agents (561) + nk̓e allomorph of ink̓e non-visual evidential (indicating basis for statement is evidence arrived at through sense other than sight--here that Coyote feels through his hand [which is stuck into the burrow and out of sight] the ground squirrels plurally getting on it) (573.8) + ·le hearsay evidential, cf. FN 1. Head of independent clause which together with following juxtaposed independent clauses constitutes an independent sentence.

When McLendon 1975 was written ink̓e and ·le were described as members of the same position class or morphemes, and therefore mutually exclusive in occurrence. This form and the following independent verb provide evidence that in fact these two morphemes can co-occur and therefore must be in different position classes.

[74]bi·ṭém (<bi· cf. FN 70 + ṭé 'distributed movement along a surface' + m 'arrested development,' cf. FN 41) with k^h punctual (536) + ma extentive plural agents (indicating plural agents, each acting individually, are involved in an extended action or continuing state) + nk̓e cf. FN 73 + ·le hearsay evidential, cf. FN 1. Head of juxtaposed clause.

[75]du·bá cf. FN 29 with yk̓ cf. FN 38 + ·le hearsay evidential, cf. FN 1.

[76]ʔí cf. FN 4 with k^h punctual (536) + ki·mà plural habitual (referring to an action which is regularly or habitually done by plural agents) + ba purposive, cf. FN 6.

[77]Cf. FN 385.

[78]xa·dí (<xa· 'approaching, bringing together, into contact,' instrumental prefix [438] + dí cf. FN 23 + yaki plural agents, cf. FN 73 + ·le hearsay evidential, cf. FN 1; i → e__/·le. Head of independent clause which together with the two following juxtaposed clauses constitutes an independent sentence.

[79]mér 'one to lie' + kìl habitual, cf. FN 23 (562), Head of juxtapose clause, cf. FN 4.

[80]Cf. FN 47 + k^h punctual (536) + kìl cf. FN 79--with compounding of negative secondary stem k^hùy cf. FN 117.

[81]Cf. FN 78 with qan switch reference sentence connective, cf. FN 14.

[82]ʔí cf. FN 4 + ·le hearsay evidential, cf. FN 1. Head of independent clause which together with the preceding dependent clause and following juxtaposed independent clause constitutes an independent sentence.

[83]Cf. FN 41. Head of juxtaposed independent clause.

84 Possessive statements lack a finite verb, as here, and merely juxtapose the possessor + the thing possessed in that order. Cf. McLendon in press, Section 15.1.

85 do·kʰȍť 'trick, fool' (< du· cf. FN 5 + kʰô 'with short, thrusting motion of the head end of a long object which generally contacts violently' + ť 'from/with pressure, particularly pressure that flattens or squeezes against a surface,' manner suffix (486) with ki semelfactive cf. FN 40 + kìl habitual, cf. FN 23 + a allomorph of ya indicative, cf. FN 24 head of independent clause which together with the following independent clause constitutes an independent sentence.

86 dú·riqal 'mislead, deceive' + kìl cf. FN 23 + a allomorph of ya indicative, cf. FN 24. Head of independent clause.

87 šu·mú 'pull' (< šu· 'involving simultaneous pull in two opposite directions along an axis, generally between two polarities of tension/force/pull,' instrumental prefix (453) + mú 'to attempt some motion, generally against resistance') with kʰ punctual (536) + aki allomorph of yaki plural agents (561) + baʔ jussive (573.10). Head of independent clause.

88 Cf. FN 74 with aki allomorph of yaki plural agents (561) + y allomorph of iy coreference sentence connective, cf. FN 8.

89 Cf. FN 87 + y allomorph of iy co-reference sentence connective, cf. FN 8.

90 šu·mú cf. FN 87 + R partial stem reduplication, i.e., of instrumental prefix and root (520, 523) + yk cf. FN 12 + iy co-reference sentence connective, cf. FN 8.

91 šu·qúpʰ 'pull up/out something, (such as tule roots from under water)' (< šu· cf. FN 87 + qû 'contacting motion in short segments' + pʰ cf. FN 54) with ki semelfactive, cf. FN 40 + yaki plural agents (561) + ·le hearsay evidential, cf. FN 1; i → e _/·le. Head of independent clause which together with the three preceding dependent clauses constitutes an independent sentence.

In transcribing, Mr. Holder recalled that he had left out a line at this point in which Coyote says, with pleasurable anticipation of the large amount of food he is to get (when he feels the intensive pulling of the ground squirrels):

"dó·l - kʰu·Làw	mé·rémin	ʔikʰuyťa	síy	šu·ťanke ."
four - pointer [deer]	lying [in there]- that's why	I guess	strong	pull-feel- personal perception

"Four-pointer deer must be lying in there, that's what makes it pull so hard."

92 qa·líY 'up,' directional preverb (840) + cf. FN 60 + ki semelfactive, cf. FN 40 + y allomorph of iy co-reference sentence connective, cf. FN 8.

93 ki·mâl 'run around' (< ki· 'uninterrupted, smoothly or consistently extended movement' instrumental prefix [419] + má 'within bounds,' cf. FN 76 + l durative manner suffix cf. FN 5) with iy co-reference sentence connective, cf. FN 8.

94 pʰu·ćá· (< pʰu· 'with energy of a moving current as locus, particularly with the plosive force resulting from the sudden release of air,' instrumental prefix (429) + ćâ· 'break by twisting'). Head of embedded clause (cf. FN 4, 2nd para.) which translates as a relative, i.e., 'which had blown off,' and is itself embedded in the embedded clause of which mér is the head.

95 mér 'lie.' Lexical main verb of verb phrase mér ʔi· which translates as a relative, i.e., 'which was lying there' and head of embedded clause which itself contains an embedded clause (cf. FN 4, 2nd para.), which translates: the stick which had blown off which was lying (there).

96 kó 'long object to be perpendicular + kʰ punctual (536) + ki semelfactive, cf. FN 40 with y allomorph of iy co-reference sentence connective, cf. FN 8. Head of dependent clause containing an embedded clause.

[97]Cf. FN 31. Head of independent clause which together with the three preceding dependent clauses (the third of which contains an embedded [relative] clause which itself contains an embedded [relative] clause) constitutes an independent sentence.

[98]má·l cf. FN 1 + kìl habitual, cf. FN 23. Head of embedded clause, cf. FN 4, 2nd para.

[99]kʼém 'long object to continue in a state' (<kʼé 'affecting a long object' + m 'arrested development,' cf. FN 41) + iday switch reference sentence connective, cf. FN 2.

[100]qʼó·y 'something previously unseen to appear,' directional preverb (840) + cf. FN 9. Head of independent clause which together with the preceding dependent clause and following juxtaposed independent clause constitutes an independent sentence.

[101]Cf. FN 34 + kʼ 'with/from short segments of reciprocating motion or energy, especially oscillating, which is inherently repetitive in nature (but need not be repeated in any single instance),' manner suffix (473) with ·le hearsay evidential, cf. FN 1. Head of juxtaposed independent clause.

[102]kʼál cf. FN 27 + epenthetic vowel harmonic with root vowel + kʼé cf. FN 99 with qà causative (545) + · stative mode (573.3). Head of independent clause which together with following dependent clause constitutes an independent sentence.

xʼáy kʼál-akʼé· was translated by Mr. Holder idiomatically as 'going to dance at another rancheria (village).' It literally refers to the act of carrying what has been called an 'invitation stick' used in preparing for ceremonies (Barret 1952:352-353). Barrett says it was used in inviting guests from another village to a ceremony, but here it is used to announce the arrival of guest ceremonialists at their own initiative. The 'invitation stick' is described by Barrett as consisting of short sticks of wormwood or willow, tied, each separately, into a string which was sometimes attached to a short wand, and which always had attached a short section of yellowhammer-feather mat as ornament. The number of sticks used was equal to the number of days intervening before the ceremony was to begin, according to Barrett usually not fewer than two nor more than eight. Each day subsequent to receipt a stick was broken off. According to Barrett the same sort of 'invitation stick' was used to invite people of another village in the case of a superabundant crop of fish or acorns for a trading feast, in which case a fish tail or an acorn would replace the yellowhammer-feathers as decoration.

[103]kʼi·yá general verb of doing + ba purposive, cf. FN 6.

[104]de·hél 'dig (in pre-contact time with digging stick)' with compounding of secondary stem du·kì· 'inceptive' (590, 593) + ·le hearsay evidential, cf. FN 1. Head of independent clause which together with preceding dependent clause constitutes an independent sentence.

[105]Cf. FN 104 + iy co-reference sentence connective, cf. FN 8.

[106]tʼé cf. FN 5 + ·l continuative manner suffix (475) + qà causative (545) + ·l hearsay evidential, cf. FN 1. Head of independent clause which together with the two preceding dependent clauses constitutes an independent sentence.

I asked in transcribing if Coyote found anything while digging the foundations for the Márakʰ (since in the other two versions he finds ta·ná· 'teal duck') and then suggested ta·ná· and Mr. Holder replied, "Yes, when he's digging he find that ta·ná· and he put him to work."

[107]kʼé cf. FN 99 + ·l continuative manner suffix (475) with aki allomorph of yaki plural agents (561) + ·le hearsay evidential, cf. FN 1. Head of independent clause which together with the preceding dependent clause constitutes an independent sentence.

[108]ló 'several to say' + m arrested development, cf. FN 41 with compounding of secondary stem du·lì constative, cf. FN 67 + ·le hearsay evidential, cf. FN 1.

Mr. Holder volunteered in transcribing that the squirrels are inviting Coyote for a dance just as the Eastern Pomo used to do, and are approaching as the Eastern Pomo used to approach. The visitors would go close to the visited village, stop, dress up in dance regalia and then dance as they moved along towards the Mârakʰ, singing. The chief would be standing there to welcome them and tell them to go in. They would stay there four nights and dance each night and finish up the morning of the fourth night at which time a big feast called ma·ʔáy di·qâ·kʰ would be served. During the period of four nights of dancing the visitors would be given something to eat twice a day--morning and evening--but not ma·ʔáy di·qà·kʰ.

A ground plan of a traditional Eastern Pomo Mârakʰ 'ceremonial house' is given below.

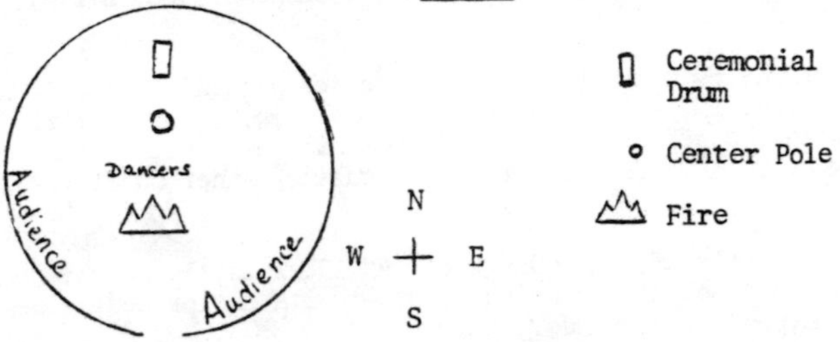

[109]ti·lí· 'make a clear, jingling sound' + m arrested development, cf. FN 41 + in co-reference sentence connective, cf. FN 18.

[110]ti·só· 'make a dull, jangling sound,' cf. FN 109.

[111]ló 'several to say' + yk̓ distributive plural continuative (cf. FN 12) with compounding of secondary stem du·lì, cf. FN 67 + ·le hearsay evidential, cf. FN 1: i → e/__·le. Head of independent clause which together with the two preceding dependent clauses in the song and the following juxtaposed dependent clause constitutes an independent sentence. The use of yk̓ here focuses on the individual voices of the ground squirrels singing (which presumably become more apparent as they approach) while the use of m with the same root in Sentence (43) emphasizes the constant, continuing sound they all make singing together, in which the individual voices are presumably not so distinct, as when heard initially at a greater distance.

[112]Cf. FN 107 + n allomorph of n co-reference sentence connective, cf. FN 18.

[113]káw 'towards/in enclosure,' directional preverb (840) + a + k̓è cf. FN 102 + ·le hearsay evidential, cf. FN 1. Head of independent clause which together with the following juxtaposed independent clause constitutes an independent sentence.

[114]káw cf. FN 113 + pʰi·lí 'several to travel' + ·le hearsay evidential, cf. FN 1. Head of juxtaposed independent clause.

[115]k̓i·yáyk̓ cf. FN 103. Head of verbal phrase, repeated for rhetorical reduplication, cf. FN 308.

[116]xa·ʔá· 'be dawn' + yax future suffix (565) + aday allomorph of iday switch reference sentence connective (cf. FN 2); x → q/__V. The aday allomorph of iday which follows post-velars had not been identified when McLendon 1975 was written.

[117]ba·qó cf. FN 15 + ·le hearsay evidential, cf. FN 1. Head of independent clause which together with the two preceding verbal phrases and the preceding dependent clause constitutes an independent sentence.

[118]pʰi·ráy 'laugh' with compounding of secondary stem k̓ì·yá + yk̓ cf. FN 103. Head of verbal phrase.

[119]c̓óqaxa 'tease by words, make fun of someone' + yk̓ cf. FN 12. Head of verbal phrase.

[120]Cf. FN 117. Head of independent clause which together with the preceding two verbal phrases constitutes an independent sentence.

[121]ma· cf. FN 31 + cʰé· 'second or third person's mother's brother,' kinship term

(654,670) + kinship reciprocal suffix (deriving a form descriptive of the relationship between an individual and the reciprocally related kinsman named) (668) + ma extentive plural (541) + qà causative + ·le hearsay evidential, cf. FN 1. Head of independent clause which together with the preceding dependent clause constitutes an independent sentence. This sentence then translates literally: The skunk girls [with] him were in mother's brother relationship, two [of them].

[122]Cf. FN 439 + x locative manner suffix (489) + ba purposive (572.3). Head of dependent clause.

[123]š̓a·t̓ó· 'burn brush, burn the house of a deceased person' (probably with a torch [cf. McLendon 1975:54, FN. 8]) (<ša· 'with a long object, particularly its point in close contact with the affected material, generally used with a thrusting, poking motion' + t̓ó 'reduce, take off a layer' + · focusing manner suffix (460) with ba purposive (572.3).

[124]xów cf. FN 47 + p^hi·lé cf. FN 309 + x cf. FN 122 with ·le hearsay evidential, cf. FN 1. Head of independent clause which together with the preceding dependent clause constitutes an independent sentence.

[125]k̓i·yáyk̓ cf. FN 115 + iday switch reference sentence connective, cf. FN 2.

[126]ki·má cf. FN 93 with compounding of secondary stem du·kí inceptive (594) + ·le hearsay evidential (cf. FN 1): i → e/__·le. Head of independent clause which together with the preceding dependent clause constitutes an independent sentence.

[127]$č^h$í adverbial indefinite interrogative, 'somehow, someway, how, what, which' (811) + ? ? + ki·yá· 'general verb of doing' + nk̓e allomorph of ink̓e non-visual evidential (of personal perception) (573.8), cf. FN 73. Head of independent clause within a sentence consisting of three independent clauses punctuated as a single sentence to reflect the fact that they were uttered separated by comma junctures (128) rather than period junctures (129).

[128]ká·y bi·t̓á idiom 'to feel good' (<bi· cf. FN 74 + t̓á 'feel, touch, have contact with' + · focusing manner suffix (460) with k^h punctual (536) + in co-reference sentence connective, cf. FN 18.

[129]k^húy negative verb stem with ink̓e personal perception, cf. FN 127. The appearance of the negative verb clause finally rather than clause initially, indicates it is acting as an independent verb, rather than as a negative marker (cf. McLendon in press, Section 17, 17.2).

[130]ká·y lé·m idiom 'to perceive activity (non-visually)' + epenthetic vowel with compounding of negative secondary stem k^húy cf. FN 117.

[131]yóx 'become' with compounding of secondary stem du·lí cf. FN 67 with nk̓e allomorph of ink̓e personal perception, cf. FN 127.

[132]ka·Nù cf. FN 83 + l durative manner suffix (474) with ·le hearsay evidential, cf. FN 1. Head of independent quotative clause which together with the preceding three quoted independent clauses and the following juxtaposed independent clause constitutes an independent sentence.

[133]ki·má cf. FN 93 + ·l continuative manner suffix (475) + in co-reference sentence connective, cf. FN 18.

[134]Cf. FN 1 with iy co-reference sentence connective, cf. FN 8.

[135]xól cf. FN 10 + epenthetic vowel + ká cf. FN 60 with y allomorph of iy co-reference sentence connective, cf. FN 8.

[136]Cf. FN 123 with ·le hearsay evidential, cf. FN 1. Head of independent clause which together with the two preceding dependent clauses constitutes an independent sentence.

[137]Cf. FN 59.

138 si·q̓á·l cf. FN 260 with ma extentive plural (541) + ňke allomorph of inǩe personal perception, cf. FN 73 + ·le hearsay evidential, cf. FN 1. Head of independent clause which together with the following juxtaposed clause constitutes an independent sentence.

139 Cf. FN 138. Head of juxtaposed clause.

140 Cf. FN 437. Head of independent clause which together with the preceding dependent clause constitutes an independent sentence.

141 Cf. FN 81 with ·le hearsay evidential, cf. FN 1. Head of independent clause which together with the following dependent clause constitutes an independent sentence.

142 qa·qá 'place in a container' + ba purposive (572.3), cf. FN 76.

143 kál cf. FN 31 + kʰi·dí cf. FN 32 + y allomorph of iy co-reference sentence connective, cf. FN 8.

144 qól 'downwards' directional preverb (840) + a epenthetic vowel, cf. FN 102 + ne 'long object to be extended, spread, frequently horizontally' + qan switch reference sentence connective, cf. FN 14.

145 kʰi·díl cf. FN 32. Head of embedded clause which translates as a relative, cf. FN 49.

146 ba·kú· 'something to fall' (<ba· cf. FN 24 + kú· verb of location indicating displacement down, away') with qan switch reference sentence connective (cf. FN 14).

147 ma·kʰú·l (<ma· 'with or affecting the foot' [424] + kʰú 'separate' + ·l continuative manner suffix [475]) with kʰ punctual (536) + ·le hearsay evidential, cf. FN 1. Head of independent clause which together with the three preceding dependent clauses--the last of which includes an embedded (relative) clause--constitutes an independent sentence.

148 du·bé (<du· 'with or affecting the fingers,' instrumental prefix [416] + bé verb of plural motion + · focusing manner suffix [460]) with R partial stem reduplication (520, 523) with ·le hearsay evidential, cf. FN 1. Head of independent clause which together with the following juxtaposed independent clause constitutes an independent sentence.

149 da·kʰo (<da· 'with or affecting the hand' + kʰó cf. FN 52) with ·le hearsay evidential, cf. FN 1. Head of juxtaposed independent clause.

THE COYOTE AND THE FLOOD

(Serrano)

Kenneth C. Hill

University of Michigan

Serrano is a Uto-Aztecan language formerly spoken around the San Bernardino Mountains in southern California. With the advent of the Missions, some speakers of this language retreated into the mountains, whence their name, Spanish for 'mountaineer'. Aboriginally Serrano may have had 1500 speakers (Kroeber 1925:617), but at the time of my field work in 1963-64, on the Morongo Indian Reservation at Banning, California, there were only about a half dozen speakers. How many of these survive today I don't know.

This story was told to me during the summer of 1963 by the late Mrs. Sarah Morongo Martin, who had learned it from her mother, Rosa Morongo. When I worked with her, Mrs. Martin had not been an active Serrano language story teller for some time. She was able to remember a number of stories without any help, but to refresh her memory for others, she referred to a copy of Ruth Benedict's 'Serrano tales' (1926), which she had been given some years earlier. The stories which Benedict published were in English and were rather sketchy. They had been told to her also by Mrs. Martin's mother, Rosa Morongo. The present story was published by Benedict as 'Coyote and Frog' (1926:15).

The story was tape recorded and the transcription is just what I hear on the tape. Here and there mistakes were of course made. Those mistakes have all been left in the written form of the story. Parentheses ( ) surround sounds that for some reason or other were omitted. (Word-initial glottal stops, though, are so highly unstable that I have simply written each word the way it occurred, without any special notation.) Fragments of words occurring in false starts (FS) are marked with a following slash /.

The transcription used here differs from transcriptions used elsewhere for Serrano (e.g. Hill 1967, 1969), the present transcription being a compromise between the technical symbols of linguistics and a practical spelling system. The sounds of Serrano are here represented as follows:

Vowels:		short:					long:				
	high	i		y	ỳ	u	ī		ȳ	ŷ	ū
	non-high	e	ə̀	a	à	o	ē	ə̂	ā	â	ō

Consonants:											
	stops & affricates	p	t	ţ	c̬	k	kw	q	qẁ	'	
	fricatives	f	s	ş	š	x		q̵	q̵ẁ	h	hw
	nasals	m	n		ñ	ng					
	laterals		l		ľ						
	tap (flap)			r							
	approximants	v	đ		j	ǥ	w				

đ, f, ǥ are found only in loanwords.

Notes on the vowels:

The vowels *à, â, ə̀, ə̂, ỳ, ŷ* are retroflexed, that is, they have a simultaneous *r*-like coloring, something like the American English vowels of *curve, star*. (The vowels *ə̀, ỳ* (and *ə̂, ŷ*) are somewhat difficult to distinguish in some contexts and I have probably made some errors here.) The use of the grave accent (ˋ) to mark retroflexion is based on the use of that diacritic by Miller 1967. The mark ˆ should be understood as a combination of ˋ, marking retroflexion, and ˉ, marking length.

The use of the letter *y* for the vowel [ɨ] (or [ɯ]) is for typographical simplicity. The palatal glide is represented with *j*. *Y* and *j* have these values in current transcriptions of a number of Californian and Great Basin area languages. I have chosen to use *y* and *j* in this way partly on the suggestion of M. Nichols.

Notes on the consonants:

Serrano *r* is a tap like Spanish *r* (not a trill like Spanish *rr* and not a retroflex glide like English *r*, Serrano *r* being unrelated to the retroflexion feature of Serrano vowels).

Kw, *hw* are *k*, *h* with *u* coloring and *qw̃*, *q̶w̃* are *q*, *q̶* with *∂* coloring. The vowel coloring symbol is not written when these consonants occur next to the vowel within a syllable. Thus *kwā'ţ* 'condor' and *kut* 'fire' begin with the same sound. Similarly, the *hw* of *maqahwt* 'dove' is the same sound as the *h* of *maqahum* 'doves' and the *qw̃* of *cēqw̃t* 'twin' is the same sound as the *q* of *cēq∂m* 'twins'. Also, *hu* before vowels, as in *māhua'n* 'burn', is the same sound as the *hw* of *maqahwt*, but *hw* before vowels, as in *wihwi'n* 'be shouting', is *h* followed by *w* (with *h* ending one syllable and *w* beginning the next).

F is labiodental but the other members of the *p* column are bilabial.

Sounds of the *t* column are dental, with *t*, *đ* being interdental (as in Spanish).

N has a retroflex allophone in non-stem-initial position next to retroflexed vowels (with or without an intervening glottal stop), e.g. *t∂̀n∂̂n∂̀'n* 'be black'.

Sounds of the *ţ* column are apicoalveolar and are conspicuously retroflex next to retroflexed vowels. (Does *n* belong here rather than in the *t* column?) *Ţ* itself varies from an apicoalveolar stop or affricate to a retroflex affricate next to retroflexed vowels. *Ţ* does not occur in stem-initial position.

Sounds of the *c* column are alveopalatal or palatal. *C* is [$t^{\check{s}}$]. *J* is voiceless when it occurs after a vowel within a syllable, e.g. *pājka'* 'to the water'.

Q is a uvular stop or affricate. The border between *q* and *q̶*, the uvular fricative, is unclear; perhaps they are the same phoneme. Similarly with *qw̃* and *q̶w̃*.

Other symbols:

A hyphen inside a word marks the division between a prefix and a stem or between a stem and a phonologically intimately connected enclitic.

Outside of words, hyphens (dashes) mark breaks in tempo within intonation contours or with incomplete contours. That is, external hyphens mark hesitation points.

A raised acute accent ( ) marks the peak of an intonation contour when it occurs on some syllable other than the contour-initial syllable. (Stress in Serrano automatically falls on the beginning of the word. If the first syllable is short, that is, if it consists of no more than a consonant followed by a short vowel, the second syllable is also stressed. Later syllables are more weakly pronounced.)

A period (.) marks the end of a descending intonation contour associated with a break in tempo. When there is no break in tempo at the end of such a contour a comma (,) is used.

A semicolon (;) marks the end of a (somewhat) ascending contour associated with a break in tempo. At the end of such a contour in the case of questions (where a somewhat greater rate of ascent seems to take place), a question mark (?) is used.

Glosses of certain grammatical categories are written in capital letters, usually abbreviated. The following abbreviations are used: ACC(usative case), DUB(itative modal), GEN(itive case), INF(erential modal), PL(ural number), QUOT(ative modal). Another abbreviation is FS (False Start).

I have attempted to gloss words in an invariant way (except for the introduction of English gender for pronouns and the occasional use of English 'the, a'). This leads at times to glosses that may be somewhat confusing, e.g. *hīt* 'what' may also mean 'something', *'ama'* 'that' may also mean 's/he', 'it', or 'the'.

My field work on Serrano was supported by the American Council of Learned Societies.

(1) Wahi' kwynyvy' - pājika' pôqp nym. (2) Kwynyvy' hakup hakwān.
coyote QUOT he PAST away on a road walk QUOT he PAST very be hungry

(3) Qai kwyn hīt 'a-rākw wyn. ajayp a-kī kwyn rȳwy'q. (4) Qai kwyn haīp
not QUOT what his food be because his house QUOT be gone not QUOT where

a-kī qaţ (5) Ama' kwyn - mia nymyi kwyn. (6) Qai kwyn hīt(i) haīp hī,
his house be that QUOT may walk QUOT not QUOT what (ACC) where see

(7) Qai kwyn huĭ'ti - tiŷha(q)ti - ąai kwyn hĭti hĭhĭ. (8) Kwyn oūp
not QUOT jackrabbit ACC cottontail ACC not QUOT what ACC see QUOT there

miāţu' (9) Kwyn "Uvia n hakwān mymy'q," qyi kwyn. (10) "'Ynānyi n tan hamin
go QUOT already I be hungry die say QUOT know I DUB I how

ñĭv," qyi kwyn. (11) "Tan ni-taą koutkiniv, (12) Ni-tŏ'ci tan koutkin(iv)
will do say QUOT DUB I myself will cut my belly ACC DUB I (will) cut

(13) Ami' tan - kuţiā'niv (14) Ami' tan - ny-şĭi tan - tyĭ'v. (15) Tan
and DUB I will make a fire and DUB I my guts ACC DUB I will roast DUB I

kwei'v," qyi kwyn. (16) Kwyn ajay' - kuţiā'nai kwyn; (17) Ajay' kwyn - 'a-/
will eat say QUOT QUOT then make a fire QUOT then QUOT his

'a-tŏ'ci koutkin; (18) Kwyn a-şĭv - 'a-şĭ kwyn húcq (19) Ani kwyn
his belly ACC cut QUOT in his guts his guts QUOT fall and then QUOT

amai tŷ' (20) Ani kwyn - kwa'i. (21) Ama' - uvia kwyn mŷ́nŷ', (22) Ama'
that ACC roast and then QUOT eat that already QUOT swallowed that

- ąai kwyn hamin qaţ, (23) Ivi' kwyn 'a-tŏ' mia 'ânŷ́'q, (24) Ama' kwyn āpiu' -
not QUOT how be this QUOT his belly may be open that QUOT from there

hucq - a-şĭ. (25) Mŏc kwyn curupkin (26) Kwyn - ama' uvia hucq, (27) A'/ -
fall his guts again QUOT put in QUOT that already fall FS

ajay' kwyn kuţān hŏ'ai 'amai 'a-tŏ'ci; (28) Kwyn ajay' miāţu'. (29)
then QUOT with a stick sew that ACC his belly ACC QUOT then go

"Ny-hun kiti' a'ai" qyi kw(yn). (30) Pājika' kwyn miāţu' (31) Ani;
my heart a little good say QUOT away QUOT go and then

āpiu' waqàt kwyn pyjyka' wĭ'n, (32) "Eja' wahi', qai cū́'n (33) A-taą
from there frog QUOT to him shout Hey! coyote not be ashamed himself

kwei't," qyi kwyn. (34) Qai kwyn jóū'kin, (35) Kwynyvy' oup miāţu'.
have just eaten say QUOT not QUOT pay attention QUOT he PAST there go

(36) Mŏc kwyn pyjyka' wĭ'n - (37) "Qai m' cū́'n, (38) My-tŏ'ci m' koutkin
again QUOT to him shout not you be ashamed your belly ACC you cut

(39) Ani m' my-taą kwa'i - (40) Qai m' cū́'n," qyi kwyn. (41) "Noū," qyi
and then you yourself eat not you be ashamed say QUOT no say

(kwy)n - (42) "Hakwānai n" qyi kwyn. (43) Kwyn ajay' miāţu'. (44) Ani mŏ́c
QUOT be hungry I say QUOT QUOT then go and then again

kwyn - pana' qyi; (45) "Tuma'q paika' tan mŷ́nŷ'kiniv," qyi kwyn. (46) "Ci'
QUOT like that say shut up away DUB I will swallow say QUOT you me

mŷnŷ'kiniv wary' jangq pāţ pūtkiv," qyi kwyn ama' waqàt. (47) Kwyn miāţu', (48)
will swallow yes but water will fill say QUOT that frog QUOT go

Mŏc kwyn qyi; (49) Ani kwyn ajay' w-/ - wahi' huânkin (50) Ani kwyn
again QUOT say and then QUOT then FS coyote jump at and then QUOT

wòpkin ama' waqàti ani mŷnŷ'kin. (51) Kwyn miāṭu'; (52) Kwyn pāṭ - 'à-nâvp.
grab that frog ACC and then swallow QUOT go QUOT water at his foot

(53) Pāv uvia miāṭu'. (54) À-nâvŷ' kwyn mī́ṣq. (55) Puju uvia kwyn
in water already go his foot QUOT get wet all already QUOT

a-tâmṭi picūṭu' pāṭ. (56) Uvia - tykuhpaka' kim; (57) Qaīv kwyn
his knee ACC arrive water already up come on the mountain QUOT

huâcq, (58) Kwyn óūp - huâcqṭu'. (59) Kwyn - wamat óūp wyn. (60) Kwyn ap
climb QUOT there go climb QUOT tree there be QUOT there

wamapa' huâcq. (61) Ap kwyn ngàqŷ'q a-kupiava', (62) Pāṭ wiṣip pūtq
on the tree climb there QUOT be perched above it water (?) fill

pyjān tykuhpaka'. (63) Wahi' kwyn qaṭ. (64) Pyṭ kwyn hahoūngan a-qaṭy', (65) Kwyn
far up coyote QUOT be so QUOT sad being QUOT

'a-wad pāv jū́vu'q. (66) Oūpiu' kwyny kim mahaqam. (67) Ani
his tail in the water be dangling from there QUOT they come cranes and then

kwyny pȳ-māi vâckin. (68) "Huânq 'īp. (69) Tac paika' jeī'v pāṭ
QUOT they their hands ACC spread jump here DUB we away will take water

'a-/ tiŷvaṭ 'a-wākīka'," qyi kwyny. (70) "Noū," qyi kwyn. (71) "Wary', tac ym-/ -
FS earth to dry say QUOT they no say QUOT yes DUB we FS

'ymȳmia(') hīñ'kiv, pajika' pyjān," qyi kwyny. (72) Ama' kwyn jyry'q ama'
with you will fly away far say QUOT they that QUOT try then stop that

wahi', (73) Kwyn mòc tiŷmq. (74) "Huân, huân," qyi kwyny. (75) Ajay' kwyn huânkin
coyote QUOT again fear jump! jump! say QUOT they then QUOT jump at

(76) Pynu' kwyny hīñi'k, (77) Kwyn ama' wahi' pāv hucqṭu', (78)
from him QUOT they fly QUOT that coyote in the water go fall

Pajika' kwyn - mymy'qṭu', (79) Ama' kwyn pāṭ ôvai't wā́q. (80) Oup kwyn āp
away QUOT go die that QUOT water right away dry there QUOT there

wahi' ýk - a-wāki'. (81) Cikṭ kwynymy' mū́cam oūvp. (82) Kwyn 'yk 'oū́p.
coyote lie dry just QUOT they PAST worms in his eye QUOT lie there

(83) Kwyn hawei't 'yk 'uvia 'a-wāki' (84) Ani kwyn 'a-pār - kim.
QUOT always lie already dry and then QUOT his older brother come

(85) Ama' - wanaṭ - kwynyvy' a-pār. (86) Kwyn picyi; (87) Kwyn
that mountain lion QUOT he PAST his older brother QUOT arrive QUOT

pyhpa' juhju', juhju'. (88) Kwyn cā́ṭu', (89) Kwyn cā́ṭu'. (90) Kwyn cáhcṭu' (91)
on him be crying be crying QUOT sing QUOT sing QUOT be singing

Ajay' kwyn - wahi't 'a-qâv kwāra'q; (92) Kwyn a-taqtqa' kwāra'q; (93) Puju
then QUOT coyote GEN his ear shake QUOT his body shake all

'a-taqtqa' kwāra'q; (94) Kwyn uvia hīk ama'. (95) Ajay' kwyn - hunei'
his body shake QUOT already come to life that then QUOT still

ama' - cāṭu' a-pār (96) Ama' kwyn uvia - kwȳṭqy' (97) Wahi' kwyn nȳpq.
that sing his older brother that QUOT already get up coyote QUOT sit

(98) "Tęany' kūman," qyi kwyn. (99) "Wary' - àṭa'kia'nai n (100) 'Ani -
INF I PAST sleep say QUOT yes be tired I and then

tęany' hucq (101) Ani n kūman." (102) "Kūman qyit. (103) A-mym'ki
INF I PAST fall and then I sleep sleep have just said dead

m'. (104) Pat 'ani n - cāṭu' ani m' hīk" qyi kwyn pyika'. (105)
you that and then I sing and then you come to life say QUOT to him

Kwyn ama' wahi' kwȳṭqy, (106) Paika' kwyn pynu' míh 'a-pāhi, (107 Ama'
QUOT that coyote get up away QUOT from him go his older brother ACC that

a-pār kwyn 'ap pynuk ap qaṭ.
his older brother QUOT there alone there be

Free translation

(1) A coyote was walking along a road. (2) He was very hungry. (3) There was nothing for him to eat because he had no house. (4) He had no house anywhere. (5) He was walking along. (6) He didn't see anything anywhere. (7) No jackrabbit, no cottontail - he didn't see anything. (8) He walked along there. (9) "I'm dying of hunger," he said. (10) "I know what I'll do," he said. (11) "I'll cut myself. (12) I'll cut my belly. (13) And I'll build a fire. (14) And I'll roast my guts. (15) I'll eat them," he said. (16) Then he built a fire. (17) Then he cut his belly. (18) His guts fell out. (19) And then he roasted them. (20) And then he ate them. (21) He had swallowed them. (22) There was no helping it. (23) His stomach was open. (24) His guts fell out of there. (25) He put them back in. (26) They fell out. (27) Then he sewed up his belly with a stick. (28) Then he went. (29) "I feel a little better inside," he said. (30) He went on. (31) And then a frog shouted over to him. (32) "Hey coyote! He's not ashamed. (33) He has just eaten himself," he said. (34) He didn't pay any attention. (35) He went on there. (36) Again he shouted at him. (37) "You're not ashamed. (38) You cut your belly. (39) And you ate yourself. (40) You're not ashamed," he said. (41) "No," he said. (42) "I'm hungry," he said. (43) Then he went on. (44) Again he said it like that. (45) "Shut up or I'll swallow you," he said. (46) "If you swallow me water will rise," said the frog. (47) He went on. (48) Again he said it. (49) And then the coyote jumped at him. (50) And then he grabbed the frog and swallowed him. (51) He went on. (52) Water was at his feet. (53) He was going along in water. (54) His feet were wet. (55) The water reached all the way to his knees. (56) It came up. (57) He climbed up a hill. (58) He climbed up there. (59) A tree was there. (60) He climbed in the tree. (61) He perched there on top. (62) The water had risen way up. (63) The coyote was there. (64) He was so sad as he was there. (65) His tail dangled in the water. (66) Some cranes came. (67) And then they spread their wings. (68) "Jump here! (69) We'll carry you off to dry land," they said. (70) "No," he said. (71) "Yes, we'll fly far away with you," they said. (72) The coyote tried then stopped. (73) He was afraid again. (74) "Jump! Jump!" they said. (75) Then he jumped. (76) They flew away from him. (77) The coyote fell in the water. (78) He died. (79) Right away the water dried up. (80) There the coyote lay dried up. (81) It was just worms in his eyes. (82) He lay there. (83) He just lay there dried up. (84) And then his brother came. (85) His brother was the mountain lion. (86) He arrived. (87) He cried and cried over him. (88) He sang. (89) He sang. (90) He sang a lot. (91) Then the coyote's ears shook. (92) His body shook. (93) His whole body shook. (94) He came back to life. (95) His brother was still singing. (96) He got up. (97) The coyote sat up. (98) "I must have slept," he said. (99) "Yes, I was tired. (100) And then I must have fallen. (101) And then I slept." (102) "Slept you say. (103) You were dead. (104) It's that I sang that you came back to life," he said to him. (105) The coyote got up. (106) He went away from his brother. (107) His brother sat there alone.

COYOTE BAPTIZES THE CHICKENS

(La Huerta Diegueño)

Leanne Hinton

University of Texas, Dallas

La Huerta Diegueño is a Yuman language spoken in Baja California, partially mutually intelligible with other dialects labeled as Diegueño. The language has not been described in detail; one other text is in print (Hinton, 1976), and a description of person-marking was published the same year (Hinton and Langdon, 1976). The present text was recorded by Sra. Alejandrina Murillo Melendres in 1969 and translated into Spanish by Sra. Maria Aldama.

(1) nčəʔák[1] šin--gayí·n šin ga·y xʷákəm[3] nʸɪhát[4] tuwátʸ[5]--- (2)
old woman one hen(Sp.)[2] one rooster (Sp.) together her stock they were

gayí·nhətʸ[6] poyí·t pəxkáy uʔwítʸ[7]--- (3) waná·č[8] saʔmáɨʸ sɔw a·r
hen chicks(Sp.) seven she had they went herbs eat go about

anʸíw saʔmáɨʸ sɔw taní·wčʸum[9] (4) xtpá šin pa· malík
they were doing it herbs eat they were doing it coyote one he came he was

kčám a·k[10] sɔw ma·wx ɨwárcum[11] (5) wi·w toyáw
unable all carry off eat not he was unable he saw (her) he was doing it

waʔa wi·š poyí·t šin nʸikʔínkum[12] a·k xašʔunúpx[13]---
door he said (emphatic) chick one you give me I'll carry it off I'll baptize it

nʸowáha[14] ma·p xašʔunúp waʔawʔwí xatəpáʔhač--- (6) exániyá·kum[15] ká·[16]---
my house carry it baptize it he said coyote very well take it away

(7) a·č[17] sa·w poyí·tha---(8) nʸɪʔiyá·yčəm[18] pa·č[19] šínkum
he carried it away he ate it the chick the next day he came another

ʔá·yəmʔeš[20] (9) komá·r---poyí·t nʸɪʔmít a·k
he took away again (emphatic) comadre chick another I'll carry it away

xašʔunúp šin tuwátʸ yeyɨít məsəʔɔ́wxəč[21]--- (10) ya·w a·č
I'll baptize it alone he is sad your son he took it he carried it away

sɔw--- (11) xašiyá·w xašunúp (12) nʸiʔinyá·yčum pa·č nʸɪʔmítʸ
he ate it deceive baptize the next day he came another

a·--- (13) na·č[22] kčáməɨ nʸa·č sɔw nʸucɔ́wč
he carried away he went all he carried them away he ate them he finished

(14)nʸapátʸ[23] i·· komá·r ka· kwɨw mɪnčakʷá·ɨ[24] nʸakúr xaɨunúp
them all when he came ah, comadre go see your children already baptized

nʸoá·y kʷaʔtá·y ɪnxá·s wa·r muʔwúwxʷítčəm[25]--- (15) exániyákom ka·
now they are(Sp?) big beautiful very they want to see you very well, go,

wʔawís gá·yhɪč--- (16) gayínxʌ ya·wč a· xətəpáxač ya·wč
he said the rooster the hen he took her he carried her off coyote he took

a· sáwya--- (17) sa·w nʸɪčáw pa·č--- (18)
her he carried her off he ate her too he ate when he finished he came

kompá·r piɬ mkomá·r msəʔtúm[26] yíwʔyus komá·r má·xʷítʔ[27]
compadre now your comadre she cries for you to come comadre she wants you to go

pɛy mayá·y mowahuʔič ma·k minčxakʷáɬ muwɨw--- (19) xaʔkʷáɬə
to them you reunite you will be you go your children you see your children

pɛy muwɨwyax[28] kur kʷatá·y nʸoá·y poyí·thætʸ--- (20) exániyʌ
to them go to see them too already big now they are the chicks very

witʸ gá·yhɪtʸ wa·--- (21) ya·wj a· hatpáhəč
well he said the rooster he went he took him he carried him off coyote

a·č sá·wye--- (22) nʸosá·w nʸočɔ́wčɪm[29] nʸá·mʌʔ---
he carried him off he ate him too when he ate him when he finished then

kʷnʸɪxá·tətʸ[30] pa muyú·č gayi·n nʸexát perdé·r
the owner of the chickens came what happened the chickens my stock to lose(Sp.)

awát̯ omoyú--- (23) maʔíč skʷič nʸinʔá·r[31]--- (24) šmɛy
they are gone what happened (?) who stand (?) robbed me to search

yuwá·čəm ɛ··· kʷɛvo kʷaʔtɛ́yš ʔwi kuwá·y ləmísʌ čiyɛ́yuwá·r
she went Ahh cave(Sp.) big stone underneath feathers there were a lot

(25) nʸípi nam sa·w nam poyí·t gayí·n čam ga·y kčám sá·wyə čam
they go (pl.) eat go (pl.) chicks hen all rooster all eat all

(26) pam nʸičaʔqhač tuwɨw nəmí yeyá·w nʸá·mʌ maʔíč
she arrived the old woman she saw she got furious she was now what

rárimǝs nʸámʌ lxox---
to do (emphatic) now all gone

Free Translation

(1) An old woman had a hen and a rooster. (2) The hen had seven chicks. (3) They went about eating herbs, eating herbs. (4) A coyote came; he was unable to carry off all of them. (5) He saw her at the door and said, "Give me one chick and I'll carry it off and baptize it---I'll carry it to my house and baptize it," said Coyote. (6) "Very well, take it away." (7) He carried the chick away and ate it. (8) The next day he came and took away another one. (9) "Comadre, I'll carry another chick away and baptize it. Your son is lonely." (10) He took it and carried it away and ate it. (11) He was deceiving them about baptizing. (12) The next day he came and carried away another. (13) He went and carried them all away and ate all of them, finished them all off. (14) When he came (next, he said) "Ah, Comadre, go see your children; they are all baptized now; they are very big and beautiful; they want to see you." (15) "Very well, go," said the rooster. (16) He took the hen and carried her off; Coyote took her and carried her off and ate her too. (17) When he had finished eating her, he came (again). (18) "Compadre, now your comadre cries for you to come; Comadre wants you to go and reunite with them, for you to go and see your children---(19) For you to go see your children, now the chicks are all grown up." (20) "Very well," said the rooster; he

went. (21) He took him and carried him off; the coyote carried him off and ate him too. (22) When he finished eating him, then the owner of the chickens came: "What happened to my chickens? They are lost, gone; what happened? (23) Who robbed me?" (24) She went to search for them; Ahh, a big cave, underneath a stone there were a lot of feathers. (25) They went and ate all the chicks, the hen; all of them; the rooster, all, they ate them all. (26) The old woman arrived and saw that, and she got furious; now what could she do? They were all gone.

Footnotes

[1] I have chosen to present this text in broad phonetic transcription, to make it as close as possible to the raw data. Dashes in the text stand for pauses. Below is a key that will allow an easy rewriting of the text in either phonemic (Americanist) or practical Diegueño orthography.

text symbol	phoneme (Americanist symbol)	Practical Diegueño symbol	text symbol	phoneme (Americanist symbol)	Practical Diegueño symbol
p	--*	--	w	--	--
t	--	--	y	--	--
ṭ (retroflex)	--	tt	ʔ	--	'
k	--	--	i	--	--
k^w	--	kw	ɨ	i	i
č	--	ch	ɪ	i	i
t^y	č	ch	a	--	--
v	--	--	æ	a	a
s	--	--	ɔ	a	a
š	--	sh	ɛ	a,e	a,e
x	--	--	ʌ	a	a
h	x	x	u	--	--
l	--	--	ʊ	u	u
l^y	--	ly	e	--	--
ɬ	--	ll	o	--	--
$ɬ^y$	--	lly	ə	--	e
r	--	--	i·	--	ii
m	--	--	a·	--	aa
n	--	--	u·	--	uu
n^y	--	ny			

The phonology of La Huerta Diegueño vowels can be sketched as follows:

(1) a --→ ɔ / ___w

(2) a --→ ɛ / ___y

(3) a --→ ʌ / [-stress] # (optional)

(4) a --→ æ / [-stress] [C, -back] (optional)

(5) i --→ ɪ / [-stress] (optional)

(6) i --→ {ɨ, u} / w___w

Note that all these rules apply only to short vowels. Long vowels are stable.
[2] Spanish loan words are marked in the translation by the abbreviation (Sp.).
[3] x^wak-m (two-comitative)
[4] n^y-xat (possessive-stock)
[5] t-wa-č (continuative-sit-past/present)
[6] gayi·n-xa-č (hen-demonstrative-subject)

*A dash means that the symbol used is the same as that in the first column.

7 u-wi-č (3-have-past/present)
8 u-na·-č (3-go(pl)-past/present)
9 t-ni·w-č-yu-m (continuative-continue-past/present/be(emphatic))
10 a·-k (carry: it: away-dependent-future-switch:reference)
11 ɬwar-č-yu-m (be: unable-past/present-be(emphatic)-switch: reference)
12 $n^{y}k^{?}$-in-k-m (you: to: me: (command)-give-dependent: future-switch: reference)
13 . . . $^{?}$-xašunup-x (I-baptize-future) (For person-prefixes containing /$^{?}$/, the /$^{?}$/ is infixed to a position just before the verb root. See Hinton and Langdon, 1976, for a more complete discussion of this phenomenon.)
14 n^{y}-wa-xa (possessive-house-demonstrative)
15 exaniya·-k-m (good-dependent: future-switch: reference)
16 k-a· (you(command)-take: it: away)
17 a·-č (take: it: away-past/present)
18 n^{y}-$^{?}$ya·y-č-m (temporal-next: day-past/present-temporal)
19 pa·-č (come-past/present)
20 a·-ya-m-$^{?}$-š (take: it: away-again-switch: reference?-?-emphatic)
21 m-sə$^{?}$aw-xa-č (your-offspring-demonstrative-subject)
22 na·-č (go(pl)-past/present)
23 n^{y}-pa·-č (temporal-arrive-past present)
24 m-nčak^{w}a·ɬ (your-children)
25 m . . . $^{?}$-wiw-x^{w}it-č-m (he: to: you-see-want-past/present-switch:reference)
26 m . . . $^{?}$-s-tú-m (she: to: you-formative-cry-switch:reference)
27 m-a·-x^{w}it (you-go-want)
28 m-wiw-ya-x (you-see-too-future)
29 n^{y}-čaw-č-m (when-finish-past present-switch: reference)
30 k^{w}-n^{y}-xat-č (the:one: who-possessive-stock-subject)
31 n^{y}. . . $^{?}$-n-a·r (he: to: me-formative-rob)

COYOTE AND CRANE

(Mohave)

Judith Crawford

Athens, Georgia

This short Mohave story about Coyote was told to me by the late Robert S. Martin and was recorded on tape, November 15, 1968, at his home near Ehrenburg, Arizona. Mr. Martin helped me with the transcription and translation of the story in January 1972.

The Mohave language is a member of the Yuman language family and is spoken by several hundred speakers living along the Colorado River from Needles, California to Ehrenburg, Arizona.

For more detailed grammatical information than I can present here, the reader is referred to Topics in Mojave Syntax by Pamela Munro. I have included in footnotes following the text and translation grammatical and lexical information on only special or unusual forms. I have presented this text in the same orthography as that of the preliminary version of A Mojave Dictionary by Pamela Munro and Nellie Brown.

I gratefully acknowledge the financial support given to me by the Survey of California Indian languages, University of California, Berkeley, enabling me to do field work on the Mohave language.

(1) nyakw?ech[1] ?aha kwa?uurly ivak. (2) ?achii satok[2] istuum.
crane water on the edge he sits fish he spears he gets

(3) ?achiihaan a?wetk ?achii chahnap[3] a?wetk istuum. (4) ithook
salmon he does humpback he does he gets he eats meat

vuwaam[4] isamk. (5) hukthar chudoorm, iyuuk
he moves here he looks at him coyote he spies on him he sees him

thuwaak. (6) 'kaa?we ke?eeyk[5] a?wim va?' im. (7) thinyuwaak,
he moves there how did he do it he did it huh he said then he moves there

'tha?a?wetpat?e, ?inyech!' etk. (8) thinyuwaak, iyemk ?a?iis
I can do that too I he said then he moves there he goes screwbean

takwerakwerk, ta?akyuulyk ta?ahaank[6] uunuuk aaviirk. (9) iyemk
he sharpens it he makes it long really he is present he finishes he goes

?ahpily[7] iyaak kamim, iihunyk tahpilym uunuuk
pitch he goes after he brings it on his nose he sticks it he is present

nyaaviirk. (10) kor[8] ?aha kwa?uurly ivak, uudoorm[9] vivak.
then he finishes now water on the edge he sits he waits he sits here

(11) ?achii chaam iyuuk vivake. (12) ?achii inyto?och idotm iyuuk.
fish a lot he sees he sits here fish little it is he sees

(13) 'humer valytaaytaahaanch vidiit ?iyuuk ?a?wiis,[10] duum
later very big one it comes this way I see I will do it then

?ithootahaank ?atootahaank,' etk, vivak iduum. (14) ?achiich
I'll really eat I'll be very full he said he sits here he is fish

viyaam nomaktk, vivakete,[11] ?achiihaan kwavalyteetahaan
it goes by this way he lets it go he sits here salmon which is very big

vidiikum,[12] iyuukum, 'nyath ta?ahaan ?a?wiith,'[13] etk.
it comes this way he sees it that one really I'm going to do he said

(15) kor uusaaptk, nyasachooqm, ?achiihaanch ithpeertk iduum.
by-and-by he spears it then he speared it the salmon strong it is

(16) kor idaawptk aawemk a?wim. (17) ?ahpily ulhuyulhuymotm.
then it takes him it takes him it does pitch he cannot loosen

(18) hamahak aawemm, ?ahaly ipuyk. (19) haly?anyoomtk, ?anyook
down it takes him in water he dies he disappears he is gone

uuwaalymotm. (20) kor nyamaamk.
he does not appear now that is all

Free Translation

(1) Crane sat on the river bank. (2) He speared fish with his beak and got them. (3) He got salmon and humpback fish. (4) He [Coyote] looked at him eating [fish], walking back and forth. (5) Coyote was spying on him and he saw him as he moved about there. (6) 'How did he do it, poor thing?' he said. (7) As he was walking back and forth there, he said, 'I can do that too!' (8) Then he walked around there, he went and sharpened a screwbean [branch], making it really long. (9) He went and fetched pitch and brought it back, and stuck it [screwbean branch] on his nose. (10) Now he sat on the river bank, waiting here. (11) He saw a lot of fish [go by] as he sat here. (12) He saw little fish [go by]. (13) 'Later I will see a very big one come this way and I will do [spear] it, then I'll really eat and be very full,' he said, as he sat here. (14) A fish went by him and he let it go, and as he sat here, a very big salmon came toward him, and he saw it, saying, 'that's the one I'm going to get!' (15) By and by he speared it, and after he speared it [a second time], the salmon was too strong. (16) Then it took him. (17) He could not loosen the pitch [from his nose]. (18) It took him down, and he drowned. (19) He disappeared, was gone, and never showed up any more. (20) Now that's all.

Footnotes

[1]Miscalled 'crane', or sometimes 'stork', this bird is actually Ardea herodias 'great blue heron'. The cognate form in Cocopa is $n^{y}ak^{w}$?á 'great blue heron'.

[2]satok 'he spears or catches it with his beak'. s- is an instrumental prefix 'to do with the hand, or with a small instrument (held in the hand)'.

[3]?achii chahnap is also sometimes glossed as 'suckerfish'.

[4]v- 'here, this way', uwaa 'be located moving here and there or back and forth'; -m denotes that the following verb has a different subject.

[5]ke?eey (sometimes recorded ke?ee) is variously translated 'poor thing! alas! ah me! he did his best!'

[6]ta?ahaan is variously translated 'real, really, good, very'.

[7]?ahpily is the pitch or glue-like substance from ?ithaav 'arrowweed' (Pluchea sericea).

[8]kor can be translated 'now, then, by and by'.

[9]uudoor 'to wait to ambush; to stalk game; to peek, spy upon, sneak up on'.

[10]-s 'evidential' indicates that the speaker has knowledge or evidence of the certainty or truth of an event.

[11]-ete is a complex and puzzling suffix which I tentatively analyze as: e a reduced form of i?i 'say', -t 'assertive', -e a reduced suffixal form of i?i 'say'.

[12]I have elsewhere hypothesized that /kum/ might be analyzed as -k 'present-past', /u/ a reduction of iduu 'be', and /m/ as -m 'different subject' (Crawford 1976).

[13]The use of -th here seems to support Munro's analysis of -h and -th as indicating 'unreality--clauses so marked include expressions of desire, hypothesis, or occasionally the future' (Munro 1976). This use of -th is rare in my notes, where it almost always indicates contrast and is translated 'but'.

COYOTE AND QUAIL

(Yuma-Quechan)

Lee Emerson A. M. Halpern*

Winterhaven, Calif. University of California, San Diego

The text that follows was narrated for tape recording by Lee Emerson in May 1976. A preliminary transcript was made from the tape by Halpern. In November 1976 the co-authors reviewed the tape and transcript together. In the course of this review Emerson corrected errors in the transcript and suggested some changes or emendations. A basic free translation was agreed on. Final editing of the text and translation as well as annotation were done by Halpern, who is therefore responsible for errors. The effort has been made to adhere as closely as possible to the originally recorded text, but the final version, as emended, is not an exact rendering of what is on the tape.

At the time of first recording the tempo of Emerson's narration was very rapid. Immediately following the first narration he gave a second version, at a somewhat slower tempo, of the same tale. The text presented here is the first version. Since the variation between the two versions is minor, the second version is not presented in full, but some of the variations, which are of grammatical interest or contain fresh detail, are presented separately or referred to in the notes.

In 1976 Emerson was in his mid-60's. He is thus somewhat more than one full generation younger than narrators recorded by Halpern in 1935 and 1938. These earlier recordings were made manually, therefore spoken at a slower tempo than the 1976 tapes. Reference is made in the notes to changes which appear attributable to either the generation or the tempo differences.

Emerson is a substantially complete bilingual, almost equally at home in English and Quechan. He has some Mohave blood. His clan affiliation is with a Mohave clan, and he is relatively fluent in Mohave, but he grew up as a speaker of Quechan. He belongs to the northerly (matxál^y cadóm) division of the tribe, and his speech contains some subdialectal differences from that of the southerly (kavé·l^y cadóm) division, to which most of Halpern's earlier narrators belonged. These subdialectal differences apparently were at one time greater than Halpern previously thought, but the matter has not been sufficiently studied to specify the differences in precise detail.

The story is a Coyote Story (xatalwé ku·ná·v) of the type told to children for their amusement. It reflects only one aspect of the Coyote character in myth and folklore--the buffoon, lazy, capricious, rather stupid, and without spiritual depth. In more serious tales the buffoon element is usually present but not necessarily dominant. The narrative style of the present tale is highly colloquial.

As many Yumanists have commented, sentence division in Yuman narrative often needs to be arbitrarily imposed by the editor. Narrators have the freedom to use various devices, including verb sequences, transition words and quotatives, to subordinate an apparent main verb to a following or preceding utterance. They may

*A. M. Halpern is deeply indebted to the American Philosophical Society and to the American Council of Learned Societies for financial support which enabled him to reestablish relations with the Quechan tribe.

also do the reverse, shifting from one actor to another without indicating subordination--in effect, from one sentence to another with no intervening pause. In the present text the editor has settled for a relatively fine division, relying as much as possible on intonational cues but overriding these at times in order to arrive at something that can be defended as having a discernible sentence structure and being short enough to present the minimum of difficulty to anyone who wants to try his hand at analysis.

The notes deal primarily with points not covered or not adequately dealt with in Halpern's previous publications. For basic morphology the reader is referred to Halpern 1946-47, which will be cited by numbers of sections of the grammar. In the notes to "Kukumat Became Sick" (Langdon 1976: 5-25) Halpern commented on some points of syntax not covered in earlier publications.

The orthography used here is as in Langdon 1976, differing from Halpern 1946-47 in the use of d rather than ð for the interdental spirant.

(1) xatalwé	ku·ná·v	vadán^{y},	xatalwéc[1]	ʔaxmám[1]	u·tú·rətək[2]
coyote	story	this one	coyote-nom	with quail	he plays hoop-and-pole

su·nó·k[3].	(2) u·tú·rək	su·nó·m[3],	u·tú·rək	su·nó·m	ʔaxmán^{y}[1]	amá·rək[4],
there they remain	he plays h-and-p	there they remain, and	he plays h-and-p	there they remain, and	the quail	he wins from him

amá·rək	vu·nó·n^{y}k[3],	ʔaxmán^{y}c[1]	ka·wíc	amá·r al^{y}aʔémət	k^{w}aʔe·y[5].
he wins from him	here he goes on doing until	the quail	anything	he doesn't win from him	poor thing!

(3) xatalwén^{y}c	ka·wéxayk	amá·rtək	amá·rtək,	n^{y}a·yú·c --	ʔaxmán^{y}c
the coyote	he still does something	he wins from him	he wins from him	things	the quail

n^{y}a·yú·	n^{y}u·wíc	cá·mel^{y}[11]	camí·m,	amá·rtək	amá·rtək	vu·nó·n^{y}k
things	he owning	all	he lays, and	he wins from him	he wins from him	here he goes on until

i·mís[6]	cá·məl^{y},	i·mísən^{y}	cal^{y}ók,	i·mís	caméxá[7],	ʔaxmán^{y}c	aʔí·m.
his pelt	all	his pelt	he plucks out	his pelt	he will lay	the quail	he says

(4) xatalwén^{y}c	amá·rtək	van^{y}a·yá·vək[8]	n^{y}a·dú·m[9],	"ʔi·má·ṭ
the coyote	he wins from him	when he keeps going along	when he does	my body

ʔacaméxa[7],	ʔi·má·ṭ	ʔacaméxa	n^{y}a·dúm[9],"	aʔétəm,	u·tú·rək	vu·nó·k.
I will lay	my body	I will lay	when it does	he says, and	he plays h-and-p	here they remain

(5) xatalwén^{y}c	n^{y}a·má·rtəntik,	n^{y}a·yú·k	van^{y}a·vák,	i·mís	ka·yúməm[10]
the coyote	when he wins from him again	when he sees	when he sits here	his pelt	he cannot see any, and

á·m[11]	ʔaxmán^{y}c	van^{y}a·vák,	"ʔé·,	ʔan^{y}vál^{y}[1]	mayémək,	ʔa·kó·y	mu·kaná·vəm
it ends	the quail	when he sits here	hey!	to my house	you go away	old lady	you tell her, and

si·vám,	mi·má·ṭ	aván^{y}	n^{y}amá·rtəm	adúm[9],	vi·mayá·k	maṭmakaná·vəm,
she sits there, and	your body	that one	I win from you, and	it is, and	here you go	you tell about yourself, and

ma·k^{y}íṭk[12]	van^{y}u·nó·k	mal^{y}úl^{y}cək[13].	(6) ʔavá·k	ʔan^{y}a·xá·mək[14]	ʔavá·mək
she cuts	when she goes on (doing) so	she cooks you	I arrive	at sundown	I arrive there

ʔasó·xá[7],"	aʔét,	xatalwén^{y}c	aʔí·m.
I will eat	he says	the coyote	he says

(7) n^{y}i·mánək	a·sawikawík,	ʔaxmán^{y}c	a·sawikawík	vi·yá·tk	van^{y}a·yá·k
there he goes	he waddles	the quail	he waddles	here he goes	when he goes along here

van^{y}ɜ·yá·k	ʔa·kó·yən^{y}c	si·vám	avá·m,	xatalwé	ʔa·kó·yən^{y}c	si·vám
when he goes along here	the old lady	there she sits, and	he arrives, and	coyote	the old lady	there she sits, and

avá·mkəm[15],	"ʔéy,	kamaláyəm	ʔu·tú·rək	vaʔu·nó·n^{y}k[3]	n^{y}a·má·m[11],
he arrives there, and	hey!	with rascal	I play h-and-p	here I go on (doing) until	it ends there

n^{y}amá·rək,	aʔím[15]	x^{w}ép[16]	aʔét,	ʔi·má·ṭ	ku·ʔé·y[5]	n^{y}amá·rtək	awétəm
he wins from me	he says	he finished it off		my body	poor thing!	he wins from me	he does, and

adú·m[9]	á·m[11],	viʔadí·k	n^{y}u·kaná·v	aʔím[17],	'avkayá·k	ku·kaná·vək'	aʔím.
he does, and	it ending	here I come	I tell you	he says	go somewhere!	tell her!	he says

(8) má·n^{y}c	n^{y}axman^{y}éwəc	mak^{y}í	adáwk	vi·dáwəm,	xaman^{y}éw	arúvəc
you	his sandal	anywhere	it sits	here it sits, and	sandal	dry one

vi·dáwəm	n^{y}á·va,	mal^{y}úl^{y}	madúm,	ʔan^{y}a·xá·vəm[4]	avá·k	asó·w	ʔéta[17]."
here it sits, and	this one	you cook	you do, and	at sundown	he arrives	he intends to eat	

(9) "tére,"	ʔa·kó·yən^{y}c	aʔí·m,	"tére	a·cu·vá·rəm[18],"	aʔét,
goodness!	the old lady	she says	goodness!	with his causing trouble	she says

"mak^{y}í	ka·wíc	kamí·m,	xal^{y}ʔáw	ka·wíc	awí·m	ʔasó·l^{y}[19],"	aʔétəm,
anywhere	anything	he brings, and	rabbit	anything	he does, and	I would eat	she says, and

"n^{y}axman^{y}éwvəc	ʔi·wá·	n^{y}i·péṭsa·[20]	u·ʔíc[18]	adótəm,	ʔal^{y}úl^{y}k	ʔawé·yxá[7],"
this his sandal	although	it confuses me	his saying	it is, and	I cook it	I will do it for him

ʔa·kó·yən^{y}c	aʔím.	(10) van^{y}a·vák	awí·m	al^{y}úl^{y}k	vi·dáwk,	n^{y}i·šadómpək.
the old lady	she says	as she sits here	she does (with it)	she cooks	she sits here	she goes straight ahead

(11) vadám[1]	xatalwéc	ʔan^{y}á·c	n^{y}a·xá·vəm	avá·k,	al^{y}úl^{y}m[37]	á·m[11]
by this	coyote	sun	when it sets	he arrives	she cooks, and	it passes

amák,	xaman^{y}éw	avác	amák	vi·vám	avá·k	xatalwén^{y}c.	(12) i·šá·l^{y}
it is ready	sandal	that	it is ready	here it sits, and	he arrives	the coyote	his hand

canák	a·cúpk,	"x^{w}ó·ţ,	xamá[21]	mu·n^{y}é·n^{y}[18]."
he puts down	he licks	gosh!	quail	its tastiness

(13) "'ʔaxmác'[21]	maʔétk,"	ʔa·kó·yen^{y}c	aʔím,	"man^{y}xaman^{y}éwən^{y}c
quail	you say	the old lady	she says	your sandal

adópk	a·dú·va[22].	xamác[21]	adú·l^{y}aʔém."	(14)	xatalwén^{y}c	n^{y}a·ʔávkəm[15],
it is entirely	it is doubtless so	quail	it isn't		the coyote	when he hears

"ʔé·,	xaman^{y}éwəc	adúm,"	aʔét.	(15)	"n^{y}á·n^{y}	ʔaʔí·l^{y}ʔaʔémək,	i·má·ţ
hey!	sandal	it is	he says		that	I don't say	his body

ʔamá·rtək	vadúm[9]	n^{y}á·n^{y}	ʔakanácəm,	mu·kaná·vək	n^{y}á·n^{y}	al^{y}úl^{y}	ʔaʔépk
I win from him, and	it is so	that	I instruct him, and	he tells you	that	cooking	I entirely say

ʔaʔávn^{y}ək[23].	(16)	n^{y}i·matí·š aʔétk	n^{y}a·dúm[9],	mak^{y}ím	ayémám,"	aʔét.
I hear until now		he wants to deceive you	if it is so	by where	did he go away?	he says

(17) "vadám[25]	ayémək	vi·yá·š[24],"	aʔétm[37]	u·šaʔórəm	n^{y}a·yú·k,
by this	he goes away	here he went	she says, and	she points with finger, and	when he sees

xatalwén^{y}c	san^{y}a·vʔáwk,	"ʔu·tí·š	ʔadáw	ʔayá·k	ʔak^{y}éxa	n^{y}a·dúm[9],"
the coyote	when he stands there	bow	I taking	I go	I will shoot him	when it is so

n^{y}a·ʔí·m	ʔu·tí·š	n^{y}a·štú·m	kan^{y}ú·mək[26]	vi·yá·k.
when he says	bow	when he gathers	he follows him closely	here he goes

(18) vi·yá·k	vi·yá·k	vi·yá·k	vi·yá·xayəm,	ʔaxʔá·c	ʔaxá	xan^{y}ól^{y}
here he goes	here he goes	here he goes	here while he still goes,	cottonwood	water	in pool

avʔáwk	al^{y}avʔáwk.	(19) n^{y}á·l^{y}[27]	ʔaxmán^{y}c	akúl^{y}k	ʔamá·y[28]	al^{y}vák,
it stands	it stands in it	onto that	the quail	he climbs	'way up	he sits on

i·mís	ka·yú·mək[10]	avadúm	xamér[29]	akúl^{y}k	van^{y}a·vák,	aván^{y}	ʔamá·y[28]
his pelt	he cannot see any	what he does	lacking	he climbs	when he sits here	that one	'way up

al^{y}vák.	(20) xatalwé	n^{y}a·vá·mək	ayú·kəm[15],	ʔamáţi·[30]	ʔxá[37]	n^{y}a·yú·xáyəm	
he sits on	coyote	when he arrives there	he sees, and	downwards	water	while he is still looking	

maţk^{w}i·šán^{y}c	al^{y}vák	n^{y}á·va	--	n^{y}á·n^{y}c	ʔaxmán^{y}c	adú·kəm[31]	--	n^{y}á·va
his shadow	it sits in	this one		that one	the quail	it is, and		this one

ak^{y}á·m.	(21) ʔaxál^{y}	ak^{y}á·m	vu·nó·k	maţk^{w}adáw	ʔi·pá	n^{y}a·ví·r	
he shoots	into water	he shoots	he goes on doing	in vain	arrow	when he finishing	

láwxəm[32],	xamán^{y}c	u·vák.
he looks back, and	the quail	he sits wherever

(22) "kaʔdómək	ʔawémək	ʔadáwel^{y}a	ʔayú·wú,"	n^{y}u·vá·k,	ʔaxá
I do how?	I can do	I would get him	let me see	when he remains	water

maxákəl^y	ʔapénəc	u·vám	kanáck,	xatalwə́n^{y}c.	(23) n^{y}a·kanáck	aʔím,
in underneath	beaver	where he sits, and	he instructs	the coyote	when he instructs him	he says

"ʔal^{y}šúca·[33],	aván^y	kakacʔíl^{y}k	avku·nó·k,	ká·p[16]	ʔayú·k	ʔaxmán^y
my y. bro.-voc.	that one	gnaw!	where go on doing!	fall	I see	the quail

ʔadáwú."	(24) "ʔaxóţk."	ʔapénəc	n^{y}i·ca·mánək	kacʔíl^y[34]	vu·nó·n^{y}k
let me get	it is good	beaver	there he starts it	he gnawing	here he goes on until

vu·nó·n^{y}k	vu·nó·n^{y}k,	n^{y}a·má·m,	ʔaxʔá·n^y	u·qalaqálələm[35]	ayá··š[24,28],
here he goes on until	here he goes on until	it passes that	the cottonwood	he makes it thin, and	it went

n^{y}a·pámək --
when it falls over

(25) n^{y}á·vil^y	awí·[34]	van^{y}u·nó·m	ʔaxmán^{y}c	n^{y}a·vák	ayú·kəm[15]
in here	he doing	when he goes on doing so	the quail	when he sits	he sees, and

a·švá·rək.	(26) n^{y}á·va	ʔa·švá·rək	ʔu·xáymətək[10]	ʔaʔím	ʔa·švá·r	al^{y}ʔaʔéməxa.
he sings	this one	I sing	I don't know how to	I say	I won't sing	

(27) ʔaca·švá·r[34]	ʔašéntək[36].	(28) n^{y}a·ví·rək	maţacé·vək	ʔaxmán^{y}c.
he singing things	it is one	when he finishes	he cures himself	the quail

(29) a·švá·r	xavík[36],	a·švá·r	xamók[36],	a·švá·r	a·cu·mpáp[36],	n^{y}á·va
he singing	it is two	he singing	it is three	he singing	he doing four times	this one

a·šu·vá·r	k^{w}aší·ntəm[18]	i·mísən^{y}c	acpá·m,	pús aʔím[16].	(30) n^{y}a·si·mánək
his singing	by the single one	his pelt	it emerges	it sprouts forth	it arises there

vi·dí·n^{y}k	vi·dí·n^{y}k,	a·švá·r	a·cu·mpáp	n^{y}a·má·m,	i·mís	mal^{y}xón^{y}c
here it comes until	here it comes until	he singing	he doing four times	it passes this	his pelt	his wing feathers

n^{y}a·má·m	l^{y}aví·k	ʔaxóţk	vi·vátk.	(31) n^{y}a·švá·rək	n^{y}a·ví·r	aʔím
it passes this	it is ready	it is good	here it sits	when he sings	when he finishing	he says

n^{y}i·mánək	ayérək	vi·yémək.
there he arises	he flies	here he goes away

(32)	xatalwén^{y}c	ʔamáṭ k^{w}adáwt	si·vʔáwk	canál^{y}k.	(33)	avác
	the coyote	empty-handed	he stands there	he loses him		that one

sak^{y}ín^{y}k	vi·yémtək.	(34) mó·,	n^{y}a·má·m,	vadám[25]	apáyəx[38].
he runs away	here he goes away	well!	it ends here	by this	it is used up

Free translation

(1) This Coyote story, Coyote and Quail were playing hoop-and-pole over there. (2) They were playing hoop-and-pole, playing hoop-and-pole, and he (the coyote) beat the quail, he kept winning until the poor out-of-luck quail didn't win anything. (3) No sooner did the coyote do anything than he won and won, things -- the quail bet everything he owned, and he (the coyote) kept on winning and winning until the quail plucked out his feathers, all his feathers, and said he was going to bet his feathers.

(4) When the coyote kept on winning (all the way), then, "I'll bet my body, I'll bet my body, that's what (I'll do)," (the quail) said, and they kept playing hoop-and-pole. (5) When the coyote won again and saw, as he sat there, as the quail sat there finally without any feathers at all, "Hey! You go to my house and tell the old lady who's there, I won that body of yours, and so, you go there and tell her about yourself, and she is to cut you up and cook you. (6) I'll arrive, I'll get there at sundown and eat," he said, the coyote said.

(7) From there he waddled, the quail went waddling along and went on and on and got to where the old lady was,--he got to where Old Lady Coyote was and said, "Hey! I was hoop-and-poling with the rascal, and finally he beat me, he cleaned me out, and in the end he won my poor body, so he wanted me to come here and tell you, he said, 'Go on over and tell her!' (8) His sandal is around here somewhere, there's a dried-up sandal here, and that (is what) you are to cook, and he intends to get here at sundown and eat it."

(9) "Goodness," the old lady said, "my goodness, the trouble he makes. He ought to bring something (from) somewhere--he should use a rabbit or something--for me to eat," she said, and, "This sandal of his bewilders me, but that being what he said, I'll cook it for him," the old lady said. (10) So, there she was cooking it, she went straight ahead.

(11) At this point, when the sun set, (Coyote) arrived, it was finished cooking and ready, he arrived when the sandal was ready there, the coyote. (12) He put his hand down on it and licked (his finger), "Gosh, what a delicious quail!"

(13) "You say 'quail'!" the old lady said, "It's your sandal, for sure. It's not a quail." (14) When the coyote heard (that), "Hey, it's a sandal," he said. (15) "That's not (what) I said. I won his body from him, and so, that's (what) I ordered him (to do), I most certainly (said that I) wanted him to tell you that that's what I wanted (someone) to cook. (16) He wanted to trick you, that's what. Which way did he go?" he said. (17) "He took off and went this way," she said, and the coyote, as he stood there, when he saw her pointing, said, "I'll get a bow and go and shoot him, that's what," and then he gathered up a bow and went following right behind (the quail).

(18) He went along, went along, went along, and no sooner did he go along than there was a cottonwood standing in a pool of water. (19) That (is what) the quail climbed up onto and sat 'way up on top of, without any feathers, (just) as he was (in his) bare (condition), he sat 'way up on top of that. (20) When Coyote arrived and looked, no sooner did he look down into the water than there was his (Quail's) shadow sitting in it, that--thinking that that was the quail, that (is what) he shot. (21) He went on shooting into the water, and when he had used all his arrows for nothing, he looked back, and there sat the quail.

(22) (Saying) "Let me see (if there's) something I can do to catch him," as he stayed there, he called on Beaver who was somewhere under the water, the coyote (did). (23) Calling on him he said, "Little brother, keep gnawing that so that I can look (for) it to fall and catch the quail." (24) "All right." Beaver started there and kept on, kept on, kept on gnawing until finally he whittled it down, and (there) it went, when it fell over--

(25) While (Beaver) was doing this, as the quail sat here, he saw it and sang. (26) I don't know how to sing that (song), so I won't sing it.

(27) He sang something once. (28) When he finished (that one) he doctored himself, the quail (did). (29) He sang two, he sang three, he sang four times, with each singing of this (song) his feathers grew, came sprouting out. (30) From that point it came on, came on until at the fourth singing, finally, his feathers and wing feathers were finally complete and sitting there in good shape. (31) When he finished singing, then, he started from there and went flying away.

(32) The coyote stood there empty-handed, he had lost him. (33) He (Quail) escaped and went away.

(34) Well, it's over, now it's all gone.

Footnotes

[1]Quechan case suffixes are described in Halpern 1946-47, 30. Hereafter -c *nominative* will not be specified in the word-for-word translation. Further explanation is needed concerning the base meanings of -m *ablative*, -k *locative* and -l^{y} *allative*. In broad terms, -m designates the point through which motion or action proceeds. Depending on the associated verb, -m can be glossed as *with*, *by*, *through*, etc. In some of the recent Yuman literature -m is designated as *comitative*; in Quechan the comitative meaning can be subsumed under the more general definition. *Locative* -k designates the point at which motion or action occurs. Depending on the associated verb, e.g., amán *arise* or adí· *come*, the most convenient gloss may be *at* or *from*. I have unfortunately used *locative* also as the label for the nominal suffix -i, which is not a case ending but supplies a more substantive element of meaning; perhaps it would be best to gloss it as *site*, *locus*, retaining the term locative to refer only to -k. *Allative* -l^{y} designates the point at which motion ends and can be glossed as *in*, *into*, *on*, *onto*.

For demonstrative suffixes of the noun see Halpern 1946-47, 28, 31. Suffix -n^{y} is glossed here as *the*, i.e., a person or thing already identified.

[2]Cf. verb u·tú·r with noun ʔu·tú·r *hoop-and-pole game*. See also Halpern 1946-47, 63, where the verb is recorded as u·tú·rv. In current Quechan, post-stress suffixed -v following a consonant appears to be regularly syncopated, a development already foreshadowed in the 1930's.

[3]Verb suffixes -k and -m interest all Yumanists. The distinction between them is stated by many as *same subject* vs. *different subject*. I prefer to distinguish between *predicative* (and coordinating) -k vs. *subordinating* -m. See further my discussion in Langdon 1976, 21-3. Here, as in Langdon 1976, I adopt the convention of glossing forms in -m as *...,* *and*.

The treatment of verbs containing -n^{y} *until* seems to contravene the normal distinction between -k and -m forms. I recall no case of -n^{y} followed by -m, while forms in -n^{y}k appear (only?) in subordinate clauses.

Note that stem u·nó· has the base meaning *be present (pl.)* but is often used to mean *be engaged in (sg. or pl.)*.

[4]There appears to be a trend toward lengthening stressed vowels of the stem when followed by r, also when followed by v, l^{y} and perhaps some other liquids. In the

1930's I recorded amár *win s.t. from*. Similarly I recorded ʔan^{y}a·xávəm rather than ʔan^{y}a·xá·vəm.

[5]*Diminutive* k^{w}aʔé·y~ku·ʔé·y was not recorded in the 1930's, doubtless fortuitously. Since it occurs following either verbs or nouns, sometimes encliticized with loss of accent, it can be regarded as a free form comparable to taʔaxán, k^{w}aʔác, etc., for which see Langdon 1976, 22.

[6]i·mís refers to human body hair, the pelts of animals, and the plumage of birds. There are specialized terms, e.g., mal^{y}xó *wing feather* and ša·víl^{y} *plume* for feathers other than down.

[7]The accent on -xa *future probable* appears variable and may be a rhetorical feature. I have no record of such an accent from the 1930's. On the other hand, in 1976 I consistently heard -úm *future probable*, which I never recorded as accented in the 1930's. Cf. Halpern 1946-47, 59.

[8]Evidently va-n^{y}a·-Ø-ayá·v-k, of which stem ayá·v appears clearly derived from ayá· *go, go along*; but I cannot connect the v of ayá·v with any previously identified morpheme.

[9]van^{y}a·yá·vek n^{y}a·dú·m appears as a normal case of the use of a behavioral auxiliary, since the two verbs agree in person. In ʔacaméxa n^{y}a·dúm there is no such agreement. There seems to have developed a pattern of using such forms in ways similar to English conjunctions, or as emphatics. Both n^{y}a·dú·m and n^{y}a·dúm could be glossed as *if that's the way it is; in that case; that's what (it is)*. Similarly vadúm (rapid speech for avadú·m ?) *it is so* comes to parallel the use of English *because*.

The forms aʔí·m, adú·m and awí·m, whether used as main verbs or as auxiliaries, are particularly subject to shortening of the accented vowel in rapid speech.

A possible prototype of this kind of usage of n^{y}a·dú·m and related forms is found in verb sequences of which the first member ends in -təm and the second is the auxiliary adú·m, the sequence being translatable as *because, inasmuch as (he does s.t.)*. In 1930's materials occasionally, at present quite frequently, the ending-plus-auxiliary, detached from the preceding verb, is used to introduce a new sentence, when it can be glossed tamadú·m (or təmadú·m) *therefore*. Similarly the ending -təsá· (-t *assertive* -as *dubitative* -á· *emphatic*) detached from any verb introduces a new sentence, when it can be glossed tasá· (or təsá·) *however, nevertheless*. These detached uses of təmadú·m and təsá· raise questions about the non-occurrence of schwa in pre-stress position (cf. Halpern 1946-47, 10, 11) and suggest a need to reconsider some other phonological questions.

[10]ka·yúməm~ka·yú·məm analyzable as ka- *anything* Ø- *3p* ayúm (< ayú· *see* -m *privative*) -m *subordinating*, the whole form = *he cannot see any*, which, in view of the wide range of meaning in Yuman languages of verbs of sensing, saying, etc., can be rendered *he cannot know, feel any*, hence, *he has none*. For *privative* -m, = 1930's -ma, see Halpern 1946-47, 41.8, 62.

Note privative -m in ʔu·xáymətək I don't know how to < u·xáy know how to. The schwa of -mə- is explicable phonologically as avoidance of an impermissible consonant cluster. The morpheme formerly had the shape -ma and yielded a "strengthened" m, equivalent to a consonant cluster in selecting a following ending, for which see Halpern 1946-47, 11. A form like walʸaʔə́miyú is at present more likely to be actualized as walʸaʔə́mú.

[11]The base meaning of á·m (which possibly includes -m away from speaker) is pass by, go past, e.g., si·ká·mek go on by over there! With prefixed nʸam-, containing -m ablative, the whole form nʸamá·m comes to mean it ends, it passes away, that's all, only that. Prefixed nʸam- can be regarded as a substitute for a noun with ablative ending. nʸa·má·m‿nʸá·má·m is clearly rapid speech for nʸá·vəm á·m ending with this, finally.

A verb subordinated by -m followed by a form of á·m yields a similar meaning. Thus i·mís ka·yúməm á·m In the end he had no feathers; finally he was featherless. Similarly alʸúlʸəm á·m She had just finished cooking.

cá·məlʸ, glossed as all, or more analytically in its entirety, contains the theme cá·m. If c- cause a bunch or cause (general), then perhaps cá·m to carry things to an end, a culmination; to accumulate; to aggregate.

[12]Theme a·kʸíṭ < a·-akʸíṭ was recorded in the 1930's as a·kʸéṭ. A shift from é to í after kʸ is found also in cakʸíw bite, earlier cakʸéw. Whether this shift reflects substitution of one pronunciation for another or a subdialectal difference is not clear.

[13]m- she→you alʸúlʸc (< alʸúlʸ cook -c ?) -k present-past. Thematic suffix -c in this case is evidently not collective plural but some kind of transitivizer not previously identified. Emerson commented that the morpheme specifies quail as the object to be cooked.

[14]ʔanʸa·xá·m probably rapid speech for ʔanʸa·xá·vəm < ʔanʸá· sun + axávəm it enters, and. The -k ending in sentence 6 ʔanʸa·xá·mək is unexplainable. Cf. sentence 11 ʔanʸá·c nʸa·xá·vəm. Version II also contains ʔanʸá· kʷaxá·m sundown, i.e., by the setting sun and ʔanʸá· kʷaxá·vəm.

[15]Verbs ending in -kəm are surprising, inasmuch as they appear to combine the -k and -m suffixes, which should be mutually exclusive. When questioned about such forms, speakers show discomfort and either deny they used them or suggest changes. Often they suggest substituting -təm (-t assertive) or simply eliminating -k and retaining -m. Possible explanations, none convincing, are: the Quechan have adopted a Mohave ending; the -əm is a collapsed form of aʔím and serves as if saying and so, and then; the -k suffix is so frequent that there is a tendency to transfer it to the stem. Cf. fn. 31.

[16]For reduced themes and their treatment see Halpern 1946-47, 42. Sentence 23 ká·p ʔayú·k where one would expect ká·p aʔí·m ʔayú·k.

[17]For verb phrases consisting of bare verb + aʔí·m see Langdon 1976, 22. viʔadí·k nʸu·kaná·v aʔím contains the further complication that viʔadí·k is coordinate with

n^{y}u·kaná·v and therefore is contained in the phrase, whose full translation becomes: *He wanted me to come here and tell you.*

asó·w ʔéta, rapid speech for asó·wú aʔéta.

18 In form a·cu·vá·rem is a gerund < a·cavá·r, which in turn < a·-c-avá·r. cavá·r (in the past or from other speakers recorded as cavár~cavárv) means *to fall short, be unable to manage*, hence, a·cavá·r *to make difficulties for s.o.* The gerund, being a noun form, is found with nominal endings, but rarely, as here, with *ablative* -m. See Halpern 1946-47, 65a. Cf., however, a·šu·vá·r k^{w}ašî·ntəm *with each (single) singing*, where -m applies to the phrase as a whole.

Note that with transitive verbs the gerund frequently refers to the object acted on, e.g., u·ʔíc *what he says*, whereas with intransitives it refers to the action, e.g., mu·n^{y}é·n^{y} *its tastiness* < man^{y}é· *to be sweet, pleasant*.

19 The construction of the quoted material appears simple, containing two dependent clauses and a main clause consisting of the one word ʔasó·l^{y} (ʔ- *1p* asó· *eat (meat)* -l^{y} *optative*). Emerson translates, *Whatever he brought, he should have brought a rabbit for me to eat.* This suggests that the tense-mode of the main verb controls the tense-mode of the subordinate verbs, so that one could translate, *He ought to bring something from somewhere--he should use a rabbit or something--for me to eat.* awí·m *do, perform, make* is here taken in the meaning *do s.t. with s.t., use (for a purpose)*. If the main verb were in the 3p, asó·l^{y} *he would eat*, the sequence would be coordinate, and there would be no problem. Cf. Langdon 1976, 23. But I have no other instance of the control of subordinate verbs by the main verb.

20 ʔi·wá· n^{y}i·pétsa·, with *dubitative* ending -sa·, is an example of a limited class of impersonal verbs, for which see Halpern 1946-47, 56b. The more frequent meaning is *to forget*.

21 The tape has ʔaxmá, but Emerson later corrected to the nominative, treating the word as quoted material, the nominative form being predicative, *(it is) quail*. Note also that the absolute form is sometimes given as xamá, which in the 1930's occurred only as a possessed form. Cf. Halpern 1946-47, 27.

22 Emerson stated that the form a·dú·va is identical with n^{y}a·dú·va, which is the form that occurs in the corresponding passage of Version II. There is now a tendency to drop initial n^{y} in context, especially after a word ending in k. Version II contains, e.g., pús aʔétk i·mánək (for n^{y}i·mánək) *it sprouted and starting from there* (cf. sentence 29, 30 above), and ʔamáṭ k^{w}adáwtək i·cpámtək (for n^{y}i·cpámtək) *he went out of there empty-handed* (cf. sentence 32 above). A possibly parallel development is the omission of prefix n^{y}i·-, for which see Halpern 1946-47, 55, from verb forms in which it used to occur regularly: al^{y}n^{y}i·dú·ck > al^{y}adú·ck *he thinks it over*, maṭn^{y}i·céwk > maṭacéwk *he transforms himself into*.

23 Again an unusual construction. ʔaʔépək ʔaʔávn^{y}ək alone is normally glossable *I am known to have said*. See Halpern 1946-47, 58. In the present occurrence it also follows al^{y}úl^{y} in a phrase with the structure bare verb + aʔí·m; thus, *I most certainly wanted (someone) to cook that*. It appears also, however, to be linked

in a similar phrasal construction with mu·kaná·vək, which, ending in -k, is coordinate in a sequence with al^{y}úl^{y}; thus, *I most certainly (said that I) wanted him to tell you that that's what I wanted (someone) to cook*. The corresponding passage in Version II is i·má·ṭ kal^{y}úl^{y}k ʔaʔépk ʔaʔáve *I certainly said "Cook his body!"*

[24] *Evidential* -š is at present used frequently with perfective force or by younger speakers as an all-purpose present-past indicator. The older shape of the morpheme was -ʔaš, and it typically occurred following *assertive* -t. Cf. Halpern 1946-47, 60. The steps by which -ʔaš > -š can be reconstructed as having followed two routes. By one route the glottal stop after -t was dropped and the vowel quality muted, whether or not simultaneously, a > ə. Thus from adú·m, adótʔaš *it did* > adótaš > adótəš, the last being a form in current use. By the second route, forms without -t became more frequent than those with it; glottal stop and vowel quality changed as in the first route: thus, ʔa·ví·rʔaš *I have finished it* > ʔa·ví·raš > ʔa·ví·rəš. Verbs with alternating stem-vowel quality which select *present-past* -^{V}m rather than -k (cf. Halpern 1946-47, 59) retain the lower quality appropriate to following -t: thus, adótʔaš > adóʔaš > adóʔš (a form still occasionally heard but requiring an inconvenient final consonant cluster) > adóš.

[25] vadám (vadá- *this* -m *ablative*) has both space and time reference, thus either *through here, in this direction* or *now, at this point*.

[26] Theme kan^{y}ú·m *follow closely* evidently < kan^{y}ó *follow (on foot)*, but the morphemes involved in the derivation are not identifiable. In the corresponding passage of Version II the verb is kan^{y}ók.

[27] n^{y}á·l^{y}, rapid speech form for n^{y}á·n^{y}ɨl^{y}.

[28] ʔamá·y for normal ʔamáy with rhetorical lengthening of the accented vowel. In the first transcription from the tape, aván^{y} ʔamá·y al^{y}vák was rendered as van^{y}má·l^{y}vək, later corrected by Emerson. Similarly ayá··š, with overlong accented vowel, for normal ayá·š.

[29] Emerson suggests emending to watxamér, but the difference between the terms is not clear to me.

[30] ʔamáṭi·, probably rapid speech for ʔamáṭn^{y}i. Cf. fns. 22, 27.

[31] Cf. fn. 15; of this form, however, Emerson comments that it means adú·k a·l^{y}ʔí·m *he thinks that it is, and*. The comment gains credence from the fact that adú/ó does not normally select *present-past* -k, but that adú·k (also aʔí·k *he says* and awí·k *he does*) indicates indirect quotation in circumstances where adú·m indicates direct quotation: adú·k aʔí·m *he says that it is* vs. adú·m aʔí·m *he says "It is."* This instance of -kəm supports the analysis -kəm ⩵ -k aʔím. The analysis suggested in Halpern 1946-47, 59 fn. 10 is insufficient. Cf. also sentence 25, ʔu·xáymətək ʔaʔím.

[32] láwxəm, perhaps rapid speech for láwxayəm *no sooner does he look back than*. But láw being a reduced theme, one would expect láw aʔéxayəm.

[33]Intercalated -l^y- characterizes Coyote's diction as compared with normal ʔašúca·.

[34]For verb sequences whose first member is a bare verb see Langdon 1976, 23. awí· van^{y}u·nó·m, however, may be explicable phonologically, final m being absorbed by following v.

[35]u·qalaqálelem, u·- causative qalaqál be thin, thinned down -m subordinating, but the second l is unexplained.

[36]1930's precedents would lead one to expect a prefixed a·- causative with each of the numerals, i.e., a·švá·r a·ʔašéntek, a·xavík, a·xamók as well as a·cu·mpáp; but there may be an undetermined semantic difference involved here. Cf. Halpern 1946-47, 37.

[37]Misc. phonological items: Sentence 30, n^{y}a·si·mánek = n^{y}á·si amának illustrates a common sandhi phenomenon, though in the 1930's the accent on n^{y}á·si was normally retained; cf. Halpern 1946-47, 18(c). Similarly sentence 14, xaman^{y}éwec (xaman^{y}éw sandal -c nominative), sentence 8, n^{y}axman^{y}éwvec (n^y- his xaman^{y}éw -va demonstrative), and sentence 13, man^{y}xaman^{y}éwen^{y}c (man^y- your xaman^{y}éw -n^y demonstrative -c) illustrate the rule that a series of three short open pre-stress syllables is avoided by syncope; see Halpern 1946-47, 13 (d).

There appears recently a tendency to avoid two open pre-stress syllables by the same process, especially if the second syllable begins in ʔ: kaʔdómek (ka- what? ʔ- 1p adóm can do -k) and ʔamát̪i· ʔxá (= ʔamátn^{y}i ʔaxá). Sentence 7, viʔadí·k can become viʔdí·k in rapid or, with some speakers, normal speech. There is a further tendency to eliminate ʔ when initial in a consonant cluster and at the same time to mute the preceding vowel: thus, viʔadí·k > viʔdí·k > vadí·k. If this tendency should become dominant, it could result in a peculiar paradigmatic shift affecting the pronominal prefixes:

ka-Ø-adóm-k = ka·dómek > ka·dómek how can he?
ka-m-adóm-k = kamadómek > kamadómek how can you?
ka-ʔ-adóm-k = kaʔadómek > kadómek how can I?
vi·-Ø-adí·-k = vi·dí·k > vi·dí·k here he comes
vi·-m-adí·-k = vi·madí·k > vi·madí·k here you come
vi·-ʔ-adí·-k = viʔadí·k > vadí·k here I come

See Halpern 1946-47 for shortening of long vowels of prefixes before ʔ.

In connected speech the final consonant of one word is often heard as the initial of the following word, a schwa which would appear in isolated pronunciation of the first word being dropped; thus, al^{y}úl^{y}em á·m > al^{y}úl^y má·m, aʔétem u·šaʔórem > aʔét mu·šaʔórem. In the present text, to avoid confusion regarding the status of -m, I have preferred to attach it to the preceding word, where it belongs morphologically.

[38]The sentence is the standard formula for ending a story, except that n^{y}u·páyk it is exhausted is normally used rather than apáyex. The final x of apáyex is unexplained.

Version II variants

The two versions do not correspond exactly in sentence division. Sentence numbers below refer to the Version I sentence to which the Version II material corresponds.

(3) i·mís cá·m calʸów vanʸu·nó·k vanʸu·nó·kem calʸˀíšketem, ˀaxmánʸc. As he went on and on trying to pluck out all his feathers, he became naked, the quail. calʸów = calʸówú let him pluck. Theme calʸˀíšk be naked.

(4) xatalwénʸc nʸa·má·rtentik, aˀím xatalwénʸc u·kaná·vkem, "i·má·ṭ macamí·m nʸamá·rem á·mxa." When the coyote won again, then, the coyote told him, "It (the) game) will be over when I beat you out of the body you are betting."

(5) kavá·m ku·kaná·vem mi·má·ṭ avánʸ alʸúlʸceva. Go and tell her she should cook that body of yours. kavá·m and ku·kaná·vem, both subordinated imperatives; cf. Halpern 1946-47, 59.

(6) ˀanʸa·xá·mek ˀavá·k nʸasó·wú. At sundown I'll come to eat you.

(7) nʸamá·rectem adúm ˀavá·tk nʸu·kaná·vek. Because he beat me, I come and tell you. For the -c in nʸamá·rectem, cf. fn. 13 above.

(9) ka·wíc akʸá·m kamétk, xalʸˀáw ka·wíc awí·m awí·lʸaˀémek, nʸaxmanʸéw aˀétk. He (should) shoot something and bring it, he (should) use a rabbit (or) something, (but) he doesn't do it, he says (to use) his sandal. ˀi·wá· nʸi·péṭsa· u·ˀíccem ˀawé·yk ˀalʸúlʸxá. It bewilders me, but I'll cook it for him according to what he told (you?). Of the geminate -cc- in u·ˀíccem, one -c is possibly a transitivizer; cf. fn. 13 above.

(21) láw aˀím nʸa·yú·k, ˀaxmánʸc u·vák, ka·ˀévalʸ calʸˀíškek. When he turned his head and looked, there sat the quail, unashamedly naked. Emerson translates ka·ˀévalʸ he didn't care, indifferent, unconcerned, unheeding. Analysis is uncertain: ka- what? Ø- 3p aˀé say -va ? -lʸ ? -va is possibly inferential, for which see Halpern 1946-47, 60. -lʸ could be either optative (Halpern 1946-47, 60) or in one's ...ing (Halpern 1946-47, 65b). The latter identification would be in better accord with the rules for suffix positions if -va is indeed inferential.

(22) Version II adds after this sentence: "ˀapéna·, ˀalʸšúca·." "á·," ˀapénec si·vák aˀávkem, "á·, ka·wíc má·rek, ˀancéna·." "Beaver, little brother!" "Yes," Beaver heard as he sat there, and, "Yes, what do you want, big brother?"

(23) For ká·p ayú·k Version II substitutes: avác awí··š apámem ˀayú·k,... I see that sway and fall down,... awí··š, rhetorically overlengthened awí·š sway, move spirally.

(24) For kacˀílʸ vu·nó·nʸk Version II substitutes: i·dó·nʸm i·dó· kʷašalašál nʸamawí·m kacakʸéṭ vanʸu·nó·k vanʸu·nó·k. With his teeth, using his protruding teeth, he kept on and on breaking it to pieces. i·dó·nʸm i·dó·, originally heard as i·dó·nʸ mi·dó·, cf. fn. 37 above.

COYOTE AND HIS DAUGHTER

(Cocopa)

James M. Crawford

University of Georgia

The Cocopa language is a member of the Yuman family. In earlier times the Cocopa lived in Mexico in the delta region of the Colorado River. Several hundred Cocopa still live in Mexico in this same general region. About an equal number are located in the vicinity of Somerton, Arizona. A few families live in the Phoenix area, for the most part, in the area west of Phoenix, between Phoenix and Buckeye.

In Arizona the language is viable and is spoken by all age groups. As a rule, Cocopa children do not become fluent in English until after they enter school. Many older speakers, as well as a number of middle-aged speakers, know little or no English, but are fluent in Spanish.

My field work on the language was conducted in Somerton and in Phoenix in 1963-65, 1967, and 1973. The text presented here is one of several told by Charlie Huck and recorded on tape in Phoenix in 1967. Born in Mexico, Mr. Huck has lived in Arizona for many years. Mr. Huck is relatively fluent in Spanish, but speaks little English. His ignorance of English, together with his reluctance to repeat verbatim from the tape the words and sentences of his tales, required the assistance of other speakers to put Mr. Huck's tales down in writing and to translate them. I am indebted to Victor Hayes, who, in the summer of 1973, worked with me in the transcription and translation of the present text. The specific wording of the translation is in most cases my own. Being already familiar with Cocopa syntax, I found Mr. Hayes's greatest contribution to be in providing the English for new lexical items. There are a few passages which Mr. Hayes found puzzling or ambiguous and there are a few which I did not inquire about, thinking I understood them, but later on became less certain of their analysis. However, in all cases I have provided translations and have remarked on the difficulties and uncertainties in the notes.

On the whole, a Cocopa text analysis presents few difficulties for an interlinear translation of morphemes. Being synthetic, its technique is mainly agglutinative and the affixes employed can usually be matched by approximate equivalents in English. The difficulties in the present text are caused mostly by the fixed position of the third person subject prefix, which is always before the consonant of the stem that immediately precedes the stressed stem vowel. In stems with two or more consonants before the stressed vowel, the third person subject is in effect an infix and the stem is discontinuous. In order to indicate interlinearly this discontinuity, I have resorted to the device of placing 'X' before the gloss of this prefix. 'X' in the interlinear translation means, therefore, that the Cocopa segment it matches is part of the stem morpheme whose gloss is given immediately after that of the prefix.

Hyphens separate the Cocopa segments and the corresponding interlinear glosses. 'Equal' symbols separate glosses of more than one word. The glosses in upper case letters are abbreviations. They are: 1PO first person object, 3PO third person object, 3PS third person subject, ADV adversative, AP animate possessive, CONT continuative, DES desiderative, DUR durative, EV evidential, FC future coordinating, FPP first person pronoun, FUT future, IMPER imperative, INTER interrogative, IN=P indefinite pronominal, IP indefinite pronoun, NEG negative, OBJ object (pronominal), PL plural, PPC present-past coordinating, REL=D definite relativizer, REL=I indefinite relativizer, S subject, SUB subordinating (switch-referent), TER terminal, TV thematic vowel. The functions of most of these categories have been described (Crawford 1976b:151-52). The functions of those not described are, except for TV thematic vowel, I believe, self-evident. The term 'thematic vowel' is described in note 7.

Support for field work was provided by the Survey of California Indian Languages (1963-65), Idaho State University (1967), and the Franklin College of Arts and Sciences of the University of Georgia (1973). This support is gratefully acknowledged.

(1) xṭpa-c ṣa-·-wá-c. (2) xṭpa-c ṣa-·-wá ma·m.
coyote-S there-3PS-sit-PPC coyote-S there-3PS-sit now

(3) n^{y}awí· p-u-sá·-p[1] kmuɨ^{y}[2] ṣa-·-wá-c y-u-xán^{y}[3]
thing X-3PS-daughter-? believe=it=or=not there-3PS-sit-PPC X-3PS-pretty

ʔin^{y}á·m-xan^{y} ṣxá·-ṣi-c. (4) y-u-xán^{y} n^{y}am[4] ma·m ṣy-u-xáy[5]
much-very girl-that-S X-3PS-pretty much now X-3PS-become=a=girl

pr-u-wí·-c[6] ṣa-·-wá-m xṭpá-pi-c p-a-·-wí·-c[7]
X-3PS-be=like-PPC there-3PS-sit-SUB coyote-this-S 3PO-TV-3PS-see-PPC

pwá·-c.[8] (5) 'xuṭ[9] psa·-c y-u-xán^{y} ʔin^{y}á·m. (6) kṭ-ʔi-k
he=hangs=around-PPC Gee! my=daughter-S X-3PS-pretty much IN=P-I=do-FC

wayá·-k p-a-n^{y}ín-x-ɨ^{y}' ʔa-c. (7) 'kṭ-ʔi-k
I=am=around-FC 3PO-TV-I=copulate-FUT-DES he=says-PPC IN=P-I=do-FC

p-a-n^{y}ín-x lu-yá·-m[10] pa-yá·-c'[11] ɨ^{y}-u-yú·m. (8) p-a-·-wí·-c
3PO-TV-I=copulate-FUT NEG-happen-NEG now-happen-PPC X-3PS-think 3PO-TV-3PS-see-PPC

šaɨ^{y} p-a-·-ʔá-m[12] ʔin^{y}á·m ṣ-pwa·-ṣ ma·m
crave 3PO-TV-3PS-he=says-SUB much there-he=hangs=around-ADV now

kṭ-u-ʔá-k ʔu-ʔá-x[13] lu-yá·-m. (9) ṣxá·-pi-c px^{w}ay
IN=P-3PS-he=does-FC 3PS-he=does-FUT NEG-happen-NEG girl-this-S good

ʔa-x lu-yá·-m n^{y}-u-wíɨ. (10) ma·m p-a-·-wí·-c
she=says-FUT NEG-happen-NEG X-3PS-refuse now 3PO-TV-3PS-see-S

ṣ-pwa·-c ṣ-pwa·-c.
there-he=hangs=around-PPC there-he=hangs=around-PPC

(11) cn^{y}am š-u-má-m ma·m wa-y waʔá· maká-y ʔu-yák
dark X-3PS-sleep-SUB now house-at door IP-at 3PS-lie

š-u-má-n^{y}. (12) n^{y}-ṣxá·-pi-c n^{y}y-u-yák[14] š-u-má-c.
X-3PS-sleep-also AP-girl-this-S there-3PS-lie X-3PS-sleep-PPC

(13) š-u-má-c ṣ-pwa·-m p-a-·-wí·-c
X-3PS-sleep-PPC there-she=hangs=around-SUB 3PO-TV-3PS-see-PPC

ṣ-pwa·-c ʔa-c 'ʔu· mapíl^{y} cn^{y}am n^{y}i·-p-a-pám-k
there-he=hangs=around-PPC he=says-PPC Oh! now dark there-3PO-TV-I=fall-FC

ʔi·ʔí·p[15] lu-ʔá-m[16] ʔi·ʔí·p-x pu-yá·-m'[17] ʔa.
I=hear what-she=says-SUB I=hear-FUT then-happen-CONT he=says

(14) ṣ-pwa·-c š-u-má-c. (15) xṭpá-pi-c wa-ɨ^{y}
there-he=hangs=around-PPC X-3PS-sleep-PPC coyote-this-S house-in

ʔu-yák š-u-má-m ma·m n^{y}-ṣxá·-pi-c cʔar maká-y ʔu-yák
3PS-lie X-3PS-sleep-SUB now AP-girl-this-S outside IP-at 3PS-lie

š-u-má-c ṣa-·-yák. (16) ṣa-·-yák ṣa-·-yák. (17) xṭpá-pi-c
X-3PS-sleep-PPC there-3PS-lie there-3PS-lie there-3PS-lie coyote-this-S

ʔu-páṭ š-u-má ka-·-yú la·x. (18) ṣa-·-yák ma·m.
3PS-lie=down X-3PS-sleep IN=P-3PS-be not there-3PS-lie now

(19) ʔaṣú-x ʔi-m s-u-pá-c pa-y wa-m.[18]
later-FUT it=says-SUB X-3PS-emerge-PPC here-at he=goes-away=from

(20) p-u-ṣí·-x ʔa-c. (21) ʔu-yú-c s-u-pá-c
X-3PS-urinate-FUT he=says-PPC 3PS-be-PPC X-3PS-emerge-PPC

p-a-·-yí·-c n^{y}-m-p-a-·-xáp[19] p-a-·-wí·-c.
here-TV-3PS-come-PPC then-away=from-3PO-TV-3PS-pass=by 3PO-TV-3PS-see-PPC

(22) ʔu-pú·-c[20] š-u-má-c ṣ-u-wán pu-·-yák-m
3PS-that=one-S X-3PS-sleep-PPC X-3PS-unaware there-3PS-lie-SUB

p-a-·-wí·-c p-u-ʔá·-c. (23) n^{y}-m-u-xáp
3PO-TV-3PS-see-PPC X-3PS-stand-PPC then-away=from-3PS-pass=by

pa·-c[21] maká-y p-u-ʔá·-c p-u-ṣí·-c ṣ-p-u-ʔá·-c
he=goes=along-PPC IP-at X-3PS-stand-PPC X-3PS-urinate-PPC there-X-3PS-stand-PPC

n-u-mák. (24) pa-·-yí·-c pwa-c[22] n^{y}-p-u-ʔá·-c
X-3PS-quit here-3PS-come-PPC he=arives-PPC then-X-3PS-stand-PPC

p-a-·-wí·-c p-u-ʔá·-c ma·m. (25) n^{y}y-u-páṭ-x[23] ʔa-c
3PO-TV-3PS-see-PPC X-3PS-stand-PPC now there-3PS-lie=down-FUT he=says-PPC

p-u-ʔá·-ṣ ma·m lá·x-c-a. (26) la·x-m n^{y}-m-u-xáp.
X-3PS-stand-ADV now not-PPC-TER not-SUB then-away=from-3PS-pass=by

(27) pa·-c[24] ʔu-páṭ ṣa-·-yák-ṣ 'láx-xan^{y}[25] ɨ^{y}-u-yú·m.
he=goes=along-PPC 3PS-lie=down there-3PS-lie-ADV not-very X-3PS-think

(28) 'xuṭ pi·-m n^{y}a-ʔá·-y-k n^{y}a-páṭ n^{y}ca·m-x.'[26]
Gee! this-SUB then-I=go-again-FC then-I=lie=down for=sure-FUT

(29) ṣa-·-yí·-k ma·m ṣa-y ʔu-mán[27] ma·m ku·r
there-3PS-come-toward now there-at 3PS-begin now little=while

ʔi-m s-u-pá-y-c ma·m. (30) ʔux l-p-u-ṣí·-m-x-ɨ^{y}
it=says-SUB X-3PS-emerge-again-PPC now Oh! NEG-X-3PS-urinate-NEG-FUT-DES

cu-·-yú-c[28] pa·-c[29] maká-y p-u-ʔá·-k-ṣ[30] p-u-ʔá·-c
DUR-3PS-be-PPC he=goes=along-PPC IP-at X-3PS-stand-FC-ADV X-3PS-stand-PPC

k-u-wá·k. (31) pa-·-yí·-c pwa-c[31] p-a-·-wí·-c
X-3PS-come=back here-3PS-come-PPC he=arrives-PPC 3PO-TV-3PS-see-PPC

p-u-ʔá·-c ma·m. (32) p-u-ʔá·-c p-a-·-ṣí·-c ma·m
X-3PS-stand-PPC now X-3PS-stand-PPC 3PO-TV-3PS-respect-PPC now

n^{y}-m-u-xáp-y-a. (33) pa·-c[32] wa ʔu-xáp
then-away=from-3PS-pass=by-again-TER he=goes=along-PPC house 3PS-enter

wa-ɬ^{y} ʔu-páṭ ṣa-·-yák ṣa-·-yák.
house-in 3PS-lie=down there-3PS-lie there-3PS-lie

(34) ku·r ʔi-m s-u-pá-c n^{y}-m-wa-m[33]
little=while it=says-SUB X-3PS-emerge-PPC then-away=from-he=goes-away=from

n^{y}-p-u-ʔá·-c p-a-·-wí·-c p-u-ʔá·-c p-u-ʔá·-c
then-X-3PS-stand-PPC 3PO-TV-3PS-see-PPC X-3PS-stand-PPC X-3PS-stand-PPC

p-u-ʔá·-c. (35) lax.[34] (36) n^{y}-m-u-xáp. (37) ṣu·-k
X-3PS-stand-PPC not then-away=from-3PS-pass=by there-toward

ʔu-yí·-c ma·m k^{w}-a-šíṭ[35] ɬ^{y}-u-wí·-c[36] ṣa-·-yí·-c
3PS-come-PPC now REL=D-TV-one X-3PS-seem=like-PPC there-3PS-come-PPC

p-u-ʔá·-c p-u-ʔá·-c ma·m n^{y}a-n^{y}á·k-x[37] pa-yí·-a.
X-3PS-stand-PPC X-3PS-stand-PPC now then-do=until=daybreak-FUT here-it=comes-TER

(38) l-š-u-má-m-c-a.
NEG-X-3PS-sleep-NEG-PPC-TER

(39) pwa·-c pwa·-c pwa·-c ma·m.
he=hangs=around-PPC he=hangs=around-PPC he=hangs=around-PPC now

(40) ma·m q^{w}lšaw-c psa·wp ʔi-c ma·m. (41) la·x xṣkay-c ma·m.
now daylight-PPC peep it=says-PPC now not still-PPC now

(42) q^{w}lšaw p-n^{y}a-yá·-m ʔa-c ma·m p-u-ʔá·-c ma·m
daylight here-then-happen-SUB he=says-PPC now X-3PS-stand-PPC now

'ʔu· pi·-m ʔa·-y-k ma·m n^{y}i·-p-a-pám n^{y}ca·m-x
Oh! this-SUB I=go-again-FC now there-3PO-TV-I=fall for=sure-FUT

pu-yá·-m.'[38] (43) ma·m ma·m q^{w}lšaw psawp[39] ʔi-m
then-happen-CONT now now daylight peep it=says-SUB

p-n^{y}a-·-yí·-c p-n^{y}a-·-yí·-c pwa-c[40] n^{y}-p-u-ʔá·-c
here-then-3PS-come-PPC here-then-3PS-come-PPC he=arrives-PPC then-X-3PS-stand-PPC

p-a-·-wí·-c p-u-ʔá·-c. (44) ʔuy ma·m n^{y}-p-a-·-ṣí·-c
3PO-TV-3PS-see-PPC X-3PS-stand-PPC Oh! now then-3PO-TV-3PS-respect-PPC

n^{y}-m-u-xáp-i·-c ma·m pa·-c.[41] (45) maká-y
then-away=from-3PS-pass=by-again-PPC now he=goes=along-PPC IP-at

p-u-ʔá·-c n^{y}xma[42] s-u-pás[43] šu-·-wín[44] ṣ-p-u-ʔá·-c.
X-3PS-stand-PPC penis X-3PS-pull=out X-3PS-hold there-X-3PS-stand-PPC

(46) ṣ-p-u-ʔá·-c ṣ-p-u-ʔá·-c ṣ-p-u-ʔá·-c.
there-X-3PS-stand-PPC there-X-3PS-stand-PPC there-X-3PS-stand-PPC

(47) ʔaṣú-x 'xuṭ pi··c n^{y}ma·m pi··n^{y} n^{y}kwin^{y} ma·m-c yu-ṣ.'
later-FUT Gee! this-S now this-OBJ finish complete-PPC be-EV

(48) l^{y}wa·y-c[45] pa-·-yí·-c pwa-c[46] n^{y}-p-u-ʔá·-c.
he=is=slow-PPC here-3PS-come-PPC he=arrives-PPC then-X-3PS-stand-PPC

(49) ṣ-u-wán-xan^{y} š-u-má-c pu-·-yák-c. (50) pu·-c
X-3PS-unaware-very X-3PS-sleep-PPC there-3PS-lie-PPC that=one-S

ṭu-·-mák pu-·-yák-m p-a-·-wí·-c
X-3PS-turn=over=onto=one's=back there-3PS-lie-SUB 3PO-TV-3PS-see-PPC

p-u-ʔá·-c. (51) ma·m l^{y}wa·y-c pu-·-wá-c n^{y}a·k[47] ʔa-c
X-3PS-stand-PPC now he=is=slow-PPC there-3PS-sit-PPC sit=down he=says-PPC

máṭ-i š-u-n^{y}á·p-c n^{y}y-u-wá-c[48] p-a-·-wí·-c.
ground-on X-3PS-lean-PPC there-3PS-sit-PPC 3PO-TV-3PS-see-PPC

(52) n^{y}-p-a-·-ṣí·-c pʔaw[49] ʔa-c p-u-ʔá·-c.
then-3PO-TV-3PS-respect-PPC stand=up he=says-PPC X-3PS-stand-PPC

(53) 'ʔuy n^{y}-n^{y}-a-wá·m-x[50] ʔí-y-a'[51] ʔa-c. (54) ʔawṣáy[52]
Oh! AP-1PO-TV-overpower-FUT it=says-again-TER he=says-PPC he=laughs

wa-ɨ^{y} ʔu-xáp. (55) pu·-c ṣ-u-wán š-u-má-c pu-·-yák.
house-in 3PS-enter that=one-S X-3PS-unaware X-3PS-sleep-PPC there-3PS-lie

(56) ʔu-yák ma·m. (57) wa-ɨ^{y} ʔu-yák ṣa-·-yák ṣa-·-yák ma·m.
3PS-lie now house-in 3PS-lie there-3PS-lie there-3PS-lie now

(58) q^{w}lšaw ma·m. (59) pu·-c ʔawk^{w}ák-i·[53] š-u-má-s[54]
daylight now that=one-S she=woke=up-again X-3PS-sleep-PL

ma·m š-u-má-s ma·m ʔu-mán. (60) p-a-·-wí·-c. (61) 'xuṭ ma·m
now X-3PS-sleep-PL now 3PS-get=up 3PO-TV-3PS-see-PPC Gee! now

n^{y}awí· l-kṭ-ʔí-m-xan^{y} ʔa-n^{y}á·k-m[55] pa-yá·-c[56] yu-ṣ.
something NEG-IN=P-I=do-NEG-very TV-do=until=daybreak-SUB now-happen-PPC be-CONT

(62) pa-yá·-m lu-ʔí-k wayá·-k p-a-xá·l^{y}
now-happen-SUB what-I=say-FC I=am=around-FC 3PO-TV-I=fool

p-a-n^{y}ín-x-ɨ^{y}' ʔa-c ɨ^{y}-u-yú·m pu-·-wá-c.
3PO-TV-I=copulate-FUT-DES he=says-PPC X-3PS-think there-3PS-sit-PPC

(63) ʔaṣú·[57] ʔi-m ma·m maká-y ku-·-yúm[58] pa·-c.[59]
later it=says-SUB now IP-at X-3PS-go=off he=goes=along-PPC

(64) xa-c ṣa-yák-m pwa-m. (65) xá-pi-c
water-S there-lie-SUB he=arrives-away=from water-this-S

ka-yú-m-x-a.[60] (66) si·ʔíɨ^{y} n^{y}awí·[61] ɨ^{y}-u-yák-m ka-yú-k
IN=P-be-CONT-FUT-TER fish something in-3PS-lie-SUB IN=P-be-toward

lu-yú-m ɨ^{y}-a-yák-m pwa-m-c[62] ʔu-wí·-c

NEG-be-NEG in-REL=I-lie-SUB he=arrives-away=from-PPC 3PS-see-PPC

ṣ-wa-·-yá·-c. (67) 'ʔu-pí·-ɨ^{y}[63] cpá-xan^{y} p-a-n^{y}ín-x-m

there-X-3PS-be=around-PPC 3PS-this-in for=sure-very 3PO-TV-I=copulate-FUT-SUB

n^{y}a-yá·-m xá-pi-ɨ^{y}' ʔa-c.

then-happen-CONT water-this-in he=says-PPC

(68) k-u-wá·k pa-·-yí·-c pwa-c.[64] (69) 'psa·'

X-3PS-come=back here-3PS-come-PPC he=arrives-PPC my=daughter

ʔa-c. (70) kmuɨ^{y}[65] p-awyá·-ṣ[66] ʔa-c ʔá-c-a.

he=says-PPC believe=it=or=not 3PO-he=knows-ADV he=says-PPC he=says-PPC-TER

(71) 'xa-c pu-yák. (72) si·ʔíɨ^{y} ɨ^{y}-wa-·-yá·-c ʔu-yú-ṣ.'

water-S there-lie fish in-X-3PS-be=around-PPC 3PS-be-EV

(73) 'n^{y}axán^{y}-a.' (74) 'waɨ pa-yá·-ṣ[67] n^{y}a·k[68] ra·r[69] p-a-yá·-k

really-INTER yes now-happen-ADV tomorrow we=work 3PO-TV-we=catch-FC

p-a-ṣáw-x-m[70] pa-yá·-c[71] yu-ṣ.' (75) ṣxá·-pi-c mṣ-u-pá-xan^{y}-c[72]

3PO-TV-we=eat-FUT-SUB now-happen-PPC be-EV girl-this-S X-3PS-excited-very-PPC

'px^{w}ay-c' ʔa ʔa-c.[73] (76) 'px^{w}ay-c' ʔa.

good-PPC she=says he=says-PPC good-PPC she=says

(77) ṣa-·-yá·w-c[74] ma·m. (78) ṣa-·-yá·w-c ma·m.

there-3PS-be=located-PPC now there-3PS-be=located-PPC now

(79) ṣa-y n^{y}a-·-mán[75] p-n^{y}-u-yíw-c-a.[76] (80) p-n^{y}-u-yíw-c

there-at then-3PS-get=up here-then-3PS-come-PPC-TER here-then-3PS-come-PPC

p-n^{y}-u-yíw-c n^{y}k-u-mís[77] ma·m. (81) xá-pi-c pu-yák

here-then-3PS-come-PPC X-3PS-arrive now water-this-S there-lie

k^{w}ʔás-a.[78] (82) pu-yák-m ʔa-c. (83) 'ʔu-pí·-ɨ^{y}[79]

that=which=he=said-TER there-lie-SUB he=says-PPC 3PS-this-in

wa-·-yá·-c ʔu-yú-m-a. (84) xa k^{w}-yák-pi-ɨ^{y}.' (85) 'm̥hm̥

X-3PS-be=around-PPC 3PS-be-CONT-TER water REL=D-lie-this-in Uh=huh

ka-yú lu-ʔí-m pu-yák yu-ṣ xá-pi-c.' (86) si·ʔíɨ^{y}

IN=P-be NEG-say-NEG there-lie be-EV water-this-S fish

wa-·-yá·-ṣ-m ṣxá·-pi-c l-awyá·-y-m-c.[80] (87) 'ʔą́hą

X-3PS-be=around-ADV-SUB girl-this-S NEG-she=knows-again-NEG-PPC Uh=huh

px^{w}ay-c ʔu-pá-y[81] k-pʔa·-k. (88) n^{y}a·-c ʔa·-k ṣu·-k man-k[82]

good-PPC 3PS-this-at IMPER-stand-FC FPP-S I=go-FC that-toward I=start-FC

n^{y}wil-k pa-yí·-k wi·-x pa-yá·-m.'[83] (89) 'px^{w}ay-c.'

I=shoo-FC here-I=come-FC I=see-FUT now-happen-CONT good-PPC

(90) pa·c[84] muxám ṣa-y ʔu-mán[85] ma·m n^y-u-wíl
he=goes=along-PPC a=short=distance there-at 3PS-start now X-3PS-shoo

k^wʔas.[86] (91) pa-·-yí·-c cu-·-yú-xan^y-c-a.[87]
that=which=he=said here-3PS-come-PPC DUR-3PS-be-very-PPC-TER

(92) pa-·-yí·-c pa-·-yí·-c ma·m. (93) n^y-ṣxá·-pi-c muxám.[88]
here-3PS-come-PPC here-3PS-come-PPC now AP-girl-this-S a=short=distance

(94) 'n^y-ṣxa· k-p-wa-k ṣ-k-n^ycín^y-xan^y[89] ṣ-k-yu-k yu-x-m
AP-girl IMPER-here-sit-FC X-IMPER-squat-very there-IMPER-be-FC be-FUT-SUB

maká-ɨ^y m-a-·-xáp-x-m p-m-ya·-x.' (95) 'px^{w}ay-c.'
IP-in you-TV-3PS-enter-FUT-SUB 3PO-you-catch-FUT good-PPC

(96) xá-pi-ɨ^y ʔu-wá-c ma·m ṣn^y-u-cín^y-c ṣa-·-wá-c ma·m.
water-this-in 3PS-sit-PPC now X-3PS-squat-PPC there-3PS-sit-PPC now

(97) pu-·c pu-·-yí·-c pu-·-yí·-c. (98) 'xuṭ psa·
that=one-S there-3PS-come-PPC there-3PS-come-PPC Gee! my=daughter

n^yi·-pwá·-c[90] ʔu-yú-ṣ. (99) p-u-táy-xan^y[91] ɨ^y-u-wí·-c[92]
there-he=hangs=around-PPC 3PS-be-EV X-3PS-big-very X-3PS-seem=like-PPC

ʔu-yú-ṣ.' (100) 'n^yaxán^y-a.' (101) 'm̥hm̥.' (102) 'px^{w}ay-c.'
3PS-be-EV really-INTER Uh=huh. good-PPC

(103) 'k-i·ʔí·p-k[93] m-a-·-xáp-x-m.'[94] (104) ma·m ṣa-y ʔu-yí·-c
IMPER-hear-FC you-TV-3PS-enter-FUT-SUB now there-at 3PS-come-PPC

ṣn^y-u-ʔúṭ ʔin^{y}á·m-xan^y xṭpá-pi-c-a. (105) ma·m n^y-ṣxá·-pi-c
X-3PS-have=an=erection much-very coyote-this-S-TER now AP-girl-this-S

ma·m l-awyá·-m n^yma·m pa-y n^ya-·-yí·-c. (106) 'k-i·ʔí·p-xan^y
now NEG-she=knows-NEG now here-at then-3PS-come-PPC IMPER-hear-very

m-a-·-xáp-x-m k-i·ʔí·p-xan^y' ʔa-c ma·m. (107) ka·p
you-TV-3PS-enter-FUT-SUB IMPER-hear-very he=says-PPC now quickly

pwa-c[95] p-šu-·-wín ṣxa· p-šu-·-wín-xan^y nap.[96] (108) ṣa-y
he=arrives-PPC 3PO-X-3PS-grab girl 3PO-X-3PS-grab-very hold=tight there-at

p-s-u-mí-c[97] p-a-·-n^{y}ín wa-·-yá·. (109) n^y-n^{y}wam-x[98]
3PO-X-3PS-lay=down-PPC 3PO-TV-3PS-copulate X-3PS-be=around AP-he=is=much-FUT

ʔa-c wa-·-yá·-ṣ n^y-ṣxá·-pi-c kan^{y}ác[99] ʔu-mí-c
he=says-PPC X-3PS-be=around-ADV AP-girl-this-S really 3PS-cry-PPC

p-a-·-n^{y}úp-c. (110) xṭpá-pi-c l-y-u-ʔí·p-m[100] ɨ^y-u-yák
3PO-TV-3PS-fight-PPC coyote-this-S NEG-X-3PS-hear-NEG in-3PS-lie

kr-u-ʔárk-xan^y[101] wa-·-yá·-c n-u-mák. (111) ṣxá·-pi-c ʔu-mán[102]
X-3PS-rigid-very X-3PS-be=around-PPC X-3PS-quit girl-this-S 3PS-get=up

p-a-·-nʸúp-c kmuɨʸ[103] wa-·-yá·-c ma·m.
3PO-TV-3PS-fight-PPC believe=it=or=not X-3PS-be=around-PPC now

(112) ṣ-u-kán ɨʸxa·y[104] ʔa-c pa·[105] ma·m.
X-3PS-run=away go=away she=says-PPC she=goes=along now

(113) xṭpa-c ma·m k-u-wá·k pwa-c[106] ṣa-·-wá.
coyote-S now X-3PS-come=back he=arrives-PPC there-3PS-sit

(114) ṣa-·-wá-c ma·m. (115) ṣkʷi·[107] ʔa-c ma·m.
there-3PS-sit-PPC now make=no=difference he=says-PPC now

(116) ʔu-šíṭ ṣa-·-wá ma·m. (117) pi·-m ma·m.[108]
3PS-one there-3PS-sit now this-away=from now

Free Translation

(1) There was a coyote. (2) There was a coyote now. (3) He, believe it or not, acquired a daughter who was a very pretty girl. (4) She was very pretty, right at puberty, and coyote hung around looking at her. (5) 'Gee! My daughter is very pretty. (6) How can I manage to copulate with her?' he said. (7) 'There is no way that I can copulate with her,' he thought. (8) He looked at her and craved her desperately as he hung around there, but there was no way he could do it. (9) [He knew] the girl would not agree and [would] refuse. (10) He kept on hanging around there now looking at her.

(11) At dark they slept and she too lay down somewhere near the door of the house and went to sleep. (12) The girl lay there and slept. (13) As she slept, he continued to look at her and said, 'Oh! Now it's dark and I'll fall down on her and find out what she says,' he said.

(14) She continued to sleep. (15) Coyote lay down to sleep in the house while the girl lay down to sleep somewhere outside. (16) She kept on lying there. (17) Coyote lay down and sometimes slept, sometimes didn't. (18) He lay there now.

(19) Later he came out and went off. (20) He had to urinate. (21) To do so, he came out, passed by her, and looked at her. (22) She lay there sleeping unaware as he stood looking at her. (23) He passed on by, went off somewhere, and urinated. (24) He came back and then stood there looking at her. (25) He intended to lie down there, but didn't. (26) When he didn't, he passed on by. (27) He went on and lay down and as he lay there thought, 'Not at all!'[109] (28) 'Gee! This time I'll go and lie down for sure.' (29) He came and started out and in a little while came out again. (30) He only pretended he wanted to urinate and went off somewhere and came back. (31) He came up and stood looking at her. (32) He respected her now and again passed by. (33) He went on into the house, lay down, and lay there for a while.

(34) In a little while he came out, went alongside [her], and stood for a long time looking at her. (35) Nothing [happened]. (36) Then he passed on by. (37) From then on now he kept doing the same thing until daybreak. (38) He didn't sleep.

(39) He kept on hanging around now. (40) Now daylight began to appear. (41) And still nothing [had happened]. (42) Then when daylight came, he said, 'Oh! This time I'll go and fall down on her for sure.' (43) So when daylight appeared, he came up and stood looking at her. (44) Oh! He respected her, passed by again, and went on. (45) He stopped somewhere, pulled out his penis, and stood there holding it.

(46) He kept on standing there. (47) Later [he said], 'Gee! This time it's got to be it!' (48) He slowly came up and stood there. (49) She lay there sleeping totally unaware. (50) He watched her turn over onto her back. (51) He slowly sat down on the ground and sat there leaning forward looking at her. (52) Then he respected her and rose to his feet. (53) 'Oh! It's going to get the best of me again!' (54) He laughed and went into the house. (55) She was unaware and lay there sleeping. (56) He lay down now. (57) He went into the house and lay down for a while.

(58) It was daylight now. (59) She awoke from her sleep and got up now. (60) He looked at her. (61) 'Gee! I didn't do a thing all night long. (62) What can I do to fool her so I can copulate with her?' he thought.

(63) Later he went off somewhere. (64) He went to where there was some water.

(65) There was not much water. (66) He went to some water where there was nothing but fish and other things in it. (67) 'I will copulate with her for sure in this, in this water,' he said.

(68) He came back. (69) 'Daughter,' he said. (70) Believe it or not, he knew who she was and said [her name]. (71) 'There is some water there. (72) There are some fish in it.' (73) 'Really?' (74) 'Yes, and tomorrow we will catch them and eat them.' (75) The girl was very excited and said, 'All right.' (76) She said, 'All right.'

(77) They were there now. (78) They were there now. (79) Then they started off and came toward it. (80) They came on and on until they got there. (81) The water was there like he said. (82) He said it was there. (83) 'They are in here. (84) In the water here.' (85) 'Uh huh. There's not much water here.' (86) The girl doubted if there were any fish there. (87) 'Uh huh. That's all right. Stand here. (88) I'll go over there and start shooing them as I come and let's see what happens.' (89) 'All right.' (90) He went a short distance and started to shoo like he said. (91) He came [toward her] really pretending [he was shooing fish]. (92) He kept on coming now. (93) The girl was a short distance away. (94) 'Girl, squat down with your legs spread and one of them might come into you and you'll catch it.' (95) 'All right.' (96) She squatted down in the water with her legs spread. (97) He kept on coming. (98) 'Gee, daughter! There's one around here somewhere. (99) It looks like a real big one.' (100) 'Really?' (101) 'Uh huh.' (102) 'All right.' (103) 'Be ready, for it might come into you.' (104) Coyote was now coming with a huge erection. (105) The girl didn't know about it as he was coming. (106) 'Be real ready, for it might come into you, so be real ready,' he said. (107) He came up quickly, grabbed the girl and held her tightly. (108) He stretched her out and copulated with her. (109) He was going to go at it strong even though the girl really screamed and fought at him. (110) Coyote, hearing and feeling nothing, lay in there very rigid and finished. (111) The girl got up fighting him and staggered around. (112) Then she ran off and went away. (113) Coyote went back home.

(114) He stayed there now. (115) It didn't matter to him. (116) He was all alone there now. (117) That's all now.

Footnotes

[1]nʸawí· pusá·p is literally 'he had something for a daughter; he daughtered something'. pusá·p is from psa· 'daughter'. I do not know the function of the suffix -p.

[2]kmuɨʸ is an invariable form, almost defying translation, which expresses ridicule, scorn, jocosity, amazement, and similar concepts.

[3]The stem is ʔi·xáʼnʸ 'be pretty'. Unstressed /i·/ becomes /y/ before a vowel.

[4]nʸam is a reduced form of ʔi·nʸá·m. It is pronounced here with high stress and high pitch, which, along with the shortening of the vowel, denote emphasis.

[5]The stem is ṣi·xáy 'be, become a pubescent girl' from ṣxa· 'girl who has reached puberty'.

[6]The stem is pri·wí· 'be similar to'. Unstressed /i·/ is dropped after /r/ before /u/.

[7]The term 'thematic vowel' glosses the vowel /a/ which is present before the onset of stems with the shape CV(C) upon the affixation of certain prefixes. Halpern (1946, 1947) treated Yuma stems (or themes, as he called them) of this sort as having initial /a/. This vowel appears to be epenthetic in Cocopa, but historically for Yuman it may be thematic.

[8]The only gloss I was able to get for pwa· is 'he hangs around'. Elicitation of 'I hang around' and 'you hang around' produced, respectively, pʔa· 'I stand' and mpʔa· 'you stand'. pwa· apparently means 'he stands around continuously' (cf. puʔá· 'he stands').

[9]xuṭ is a mild exclamation of surprise. 'Gee!' and 'Gosh!' were the only English glosses I was able to obtain.

[10]l(u)-...-m 'negative' is discontinuous. /u/ is present only when the prefixal element immediately precedes a stem of the shape CV(C).

[11]The prefixes pa-, pu-, and ṣa- ordinarily have temporal reference when affixed to ya· 'happen'. See Crawford (1976a) for a description of this usage.

[12]The stem is šaɨʸ ʔi 'crave', one of a large number of periphrastically inflected verbs, whose inflection for person takes place in the second element ʔi 'say'.

[13]ʔa 'he says' with the third person subject prefix ʔu- means 'he does'.

[14]The prefix is nʸi·- 'there, in an unspecified location'. /i·/ becomes /y/ before a vowel.

[15]ʔi·ʔí·p has the basic meaning 'hear', but is used also to express such notions as 'feel, discover, taste, try, be on guard'.

[16]This is homonymous with luʔám 'he didn't say'. 'He didn't do' is lawʔám.

[17]See n. 11.

[18]wa is the third person form of ʔa· 'go'.

[19]The basic meaning of xap is 'enter'.

[20]ʔupú·- is a pronoun, not a verb. The prefix ʔu- is probably not 'third person subject', as I glossed it here. I don't know what it is. It occurs also in ʔulú- (interchangeable with yulú-) 'that one (you know who I mean)'.

[21]The stem is paʔá· 'go along'. See Crawford (1976b:146, n. 2) for its analysis.

[22]The stem is pa· 'arrive'. See Crawford (1976b:146, n. 2) for its analysis.

[23]See n. 14.

[24]See n. 21.

[25]lax, reduced from la·x, here has high stress and high pitch, which denote emphasis.

[26]nʸca·m is a verb which is uninflected for person with the meaning 'it is certain, there can be no doubt'.

[27]The basic meaning of man is probably 'get up, arise', but it also means 'fly, begin, start out'.

[28]I have arbitrarily labeled c(u)- as 'durative', being aware that this notion does not cover all its functions. In its usage here it denotes pretence or deception. See Crawford (1976b:150, n. 95) for a discussion of this prefix.

[29]See n. 21.

[30]Even though -x 'future' does not appear further on in the sentence, I believe -k here is 'future coordinating'. I think that the narrator anticipated a form with -x, but failed to come through with it. The alternative analysis of -k as 'toward a point of reference' is unsatisfactory.

[31]See n. 22.

[32]See n. 21.

[33]This analysis of nʸmwam is undoubtedly correct, but scarcely reveals its meaning 'go alongside of'.

[34]lax is reduced from la·x. The shortening of the vowel adds emphasis.

[35]The meaning of kʷašíṭ is 'the same'.

[36]ɨʸwi· 'be like, seem like, resemble', homonymous with ɨʸwi· 'see in, look into', is apparently not further segmentable.

[37]nʸa·k 'do, remain until daybreak' is perhaps from nʸak 'east (toward the sun)'. nʸa·k also means 'tomorrow'.

[38]See n. 11.

[39]psawp is reduced from psa·wp, with the shortening of the vowel apparently indicating completive aspect.

[40]See n. 22.

[41]See n. 21.

[42]nʸxma is probably reduced from nʸnʸxma 'his penis', with loss of the first /nʸ/ (nʸ- 'third person possessive'). Prefixation of nʸ- 'animate possessive' to xma 'quail' changes the meaning to 'penis'.

[43] spas is more literally 'cause to emerge', with -s undoubtedly segmentable as a causative suffix. Cocopa has also cxpaɨ^{y} 'pull out'.

[44] šuwín has the additional meanings 'grab, stop'.

[45] This is the third person form of l^{y}a·y 'be slow'.

[46] See n. 22.

[47] n^{y}a·k ʔi 'sit down' is inflected periphrastically. See n. 12.

[48] See n. 14.

[49] pʔaw ʔi 'stand up' is inflected periphrastically. See n. 12.

[50] A large number of verbs have in prefixal position the element /n^{y}/ which seems to be part of the stem. In many verbs n^{y}- is segmentable and is present only when the reference is animate. Its function with verbs resembles that of n^{y}- 'animate possessive' with nouns. Although possession is not denoted when affixed to verbs (and not always when affixed to nouns), I have nevertheless retained the gloss 'animate possessive' to indicate this resemblance in function.

[51] Mr. Hayes took ʔíya to be a separate word, but an alternative and more satisfactory analysis would be to consider it part of the preceding word: -iy (from -i·) 'again' and -a 'terminal'.

[52] ʔawṣáy is the third person form of ʔu·ṣáy 'laugh'. Verbs whose stems have /u·/ in the syllable immediately before the stem syllable form the third person subject by changing /u·/ to /aw/.

[53] The stem is ʔu·k^{w}ák 'wake up'. See n. 52.

[54] šumás is undoubtedly a nominalization, which generally requires the plural form of a verb.

[55] See n. 37.

[56] See n. 11.

[57] This impersonal periphrastically inflected verb generally takes -x 'future', e.g., sentences 19 and 47, in which case /u/ is short. Without -x, /u/ is long.

[58] kuyúm is a verb of motion. It appears to be segmentable, but it is hard to know what to make of the segments. What is /k/? Is /yu/ the verb 'be'? Is /m/ the suffix -m 'away from a point of reference'? I do not know.

[59] See n. 21.

[60] ka- 'indefinite pronominal' apparently signifies here the scarceness of water. It is not clear why -x 'future' is suffixed. Perhaps the narrator anticipated the use Coyote intended to make of the water.

[61] n^{y}awí· 'thing, something' denotes the unnamed 'other things'.

[62] See n. 22.

[63] See n. 20.

[64] See n. 22.

[65] See n. 2.

[66] The stem is ʔu·yá· 'know'. See n. 52.

[67] See n. 11.

[68] See n. 37.

[69] ra·r is the collective plural of rar 'work'.

[70] ṣaw is the collective plural of ṣa· 'eat hard things'.

[71] See n. 11.

[72] The stem is mṣpa whose basic meaning is 'die'. This verb is frequently used to express anger, excitement, joy, and similar strong emotions.

[73] ʔac here, and probably also áca in sentence 70, is a quotative used by the narrator, which can be translated as 'they say' or 'it is said'.

[74] ya·w 'be located sitting, standing, or lying' is the collective plural of the verbs:

wa 'sit', pʔa· 'stand', and yak 'lie'.

[75]See n. 27.

[76]yiw is the collective plural of yi· 'come'.

[77]nʸkmis is the collective plural of pa· 'arrive'.

[78]kʷʔas contains the elements kʷ- 'definite relativizer', ʔa 'he says', and -s 'plural'.

[79]See n. 20.

[80]I do not understand the function of and need for -y 'again' in this word. The stem is ʔu·yá· 'know'. See n. 52.

[81]ʔupá- is a pronoun, not a verb. See n. 20.

[82]See n. 27.

[83]See n. 11.

[84]See n. 21.

[85]See n. 27.

[86]See n. 78.

[87]See n. 28.

[88]Some element or word seems to be missing in this sentence. muxám is an invariable form, not inflected for person.

[89]The stem is ṣnʸcinʸ 'squat with legs spread apart'. The position of k- 'imperative', which is the same as m- 'second person, subject/object', is unusual here. These two prefixes generally precede all other prefixal elements except the 'locative-temporal' prefixes p(a)-, p(u)-, and ṣ(a)-. They always follow the 'locative-temporal' prefixes, as illustrated in ṣkyuk, the next word in the text.

[90]See n. 14.

[91]The narrator gave the syllable /tay/ high stress and high pitch for emphasis.

[92]See n. 36.

[93]See n. 15.

[94]-m 'subordinate' (or 'switch-referent') is undoubtedly used here because the narrator intended to follow this word with one whose subject was different, but did not do so. Cf. sentence 106.

[95]See n. 22.

[96]ka·p, the first word in sentence 107, and nap are inflected periphrastically, but are frequently used alone, without ʔi 'say'.

[97]The stem is smi 'lay down a long object'.

[98]nʸnʸwam is the third person form of ʔinʸá·m 'be much'. See n. 50.

[99]kanʸác apparently cannot be segmented. It denotes emphasis and the sudden occurrence of an event.

[100]The stem is ʔi·ʔí·p. See n. 15.

[101]The stem is krʔark 'be in a rigid position with arched back', or as one speaker said, 'standing like a ground squirrel'.

[102]See n. 27.

[103]See n. 2. kmułʸ is used here to ridicule her movements after getting to her feet.

[104]The stem is łʸxa·y ʔi 'go away, run off'. See n. 12.

[105]See n. 21.

[106]See n. 22.

[107]The stem is ṣkʷi· ʔi 'be indifferent to something, have no choice'. See n. 12.

[108]pi·m ma·m is one of several stereotyped phrases used by narrators to signal the end of a tale.

[109]Mr. Hayes's freer rendition of Coyote's thought was 'I just couldn't do it!'

MOLLY FASTHORSE'S STORY OF THE GREAT WRESTLING MATCH

(Tolkapaya Yavapai)

Pamela Munro

University of California, Los Angeles

Yavapai is a language of the Upland or Pai branch of the Yuman family (Hokan stock) spoken in central Arizona. Some dialects of Yavapai, particularly that of the Verde Valley, have been extensively described by Martha B. Kendall (in her 1972 dissertation[1] and later works), but very little has so far been published concerning Molly Fasthorse's Tolkapaya (western Yavapai) dialect, except for a thought-provoking paper by Chung (1976).

Molly Fasthorse is now in her late sixties and believes that she is one of the last speakers of Tolkapaya. A long-time resident of Los Angeles, she recently retired and plans to return soon to a home on the Fort McDowell Reservation near Phoenix. Molly is a good friend and a resourceful and exciting teacher, equally adept at translating, explaining fine semantic distinctions, and telling stories. She remembers many old tales and reads a lot of ethnography and Indian lore. After I had asked her a few times for a coyote story for this book, she produced the following short tale, adapted from a traditional Yuman myth she had read in a book.

Molly's story is presented here in the practical orthography developed by the U. C. L. A. Tolkapaya class[2] (with capitalization and punctuation as in English), and my glosses and notes below draw upon discoveries made by my fellow Tolkapaya students, Lynn Gordon, Heather Hardy, Bonnie Glover, Jack Kriendler, Jeni Yamada, and Barnabas Forson. My understanding of Tolkapaya grammar owes much to conversations with all of them, with Molly, and with Margaret Langdon, Sandra Chung, and Stephen Anderson. I am particularly grateful to Heather Hardy and Lynn Gordon for discussion of this text.

(1) 'Kur-th-a[3]	'chpay-che	law-k[4]	va-m	hwaav-m
long ago	animals-SUBJECT	being many	around	roam

yu-ch-t-me,[5]	tkav-k	'i-ch-k-a,	"Pa-thpirv-k-yu-ch-che[6]
when they used to-DIFFERENT	they gathered	they said	a strong person

pa-thpirv-qyat-k-yu-ch-che	'-yoo-ch-me	pa-chkwiithv-h[7]	yii-k-yu-m,"[8]
a very strong person	we get-DIFFERENT	wrestle	he will

'i-ch-k-'-m.[9]	(2) Twi-k	'i-ch-k-a,	"Pa-ny-kpit-v-che[10]
they said	being some	they said	the Turtle-SUBJECT

pa-thpirv-qyat-k-yu-m.	(3) Nytha-che	ka-v-yu-ch-me[11]	hwak-k	pa-chkwiithv-h
is very strong	he-SUBJECT	with someone	being two	wrestle

yi-mo,"	'i-ch-k-'-m.	(4) 'Sit-e-k	'i-ch-k-a,	"Pa-ny-kthar-che
he may	they said	being others	they said	Coyote-SUBJECT

pa-thpirv-ny-qyat-ch-yu-m.[12]	(5) Pa-vyam-ch-yu-m.	(6) Nytha-che	hwak-k-a
is a very strong one too	he's a runner	he-SUBJECT	being two

chkwithv-ch-h yi-mo," 'i-ch-k-'-m. (7) Yu-ch-k-a chkwith-k vak unu-k[13]
wrestle they may they said now wrestling there they were

Pa-ny-kpit-v-che Pa-ny-kthar-m hwak-k-a pa-chkwiithv-k.[14] (8) Pa-ny-kthar-che
the Turtle-SUBJECT with Coyote being two they wrestled Coyote-SUBJECT

qyat-k-a hak unu-k: Pa-ny-kpit-v-a mak-a kvwekv-k yu-th-k
being very much there he was the Turtle his back turn on do perhaps

vwar-i. (9) Vwar-me,[15] Pa-ny-kthar-che man-k yu-ny-k mii-v-a
he tried he tried-DIFFERENT Coyote-SUBJECT fall he did too his feet

mat-ra-k-a, nyha-k vya-k 'im-t-me v-lwi-th-k-yu-m.
he really dragged there there when he lay down-DIFFERENT that showed it

(10) "Pa-ny-kpit-v-che pa-tkwil-k-wi-w-k-wu-m,"[16] 'i-ch-i. (11) "Pa-ny-kthar-
the Turtle-SUBJECT has won they said Coyote-

che Pa-ny-kthar-a pa-yev-h-che[17] mshayv-k," 'i-ch-k-'-m,
SUBJECT Coyote those who he was with-SUBJECT they are angry they said

"mshayv-k.[18] (13) 'Nyach-ch-pe[19] 'kwe nya-'-kav-ch-a pay-a '-yoo-ch-h-k
they are angry we-SUBJECT something our bet all we get it

'-unu-k-'-yu-m." (14) Pa-ny-kthar-v-ch 'i-ch-k-a, "Ka-v-yu-k-a 'nyach-che
we're going to the Coyote-SUBJECT they said somehow we-SUBJECT

'kwe kav-ch-k[20] '-war-k-'-yu-ny. (15) Pami-ka-v-yu-k-upe[21] 'kwe
something we bet we did too why on earth something

nya-'-kav-a '-yoo-ch-h-a 'um-h-a?" 'i-k. (16) Nytha[22] chawv-k hak
our bet we'll get it not they said them fighting there

unu-t-k-a, tu pay-a 'kur-m yam-ch-k-a tswakv-k 'kur-m yam-ch-k-a.
they were just all then going off they scattered then they went

(17) Nyu-v-yu-m-nya-'han-me[23] 'chpay-che nytha-m-pe tnwahv-k-a
that's why animals-SUBJECT from then on they are friends

'han-ch-h-a 'um-k-yu-m. (18) Tu mshayv-i.
they are good not just they are fierce

Free Translation

(1) Long ago, when all the animals used to roam around, they gathered together and said, "We will get a strong person, a very strong person, who will wrestle." (2) Some said, "Turtle is very strong. (3) He will get someone to wrestle with him," they said. (4) The others said, "Coyote is a very strong one too. (5) He's a runner. (6) He may wrestle," they said. (7) Now the fight was on, Turtle wrestling with Coyote. (8) Coyote was trying with all his might: he tried to turn Turtle on his back. (9) After trying that, Coyote fell down and dragged his feet on the ground, and when he lay down that showed [that he had lost]. (10) "Turtle has won," they said. (11) "Coyote really lost. (12) Coyote and those on Coyote's side are angry," they said, "they are angry. (13) Those of us [who bet on Turtle] are going to get the full amount of our bet." (14) [The supporters of] Coyote said, "Well, we bet something too. (15) Why on earth don't we get what we bet?" (16) Then they got in

a fight, and then all of them went off and scattered. (17) That's why the animals haven't been good friends since then. (18) They are just hostile.

Footnotes

[1] The dissertation has been published in revised form (Kendall 1976), but I have not yet consulted the newer version.

[2] In this orthography, ch represents [č], kw (with no intervening boundary) represents [kʷ], ' represents [ʔ], th represents [θ], sh represents [š], ny represents [nʸ], and doubled vowels are long. It should be noted that in speech many consonant clusters (particularly those in inital and post-stress positions) are broken up by inserted [ə] vowels.

[3] The interlinear glosses used here are designed to give an informal feeling for the arrangement of the text while staying as close as possible to its grammatical structure. Two grammatical morphemes are indicated in the glosses to aid the reader in seeing the relationship of words and phrases: SUBJECT follows nouns marked with the subject case suffix -ch(e); DIFFERENT follows verbs marked with the different-subject subordinator -m(e), which shows that a verb's subject is different from that of some following verb. (Deviations from these accepted usages are indicated below.) Otherwise, a noun without the gloss -SUBJECT is assumed to fill some other case role than that of subject, and a subordinate verb without -DIFFERENT is assumed to have either explicit or inferred same-subject status.

I use hyphens, for the most part, to separate inflectional affixes from each other and from the stems to which they are attached. This poses a problem with various types of derived verb stems, which my glosses below generally show to be (inflectionally) non-complex. For instance, the very common -v suffix (sometimes called "passive") seems to effect many unpredictable meaning shifts (for discussion, see Yamada 1977), so I have analyzed it below as part of the verb stem. A similar problem arises with plural verbs. Most verbs indicate plural subject by the suffixation of -ch. I regard this process as regular/inflectional, and I segment all plural -ch's below. However, a minority of verbs form their plurals by quantitative or qualitative ablaut of the stressed root vowel (see Hardy 1977a). I regard this process as one which must be lexically marked, and have made no attempt to segment such vowels in the Tolkapaya text.

A very large number of Tolkapaya "adverbs" and "conjunctions" are actually verbs --consider yu-th-k in sentence (8) and yu-ny-k in sentence (9), which might, perhaps, have been glossed 'perhaps' and 'and'. Both of these are forms of yu 'be', but the problem of how to treat them in a synchronic grammar is a very difficult one. In general, I have used a verbal translation in cases when the verb involved is capable of person-marking and other verbal inflection, but if I were to make these decisions again next month, some of my glosses might well be different. (An example of a yu adverb that (I believe) fails my person-marking test is yu-ch-k-a, glossed 'now' in sentence (7) because that is how Molly translated it. But the ch in that word is suspicious, and may suggest some agreement with the plural subject of the sentence.)

[4] The '-ing' translation is used on "modifying" verbs marked with the same-subject subordinator -k (which contrasts with -m; cf. fn. 3). It is usual in Yuman for quantifiers like 'many' to receive full verbal marking--cf. also 'some' (sentence (2)), 'two' (sentence (3)). An exception in Tolkapaya is 'all' (pay-a, sentences (13) and (16) below), an uninflected particle which looks more like a noun than a verb.

[5] Hwaav-m yu-ch-t-me illustrates a habitual construction (discussed in Kendall 1975) in which a main verb marked with -m is followed by an appropriate existential auxiliary (see fn. 9)--here yu 'be'--marked with the suffix -ch-, which generally shows that a verb has a plural subject. The -ch- marking is, then, a regular feature of this construction, used even when a verb has a semantically singular subject. It is the verb before the auxiliary which shows the plurality of the nominal subject--and, indeed, hwaav 'roam' is apparently restricted to plural subjects.

The temporal relationship shown by the -t- suffix following the habitual auxiliary has been insightfully treated by Hardy and Gordon (1977) and Hardy (1977b)

--cf. also Crook (1976).

I find the different-subject -m on yu-ch-t-me puzzling, since it would seem that the subject of 'when they used to roam'--namely, 'animals'--is also the subject of both the immediately following verb, 'gather', and of the highest verb of the sentence, 'say'. There are two possible explanations for this use of -m, I think. First, it might indicate that only a subset of the many animals roaming around were actually gathered together to talk. (Langdon and Munro (1975) report that in a minority of cases Yuman speakers do use the -m suffix to show that a subset of a group is "different" from the whole group.) Second, and more intriguingly, this -m may show that the subject of the m-marked verb yu is not 'animals' but something else--possibly, then, hwaav-m yu-ch-t-me should be translated as 'there were many instances of their roaming around'. (I discuss other such instances of -m marking on sentential subjects in more detail in Munro (1976).) This would be consistent with the appearance of -m on hwaav-, which has so far resisted syntactic explanation (Kendall (1975) advances an interesting semantic explanation, followed up provocatively (for other constructions in the related language Yuma) by Slater (1977)).

[6]This word and the next one illustrate a very common Tolkapaya nominalization type which seems to be highly complex, but is always pronounced as a single word. In it, a verb is followed by k plus yu 'be' plus ch--possibly the plural suffix mentioned in fn. 5, or perhaps a (related?) nominalizer. The problem is the identity of the -k-. At first, it seems attractive to identify it with the k- subject relative prefix (cf. Kendall (1974), Kriendler (1977)), which would mean that at some level the structure of such expressions was VERB#k-yu-ch-. Although it is possible for a k- relative prefix to occur on only the last of a string of verbs in a relative sentence, Kriendler (1977) has shown that the verb preceding the k-prefixed verb in such a structure retains all its normal syntactic suffixes--and I know of no Tolkapaya constructions in which 'be' ever follows a totally unmarked verb (but VERB#yu should occur in the simple-sentence equivalent of a VERB#k-yu nominalized form). Therefore, it seems best to identify the k in such constructions with the same-subject suffix (fn. 4), which often follows a verb preceding the auxiliary yu (i.e., as VERB-k#yu), particularly in the main-clause constructions of the type discussed in fn. 9 below. One could argue that the -k-yu-ch- expressions are simply nominalized versions of sentences like Nytha-che tnyurv-a wam-ch-k yu-ch-k-yu-m (that-subject letter-nominal carry-ch-same be-ch-same-be-incomplete) 'He's a mailman'--when the final incomplete inflection (cf. fn. 9) is removed from the predicate of this sentence and the nominal ending -a added, we have the noun tnyurv-a wam-ch-k-yu-ch-a 'mailman' (non-subject form).

I do not have an explanation for why an extra -che follows both 'strong persons' here (and to avoid confusion for the casual reader I omitted the SUBJECT indication in the gloss). Lynn Gordon has suggested that these -che's are used because 'a strong person' is the subject of 'will wrestle', but this is not consistent with Molly's translation, on which she insisted.

[7]The pa- prefix usually indicates a plural object, and so this probably means 'he will wrestle with all comers'. I have glossed third-person verbs followed by the irrealis suffix -h before a modal, as here, with English unmarked verb forms.

[8]The verb yii in many contexts means 'think'.

[9]I have tried to follow the practice of marking sentence boundaries between parts of the text which could stand alone. In general, this means that the "main" verb of each numbered sentence is followed by what Chung (1976) refers to as a "compound tense marker"--essentially, same-subject -k plus an "existential auxiliary" (the term was introduced for Yuman by Langdon (1974)--the Tolkapaya auxiliaries are yu 'be', wi/wu 'do', 'i/i/' 'say') plus an aspectual ending (-m incomplete or -ny complete, to use Kendall's (e.g. 1972) terminology). (Choice of auxiliaries is discussed by Chung.) The U. C. L. A. Tolkapaya group's observation differs from Chung's, however, in that we record person markers (first person '- and second-person m-) consistently not only on the "main" verb of a sentence but also on the following auxiliary: thus, while 'he sees it' is 'u-k-yu-m (see-same-be-incomplete), 'I see it' is '-'u-k-'-yu-m (1-see-same-1-be-incomplete), with first-person '- on both 'see' and 'be', in our recordings. (Two somewhat complex examples in this text are in sentences (13) and (14) below.) The occurrence of this person-marking may in itself be enough to call into question Chung's

claim that the "tense markers" (it is a most convenient term) are synchronically unanalyzeable; in addition, however, we have learned that the auxiliary in such expressions may be preceded by the diminutive prefix n- (Munro 1977b) or, very rarely, followed by the plural -ch- (Heather Hardy, personal communication).

Another verb suffix which can allow a sentence to stand alone is -i, which not only occurs on many present- and past-tense sentences (cf. (8), (10), and (18) below) but also follows all consonant-final verb stems in their citation form. This suffix has a variant -'i (especially frequent on the verbal citations in the lexicon in Shaterian (n.d.)), suggesting a connection with the verb 'i 'say' (cf. also Kendall 1977). The distribution of this suffix is not yet well understood, however.

[10] The myth names for Turtle and Coyote used in this text, Pa-ny-kpit-a and Pa-ny-kthar-a (object forms) are complex. They begin with the morpheme pa 'man, person' (also part of pa-thpirv-k-yu-ch- in sentence (1)). The following ny might be related to a prefix which occurs on the predicates of many Tolkapaya relative clauses (discussed extensively in Kriendler (1977)). Kpit- is the normal stem for 'turtle'. Kthar- is evidently an old word for 'coyote' (cf. Mojave hukthar), but in modern-day Tolkapaya kthar- means 'dog' and kthar-'han- (literally 'good [or real] kthar') is the stem for 'coyote'.

[11] Ka-v-yu-ch- seems to be a nominalized form of the verb ka-v-yu 'be (some) how', with comitative -me.

[12] This word differs from the last one in sentence (2) first because of the -ny- 'too' suffixed to thpirv 'strong' and secondly because it carries the predicate nominal -ch-yu-m suffix instead of the "compound tense marker" -k-yu-m used in (2). As Chung (1976) has noted, however, the predicate nominal suffixes -ch-yu-m and -ch-yu-ny (which, like the tense markers discussed in fn. 9, the U. C. L. A. group records with non-third-person marking, as appropriate) seem to be acquiring the status of tense/aspect markers themselves, particularly in sentences like this one. The normal Yuman pattern for predicate nominal sentences (Munro 1977a) is for the subject to be unmarked (with no -ch(e) suffix). Kendall (1972) first observed that this pattern is frequently violated in Yavapai--the present sentence is a further example.

[13] Ordinary incompletive verbs are often given progressive translations, but a progressive sense may be made explicit in Yavapai if the main verb plus -k is followed by a demonstrative (also followed by -k, presumably in this case the locative/directional case marker) and the auxiliary verb unu. This progressive clause was translated 'now they were wrestling', but it might have also been rendered as 'now they were in the process/act of wrestling'. Some similar sentences occur without the vak (or hak, as in (8)), under conditions not yet specified. (The unu auxiliary is also used to express a 'going to' future, with the preceding verb marked with irrealis -h- plus -k, as in sentence (14).)

[14] Here is the first serious problem for the sentence-boundary-finding rules outlined in fn. 9. Both of the two clauses here end simply in (same-subject) -k. Neither can easily be argued to be "main". In deciding to consider this a separate sentence, I relied mainly on Molly's intuitions and the translation she gave. I should note, however, that sentences like (7) do occur occasionally in elicited material.

[15] This use of different-subject -me looks like another problem (cf. fn. 5), but the marking here is merely parallel to that on the verb 'im-t-me below. Both are marked with the different-subject suffix because the subject of both verbs ('Coyote') is different from that of the final (compound-tense-marked, "main") verb of the sentence, v-lwi-th-k-yu-m, whose subject is the whole preceding complex sentence.

[16] This is a common perfective construction. The main verb is followed by -k plus an existential auxiliary followed by the perfective suffix -w- followed by -k plus a second occurrence of the previous existential auxiliary with a final suffix.

[17] Pa-yeev- is a totally unmarked (oblique) relative clause form (the corresponding sentence 'he was with them' would be pa-yeev-k-yu-m), followed by demonstrative -h- and case marker -che. Notice that the two conjoined subjects here are both marked with subject -che--a somewhat unusual construction for Tolkapaya.

[18]This repetition seems very strange, and it is certainly quite marked stylistically.

[19]The -pe suffix indicates specific members selected from a larger group (Glover 1977). It is also apparently used on nytha-m-pe 'from that particular [time]' in (17).

[20]I frequently record no '- first-person prefix on verbs starting with k.

[21]-Ka-v-yu-k-means 'why' or 'how' (it is related to the nominalized 'someone' discussed in fn. 11). The pami- prefix used here seems to be some kind of intensifier--Molly volunteered pami-ka-m-i-ra-k-m-ii (intensifier-why-2-say-really-same-2-say+question) 'why on earth is it that you're saying it?' as another example. The -upe suffix is probably the same as the -pe I commented on in fn. 19.

[22]This form is not only not overtly plural, it is also not marked as a subject. Failure to indicate plurality on verbs (or on those nouns and pronouns for which such marking is an option) is relatively common in Tolkapaya, but failure to mark the subject is rare.

Sentence (14) above is probably the most interesting in this text in terms of plurality. Note that the (singular) subject 'Coyote' is used elliptically for 'those who supported Coyote' (in discussing the translation of the text, Molly volunteered this information, commenting, "Isn't that funny!"). 'Coyote' is the subject of the plural verb 'i-ch-k-a and the anaphor for 'nyach-che 'we'. Note, though, that the non-plural, non-final-marked verb 'i-k which ends sentence (15) should also have the same (plural) subject.

[23]This expression is rather puzzling. I followed Molly's intuition in presenting it as just one word, but it would seem to me to be analyzeable as nyu-v-yu-m (two demonstrative prefixes plus yu 'be' plus different-subject -m nya-'han-me (when-good-different) with the whole possibly translatable as 'when it was good/okay that it was that way' or (Molly suggests) 'that's a good reason why it was that way'.

FIVE COYOTE ANECDOTES

(Yavpe)

Martha B. Kendall

Indiana University

Yavpe is a variety of Yavapai, itself a dialect of a language called Upland Yuman or Northern Pai. Yavpe is spoken primarily in and around the present city of Prescott, Arizona; in the small reservation towns of the Verde Valley: Clarkdale, Middle Verde, and Camp Verde; and, more recently, at Ford McDowell, near Phoenix. For a variety of complex sociolinguistic reasons, it is difficult to estimate the number of people speaking this Yavapai dialect, but certainly less than 400, and probably more than 100 individuals could be said to have competence in it. Since most Yavapai speakers are over 50 years of age, the language is fairly clearly moribund.

The following anecdotes were obtained in the summer of 1977 from two native-speaker consultants: Effie Starr and Daniel Russell. Both of them currently live in Prescott. I would like to acknowledge with most grateful thanks these two fine people, in particular Effie Starr--whose patience and sense of humor saw us both through some trying times.

A grammar exists for Verde Valley Yavpe (Kendall, 1976) where abbreviations and glosses found in this article are explained. The reader is also urged to consult Kendall and Sloane (1976) in the Yuman Texts volume of this series for additional grammatical information on Yavpe. Please note that in the following transcription, as in most of my work, [v] = [ɸ]; [ñ] = [ɲ]; [?] = [ʔ] and [c] = [č]. In order to read this material smoothly, keep in mind that virtually all initial and post-stress consonant clusters contain the epenthetic vowel [ə].

I. Coyote's Spite Backfires

(1) ?pa·vce·	?wil-ta·sva	tuñyuc-h	yi·ckm	?i·ctm	(2) kθarq^{w}arac
The people	grass-flower	always-irreal	they wanted	they said	The Coyote

?ik	?umha	(3) ?mat	vmwe·-h	?imm	pira	(4) ?pa·vce·
he said	this will not be	earth	warm-irreal	when it becomes	only	The people

?i·cka	?pavc	ñ-pikθo	yuñk	sya·pe·-h[1]	yi·ckm	?i·ctm
they said	a person	when he died	then	alive-irreal	they wanted	they said

(5) kθarq^{w}arac	?ik	?umha	(6) ke	ñuvyuha	?um-h
coyote	said	this will not be	no	this thing will be	not-irreal

(7) ñ-pi·ckθo[2]	ñ-vli·θm	pi·ckm	(8) ?pa·cc	?i·ck
when-they die	then-it is fitting	they are dead	the people	they said

?k^{w}e·-vya·lc	yuñka	pe·m	?-mac-ha	?-yi·ckm	(9) ?pa·cc	?i·cka	?k^{w}e-vyalc
thing-mescal	then	ripe	we-eat-irreal	we want	the people	they said	thing-mescal

vluwim	?-mac-ha	?-yi·c	?-yukθo[3]	(10) kθarq^{w}arac	?ik	?iñka
correct	we-eat-irreal	we want	we-that it be	The Coyote	he said	speaking

vyal	nuv-h	nukm	(11) ?pa·cc	?i·ck	?iñka	tu	?-payk
mescal	baked-irreal	must be	the people	they said	saying	just	we-alive

?-spo·vc-h ?numa ?i·ctm (12) pe· kθarq^{w}arac ?ik ?iñk
we-cognizant-irreal we must be they said and Coyote he said saying

?cpaya yuck yuñk tu ?wil k-wa·c-ñu-l howa·v-h numa
animal they be and just woods rel-live-there-in roam-irreal this will be

?ik ?im (13) ?pa·cc ?i·ck ?ña· c?a·l-h yuñk num
he said he said the people they said sun emerge-irreal then along there

?a·m-ha ?-yi·km ?i·ctm (14) kθarq^{w}arac ?ik ?iñk "hipa·me·"
go-irreal we want they said Coyote he said saying Let there be night!

(15) ñθam ?-sma·c-h ?-numa (16) marma·rm kθarq^{w}arac
when that happens we-sleep-irreal we will After awhile Coyote

paca· θak pa·-ck^{w}a·ñtm (17) vce·vc ?c?ra·vk yuñk pi?
family there them-he settled down the daughter took sick then died

(18) kθarq^{w}arac mi·k yuñk ?pa·ca ?wa k-yo·-h va·mk yuñk
Coyote he cried then the people houses rel-exist-obj he came and

vkoñk (19) ?-m-kva·vc-o-m (20) ?ña ?-vce·c ?ya+pe·-h ?-yikm
he bowed his head me-you-pray-for-switch my my-daughter alive-irreal I-want

(21) ?itm ?pa·cc ?i·cka ?iñk m-vo·me (22) ma·c m-ik[4]
when he said it the people they said saying you-go away! you you-said

m-iñka ?pavc ñ-pikθo ñ-vliθm pi? yum m-ik
you-saying a person when-he dies then-it's proper dead to be you-said

m-yi-wa (23) yuha m-vce·vc pi? (24) ñ-vlitm pik
you-thought-formerly so your-daughter dead then-it's proper she died

ya·mɨ
she is gone

Free Translation

(1) The people said they wanted there always to be flowers. (2) Coyote said,"This will not be...(3) (there will be flowers) only in the Springtime (when the earth becomes warm)." (4) The people said that when a person died, they wanted him to return to life. (5) Coyote said,"This will not be.(6) This will never happen. (7) When they die, it's proper that they die." (8) The people said they wanted to eat mescal just as it ripened. (9) The people said that they wanted to eat mescal as soon as it was fit to eat. (10) Coyote decreed,"Mescal shall be baked first." (11) The people wanted to be living, thinking creatures. (12) And so Coyote said,"They will be wild animals and roam about in the forests." (13) The people wanted the sun to emerge and shine there (in the heavens) all the time, they said. (14) Coyote, however, said,"Let there be night! (15) When that occurs, we will sleep." (16) After awhile Coyote had a family and settled down with them there.(17) His daughter took sick and died.(18) Coyote cried and came around to the peoples' houses with his head bowed.(19) "Pray for me! (20) I want my daughter alive." (21) When he said this, the people said "Go away! (22) You cry (now), but you formerly thought that when a person died, it was correct for them to die. (23) So, your daughter is dead. (24) It's proper therefore that she's dead and gone."

II. Coyote Challenges the Reed to a Dancing Contest

(1) ?pa·ñkθar lha·vce· vo·k va·m ya·mtk ?wi·lce·
Mr. Coyote the fool he walked around here he was going along a reed

?ha·vl ?u·km (2) vli·wvli·wi (3) yum ?u·k (4) θak vsk^{w}i·k

in the water he saw it waved to and fro so he saw it there he stood

?wi·lc himak yin̄ka (5) yun̄k ?n̄ac pay iman̄k ?-wark ?-yum

the reed it danced he thought so then I all I dance too I-also I-am

(6) ?in̄k θak himak hono·k + hono·tk (7) marma·rm vqotk

saying this there he danced he started in then finally he dropped over

(8) θak yakk tu pik ?i·ckm (9) ?pa-ttmeli

there he lay just dead they say person-buffoon

Free Translation

(1) Mr. Coyote, the fool, went out walking, and while he was walking he saw a reed in the water. (2) It was waving to and fro. (3) So he watched it. (4) He stood there and he thought, "The reed is dancing." (5) Then (he thought), "I too can dance like anyone else." (6) Saying this he started in dancing. (7) After awhile he collapsed. (8) There he lay dead. (9) What a Buffoon!

III. Coyote Turns Linguist

(1) ?pa·n̄klha·vce· ?wa·cc ya·mk pa·-n̄-we·vk kura θe·

The foolish one Apaches he went them-when-he visited a long time there

watk (2) vo·kk va·m (3) ?ickk^{w}i·c ?in̄k ?wa·ca pa ya

he stayed he returned then they asked him saying Apache person tongue

m-?e·vmmo· ta·m-mo (4) ?ickk^{w}i·cm (5) ?e·? ?ik ?im (6) m-k^{w}a·wm

you-understand now-maybe they asked him yes he said he spoke you-talk

?e-?e·vcha ?i·cm (7) yuka n̄hn̄o·pan̄ ?sla ?ik (8) vam

We want to hear they said so his mocasins nonsense he said then

vtmakovi ?imk ?i·ckn̄

he turned his back on them he left they say

Free Translation

(1) The foolish one went to visit the Apaches, and he stayed with them a long time. (2) He returned. (3) They asked him if he could perhaps speak Apache now. (4) "Yes," he replied. (5) "We want to hear you", they said. (6) So he said, "his mocasins ?sla"[5]. (8) Then he turned his back and walked off.

IV. Coyote Eats his own Offspring

(1) ?pa·n̄lha·vce· qmwira wi·yc yuk hma·n̄ wi·yvc yum[7] kmca·ym

Foolish one old woman his was children his was hunger

puykm (2) yutm vqi wi·yc ?ik ?in̄k m-ya·mk ?k^{w}e·kav?icm

they were dying so woman his she said she spoke you-go out something or other

m-?u·k m-yo·m ?-mac-ha (3) ?ime· ?pan̄kθar-klha·vce· ya·mk

you-look for you-take we- eat-irreal when she said that Mr. Coyote-the fool he left

hma·n̄ wi·y kavolim pa· - hiye·vk ya·mtk (4) ke ?k^{w}e·θ ?u·h

children his some of them - he took along when he left not anything he saw

?umk (5) yuñka wa·mk ?wak wa·mh ?umkm (6) marma·rme ke
not so he carried to his house he carried he didn't for awhile not

?uh ?umm (7) marma·rm hmañ wiy ?sitm nehk wiñk sk^{w}a·ñk
he saw he didn't finally child his one of he killed and then he skinned it

wiñk pe· ma·tva ?wa wa·mi (8) qmwirma ?e· (9) ñvam
and then and the meat home he carries old woman he gave it to her now

mu?ulc ñwivm ?uk (10) ?pañ kθarlha ñwa va·mtk
an antelope what was done saw it Mr. Coyote the fool his house he went there

yuñka kavwi?wime· yik hiva·mk (11) yutm ?pañkθar lhac
so what will he do he thought when he gets there and so Mr. Coyote the fool

?ik ?iñk pa·- m-ye·vk ?c-m-ma·ñe· (12) mu?ulc
he said said us- you-gather together with food-you-eat too. The antelope

?ik ?iñka ?u·m-mo (13) ñθa hmañ wiy nehk ma·-h numa
he said said maybe-not that one child his kill eat-irreal he will

ma?yikm (14) tu ñulya·mkm (15) mat-k?opvc vak yum (16) ñθak vsk^{w}i·k
he thought just he ran off earth-steep there was on it he stood

?iñk vca·rk ?ikk ?iñk ?θawa kθo·ca θawa kθo·ca" ?ik ?im
and he yelled he started saying child eater child eater he said he said

(17) kθarq^{w}ara qmwirmc e·vk ?iñk pahmi wiyθa ckk^{w}i·k
Coyote oldwoman she heard and husband her own she asked

?k^{w}e·θa kav?ik?i? (18) ?itm kθarq^{w}arac̣ tiye·k ?ik mu?ulc
what is he saying when she asked Coyote he lied and said the antelope

?ik "?mu?ul θawa kθo·ca mu?ul θawa kθo·ca" ?ikm. (19) ñ?im
he says antelope baby eater antelope baby eater he said when he said it

hok^{w}ak hok^{w}atm (20) kθarq^{w}ara vqi wiyc ?ik ?iñk ckk^{w}iyk
he yelled and he yelled Coyote wife his she said she spoke she asked again

kav?ik?i? mu?ul ?ik (21) mu?ul-c ?k^{w}e·θa ka·v?i?
what is he saying antelope she said The antelope what is he saying

(22) ?paklhavc ?ik ?iñk tuña vli•wok wark "mu?ul θawa
The foolish one he said he spoke always it's the same again antelope baby

kθo·ca mu?ul θawa kθo·ca" ?ik ?im (23) ?itm kθarq^{w}ar vqic
eaters antelope baby eaters he said he said when he said coyote wife

?ik ?ñac ?e?evñk ?warm (24) yuk yuñk θak vra·vi ?i?i
said I I understand too also she did so there she rose stick

wiyha mi· k^{w}eθa wiyha wa·m vam ?a·vi (25) yum
her own or something her own she carried then she struck him and

ñθak pik yu
there he died he was

Free Translation

(1) The foolish one, his old woman and his children were starving to death. (2) So his woman spoke and said,"Go see if you can find something for us to eat." (3) When she said that, the fool Coyote left, taking some of his children with him. (4) He didn't find anything. (5) So he had nothing to carry back to his house. (6) He didn't see anything for a long, long time. (7) Finally he killed one of his children and skinned it and carried the meat home. (8) He gave it to the old woman. (9) Now an antelope saw what he had done.(10) He went to the coyote's house to see what he might do when he got there.(11) So the Coyote said (to the antelope), "join us, eat with us". (12) But the antelope replied,"maybe not." (13) "He's going to eat his own baby," the antelope thought. (14) Antelope ran off. (15) There was a hill there. (16) He stood on it and began to yell,"Baby-eaters, baby-eaters!" (17) Coyote's old woman heard and asked her husband,"what's he saying?" (18) When she asked, Coyote lied and said,"The antelope is saying,'Antelopes are baby-eaters; Antelopes are baby-eaters!'" (19) When Coyote said this,Antelope started yelling again. (20) Coyote's wife asked once more what Antelope was saying. (21) "What's Antelope saying?" she asked. (22) The foolish one said,"It's always the same thing: "'Antelopes are baby eaters; antelopes are baby-eaters!'" (23) Coyote's wife said,"Ah, I understand too!" (24) And she did, so she picked up her stick or some other object and struck him.(25) And so he died there.

V. Coyote Steals the Chief's Heart

(1) vlhe·vc vak wa·tme· mayo·r yo·vci. (2) n̄va
the old man there when he lived chief they made him that one

mayo·rc ?pa·vc ?sitk ?matk ?a·mci (3) yu·tm
the chief the people the first ones on earth they moved about so it was

?c?ravk yŭnk paca·-θa pa·-kna·vk ?in̄k ?k^{w}e·kav?ice va m-wi·ce
he was sick and then kinsmen-those them-he told said whatever I say that you-do it!

n̄-?-pikθo ?im (4) ?k^{w}e· ?mat m-tpulk m-win̄k iwayk m-cwo·cm
when-I-die he said thing earth you-make damp you-then on my heart you-put it there

(5) tya·cc n̄θak c?al-h nukm (6) yuha tya·cc n̄θak
corn there emerge-irreal will When that happens corn there

c?alkθo ?k^{w}e·ma·va la·w-h nukm (7) ?pa·cce mayo·r n̄wa·
if it emerges things to eat many-irreal will be The people chief his house

tka·vtm (8) kθarq^{w}arac n̄θak va·mn̄k tu qle·pa wa?sivn̄km.
they gathered The Coyote there he also came just evil thinking bad thoughts

(9) mayo·rc pih n̄-nuk paca· pa·-kna·vk ?in̄k kθarq^{w}ara n̄ul
The chief die when-he started to kinsmen them-he told saying coyote away

m-ya·me· m-ice ?im (10) ke n̄θak yu-h ?-m-tu·cm (11) ?u·k
you go you-tell him he said. Not there be-irreal me-you-burn see

k^{w}al-?-yi-h ?umkm (12) kθarq^{w}ara n̄ul c?a·mcm (13) ?k^{w}e· m-ya·mk
want-I-want-irreal not coyote away they sent something you-go

m-yo·mk m-win̄ka m-cpe· makyo·r-n̄u m-yuwo· ?i·ctm
you-leave you-so that you-cover up former chief-that one you-put they said

(14) ya·mtm makl vha·mi ?itk ?oha·yc n̄θam vn̄yulki
he left back he looked starting to smoke there beginning to rise

(15) yun̄ka mayo·ra ?ckra·vc pim (16) tuck wiom
then chief the sick one he died they burn him there's evidence

?ik (17) ?in̄k vya·mk makl vo·mkn̄ (18) ?pa θak tkawva
he said. And so he left back he returned. People there they gathered

tmara tkawra (19) θak tkawvk yun̄k ska·wvk tuc-l
to bury him they gathered there gathered then in a circle the middle in

cmi·kn̄ (20) tuwik ?pa ?kyulm ?pa· cckro·tk n̄maθc
they placed him The rest person tall persons short badger

kpitm hwa·k-k ckro·tcn̄ravi (21) kθarq^{W}arac pa·-?u·k θak
with a tortoise those two were very short indeed Coyote then-he saw there

tkavtm pa·-?utk θak vsk^{W}i·tk yun̄k vca·lvi ?ik ?in̄ka
gathering them-when he saw there standing then crying out he began and then

?pa· θak ktke·va pa·-ckopa· (22) yutk n̄θak
person there crossing over them-he climbed over And then there

pa·-n̄-ckopa·km yun̄k n̄maθac kpitm hwa·kk θak yucm
them-when-he climbed then badger and tortoise those two there they were

ca·cm v?o·q ?imm (23) yuk ?pa-pi? θak yakkm (24) mayo·ra
over the top he jumped he did And person-dead there lying the chief

hiwaya yo·k yun̄k ?wilk ma·kn̄ (25) hk^{W}iθk win̄k ne·ckn̄
his heart he took and then fast he ate it They seized him then they killed him

(26) yume· kθarq^{W}arac n̄θa hiway n̄-ma·m vke hiwayc ?pe·mm
So Coyote that heart when-he ate it no heart wasn't there any longer

(27) yun̄ka ?mat tpulc-h ?umkn̄ (27) yume· tyac hwa·lcc ?cura
Then earth they dampened-irreal they didn't. And corn plants winter

ke pe·-h ?umkm (28) ?n̄a·-ruyi pira yucm
not ripe-irreal not earth-hot only they are

Free Translation

(1) Hereabouts there once lived an old man, a chief. (2) He was chief of the first people who lived on earth. (3) So it was that he took sick, and (calling) his kinsmen together, he told them, "Do what I tell you to when I die. (4) Take earth, dampen it and place it over my heart. (5) Corn will grow there. (6) When that happens, when the corn grows, there will be much to eat." (7) The people were gathered at the chief's house. (8) Coyote was there too, thinking malignant thoughts. (9) As the chief started to die, he told his kinsmen to drive Coyote away. (10) "Don't let him be there when you burn me," he said. (11) "I don't want him to see it". (12) They sent Coyote away. (13) "Go get something to cover up the chief with", they told him. (14) He left, but looking back over his shoulder, he saw smoke there beginning to rise. (15) "So the sick chief died. (16) There's evidence that they're burning him", he thought. (17) So he went back. (18) The people were gathered there to bury (the chief). (19) They stood there in a circle, placing him in the middle. (20) There were tall people and short people, badger and turtle being the shortest of all. (21) Coyote saw them together standing there, so he started crying out and running around to climb over them. (22) Then he climbed over them, over the top of these two he jumped. (23) And there the corpse was lying.

(24) Coyote grabbed the heart and ate it quickly. (25) They grabbed him and killed him. (26) But when coyote ate the heart, there was no longer any heart. (27) So they didn't dampen the earth. (28) And the corn plants do not ripen (all the year) now. (29) Only in the summertime.

Grammatical Notes

1. /sya...pe·/ is a disjunctive verb, inflected for person before the second element in the stem.

2. /pi/ to die normally pluralizes suppletively as /poy/. This consultant however is consistent in using /pi·c/ as the plural form.

3. The exact meaning of this auxiliary is unclear.

4. The second person prefix /m-/ suppresses the stem-initial glottal stop in this verb. This is an idiosyncratic feature of the verb ?i to say, and a small set of similarly marked verbs; in other words, it is by no means a regular phonological process.

5. This is, of course, a nonsense word in both Apache and Yavapai, although it bears a certain phonological resemblence to Apache structure. The point of the joke is that Coyote can not in fact say anything in the language he claims to have learned.

Variants of Coyote's Name

The variants on Coyote's name:

(1) Kθarq^{w}ara "desert dog"

(2) pañkθar "dog man" or "Mr. dog"

(3) pañkθarlha "dog man fool" or "Mr. Coyote the fool"

(4) pañklha "Mr. Foolish one"

are made up of the elements

Kθar	Coyote, dog
q^{w}ara	desert
lha	fool
pa	person, Mr.
ñ-	relational prefix
k-	relativizer

COYOTE AND BULLSNAKE

(Arizona Tewa)

Paul V. Kroskrity — Indiana University

Dewey Healing — Tewa Village

Arizona Tewa is a dialect of Tewa, a Kiowa-Tanoan language, which is currently spoken in Tewa Village on First Mesa of the Hopi Reservation as well as in Polacca--a more recently (around 1900) established community located at the foot of the mesa. According to both folk historical and ethnohistorical sources (Reed 1943, Kroskrity 1976) these people represent the descendants of a group, or groups, which migrated to First Mesa from Tanoan speaking Rio Grande pueblos around 1700. The Arizona Tewa have received the ethnographic attention of several anthropological writers such as Fewkes (1899), Parsons (1926), Eggan (1950:139-175), and--most notably and comprehensively--Dozier (1951, 1954, 1955). No published grammar of Tewa yet exists though two doctoral dissertations (Yegerlehner 1957, Kroskrity 1977) have been devoted to a grammatical analysis of Arizona Tewa and a third (Speirs 1966) has been similarly devoted to an analysis of the Rio Grande dialect. Published grammatical sketches of Tewa include those by Harrington (1910), Dozier (1953), Yegerlehner (1959a, b), the Speirs (1972, 1974) and Kroskrity (1978). Though no dictionary of Tewa yet exists, the authors of this contribution are currently preparing a dictionary of Arizona Tewa. This text is the first to be published in the Arizona dialect--the previous three all represented the Rio Grande dialect (Harrington 1947).

This Coyote story was collected in the summer of 1977.[1] The story was brought to our attention by Albert Yava, a Tewa who is in his late eighties and now resides in Parker, Arizona, on one of his frequent visits to Tewa Village. When asked if he knew any good Coyote stories, Yava immediately responded by telling "Coyote and Bullsnake" in its entirety. Dewey Healing, a Tewa in his late sixties, later retold the story and provided native commentary and explication. Paul Kroskrity, an anthropological linguist in his late twenties, transcribed the stories, provided the linguistic analysis, and otherwise prepared the text for publication.

Formerly Coyote stories such as this one were told in the home for the amusement of friends and relatives--especially the young--and constituted an important source of entertainment. Today both the penetration of the mass media into the reservation and the waning influence of the family and household as a mechanism of social control and as an instrument in the socialization of young people have precipitated a decline in the use of story-telling--a skill which is now the characteristic possession of only the older speakers. Structurally all the Coyote stories in our present sample exhibit a tripartite formal structure consisting of an introduction, narrative portion, and conclusion. The introduction invariably situates the story in the remote past and introduces the main characters. The narrative consists of all the rising and falling plot-related action and optionally contains one or more digressions in which seemingly disproportionate attention is afforded to the development of a sub-plot (absent in this text). The conclusion simply notes the demise of Coyote and is optionally adorned with a didactic exhortation. The warning against imitation expressed here is especially appropriate for the Arizona Tewa and consonant with an ethnographic record which documents their ethnic and cultural persistence amidst considerable inter-ethnic interaction and widespread social change (Dozier 1951, Kroskrity 1976).

(1)	ʔó·wé·hén	ba[2]	bayɛ·nah-seno[3]	ba	na-ta·	(2)	ʔi-bí
	long-ago	DISCOURSE	coyote-old man	DISC.	3rd-be alive		3rd-'s

k'e·ge hangih-wɛ-yá[4] na·la-á ba na-ta· (3) he·dí
house nearby-there-EMPHATIC bullsnake-EMPH. DISC. 3rd-be alive then

ba nɛʔin den-mun-dí[5] k'in ʔi-wɛ-dí ba den-
DISC. these they(dual)-see-ASSOCIATIONAL so 3rd-there-ASSOC. DISC. they(dual)

k'e·ma-ʔán (4) he·dí ba hųwa den-mun-dí ba den-
friend-COMPLETIVE then DISC. again they(two)-see-ASSOC. DISC. then(dual)

tu-ʔán (5) wi·nɛ ga-kya·lac'i-mų-mí gi-ba
say-COMPLETIVE both 1st(dual)-guest-be-OBLIGATIVE QUOT.-DISC.

bayɛ·nah-senó na-tų (6) ʔi-he·dí ba na·la-dí ʔó·-tų-ʔán[6]
coyote-old man 3rd-say 3rd-then DISC. bullsnake-ASSOC. 3/3 PASSIVE-say-COMPL.

nekų· ʔų-bíʔi ʔo-kya·lac'i-pu-t'ó (7) he·dán ʔúh-hangin-ná-mí
tonight you-'s-3rd 1st-guest-go-INTENTIVE and-then you-remember-be-OBLIG.

gi-ba bayɛ·nah-senó-dí ʔó·-tų-ʔán (8) k'in ba da-
QUOT.-DISC. coyote-old man-ASSOC. 3/3 PAS.-say-COMPL. so DISC. they(dual)

tu-yɛ kidí wi·nɛ-pɛʔɛ den-ʔą́ʔ-tu·ye (9) ʔi-he·dí ba
say-DURATIVE and-then both-directions they(dual)-foot-proceed 3rd-then DISC.

bayɛ·nah-senó ʔi-ánkhaw-hón hɛlun keʔ na·-bí kya·lac'i-ʔi dó-
coyote-old man 3rd-think-PROGRESSIVE what exactly 1st-'s guest-3rd 1st/3rd

hwí·-ʔó-mí (10) ga nɛʔi-yán na·-bí hwí·-kán-ʔi na-mų
feed-PROG.-OBLIG. wonder this-EMPH. 1st-'s feed-COMPL.-3rd 3rd-be

gi-ba na-kyanpo bayɛ·nah-senó (11) he·dán ba hų-k'a
QUOT.-DISC. 3rd-realize coyote-old man and-then DISC. juniper-thicket

ʔi-pɛʔɛ na-mɛ (12) ʔin-gɛ ba mán-kwin-hón hų-ʔin-gɛ
3rd-thither 3rd-go 3rd-at DISC. 3rd/3rd-search-PROG. juniper-3rd-at

(13) he·dí ba ho ʔimoʔ na-hų-pe·k'u-mų ʔin-g baɛ mán-
and-then DISC. already much 3rd-juniper-berry-be 3rd-at DISC. 3/3-

nɛ-hón-dí ba na-ʔá-ʔi mán-khyaw (14) ʔi-he·dí ba
taste-PROG.-ASSOC. DISC. 3rd-be sweet-3rd 3/3-find 3rd-then DISC.

mán-wo·lo-hón (15) hoba hé·he mán-ʔán (16) ho·ke nɛʔi na·-bí k'e·ma
3/3-pick-PROG. finally surplus 3/3-make enough this 1st-'s friend

ʔi-kwɛ-ʔám-mí gi-ba na-tų bayɛ·nah-senó (17) ʔi-we·dán ba
3rd-fill-COMPL.-OBLIG. QUOT.-DISC. 3rd-say coyote-old man 3rd-from DISC.

ʔi-bí k'e·ge-pɛʔɛ na-mɛ (18) ʔi-he·dí hoba na-tan-c'ųn (19) ʔiʔi-yán
3rd-'s house-thither 3rd-go 3rd-then finally 3rd-sun-set there-EMPH.

ba na-c'i·ka-ʔɛn (20) tayɛ ba he·do-pídí pa·-k'edi ba na·la-
DISC. 3rd-wait-sit surely DISC. long-not hill-top DISC. bullsnake-

senó ʔi-c'i·kidi (21) ʔi-he.di ba ʔi-bí hų-pe·k'u-saʔ mán-hwik'e-
old man 3rd-show 3rd-after DISC. 3rd-'s juniper-berry-bowl 3/3-feed-

k'wi (22) he·do-pídí-moʔ po·lǫ-ʔiʔi-dí na·la-senó ba ʔi-
place long-not-ADVERB hole-there-ASSOC. bullsnake-old man DISC. 3rd-

c'i·kidi (23) ʔi-he·dán ba bayɛ·nah-senó na-tų ʔo-c'ú·wa·bɛ
show 3rd-and then DISC. coyote-old man 3rd-say IMPERATIVE-enter

(24) ʔi-he·dí ba na-c'ų·dɛ-ʔɛ́ʔɛ̨ kidí ba na·la-senó na-tų-
3rd-after DISC. 3rd-enter-come and-then DISC. bullsnake-old man 3rd-say-

yɛ wa·tadá kuwó·naʔa he·yiʔi ʔo-mų (25) ʔų-bí k'e·ge ha.dan
DUR. sorry extreme long 1st-be you''s house probably-not

wo-ʔo-pídɛ́-mí-dí (26) ʔi-he·dí ba bayɛ·nah-senó ba na-tų
NEG.-1st-fill-OBLIG.-ASSOC. 3rd-after DISC. coyote-old man DISC. 3rd-say

hohant'o na-mų-mí (27) na.-wádá ʔimoʔ he·yiʔi ʔo-khwę́n-mų (28) ʔi-
regardless 3rd-be-OBLIG. 1st-also very long 1st-tail-be 3rd-

he·dí ba bayɛ·nah-senó ʔi-bí hų-pe·k'u-saʔ ʔų́·-ʔám-powa
after DISC. coyote-old man 3rd-'s juniper-berry-bowl 3rd-think-become

(29) ?o-hwí·-yán (30) hę·wɛ̨ wí-n-hwi·k'e-k'wi (31) ʔi-he·dí ba
IMP.-eat-EMPH. there 1/2-3rd-feed-place 3rd-after DISC.

na·la mán-kwi·mɛ̨·yų ʔiʔi-dí ba man-nɛ̨ ʔi-bí hwí·-kán-ʔi
bullsnake 3/3-stare there-ASSOC. DISC. 3/3-taste 3rd-'s feed-COMPL.-3rd

we-na-mų-pí-dí (32) hoba ʔi-yo·le-hwí·-ʔó (33) wolo-gɛ
NEG.-3rd-be-DUBITATIVE-ASSOC. finally 3rd-feign-eat-PROG. action-at

ba den-hi·li-mɛ·yu we·yɛ da-yin-dɛ-ʔiʔi we.yɛ
DISC. they(dual)-talk-hold wherever they(dual)-roam-HABITUAL-there wherever

hɛ̨·lɛwiʔ den-khyaw-mɛ·yu (34) ʔi-hɛ̨.lɛ ba den-hi.li-mɛ·yu
something they(dual)-find-hold 3rd-what DISC. they(dual)-talk-hold

(35) handi·dí-moʔ ba dɛ́n-k'u· (36) he·dí hoba na·la
similar-ADV. DISC. 3rd(dual)-be dark after finally bullsnake

ha·ya déh-kwó-hon gi-ba na.la na-tų-yɛ (37) gakhwen
perhaps 1st-sleep-thither QUOT.-DISC. bullsnake 3rd-say-PROG. alright

gi-ba bayɛ·nah-senó-dí ʔó.-tų-ʔán (38) ʔi-he·dán ba
QUOT.-DISC. coyote-old man-ASSOC. 3/3 PAS.-say-COMPL. 3rd-after DISC.

na.la-senó ba na-pí·-mɛ (39) hɛmo ʔi-bí pón na-pí·-dí
bullsnake-old man DISC. 3rd-exit-go long-after 3rd-'s head 3rd-exit-ASSOC.

wa·ti ba mu·lų-gɛ na-kwisu·lu-mɛ-n na·la-senó ba na-dɛʔ-pí.
still DISC. inside-at 3rd-unravel-go-PROG bullsnake-old man DISC. 3rd-all-exit

(40) heʔi na-mɛ ʔi-he·dí ba bayɛ·nah-senó ʔi-ánkhaw-mɛ·yu (41) hanke
that-one 3rd-go 3rd-after DISC. coyote-old man 3rd-think-hold how

hą·mą déh-ʔan-dán ʔi-bí k'e·ge ʔo-pídɛ́-mí (42) gah wa·ti tándán
similarly 1st-make-EMPH. 3rd-'s house 1st-fill-OBLIG. well still tomorrow

ʔo-hų-k'wi-pą́·lún-kǫn-mɛ-mí (43) ʔi dó-kwi-saki-dí na·-bí khwę́n
1st-juniper-bark-yucca-gather-go-OBLIG. 3rd 1/3-tie-join-ASSOC. 1st-'s tail

ʔi dó-kwi-ʔán-dí ʔi-dán-t'ó we-dó-mayɛ-mí-dí
3rd 1/3-tie-COMPL.-ASSOC. 3rd-EMPH.-INTENTIVE NEG.-1/3-surpass-OBLIG.-ASSOC.

na·la-senó (44) k'in na-tų kidí ba ʔi-yóh-kwi· (45) ʔi-he-dí
bullsnake-old man so 3rd-say and-then DISC. 3rd-sleep-satisfy 3rd-after

tawendi he·dimoʔ ʔi-khawkí-dí hų-k'a na-mɛ (46) ʔiʔi-yán
next-day early 3rd-awake-ASSOC. juniper-thicket 3rd-go there-EMPH.

ba mán-hų-k'wi-yá·wɛn kidí ba pą́·lún-nádá ba mán-khyaw-ʔin
DISC. 3/3-juniper-bark-strip and-then DISC. yucca-also DISC. 3/3-find-3rd

mán-c'i·gi (47) ʔi-he·dí ba ʔi-wɛ-dí ʔi-bí k'e·ge-pɛʔɛ na-
3/3-uproot 3rd-after DISC. 3rd-there-ASSOC. 3rd-'s house-thither 3rd-

mɛ (48) ne-yán ho han na-po-dán na·la-senó-bí k'e·ge
go now-EMPH. surely will 3rd-become-EMPH. bullsnake-old man-'s house

wo-ʔo-pídɛ́-mí-dí gi-ba na-tų bayɛ·nah-senó (49) ʔi-he·dí
NEG.-1st-fill-OBLIG.-ASSOC. QUOT.-DISC. 3rd-say coyote-old man 3rd-after

ba ʔi-c'án-hwí·-ʔán (50) ʔi-kwę-mo·wa ʔi-he·dí ba hų-k'wi
DISC. 3rd-just-eat-COMPL. 3rd-fill-finish 3rd-after DISC. juniper-bark

mán-mą-ʔán mán-tę́hbí-ʔó (51) ʔi mán-mo·wa kidí ʔi-he·dí mán-
3/3-by hand-make 3/3-soften-PROG. 3rd 3/3-finish and-then 3rd-after 3/3

pą́·lún-syu (52) mán-ʔan kidí hų-k'wi ba mán-wi·nɛ-yé·sa
yucca-split 3/3-make and-then juniper-bark DISC. 3/3-both-connect

(53) ʔi-yɛ nɛʔi pą́·lún-dí ba mán-i·pa-ci·dí-hón (54) kyanadi
3rd-there this yucca-ASSOC. DISC. 3/3-tie-knot-thither gradually

he·yiʔin ba ʔų́·-po (55) ho·ke nɛhe ʔimoʔ ho na-mų-mí
long DISC. 3rd-become enough this very already 3rd-be-OBLIG.

gi-ba bayɛ·nah-senó na-tų-yɛ (56) ho·ʔo ʔo-c'i·ka-kya-mí na-
QUOT.-DISC. coyote-old man 3rd-say-PROG. now 1st-wait-sit-OBLIG. 3rd-

k'i-míʔi gi-ba na-tų-yɛ bayɛ·nah-senó (57) he·dán tayɛ
dusk-OBLIG.-3rd QUOT.-DISC. 3rd-say-PROG. coyote-old man later surely

na-tán-c'ų·n (58) ʔi-he·dí ba ʔi-k'e·-mɛ·yu ʔi-bí khwę́n pą́·lún-syu-dí
3rd-sun-set 3rd-after DISC. 3rd-garb-hold 3rd-'s tail yucca-split-ASSOC.

ba mán-kwi-ˀó (59) mán-mo·wa ki-ˀi-he·dí ba ˀiˀi-dí ˀi-bí
DISC. 3/3-tie-PROG. 3/3-finish then-3rd-after DISC. there-ASSOC. 3rd-'s

k'e·ge ˀiˀi-dí na-pí· na·la-senó-bí-ˀi-k'e·ge-pɛˀɛ ba na-
house there-ASSOC. 3rd-leave bullsnake-old man-'s-3rd-house-thither DISC. 3rd-

mɛn (60) he·dí ba ˀi na-powa-dí ˀo·-c'ų·dɛ-yón (61) ˀo-
go after DISC. 3rd 3rd-arrive-ASSOC. 3/3 PAS.-enter-invite IMP.-

so·ge gi-ba ˀó·-tų-ˀán (62) he·dí ba na·la mán-mun-dí ba
sit QUOT.-DISC. 3/3 PAS.-say-COMPL. after DISC. bullsnake 3/3-see-ASSOC. DISC.

ˀi-bí khwę́n ho ˀų́·-c'u· wemo ˀi-wɛ-dí hɛ̨lɛna wa·ti mán-
3rd-'s tail already 3rd-enter but 3rd-there-ASSOC. something still 3/3-

kwaye-hon (63) he·dí ba ˀų́·-kipo·-dí hų-k'wi-yán di-
drag-PROG. after DISC. 3rd-be visible-ASSOC. juniper-bark-EMPH. 3rd

wi·nɛ-kwi-mųˀi-yán guba bayɛ·nah-senó ˀi-háˀámána-ˀán-dí ˀi-bí
both-tie-be-3rd-EMPH. hopefully coyote-old man 3rd-copy-COMPL.-ASSOC. 3rd's

khwę́n ˀi mán-so·wɛ (64) he·dí ba ˀų́·-ya·-dí na.la
tail 3rd 3/3-lengthen after DISC. 3rd-be forced-ASSOC. bullsnake

p'ɛnu-pɛˀɛ ba na-pí· ˀiˀi-dán ba na-ˀɛn (65) he·di ba
outside-thither DISC. 3rd-exit there-from DISC. 3rd-sit after DISC.

bayɛ·nah-senó ba ˀó·-tų-ˀán ˀu-wán na·-bí-ˀi-Wɛ-dí
coyote-old man DISC. 3/3 PAS.-say-COMPL. you-EMPH. 1st-'s-3rd-there-ASSOC.

ˀų́·-da-pa·dɛn ˀi ˀų́·-mų (66) hoy gi-ba bayɛ·nah-senó na-tų
3rd-very exceed 3rd 3rd-be yes QUOT.-DISC. coyote-old man 3rd-say

(67) he·wa ha·dán we-wí-pa·dɛ-mí-dí k'in ba ˀi-ánkhaw-
see! certainly NEG.-2/1 PAS.-exceed-OBLIG.-ASSOC. so DISC. 3rd-think-

ˀán (68) ˀi-he·dán ba hą·mą na·la-dí ba ˀó·-n-kwík'e-
COMPL. 3rd-after DISC. similarly bullsnake-ASSOC. DISC. 3/3 PAS-3rd-feed

k'wi (69) guba na·la son mán-hey kidí ˀi-bí tų·
place unbeknownst bullsnake porcupine 3/3-kill and-then 3rd-'s meat

guba mán-dɛˀ-haˀ-dí son-bí ko·wa toˀ mán-me·legi-ˀán kidí
unbeknownst 3/3-all-eat-ASSOC. porcupine-'s pelt only 3/3-ball-COMPL. and-then

wati ˀin-gɛ ha·mo ˀi-bí wɛ̨ na-ni-sa. (70) hangimoˀ ˀó·-n-
still 3rd-at intact 3rd-'s quill 3rd-stick-be rooted just-so 3/3 PAS.-3rd.

hwík'e-k'wi (71) ˀo-hwí·-yán gi-ba bayɛ·nah-senó ˀó·-tu-ˀán
feed-place IMP.-eat-EMPH. QUOT.-DISC. coyote-old man 3/3 PAS.-say-COMPL.

(72) ho bi-hwí·-ˀó-dí an-hi·li-mɛ·yu-mí gi-ba ˀó·-
let's 2nd-eat-PROG.-ASSOC. 1st(dual)-talk-hold-OBLIG. QUOT.-DISC. 3/3 PAS.-

tų-ˀán (73) hą·mą ba we·yɛ da-yin-dɛ-ˀiˀi ba
say-COMPL. similarly DISC. wherever they(dual)-roam-HAB.-there DISC.

den-hi·li-mɛ.yu (74) handi·dí-moʔ ba dɛ́n-k'u· (75) he·dí
they(dual)-talk-hold similarly-ADV. DISC. 3rd-be dark after

ba bayɛ·nah-senó na-ha·yon-po (76) ho·ke na-k'un déh-kwó-
DISC. coyote-old man 3rd-yawn-become enough 3rd-be night 1st-sleep-

ku·wa-mí gi-ba bayɛ·nah-senó na-tų (77) gakhwen ho an-
lie-OBLIG. QUOT.-DISC. coyote-old man 3rd-say alright surely 1st(dual)-

yóh-kwi·-mí (78) ʔi-he·dí ba ʔiʔi-dí bayɛ·nah-senó na-pí·
sleep-satisfy-OBLIG. 3rd-after DISC. there-ASSOC. coyote-old man 3rd-exit

(79) ʔiʔi-dí ba pa·-ki-pɛʔɛ na-piyɛ-mɛn (80) pa·-ki-k'edi
there-ASSOC. DISC. hill-up-thither 3rd-ascend-go hill-up-top

ba ʔi-wí-mi·li-dí (81) wa·ti hoba ʔi-bí khwę́n na·la-senó-
DISC. 3rd-back-revolve-ASSOC. still finally 3rd-'s tail bullsnake-old man-

bí-k'e·ge-ʔiʔi-dí we-na-dɛʔ-pí·-dí (82) he.dán ba bayɛ·nah-senó
's-house-there-ASSOC. NEG.-3rd-all-exit-ASSOC. after DISC. coyote-old man

na-pa·yiʔ (83) he·wa kinan ʔo-tų-yɛ han na-po-dan we-wí-
3rd-grin see! so 1st-say-PROG. will 3rd-become-EMPH. NEG.-2/1 PAS.-

pa·de-mí-dí ʔi-wɛ́-dí ba ʔi-bí-k'e·ge-pɛʔɛ na-mɛ
exceed-OBLIG.-ASSOC. 3rd-there-ASSOC. DISC. 3rd-'s-house-thither 3rd-go

(84) he·dí guba na·la-senó pa·-ki-pɛngɛ na-k'indí-moʔ
after unbeknownst bullsnake-old man hill-up-over 3rd-be invisible-ADV.

guba ʔi-bí hų-k'wi-khwę́n na·la-dí ʔó·-n-phá-t'a.lɛ
unbeknownst 3rd-'s juniper-bark-tail bullsnake-ASSOC. 3/3 PAS.-3rd-fire-touch

(85) he·dí ba na-ʔo·ti-dí wɛngeh ba na-ko·yɛ (86) hoba
after DISC. 3rd-breeze-ASSOC. suddenly DISC. 3rd-burn finally

tayɛ̨ʔ bayɛ·nah-senó na-mɛ-n kidí ba ʔi-mi·li (87) he·dí
long-time coyote-old man 3rd-go-PROG. and-then DISC. 3rd-revolve after

ba phá-dí ʔó·-k'e-hón (88) kya·nadi-moʔ ba heʔteʔe-ʔiʔi-
DISC. fire-ASSOC. 3/3 PAS.-trail-PROG. gradual-ADV. DISC. close-there-

dí ʔų́·-kąpowa-ʔɛ̨́ʔɛ̨-dí (89) ʔi-he·dí ba ʔi-ʔɛ̨́·lų́ (90) gukeʔ
ASSOC. 3rd-approach-come-ASSOC. 3rd-after DISC. 3rd-run maybe

na·-bí khwę́n-nán dín-kó·yɛ gi-ba na-khyam-po (91) han déh-
1st's tail-EMPH. 1st-burn QUOT.-DISC. 3rd-think-become will 1st-

ʔam-mí (92) gakyan nɛ tám-pɛʔɛ-pɛngɛ na-p'o-hu·lumɛn ʔiʔi-
do-OBLIG. of-course here sun-thither-over 3rd-water-canyon-go there-

yán déh-p'o-t'ǫ·gi-dí dó-pa·-mí gi-ba na-tų-yɛ
EMPH. 1st-water-dunk-ASSOC. 1/3-extinguish-OBLIG. QUOT.-DISC. 3rd-say-PROG.

(93) he·dí ba hųwa ʔi-mi·li (94) hoba da-heʔteʔe-ʔiʔi-dí

after DISC. again 3rd-revolve already very-close-there-ASSOC.

ʔu·-ʔɛ̨́ʔɛ̨ (95) ʔi-wɛ-dí ba ʔi-da-ʔɛ̨́·lų́ (96) handi·dí-moʔ

3rd-come 3rd-there-ASSOC. DISC. 3rd-very-run similarly-ADV.

ba p'o-hu·lu-gɛ na-powa (97) we-ankhaw-ám-pí-dí-moʔ ba

DISC. water-canyon-at 3rd-arrive NEG.-think-COMPL.-DUB.-ASSOC.-ADV. DISC.

ʔi-p'o-kɛ·nu (98) ʔimoʔ ba p'o na-ke·le-dí ba ʔó·-p'o-

3rd-water-jump very DISC. water 3rd-strong-ASSOC. DISC. 3/3 PAS.-water-

hon kidí ʔó·-p'o-hey (99) nɛhe ʔi-nán nɛʔin na·la

thither and-then 3/3 PAS.-water-kill this 3rd-EMPH. this bullsnake

pę·yuʔu na-mų (100) kinan ba bayɛ·nah-senó ʔú·-po-dí-yán

story 3rd-be so DISC. coyote-old man 3rd-become-ASSOC.-EMPH.

ba towiʔ we-di·-suʔo-dɛ-dí

DISC. someone NEG.-3rd(plural)-imitate-HAB.-ASSOC.

Free Translation

(1) Long ago, so they say, lived Old Man Coyote. (2) Not far from his house Bullsnake also lived. (3) Then, since they saw each other (regularly) they became friends. (4) Then once as they met again they were talking to each other. (5) "Both of us should each invite the other as a guest," Old Man Coyote said. (6) And then, so the story goes, Coyote was told by Bullsnake, "Tonight I'm going to visit you at your place." (7) "Remember," Old Man Coyote said then. (8) So the two of them kept on talking and later walked off in opposite directions. (9) After that Old Man Coyote was thinking, "Just what should I feed my guest?" (10) "Perhaps my own food would do," it occurred to Old Man Coyote. (11) And then, so I've heard, Coyote went over to a thicket of juniper trees. (12) At that spot he was searching around among the junipers. (13) Then soon after tasting about on some juniper trees with lots of berries he found some sweet ones. (14) After that he started picking. (15) Finally he had produced enough. (16) "Maybe this will be enough to fill up my friend"--that's what Old Man Coyote said. (17) From there he went home. (18) After that the sun finally set. (19) There it was that he sat waiting. (20) Sure enough, so the story goes, it wasn't long before Old Bullsnake appeared on the hilltop (in front of Coyote's house). (21) After that he set out his bowl of juniper berries. (22) Shortly thereafter Old Man Bullsnake appeared through the opening (of Coyote's house). (23) Then Old Man Coyote said, "Come in!" (24) After that Old Man Bullsnake entered and then he kept saying, "I'm sorry that I'm so very long. (25) I probably can't help but fill up your house." (26) After that, so I've heard, Old Man Coyote said, "Never mind, that's alright. (27) I too have a very long tail." (28) After that Old Man Coyote was thinking about his bowl of juniper berries. (29) "Eat! (30) I set it out for you over there." (31) After that

Bullsnake stared at it and from there he tasted it, tasting that it wasn't his (type) of) food. (32) Finally he was pretending to eat it. (33) While so doing they kept talking about where the two of them usually roam and where they found something (of interest.) (34) About such things they continued to talk to each other. (35) In this manner night fell on them. (36) Afterwards Bullsnake was saying, "Perhaps I'll go off and sleep." (37) "Alright," Old Man Coyote said. (38) After that Old Man Bullsnake was leaving. (39) Long after his head had departed, Old Man Bullsnake was still uncoiling until he was completely gone. (40) After he had gone, Old Man Coyote kept on thinking to himself. (41) "How can I make it so that I can fill up his house. (42) Well, come tomorrow, I must gather up some juniper bark and some yucca. (43) When I fasten it all together and tie it to my tail I can't help but surpass Old Bullsnake." (44) This is the way he talked and then he went to sleep. (45) After that, when he awoke early the next day, he went to the juniper thicket. (46) There it was that he stripped off some juniper bark and uprooted the yucca which he had found. (47) After that, so the story goes, from there he went home. (48) "Now it will turn out that I can't help but fill up Old Man Bullsnake's house"--that's what Old Man Coyote said. (49) After that he just ate. (50) After finishing eating he was working the juniper bark with his hands and was softening it. (51) He finished this and then after that he split the yucca. (52) He did this and then he connected the pieces of juniper bark. (53) There (where the pieces met) he was tying knots here and there with this yucca. (54) Gradually it became long. (55) "This should already be more than enough," Old Man Coyote was saying. (56) "Now I'll just have to sit here waiting until dusk," Old Man Coyote said. (57) Later, sure enough, the sun set. (58) After that he was dressing himself up by tying it with the split yucca to his (real) tail. (59) Then, after having finished, he left his house and went out toward Old Man Bullsnake's place. (60) Afterwards, when he arrived, he was invited in. (61) "Sit!" he was told. (62) After this Bullsnake noticed that Coyote's (real) tail had already entered, yet after it he was still dragging in something. (63) Afterwards it became clear to him that juniper bark was what Coyote had joined together in the hope of copying Bullsnake by lengthening his (own) tail. (64) Having been forced out, Bullsnake went outside and there he sat down. (65) Afterwards Old Man Coyote was told, "You really are longer than I am." (66) "Yes," Old Man Coyote said. (67) "See! You couldn't help but be outdone by me," so Coyote was thinking. (68) After that, following precedent, food was offered by Bullsnake. (69) Unknown to Coyote, Bullsnake had killed a porcupine and then when he had completely eaten its meat he rolled up just the pelt--still intact with all its quills protruding--into a ball. (70) In just this manner it was served to him. (71) "Eat!" Coyote was told. (72) "Let's keep on talking while you're eating," Coyote was told. (73) Also according to precedent they talked about places where they usually roam. (74) In this manner, it got dark. (75) Then Old Man Coyote started to yawn. (76) "Enough, it's night--I must go to sleep," Old Man Coyote said. (77) "Alright, we better go to sleep." (78) After that Old Man Coyote left. (79) From there he walked up the hill. (80) When on top of the hill he turned back (to take a look.) (81) His tail was still not completely out of Old Man Bullsnake's place. (82) After (seeing) that Old Man Coyote grinned. (83) "See!; It turned out just as I said: You could not help but be surpassed by me," so saying from there Coyote went homeward. (84) Afterwards when Old Man Bullsnake was not visible from the other side of the hill, Coyote did not know it but his tail was ignited by Bullsnake. (85) After that a breeze came up suddenly and the tail was really burning. (86) Finally, after Old Man Coyote had been walking for quite a while, he turned around. (87) By then he was being "trailed" by the fire. (88) Gradually it was coming closer to him. (89) After that he ran. (90) "Maybe it's my tail that is burning," he thought. (91) "What should I do? (92) Of course! Over there--eastward--there's some water running in the canyon; that's where I can put it out by dunking myself," that's what he said. (93) It had already come very close to him. (95) From there on he really started running. (96) By so doing he arrived at the river. (97) Without thinking he jumped into the water. (98) Since the water was very strong it carried him away and drowned him. (99) This is what there is of this Bullsnake story. (100) So, they say, since this is what became of Old Man Coyote, people should never imitate anybody.

Footnotes

[1]Kroskrity gratefully acknowledges the receipt of a small grant from the Phillips Fund of the American Philosophical Society which partially supported the summer research from which the present text emanated as a by-product.

[2]DISCOURSE here refers to discourse evidential particles which convey the "second-hand" status of the information imparted by the speaker. While these occur prodigiously in the Arizona Tewa text they will only occasionally be realized in the free translation in order to avoid the redundancy that their less encodable English translation equivalents would otherwise produce. In all future occurrences of the particle DISC. will serve as an abbreviated gloss. In a similar fashion all other constituents which are glossed by English grammatical morphemes (in upper case) will be abbreviated in all instances after their initial occurrence.

[3]In Arizona Tewa two designations exist for the mythic Coyote. This one, bayɛ·nah-senǿ, employs the conventional term for the animal. The other, pȍ·sikway, designates only the mythic character.

[4]EMPHATICS are constituent morphemes in both conjunctive and focus constructions. For discussion see Kroskrity (1977:130-163).

[5]The ASSOCIATIONAL postposition /-dí/ is a polysemous constituent which can be variously translated as "by", "with", "from", "SUBORDINATION", etc. See Kroskrity (1978) for detailed discussion.

[6]The fractional notation (3/3) employed here for the gloss of /ʔǿ·-/ is to be understood as encoding a third person subject and a third person object. Except for passive and imperative verbal prefixes, Tewa generally has discrete verbal prefixes encoding the type (possessive, stative, active, reciprocal-reflexive), person (1st, 2nd, 3rd) of the subject and number (singular, dual, plural) of the subject. With the exception of the passive and imperative prefixes, the prefix type will not be represented by the English glosses. For discussion and clarification consult Kroskrity (1977:164-193, especially p. 169).

COYOTE AND JUNCO

(Zuni)

Dennis Tedlock

Boston University

The Zuni language, or šiwi?ma, is an isolate possibly within Macro-Penutian (Newman 1964). It is spoken today, as it was when the Spaniards first arrived in 1539, in the upper drainage of the Zuni River, in what is now west-central New Mexico. At present there are more than 6,000 speakers, which is twice the number at the time of the conquest. Most of the published textual material is in the works of Ruth L. Bunzel (1932a, 1932b, 1933). Stanley Newman has published a dictionary (1958) and a grammar (1965). There is an enormous ethnographic literature stretching over what will soon be a century, but The Zuñi Indians of Matilda Coxe Stevenson (1904) remains the only comprehensive work.

The text given here was taken from a tape-recording of a whole series of tales told by Andrew Peynetsa (the performer of the present story) and Walter Sanchez, speaking in alternation, on the night of January 20, 1965, near the town of Zuni. "Coyote and Junco" is a translation of the Zuni title given by the narrator (on request): suski ta·p silo. The text has been published before (Tedlock 1972:75-84), but without the word-for-word translation given here; both text and translation have been thoroughly revised through a fresh confrontation with the original recording. Any reader desiring to hear that recording (or any of the other tapes on which Tedlock 1972 is based) will find a copy on deposit in the Library of the American Philosophical Society in Philadelphia.

The opening (line 1) and closing (71, beginning with "enough") formulas identify this story as a telapnanne 'tale' rather than as a čimik?ana?kowa 'beginner'; narratives of the latter genre are sacred truths, while no such claim is made for the former. Both kinds of narrative take place ?ino·te 'long ago', but the remote past of Zuni tradition is like that of many other agricultural peoples in North America rather than like the "myth-age" so familiar among hunters and gatherers: human beings are on stage right from the very beginning rather than waiting for a transformation of "first people" into today's animals. Even when animal characters are present they seldom play leading roles, but there is a small corpus of animal tales, nearly all of them featuring Coyote. Such tales are very brief, ranging from three to twenty minutes in length (four minutes here), whereas tales with human characters take up at least half an hour and not uncommonly run a full hour or more.

Despite the brevity of the present story, the narrator runs through a wide range of verbal skills. He departs from ordinary narrative delivery to imitate the voices of the characters, giving Coyote a tone that ranges from firm to insistent to stern, while Junco's tone ranges from shy and resistive to a close-mouthed tightness. A number of lines or parts of lines (1-4, 68, 71) are chanted after the manner of public announcements, and there is also a song (26-28), novel for the unvoiced puffs of air in its last line.

In ordinary phonetic matters, the text follows Newman's orthography (1965). Sandhi, which is considerable in Zuni, is preserved. The text-making linguist is commonly tempted to fill in missing syllables and make other "corrections," conforming (in effect) to the standards of a written literature of his own invention, but in the text given here I have tried to stay with the sounds (and intervening silences) that actually exist in the performance. A number of the features I have annotated are called "paralinguistic" by linguists for no better reason than that they customarily ignore them; I include them here on the grounds that they contribute to meaning (see Tedlock 1971, 1977). CAPITALS are used for loud passages and *italics* for soft ones. Unusual vowel lengthening, running a second or more, is shown by [----]. Pauses of at least one-half second (this is about the point at which they become readily audible) are indicated in the text by [/] and in the final translation by the beginning of a new line at the left-hand margin, while pauses of two seconds or more are indicated in the text by [//] and in the translation by strophe breaks. The numbering system follows the units of sound thus divided rather than units of grammatical construction; I have elsewhere proposed calling such units "lines" rather than "breath-groups" or "utterances," since there are many pauses in natural speech in which no breath is taken, and since the "utterance" is commonly assumed to conform to major grammatical boundaries, whereas the "line" is often in disconformity with those boundaries (Tedlock 1976). The play of line against grammar gives the story a shifting rhythm, with sentence structure sometimes "on the beat" (as in 52-54) and sometimes syncopated (as in 50-52).

Solid lines running below or above syllables indicate a stabilization of pitch approaching chant, respectively representing pitches [2] and [3] on a rough ascending scale of three pitches for the text in general. For the song of Junco, pitch stabilization reaches that of the singing voice; the two notes used are a tone and a half apart. The placement of the evenly spaced beats of the song is indicated interlinearly by [x]. For those portions of the text delivered in a normal speaking voice, relative pitch contrasts are noted as follows: [,] indicates a point at which the intonation contour has dropped to [2] before rising to [3] again, and [.] indicates a drop all the way to [1]. When the word at the end of a line is followed by [—], that indicates a slight rise in the last syllable before a pause; this is a deliberate suspension of the intonational flow in mid-stream rather than an uncontrolled hesitation. Toward the end of the story, Coyote delivers line 60 with an exasperated sputter; this is indicated by dashes within the line (rather than at the end of it), representing pauses of less than one-half second. In the interlinear translation, brackets enclose hypothetical renditions of archaic formulas.

(1) SONAHČI SONTI ?INO·----TE// (2) SOPŁUWA
[now we take it up] [now we begin] long ago bottle-necked gourds standing

YAL?AN/ (3) SIL ?OKACCIK K?AK^{w}appa/ (4) ta·či SUSki/ (5) suski
at the top[1] junco[2] old lady is housed SUB[3] and coyote coyote

lak ?ala ?i·muł?an hoł ča?liye./ (6) *ča?lappa/*
there bunch of rocks where they sit down then there is a brood there is a

(7) ta·či sil ?okaccik hołi—/ (8) kawašey?a,/ (9) tešuk?o/
brood SUB and junco old lady then winnows pigweed seeds

(10) ta·p k?ušuc?i, hoł kawašey?a./ (11) *ill?anna wolun hoł lesna/*
and tumbleweed seeds then she winnows with her basket then that way

(12) kawašnan ?allačełk?akka./ (13) *?allačełk?ap* ta·či
to winnow she tossed them in the air she tosses them in the air SUB and

suski/ (14) suski s/ (15) łat ?allu?ya, yam ča?l ?a·wan łat
coyote coyote now hunting goes around his children for hunting

?allu?ya laks—/ (16) silo kawašennank^{w}in tečči./ (17) kop to
goes around this way junco where she is winnowing he arrives what you

LEYE?A, le ?anik^{w}ap, ma? ho kawašey?a, le?./ (18) k^{w}ap to
do that he says to her SUB well I winnow that what you

kawašey?a, le?, ma?// (19) tešuk?o ta·p k?ušuc?i, *le? hoł*
winnow that well pigweed seeds and tumbleweed seeds that then

?anik^{w}ap, hayi./ (20) kop to ?ik^{w}e?a, le?, ma? hom luk
she says to him SUB indeed what you say that well my this

kawašnaka tenanne, le?./ (21) ?A·MA HOM?A·N TENA?U—/ (22) ?akka ho?
to winnow with song that come on! for me sing it so that I

yam/ (23) čaw o tenna, le?./ (24) sil ?okaccik s yam/
to my children own might sing that junco old lady now hers

(25) suski ?a·n tena,/ (26) YUWAHINA YUWAHINA/ (27) YUWAHINA YUWAHINA/
coyote for sings X X X X X X X X X X

(28) YOHINA YOHINA p^{h}u· p^{h}u· YOHINA YOHINA p^{h}u· p^{h}u·/[4] (29) le? hoł ?i./
X X X X X X X X that then says

(30) E· HO? S HO ?A·KA/ (31) ma? s ho ?anne, yam ho? ča ?a·wan
yes I now I went well now I go my I children for

tena?unna./ (32) suski ?a·ka lak wi·maya·wan hoł lottikap,
will sing it coyote went this way where the oaks stick out then he gets

NI·ŠAPAK?O ?ALLAHIPPA/ (33) ta· yam tenan ?okk?a./ (34) ?ika
near mourning doves fly up SUB and his song he loses he came

?ina—/ (35) hanatte, tom?an tena?u, ni·šapak hom—/ (36) tenan
he comes SUB quick! yours sing it mourning doves my song

?okk?anapka, le?./ (37) ta· s ?an tene,/ (38) tenan
they made me lose that and now for him she sings song

ya·nik^{w}atinan ta· s a·ka./ (39) lak tešokta·wan hoł i—/
he learns SUB and now he went this way where a field is planted then

(40) ta· s ?isk?on yeyye ?an ?a? k^{w}aču./ (41) ta· s yam tenan
and now there gopher his hole he breaks through and now his song

?okk?a./ (42) ta· s k^{w}ilik?annan ?iy—/ (43) ?itekkunan/
he loses and now for the second time he comes back he asks for it SUB

(44) ta· s ?an tene./ (45) ha·?ik?annana s ?anne ta· s/
and now for him she sings for the third time now he goes and now

(46) wi·maya hoł tečč̌ippa,/ (47) K?EČČO ?ALLAHIP ta· s yam
oaks stick out then he arrives SUB blackbirds[5] fly up SUB and now his

tenan ?okk?a./ (48) *?a·witenak?annan ?iya s ?iyappa/* (49) *sil*
song he loses for the fourth time he comes now he came SUB junco

?okaccik les k^{w}ikka, ?a· lak to ?iyappa/ (50) *k^{w}a? s ho tena?šuk^{w}a,*
old lady this said oh here you come SUB not now I will not sing

le? k^{w}ana s. ?a? k?amon tešuna—/ (51) ?a? k?amon
that she says SUB now rock round she looks for on the ground rock round

?awana, yam—/ (52) sil ?uččun ?ullunan, ?an sil ?a
she finds SUB her junco blouse[6] she puts it on SUB her junco rock

?unan kala??u./ (53) *šemak yamante ko? ley ?ona.*
to look at she makes it smooth ask as for you the matter does the one who

silo yam k^{w}?ak^{w}en k^{w}ato./ (54) suski s ?a·witenak?annan ?iya./
junco her house she enters coyote now for the fourth time comes

(55) ?inan s,/ (56) hanatte tom?an tena?u, ta· s ?an tenan ?okk?an
he comes SUB now quick! yours sing it and now his song he loses

?akka, ?iya, le ?anik^{w}a./[7] (57) kwa? silo peyena?ma./
SUB so he comes that he says to her not junco does not speak

(58) hanatte, le ?anik^{w}ap, k^{w}a? pena./ (59) to·---PA le?./
quick! that he says to her SUB not she speaks one! that

(60) ?a·witenak?annan ho?— penap— k^{w}a? hom?an to? tena?ma, tom ho? ?uttenna,
the fourth time I speak not for me you do not sing you I will bite

le ?an.// (61) k^{w}ilik?annan, k^{w}i·---LI le?./ (62) hanat tom?an tena?u, le?
that to her second time two! that quick! yours sing it that

hoł./ (63) k^{w}a? tenap, ha·---I le? hoł, AŁNAT ho? PENUWA,
then not she sings SUB three! that then last time I will speak

le?.// (64) suski s, HANAT TENA?U, le? an./ (65) k^{w}a? tena./
that coyote now quick! sing it that to her not she sings

(66) silo suski ?a?u./ (67) sil ?uttep, K^{W}A·M ?a? k?amon
junco coyote bites through junco he bites SUB munch! rock round

sil ?utte./ (68) li·łno luk?anna ko· yo?nask?an, ?akka luk
junco he bites right here these several teeth come out so that these

yo?na yała k^{w}aye./ (69) luhappa ten hiš tom ho?
teeth reaching across come out this certainly very much to you I

leyanna, ?ay ?ay le? k^{w}ana./ (70) sani yam ča?lik^{w}in teččip,
would do ow! ow! that he says coyote[8] his where the brood is arrives SUB

ka·kamaš ko· ?an čawe yašekka tekk^{w}in tečči./ (71) le?n
by now several his children they died at the place he arrives in this way

?ino·te teyatikkow ?akka, k^{w}a? suski li·łno ?a·wo?nawamme
long ago the one who lived it because of not coyotes here they do not have

LE·------ SEMkonika.
teeth [enough] [the word was short]

Free Translation

NOW WE TAKE IT UP NOW WE BEGIN LO----NG AGO

WHERE THE BOTTLE-GOURD STANDS ON TOP
OLD LADY JUNCO has her HOME
and CoYOte
Coyote has his brood where the rocks are clustered.
He has his brood
and Old Lady Junco then—
she's winnowing,
pigweed
and tumbleweed seeds, she's winnowing.
With her basket, that's the way
she winnowed by tossing them in the air.
She tosses them in the air and Coyote
now Coyote
he's going around hunting, going around hunting for his children this way—
he gets to where Junco is winnowing.
"What're you DOING?" he says that to her, "Well I'm winnowing," she says.
"What're you winnowing?" he says, "Well

pigweed and tumbleweed seeds," *she says that to him then,* "I see.
What's that you're saying?" he says, "Well this is my winnowing song," she says.
"COME ON! SING IT FOR ME—
then I can
sing it to my own children," he says.
Old Lady Junco now
sings it for Coyote,
"YUWAHINA YUWAHINA
YUWAHINA YUWAHINA
YOHINA YOHINA puff puff YOHINA YOHINA puff puff"
she says that then.
"YES I, NOW I'M GONE
well I'm going now, I'll sing it for my children."
Coyote went this way, then he gets near where the oaks stick out, MOURNING DOVES FLY up
and he loses his song.
He came back, he comes back—
[muttering] "Quick! Sing your song, mourning doves, my—
song, they made me lose it," he says.
And now she sings for him,
he learns the song and now he's gone.
This way, where a field is planted then—
and now a gopher hole is there, he breaks through.
And now he loses his song.
And now he comes back for the second time—

he asks for it
and now she sings for him.
Now for the third time he goes and now
he gets to the oaks sticking out then,
BLACKBIRDS FLY UP and now he loses his song.
When he came for the fourth time
Old Lady Junco said this, "Aw, here you come
but now I won't sing," she says that now. She looks around for a round rock—
she finds a round rock, she—
puts her junco-blouse on it, she makes her junco-rock look smooth.
"Go ahead and ask, it's up to you." Junco goes inside her house.
Coyote now comes for the fourth time.
He comes, now,
[muttering] "Quick! Sing your song," now he's lost his song, so he's back, he tells her that.
But Junco doesn't speak.
"Quick!" he says that to her, but she doesn't speak.
"ONE!" he says.
"The fourth time I—speak—and you don't sing for me, I'll bite you," he says to her.

"Second time, TWO!" he says.
"Quick! Sing your song," he says then.
When she doesn't sing, "THREE!" he says then, "I'll SPEAK for the LAST TIME," he says.

Now Coyote says, "QUICK! SING IT," to her.
She doesn't sing.
Coyote bites Junco right through.
He bites Junco, MUNCH! He bites the round-rock Junco.
Right here [points to molars] these here all the teeth come out, so this row of teeth comes out.
"This is exactly what I wanted to do to you." "Ow! Ow!" he says that.
Prairie Wolf gets back to his brood, and by the time he gets back to that place all his children have died.
In this way, because of the one who lived it, coyotes have no teeth here [points to molars] eNOU------GH THE WORD WAS short.

Footnotes

[1]This place is on the northern edge of the town of Zuni.
[2]The Oregon junco.
[3]SUB indicates subordination to a later verb.
[4]The puffs of air, pʰu· pʰu·, are unvoiced.
[5]Brewer's blackbirds.

[6]The Oregon junco has a hood of darker feathers covering its head and part of its breast.

[7]From ?an tenan to the end, line 56 represents an extremely rare example of indirect discourse.

[8]The ordinary term for the coyote is suski; sani, used here, is an esoteric term, and I have rendered it in the running translation as 'prairie wolf', which is the alternative English term for this animal.

RABBIT STEALS COYOTE'S BLADDER

(Western Tarahumara)

Don Burgess

Summer Institute of Linguistics

Western Tarahumara is spoken in the southwestern part of the state of Chihuahua, Mexico, within a rough triangle formed by the Chínipas, Urique and Oteros rivers. The Guarojio Indians, who have greatly influenced the Western Tarahumara, border this group on the west, the Pima somewhat to the north, and the Central dialect of Tarahumara on the east. Considerable linguistic and cultural difference has been noted between the two Tarahumara dialects, and mutual intelligibility is low.

The present text was written by Albino Mares Trias, a 29 year old Tarahumara man from the municipio of Guazapares. It was first published in a book (1975) which he wrote in collaboration with me for the Western Tarahumara schools. It includes nineteen snake and animal stories written in Tarahumara with a free Spanish translation. Five of the stories are about the coyote. The author wrote them as separate discourses but they are often told as a single, continuous discourse where the coyote chases the rabbit from one situation to the next. Coyote stories are part of a larger complex of stories which deal with how things were long ago when the Anayáwari people, the ancient ones, lived. It was a time when all the animals talked, when the great flood occurred and when the god Riosi taught the people to dance and make corn beer.

The author heard the stories from his parents, grandparents, and great-grandparents. Stories are usually told in the evening as a family sits around the fire or early in the morning as they are huddled under their blankets waiting for the first rays of the warm sun.

The author, who is among the few Tarahumaras who can read and write (he mostly taught himself), seems to be developing a written style which is more formal than his oral style. For example, stories which he recorded on tape several years ago do not contain many instances of the word ˀlíge 'and then', which is used to connect parts of a narrative. When he later put the same stories into writing, he used the word ˀlíge a great deal more.

Coyote stories from the Central dialect of Tarahumara can be found in Lumholtz (1902:302-307) and Muñoz (1965:22).

Only brief grammatical notes are given here since a grammatical sketch of Western Tarahumara is found in Burgess (forthcoming a). An analysis of the phonology can be found in Burgess (1970).

(1) yé raˀíči-li[1] wé ˀyá nerú-game hú nápu ruwí-le alué né
this talk-NOM much before be-PART is which explain-PAST that my

umúli-la.
great-grandfather-POSS

(2) ˀlíge siné=čigo alué basačí natépa-le-ke-ˀe ˀlíge alué rowí
then once-also that coyote found-PAST-SPEC-EMP then that rabbit

ená-game alé-mi boičí-mi epó-mi. (3) ˀlíge alué rowí
walk-PART there-there road-there plain-there then that rabbit

an-é-le-ke-ˀe ˀlíge alué basačí, tačíri ˀya-mí mué jé-mi,
say-to-PAST-SPEC-EMP then that coyote what search-there you here-there
him

an-é-le rowí.
say-to-PAST rabbit
him

(4) ʔlige alué basačí nehé-le ʔlíge regá, ʔné-ka pé mué goʔ-nále
then that coyote answer-PAST then thus I-EMP just you eat-want

ní-li-ke-ʔe, aní-le-ke-ʔe ʔlíge basačí.
be-STAT-SPEC-EMP say-PAST-SPEC-EMP then coyote

(5) ʔlíge alué basačí raʔíča-ga alé alué rowí ʔyúga wihčí
then that coyote talk-CONT there that rabbit with dirt

así-ba-le-ke-ʔe ʔlíge. (6) ʔlíge alé wihčí ilí-le-ke-ʔe ʔlíge
sit-REFL-PAST-SPEC-EMP then then there dirt stand-PAST-SPEC-EMP then

alué wehčá. (7) ʔlíge alué basačí alé así-ba-ga má soʔí-le-ke-ʔe
that thorn then that coyote there sit-REFL-CONT now stick-PAST-SPEC-EMP

ʔlíge alé muyá-la-či. (8) ʔlíge alué basačí aní-le-ke-ʔe ʔlíge
then there rump-POSS-place then that coyote say-PAST-SPEC-EMP then

né-ka ma soʔí-ke-ʔe. (9) tá-ča ʔlá soʔpú-sa ní-li mué. (10) soʔí-ke
I-EMP now stick-SPEC-EMP NEG-Q good pull-SUBOR be-STAT you stick-SPEC

né hé-na muya-čí guwána-ka, aní-le-ke-ʔe ʔlíge alué basačí.
I here-close rump-place behind-EMP say-PAST-SPEC-EMP then that coyote

(11) ʔlíge alué rowí-ka wé yáti eʔwá-le-ke-ʔe ʔlíge.
then that rabbit-EMP very quick do-PAST-SPEC-EMP then

(12) soʔpú-le-ke-ʔe ʔlíge alué wehčá alé há-game. (13) ʔlíge alué
pull-PAST-SPEC-EMP then that thorn there stand-PART then that

wehčá soʔpú-ga alué rowí, ʔlíge pé aʔlíge[2] oʔpó-le-ke-ʔe[3] ʔlíge alué
thorn pull-CONT that rabbit then just then pull-PAST-SPEC-EMP then that

basačí gosíba-la. (14) ʔlíge alué basačí tabilé sayé-le-ke-ʔe ʔlíge alué
coyote bladder-POSS then that coyote not feel-PAST-SPEC-EMP then that

rowí alué gosíba-la oʔpó-či. (15) ʔlíge wé=čigo oʔkó-li-game ʔlíge
rabbit that bladder-POSS pull-CONT then much-also hurt-STAT-PART then

alué wehčá-te soʔi-sá. (16) ʔlíge alué rowí aní-le-ke-ʔe ʔlíge,
that thorn-with stick-when then that rabbit say-PAST-SPEC-EMP then

čanigá goʔ-mé olá mué ne-ʔčí. (17) aka=né ʔlá oʔká ená-pa-če bilé saʔpá
why eat-FUT do you I-ACC Q=I good carry walk-EMP-EMP one meat

wé raʔí-game napurigá kó-ni-ma, aní-le-ke-ʔe ʔlíge alué rowí.
very tasty-PART as give-STAT-FUT say-PAST-SPEC-EMP then that rabbit

(18) ʔlíge alué rowí ʔyá-le-ke-ʔe ʔlíge alué saʔpá alué basačí.
then that rabbit give-PAST-SPEC-EMP then that meat that coyote

(19) ʔlíge alué basačí goʔ-lé-ke-ʔe ʔlíge. (20) ʔlíge wé
then that coyote eat-PAST-SPEC-EMP then then much

iyá-ga-le-ke-ʔe ʔlíge. (21) ʔlíge alué rowí ruké-le-ke-ʔe ʔlíge
like-CONT-PAST-SPEC-EMP then then that rabbit ask-PAST-SPEC-EMP then

alué saʔpá kő-gi-sa alué basačí pala ʔla iyága-li-ga ʔlíge alué
that meat give-EMP-when that coyote Q good like-STAT-CONT then that

basačí alué saʔpá. (22) ʔlíge basačí ʔlíge aní-le-ke-ʔe ʔlíge ruke-lía, ʔla abé
coyote that meat then coyote then say-PAST-SPEC-EMP then ask-SUBOR good more

raʔí-gan-ti[4] ní-li-ge-če alué saʔpá nápu mué nehí-sie, aní-le-ke-ʔe
like-PART-STAT be-STAT-PAST-EMP that meat which you give-TNS say-PAST-SPEC-EMP

ʔlíge alué basačí.
then that coyote

(23) ʔlíge alué rowí an-é-le-ke-ʔe ʔlíge alué basačí,
then that rabbit say-to-PAST-SPEC-EMP then that coyote
him

áka učé ʔyá-wa-ʔe ʔlíko alué saʔpá nápu mué wé iyá-ga, aní-le
RQ again search-IMP-EMP then that meat which you much like-CONT say-PAST

rowí. (24) ʔlíge mué-ka yé pá-ri nolí-ri simi-bóa-ka ʔlíge.
rabbit then you-EMP this up-steep ridge-steep go-FUT-EMP then

(25) Wa-mí pá rabó moiná-wa-ka ʔlíge. (26) ʔlíge né-ka yé nolí-ri
far-there up mountain climb-IMP-EMP then then I-EMP this ridge-steep

si-méla ʔlíge.
go-FUT then

(27) ʔlíge ala-ni-gá simí-ba-le-ke-ʔe ʔlíge alué basačí ʔlíge alué
then thus-say-CONT go-PL-PAST-SPEC-EMP then that coyote then that

rowí sí alé pá-ri-mi nolí-ri-mi. (28) ʔlíge alué basačí
rabbit also there up-steep-there ridge-steep-there then that coyote

ená-le-ke-ʔe ʔlíge alé pá-ri amulí moyéna alé rabó čubí-či.[5]
walk-PAST-SPEC-EMP then there up-steep almost climb there ridge peak-place

(29) ʔlíge alé-ri ene-gá oʔkó níle-le-ke-ʔe ʔlíge alé nápu
then there-steep look-CONT hurt feel-PAST-SPEC-EMP then there where

oʔpó-le alué rowí alué gosíba-la.
pull-PAST that rabbit that bladder-POSS

(30) ʔlíge alué basačí aní-le-ke-ʔe ʔlíge, mué-ri-go ompáli[6] má
then that coyote say-PAST-SPEC-EMP then you-IMP-IMP compadre now

ne-ʔčí gosíbi-la oʔpó-li-n=ko. (31) ʔlíge hípe-ko tabilé eʔkái-ma=ne
I-ACC bladder-POSS pull-STAT-NOM-be then today-EMP not forgive-FUT-I

ˀlíge mué. (32) Má me ˀli-méa=ne mué, aní-le-ke-ˀe ˀlíge alué basačí.
then you now kill-FUT-I you say-PAST-SPEC-EMP then that coyote

(33) ˀlíge alué basačí wé ayó-game neˀó-le-ke-ˀe ˀlíge alé
then that coyote much mad-PART shout-PAST-SPEC-EMP then there

pá-ri nolí-ri ili-gá. (34) ˀlíge alué rowí aké-le-ke-ˀe ˀlíge
up-steep ridge-steep stand-CONT then that rabbit hear-PAST-SPEC-EMP then

alué basačí neˀó-čini-či. (35) ˀlíge alué rowí aqui-sá ˀlíge alué
that coyote shout-noise-CONT then that rabbit hear-when then that

basačí neˀó-čini-či, ˀlíge yáti ˀmá-se-le-ke-ˀe ˀlíge alé
coyote shout-noise-CONT then quick run-flee-PAST-SPEC-EMP then there

ˀlé-gana alé epó-mi. (36) ˀlíge alue basačí-ka alé-mi nihubá
below-down there plain-there then that coyote-EMP there-there behind

ˀma-le-ke-ˀe ˀlíge naháti-sia meˀli-nále-ga alué rowí. (38) ˀlíge
run-PAST-SPEC-EMP then follow-SUBOR kill-want-CONT that rabbit then

alué rowí-ka abé sapú-me ní-le-ke-ˀe ˀlíge meta-gá alué basačí.
that rabbit-EMP more fast-PART be-PAST-SPEC-EMP then win-CONT that coyote

(39) ˀlíge alé-mi ˀmá-ga alé weˀká baká hági-či
then there-there run-CONT there many cane stand-place

ˀmá-re-le-ke-ˀe ˀlíge alué rowí. (40) ˀlíge wé ˀmá-re-le-ke-ˀe
run-through-PAST-SPEC-EMP then that rabbit then much run-through-PAST-SPEC-EMP

ˀlíge alé-mi. (41) ˀlíge alué basačí-ka alé baká hági-či alé
then there-there then that coyote-EMP there cane stand-place there

nasípa ahti-gó olá-le-ke-ˀe ˀlíge alué rowí. (42) ˀlíge alué basačí má
middle be-DUB do-PAST-SPEC-EMP then that rabbit then that coyote not

eˀkósi-le-ke-ˀe ˀlíge alué baká alé há-game peˀtá iˀlibé-ko. (43) pé
set-PAST-SPEC-EMP then that cane there stand-PART little later-EMP just
fire

alé ahti-gó mayé-ga alué rowí. (44) ˀlíge alué basačí-ka tabilé
there be-DUB think-CONT that rabbit then that coyote-EMP not

gayé-na-le-ke-ˀe ˀlíge alé nasípa alué weˀká baká hági-čí bahki-á
able-MOT-PAST-SPEC-EMP then there middle that many cane stand-place enter-CONT

čá namó há-li-game ˀlíge alué baká. (45) ˀlíge alé nalí suwéke
bad together stand-STAT-PART then that cane then there below edge

bočí-gi-mi ˀyá-le-ke-ˀe ˀlíge pála asé riwi-rá ˀlá-ga. (46) ˀlíge má
all-edge-there search-PAST-SPEC-EMP then Q be find-DUB think-CONT then now
over

eˀkósi-sa alué baká alué basačí, ˀlíge noligá repú-le-ke-ˀe ˀlíge alé pála asé
burn-when that cane that coyote then all care-PAST-SPEC-EMP then there Q be
around

maʔčí-na-ra yé rowí hé-na ʔla-gá. (47) ʔlíge alué baká raha-gá
come-MOT-DUB this rabbit here-near think-CONT then that cane burn-CONT out

eʔwé-le raʔná-le-ke-ʔe ʔlíge. (48) ʔlíge alué basačí aki-sá ʔlíge
strong-PAST pop-PAST-SPEC-EMP then then that coyote hear-when then

alué raʔná-me alé aní-le-ke-ʔe, yaʔ-má aʔtá-čane alué ompáli,
that pop-PART there say-PAST-SPEC-EMP now-now pop-noise that compadre

aní-le-ke-ʔe ʔlíge alué basačí alué baká raʔná-me aki-gá.
say-PAST-SPEC-EMP then that coyote that cane pop-PART hear-CONT

(49) ʔlíge abé iʔlibé-ko alué baká má rahi-sá-o, ʔlíge bočí-gi-mi
then more later-EMP that cane now burn-SUBOR-UNR then all-edge-there over

ʔyá-le-ke-ʔe ʔlíge alué basačí alé, pála asé boʔi-gá hé-na alué
search-PAST-SPEC-EMP then that coyote there Q be lie-CONT here-near that

rowí la-gá ʔyá-le-ke-ʔe (50) ʔlíge tabilé siné rewá-le-ke-ʔe
rabbit think-CONT search-PAST-SPEC-EMP then not ever find-PAST-SPEC-EMP

ʔlíge. (51) ʔlíge alué rowí-ka péča asá-li-ga ʔlíge alé. (53) ʔlíge
then then that rabbit-EMP not be-STAT-CONT then there then

tabilé čigó alé ní-le-ko nápu alué baká rahá-le. (54) mehká ní-le
not also there be-PAST-EMP where that cane burn-PAST far be-PAST

amulí bilé kilómetro mehká.
almost one kilometer far

(55) ʔlíge arigá tabilé umé-ba-le-ke-ʔe ʔlíge alué basačí alué
then thus not able-EMP-PAST-SPEC-EMP then that coyote that

rowí meʔá. (56) ʔlíge alué rowí-ka má neyú-se-le-ke-ʔe ʔlíge
rabbit kill then that rabbit-EMP now escape-flee-PAST-SPEC-EMP then

alué basačí ʔyúga.
that coyote with

Free Translation

(1) This story, which my great-grandfather explained to me, is about long ago.
(2) Once the coyote encountered a rabbit walking along a trail on a flat place. (3) The rabbit said to the coyote, 'What are you looking for here?'
(4) Then the coyote answered him in this way, 'I just want to eat you.'
(5) Then the coyote, as he talked with the rabbit, sat himself down on the ground. (6) There was a thorn sticking up there on the ground. (7) As the coyote was sitting there, it got stuck in his rear end. (8) Then the coyote said, 'I got stuck. (9) Could you pull it out? (10) I'm stuck here behind on my rear end.'
(11) Then (so) the rabbit quickly did it. (12) He pulled out that thorn. (13) (But) as he was pulling out the thorn, he also pulled out the coyote's bladder. (14) The coyote didn't feel anything when he pulled his bladder out. (15) He was hurting so much from the thorn sticking him.
(16) Then the rabbit said, 'Why do you want to eat me? (17) Don't I have with me a piece of very tasty meat to give you?'

(18) Then the rabbit gave the meat to the coyote. (19) Then the coyote ate it. (20) He really liked it. (21) When the rabbit gave the meat to the coyote, he asked the coyote if he liked it. (22) On being asked, the coyote said, 'It's really tasty, that meat which you gave me.'

(23) Then the rabbit said to the coyote, 'Then shall we look for (some more of) that meat which you really like? (24) You go up there on this ridge. (25) Climb way up on top. (26) I will go on this other ridge.'

(27) Having said that, the coyote and the rabbit went up on the ridges. (28) The coyote walked up there, almost climbing to the highest point on the ridge. (29) As he was up there looking around, he felt pain where the rabbit pulled his bladder out.

(30) Then the coyote said, 'Hey you, compadre, you pulled out my bladder. (31) Now I'll never forgive you. (32) Now I'm going to kill you.'

(33) Then the coyote shouted, really mad, standing up there on the ridge. (34) The rabbit heard the coyote shouting. (35) When the rabbit heard the coyote shouting, he quickly fled down below to a flat place. (36) The coyote ran after him, following him, wanting to kill that rabbit. (37) But the coyote never caught the rabbit. (38) The rabbit was much faster, beating the coyote.

(39) Running away, the rabbit ran through a place where there was a lot of standing cane. (40) He ran right on through. (41) But the coyote thought the rabbit was there in the middle of the cane patch. (42) Then, a short time later, the coyote set fire to the cane. (43) He was thinking the rabbit was in there. (44) He couldn't get into the cane himself because the cane stood so close together. (45) The coyote searched all along the edge to see if he could find the rabbit. (46) When the coyote burned the cane he watched all around to see if the rabbit came out. (47) The burning cane popped loudly. (48) When the coyote heard the cane popping there, he said, 'Quickly popped that compadre.'[7]

(49) A little later, when the cane had burned, the coyote looked all over to see if the rabbit was laid out there. (50) But he never found him. (51) That rabbit wasn't there. (52) The rabbit was far away in the underground hole of a mole. (53) He wasn't there where the cane burned. (54) He was a long way off, almost a kilometer.

(55) Thus the coyote didn't catch the rabbit to kill him. (56) The rabbit escaped from the coyote.

Footnotes

[1]/r/ and /l/ are retroflexed. /ʔ/ stands for glottal stop. /b/ and /g/ are fricatives. A hyphen represents morpheme boundary; = represents clitic boundary. Stress is phonemic; it cannot be predicted. The following grammatical abbreviations are used: NOM 'nominalizer', PART 'participial', POSS 'possessive', EMP 'emphatic', CONT 'continuative', REFL 'reflexive', SUBOR 'subordinator', STAT 'stative', ACC 'accusative', Q 'question', FUT 'future', TNS 'tense', IMP 'imperative', DUB 'dubitative', MOT 'motion', UNR 'unrealized' and NARR 'narrative'.

[2]Aʔlíge 'then' is the full form of ʔlíge and is used in certain emphatic situations.

[3]Oʔpó refers to pulling out something growing naturally, such as hair, and soʔpú to pulling out something extraneous, such as a thorn.

[4]The full form of raʔí-gan-ti, before morphophonemic changes, seems to be raʔí-game-ti. Also note in line 30 oʔpó-li-n=ko < oʔpó-li-ame kó.

[5]Incorporation into stems is not discussed here, but in the case of čubí-či, ču refers to something long and pointed, such as the beak of a bird. Note čulugí 'bird' and čulé 'coati mundi' (an animal with a long snout).

[6]For a study of the use of loanwords in Tarahumara, see Ornstein (1976).

[7]The coyote thought the popping sound was from the rabbit popping apart.

THE RABBIT AND THE COYOTE

(A Jacaltec Story)

Colette Grinevald Craig

University of Oregon

Jacaltec is a Mayan language of Guatemala. It is spoken on the border of Mexico in the highland department of Huehuetenango.

This text was recorded in the village of San Marcos in 1973. It was transcribed and translated into Guatemalan Spanish by Antonio F. Mendez, a native Jacaltec speaker whose contribution is gratefully acknowledged here.

Other Mayan stories of the rabbit and the coyote may be found in Craig (1976) for Jacaltec, England (1975) for Mam, and Smith-Stark (1976) for Pocomam.

(0) no7 conejo$_1$ b'oj$_2$ no7 oj$_3$
the rabbit$_1$ and$_2$ the coyote$_3$

(1) ab$_1$ ya7le$_2$ hun$_3$ no7$_4$ ni7an$_5$ conejo$_4$ (2) i7$_1$ como$_2$ cow$_3$
they say$_1$ [it] happened$_2$ [to] a$_3$ small$_5$ rabbit$_4$ and$_1$ since$_2$ he$_5$ [is]

listocanoj$_4$ no7$_5$ jalni$_6$ (3) ab'$_1$ chi b'eyc'oj$_2$ no7$_3$ slob'iltij$_4$ yul$_5$
very$_3$ smart$_4$ as we say$_6$ they say$_1$ he$_3$ goes by$_2$ to nibble$_4$ in$_5$

te7 ssandiya$_6$ hune$_7$ ix ixnam$_8$ (4) i7$_1$ niẋtejal$_2$ xin$_3$ ab'$_4$ sto$_5$ ix$_6$
the watermelon$_6$ [of] an$_7$ old woman$_8$ and$_1$ a little later$_2$ then$_3$ they say$_4$

ya7noj$_7$ hune7$_8$ smatanoj$_9$ ya7 pale$_{10}$ hacti7$_{11}$ la$_{12}$ (5) padre$_1$
[that] she$_6$ goes$_5$ to give$_7$ a$_8$ present$_9$ [to] the priest$_{10}$ this way$_{11}$ see!$_{12}$ father$_1$

ay$_2$ hune7$_3$ ha sandiya$_4$ la$_5$ (6) ẋihab'$_1$ ix$_2$ (7) a...$_1$
[here] is$_2$ a$_3$ watermelon for you$_4$ see$_5$ they say that$_1$ she$_2$ said$_1$ ah$_1$

c'ultic'a$_2$ yuch'antiyoẋ$_3$ ta wet$_4$ (8) ẋihab'$_1$ ya7 pale$_2$
good$_2$ thank God$_3$ to you$_4$ they say that said$_1$ the priest$_2$

(9) ab'$_1$ haxa$_2$ yilni$_3$ spohnitoj$_4$ ya7$_5$ te7$_6$ xin$_7$ la$_8$ (10) ab'$_1$
they say$_1$ [that] when$_2$ he$_5$ saw$_3$ and opened$_4$ it$_6$ then$_7$ see!$_8$ they say$_1$

hopb'ilxa$_2$ yul$_3$ te7$_4$ (11) ab'$_1$ maxa slotij$_2$ no7 conejo$_3$
[that] [it was] already rotten$_2$ inside of$_3$ it$_4$ they say$_1$ [that] the rabbit$_3$

yul$_4$ te7$_5$ (12) haxa$_1$ yawten$_2$ ya7$_3$ ix ixnam$_4$
had already eaten$_2$ inside of$_4$ it$_5$ [that is] when$_1$ he$_3$ called$_2$ the old woman$_4$

xin$_5$ (13) wal$_1$ tinañ$_2$ ta7an$_3$ ma hin ha wa7 engañar$_4$ han$_0$ (14) i7$_1$
then$_5$ well$_1$ now$_2$ really$_3$ you have just fooled me$_4$ and$_1$

tinañ$_2$ la$_3$ ta7an$_4$ hopb'ilxa$_5$ yul$_6$ te7 sandiya$_7$ ma ha wa7$_8$ ayin$_9$ han$_0$
now$_2$ see$_3$ [it is] really$_4$ already rotten$_5$ inside$_6$ the watermelon$_7$ you gave$_8$ me$_9$

(15) x̌ihab'$_1$ ya7 pale$_2$ tu7$_3$
they say that said$_1$ that$_3$ priest$_2$

(16) a...$_1$ waltu7$_2$ padre$_3$ cow$_4$ mach$_5$ hin muluj$_6$ han$_0$
ah$_1$ then$_2$ father$_3$ it is not$_5$ my fault$_6$ at all$_4$

(17) cow$_1$ mataj$_2$ hin$_3$ chi wute$_4$ han$_0$
it is not$_2$ I$_3$ at all$_1$ [who] does it$_4$

(18) ay$_1$ hun$_2$ no7$_3$ ni7an$_4$ nok'$_3$ cow$_5$ chi b'eyc'oj$_6$ lonojtoj$_7$ yul$_8$ hin sandiya$_9$ ti7$_{10}$ han$_0$
there is$_1$ a$_2$ small$_4$ animal$_3$ [who] goes by$_6$ a lot$_5$ to eat up$_7$ [the] inside of$_8$ this$_{10}$ watermelon of mine$_9$

(19) toñetic'a$_1$ aycoj$_2$ no7$_3$ sloniltij$_4$ yul$_5$
he$_3$ is$_2$ always$_1$ eating$_4$ inside$_5$

(20) mach$_1$ xin$_2$ ninoj$_3$ chin tz'atoj$_4$ yiñ$_5$ han$_0$
and$_2$ not$_1$ even a little$_3$ do I make$_4$ out of it$_5$

(21) x̌ihab'$_1$ ix$_2$
they say that$_1$ she$_2$ said$_1$

(22) a...$_1$ c'ultic'a$_2$ cu potx'o7$_3$
ah$_1$ all right$_2$ we will kill him$_3$

(23) ja7ay$_1$ hunuj$_2$ strampa$_3$ ta wet$_4$
let's put down$_1$ a$_2$ trap$_3$ for you$_4$

(24) x̌ihab'$_1$ ya7 pale$_2$
they say that said$_1$ the priest$_2$

(25) a...$_1$ c'ultic'a$_2$ xin$_3$ yuch'antiyox̌$_4$ ta wet$_5$ chaltu7$_6$
ah$_1$ all right$_2$ then$_3$ thank God$_4$ to you$_5$ then$_6$

(26) x̌ihab'$_1$ ix$_2$
they say that$_1$ she$_2$ said$_1$

(27) yaj$_1$ cha witij$_2$ ninoj$_3$ ixcab'$_4$
but$_1$ you bring$_2$ a little$_3$ wax$_4$

(28) xihab'$_1$ ya7 pale$_2$ tu7$_3$
they say that said$_1$ that$_3$ priest$_2$

(29) bueno$_1$ c'ultic'a$_2$
good$_1$ all right$_2$

(30) x̌ihab'$_1$ ix$_2$
they say that$_1$ she$_2$ said$_1$

(31) xinitoj$_1$ ix$_2$ ni7an$_3$ no7 ixcab'$_4$ xin$_5$
she$_2$ brought$_1$ a little$_3$ wax$_4$ then$_5$

(32) ab'$_1$ swatx'e$_2$ ya7 pale$_3$ no7$_4$ crucifijohal$_5$
and they say$_1$ [that] the priest$_3$ made$_2$ it$_4$ into a cross$_5$

(33) lahwi$_1$ tu7$_2$ xin$_3$ ab'$_4$ yalni$_5$ ya7$_6$
after$_1$ that$_2$ then$_3$ they say$_4$ [that] he$_6$ said$_5$

(34) b'ay$_1$ cow$_2$ sb'eh$_3$ no7$_4$ tu7$_5$ xin$_6$ hat$_7$ cha wayoj$_8$
where$_1$ [is] that$_5$ animal's$_4$ very$_2$ path$_3$ then$_6$ that's where$_7$ you put it down$_8$

(35) x̌ihab'$_1$ ya7 pale$_2$ tu7$_3$
they say that said$_1$ that$_3$ priest$_2$

(36) heh$_1$ x̌ihab'$_2$ ix$_3$
o.k.$_1$ they say that$_2$ she$_3$ said$_2$

(37) yinitoj$_1$ ix$_2$ hune7$_3$ crucifijo$_4$ tu7$_5$ xin$_6$
and she$_2$ took$_1$ that$_7$ one$_3$ cross$_4$ then$_6$

(38) xto$_1$ ix$_2$ yanojayoj$_3$ b'ay$_4$ sb'eh$_5$ no7 conejo$_6$
she$_2$ went$_1$ to put it down$_3$ where$_4$ the path$_5$ of the rabbit$_6$ [is]

(39) ab'$_1$ haxa$_2$ yapni$_3$ no7$_4$ ñi7an$_5$ conejo$_4$ xin$_6$
they say$_1$ [that] [this is] when$_2$ the$_4$ little$_5$ rabbit$_4$ arrived$_3$ then$_6$

(40) ab'$_1$ pajancañ$_2$ yiñ$_3$ ssat$_4$ no7$_5$ chila$_6$
they say$_1$ [that] standing up$_2$ in$_3$ front of it$_4$ [was] he$_5$ looking$_6$

(41) elañ$_1$
move$_1$

yul$_2$ hin b'eh$_3$ han$_0$ cho7$_5$ (42) ӿihab'$_1$ no7$_2$ (43) ab'$_1$
out of$_2$ my way$_3$ he you!$_5$ they say that$_1$ he$_2$ said$_1$ they say$_1$

mach$_2$ chi b'ili$_3$ (44) chawu$_1$ elaӿ$_2$ yul$_3$ hin b'eh$_4$ han$_0$ (45) ta$_1$
[that] [it] did$_3$ not$_2$ move$_3$ you do it$_1$ move$_2$ out of$_3$ my way$_4$ if$_1$

mach$_2$ xin$_3$ tajca$_4$ cha wij$_5$ wu$_6$ han$_0$ (46) ӿihab'$_1$ no7$_2$ hacti7$_3$
not$_2$ then$_3$ otherwise$_4$ you will get hit$_5$ by me$_6$ they say that$_1$ he$_2$ talked$_1$

xin$_4$ (47) ab'$_1$ maӿtic'a$_2$ hunuj$_3$ mac$_4$ chi b'ili$_5$ paxoj$_6$
this way$_3$ then$_4$ they say$_1$ [that] nobody$_{3-4}$ ever$_2$ moved$_5$ in return$_6$

(48) cow$_1$ chach eli$_2$ (49) ta$_1$ mach$_2$ xin$_3$ cow$_4$ chi wa7a7$_5$ hunuj$_6$
you move out$_2$ for good$_1$ if$_1$ not$_2$ then$_3$ I will give$_5$ [you] for sure$_4$ this$_8$

hin k'ab'$_7$ ti7$_8$ han$_0$ (50) b'aytam$_1$ chach tojicoj$_2$ wu$_3$ han$_0$
one$_6$ hand of mine$_7$ and who knows where$_1$ you will go$_2$ because of me$_3$

(51) ӿihab'$_1$ no7$_2$ (52) ab$_1$ maӿtic'a$_2$ mac$_3$ chi b'ili$_4$ xin$_5$
they say that$_1$ he$_2$ said$_1$ they say$_1$ [that] no one ever$_{2-3}$ moves$_4$ then$_5$

(53) ya7ni$_1$ no7$_2$ sk'ab'$_3$ scancanoj$_4$ lac'noj$_5$ (54) como$_1$ ixcab'$_2$
and he$_2$ gave$_1$ [with] his hand$_3$ and it stayed$_4$ stuck$_5$ since$_1$ it$_3$ [was]

no7$_3$ xin$_4$ (55) ab'$_1$ lahwi$_2$ tu7$_3$ xin$_4$ (56) b'ejtzoj$_1$
wax$_2$ then$_4$ they say$_1$ [that] after$_2$ that$_3$ then$_4$ [he said] let go$_1$

hun$_2$ hin k'ab'$_3$ ti7$_4$ han$_0$ (57) ta$_1$ chi wa7$_2$ hunxa$_3$ hin k'ab'$_4$ ti7$_5$
this$_4$ one$_2$ hand of mine$_3$ if$_1$ I give$_2$ [you] this$_5$ other$_3$ hand of mine$_4$

(58) b'aytam$_1$ chach apnoj$_2$ (59) ӿihab'$_1$ no7 conejo$_2$ tu7$_3$
who knows where$_1$ you will arrive$_2$ they say that said$_1$ that$_3$ rabbit$_2$

(60) ab'$_1$ ya7ni$_2$ no7$_3$ hunxa$_4$ sk'ab'$_5$ canpax canoj$_6$
they say$_1$ [that] he$_3$ gave$_2$ [with] his$_5$ other$_4$ hand$_5$ [which] stayed too$_6$

(61) b'ejtzoj$_1$ hin k'ab'$_2$ ti7$_3$ han$_0$ (62) ta$_1$ mach$_2$ xin$_3$ chi wa7apaxoj$_4$
let go$_1$ of this$_3$ hand of mine$_2$ if$_1$ not$_2$ then$_3$ I will give also$_4$

woj$_5$ ti7$_6$ han$_0$ (63) ӿihab'$_1$ no7 conejo$_2$ (64) waltu7$_1$
with this$_6$ foot of mine$_5$ they say that said$_1$ the rabbit$_2$ well$_1$

b'aytam$_2$ chach apnicoj$_3$ (65) ӿihab'pax$_1$ no7 conejo$_2$ tu7$_3$
who knows where$_2$ you will arrive$_3$ they say that said also$_1$ that$_3$ rabbit$_2$

(66) ab'$_1$ ya7ni$_2$ no7$_3$ hunxa$_4$ yoj$_5$ (67) ab'$_1$ scanpaxcanoj$_2$
they say$_1$ [that] he$_3$ gave$_2$ with another$_4$ of his feet$_5$ they say$_1$ [that]

lac'noj$_3$ hunxa$_4$ yoj$_5$ no7$_6$ (68) ya7ni$_1$ no7$_2$ hunxa$_3$ yoj$_4$
his$_6$ other$_4$ foot$_5$ also stayed for good$_2$ stuck$_3$ and he$_2$ gave$_1$ [with] his$_4$

xin$_5$ (69) hactu7$_1$ yu$_2$ scancanoj$_3$ sunil$_4$ yoj$_5$ noj$_6$ b'oj$_7$ sk'ab'$_8$
other$_3$ foot$_4$ then$_5$ that [is] how$_1$ did$_2$ stay put$_3$ all$_4$ his$_6$ feet$_5$ and$_7$ his

xin$_9$ (70) ab'$_1$ matxa$_2$ chu$_3$ yel$_4$ no7$_5$ (71) ab'$_1$
hands$_8$ then$_9$ they say$_1$ [that] he$_5$ already$_2$ could$_3$ not$_2$ run$_4$ they say$_1$

haxa$_2$ yapni$_3$ ix ixnam$_4$ (72) ab'$_1$ ayxac'oj$_2$ no7 conejo$_3$
[that] that is when$_2$ arrived$_3$ the old woman$_4$ they say$_1$ [that] the rabbit$_3$

yul$_4$ trampa$_5$ (73) ab'$_1$ tzab'b'ilxa$_2$ no7$_3$ yu$_4$ hune7$_5$ crucifijo$_6$
was still$_2$ in$_4$ the trap$_5$ they say$_1$ [that] he$_3$ was already grabbed$_2$ by$_4$ that$_8$ one$_5$

ixcab'$_7$ tu7$_8$ (74) bueno$_1$ wal$_2$ tinañ$_3$ ta7an$_4$ ay$_5$ hach$_6$ chin ha wet$_7$
cross$_6$ of wax$_7$ well$_1$ then$_2$ now$_3$ if$_4$ you$_6$ are$_5$ not$_4$ [the one who] gives me

han$_0$ (75) ta7an$_1$ ila7$_2$ hachñe$_3$ ni7an$_4$ cow$_5$ chin ha wa7 canoj enganar$_6$
trouble$_7$ for sure$_1$ look$_2$ [how] small$_4$ you just are$_3$ [and] you have given me$_6$

han$_0$ (76) tinañ$_1$ hantaj$_2$ hin sandiya$_3$ cha wetacantoj$_4$ han$_0$
a lot of$_5$ trouble$_6$ now$_1$ so many$_2$ of my watermelons$_3$ you wasted away$_4$

(77) x̌ihab'$_1$ ix ixnam$_2$ tu7$_3$ (78) tinañ$_1$ chin to$_2$ wi7a7tij$_3$
they say that said$_1$ that$_3$ old woman$_2$ now$_1$ I go$_2$ to bring$_3$

ha chocolate$_4$ (79) x̌ihab'$_1$ ix$_2$ hacti7$_3$ la$_4$
your chocolate$_4$ they say that$_1$ this$_3$ [is how] she$_2$ said$_1$ see!$_4$

(80) xcancanoj$_1$ no7 conejo$_2$ schuquil$_3$ (81) ab'$_1$ lañan$_2$ tu7$_3$ xin$_4$ yec'toj$_5$
the rabbit$_2$ stayed behind$_1$ alone$_3$ they say that$_1$ that$_3$ was going on$_2$

hun$_6$ no7 oj$_7$ (82) a...$_1$ tzet$_2$ cha wu$_3$ cho7$_4$
then$_4$ [when] passed by$_5$ a$_6$ coyote$_7$ ah!$_1$ what$_2$ are you doing$_3$ he you!$_4$

(83) x̌ihab'$_1$ no7 oj$_2$ tu7$_3$ (84) a...$_1$ matzet$_2$ ayinc'oj$_3$ wechman$_4$
they say that said$_1$ that$_3$ coyote$_2$ ah$_1$ nothing$_2$ I am here$_3$ waiting for$_4$

ni7an$_5$ hin chocolate$_6$ (85) x̌ihab'$_1$ no7 conejo$_2$ tu7$_3$ (86) tzet$_1$
a little of$_5$ my chocolate$_6$ they say that said$_1$ that$_3$ rabbit$_2$ what$_1$

chocolatehal$_2$ (87) a...$_1$ tzixam$_2$ chocolatehal$_3$ (88) cow$_1$
kind of chocolate$_2$ ah!$_1$ who knows$_2$ what kind of chocolate$_3$ [it is]

c'ulmi'$_2$ cu lonicanoj$_3$ (89) yaj$_1$ haxti7$_2$ b'isc'ulal$_3$ we$_4$ yiñ$_5$ han$_0$
very$_1$ good maybe$_2$ for us to eat$_3$ but$_1$ me here$_2$ I am$_4$ sad$_3$ about it$_5$

(90) machmi$_1$ chi lahwoj$_2$ wu$_3$ han$_0$ (91) cow$_1$ nich'an$_2$ hin$_3$ han$_0$
maybe$_1$ it will$_2$ not$_1$ be finished$_2$ by me$_3$ I$_3$ [am] very$_1$ small$_2$

(92) x̌ihab'$_1$ no7 conejo$_2$ tu7$_3$ (93) wac'amta$_1$ cow$_2$ sak'al$_3$
they say that said$_1$ that$_3$ rabbit$_2$ I bet it would be probably$_1$ very$_2$

cu loni$_4$ (94) x̌ihab'pax$_1$ no7 oj$_2$ tu7$_3$ (95) sak'al$_1$
nice$_3$ if$_1$ we ate it$_4$ they say that said also$_1$ that$_3$ coyote$_2$ nice$_1$

xin$_0$ tinan̄$_2$ yaj$_3$ machmi$_4$ chi lahwi$_5$ wu$_6$ han$_0$ (96) x̌ihab'pax$_1$ no7 conejo$_2$
now$_2$ but$_3$ maybe it [can]not$_4$ be finished$_5$ by me$_6$ they say that said also$_1$

tu7$_3$ (97) hombres$_1$ canan̄$_2$ hin heleloj$_3$ han$_0$ (98) waltu7$_1$
that$_3$ rabbit$_2$ man!$_1$ stay$_2$ in my place$_3$ that way$_1$ it

chi lahwi$_2$ ha wu$_3$ (99) hach$_1$ ti7$_2$ nimejal$_3$ hach$_4$ (100) x̌ihab'$_1$
[can] be finished$_2$ by you$_3$ you$_1$ here$_2$ you$_4$ [are] big$_3$ they say

no7 conejo$_2$ tet$_3$ no7 oj$_4$ tu7$_5$ (101) c'ultic'a$_1$ xin$_2$ ocoj$_3$ hin$_4$ han$_0$
that$_1$ the rabbit$_2$ said$_1$ to$_3$ that$_5$ coyote$_4$ all right$_1$ then$_2$ I$_4$ will get in$_3$

(102) x̌ihab'$_1$ no7 oj$_2$ tu7$_3$
they say that said$_1$ that$_3$ coyote$_2$

(103) yiniloj$_1$ no7$_2$ no7 conejo$_3$
and he$_2$ pulls out$_1$ the rabbit$_3$

(104) yanicancoj$_1$ no7$_2$ sb'a$_3$ jalninayi$_4$ yin̄$_5$ hune7$_6$ crucifijo$_7$ ixcab'$_8$ tu7$_9$
and he$_2$ put$_1$ himself$_3$ in to stay$_1$ as we say$_4$ in$_5$ that$_9$ one$_6$ wax$_8$ cross$_7$

(105) haxa$_1$ yapni$_2$ ix ixnam$_3$ xin$_4$
and when$_1$ the old woman$_3$ arrived$_2$ then$_4$

(106) ha$_1$ jodidos$_2$ ta7an$_3$ mañoso$_4$
ah!$_1$ damn you$_2$ if$_3$ you$_5$

hach$_5$ (107) tinan̄$_1$ yet$_2$ ma hin hulc'uj$_3$ han$_0$ (108) cow$_1$
are not$_3$ vicious$_4$ today$_1$ when$_2$ I came by$_3$ you$_3$ [were]

ni7anch'an$_2$ hach$_3$ (109) tinan̄$_1$ cow$_2$ nimejal$_3$ hachxapaxoj$_4$ (110) ay$_1$
very$_1$ small$_2$ now$_1$ you are already also$_4$ very$_2$ big$_3$ have$_1$

ha chocolate$_2$ tu7$_3$ la$_4$ (111) x̌ihab'$_1$ ix$_2$ la$_3$ (112) ab'$_1$
that$_3$ chocolate of yours$_2$ see!$_4$ they say that$_1$ she$_2$ said$_1$ see!$_3$ they

caj$_2$ ch'en alambra$_3$ (113) ab'$_1$ sopnictoj$_2$ ix$_3$ ch'en$_4$ yul$_5$
say that$_1$ [it was] red hot$_2$ wire$_3$ they say that$_1$ she$_3$ jammed$_2$ it$_4$ in$_5$ the

syutz$_6$ no7 oj$_7$ tu7$_8$ (114) ab'$_1$ toxan̄e$_2$ ch7ok'canoj$_3$ ho7$_4$ ni7an$_5$ oj$_4$
behind$_6$ of that$_8$ coyote$_7$ they say that$_1$ the poor$_4$ little$_5$ coyote$_4$ all he

stocanoj$_6$ ho7$_7$ (115) wal$_1$ no7 conejo$_2$ xin$_3$
could do$_2$ [was] to cry$_3$ [as] he$_7$ was left running$_6$ while$_1$ the rabbit$_2$ then$_3$

(116) ab'$_1$ nahatxa$_2$ aytij$_3$ no7$_4$ tzeb'oj$_5$
they say that$_1$ already far away$_2$ he$_4$ had arrived$_3$ to laugh$_5$

(117) niẍtejal$_1$ xin$_2$ ab'$_3$ sto$_4$ no7$_5$ (118) yapni$_1$
a little later$_1$ then$_2$ they say that$_3$ he(rabbit)$_5$ had gone$_4$ and he$_2$

no7$_2$ yiñ$_3$ hune7$_4$ ch'en ch'en$_5$ (119) ab'$_1$ cawxañe$_2$ texto$_3$ yecoj$_4$ no7 conejo$_5$
had arrived$_1$ to$_3$ a$_4$ rock$_5$ they say that$_1$ that$_6$ rabbit$_5$ was standing$_4$

tu7$_6$ yalañ$_7$ hun$_8$ ch'en ch'en$_9$ tu7$_{10}$ (120) yapni$_1$ no7 oj$_2$
already hard$_2$ and still$_3$ under$_7$ that$_{10}$ one$_8$ rock$_9$ [when] that$_3$ coyote$_2$

tu7$_3$ (121) wal$_1$ tinañ$_2$ cow$_3$ chach tañcaniloj$_4$ (122) ta7an$_1$ toñe$_2$
arrived$_1$ well$_1$ now$_2$ really$_3$ you are finished$_4$ since$_1$ the only

ma hin ha wa7 engañar$_3$ han$_0$ (123) chocolate$_1$ cachi$_2$ yuxin$_3$
thing$_2$[you did was that] you tricked me$_3$ chocolate$_1$ you said$_2$ for that$_3$

ma hin can$_4$ han$_0$ (124) ta7an$_1$ cow$_2$ tinañ$_3$ ma hin mak'lax$_4$ han$_0$ (125) mato$_1$
I stayed$_4$ in fact$_1$ right$_2$ now$_3$ I was beaten$_4$ or

ch'en alambra$_2$ yul$_3$ hin yutz$_4$ han$_0$ (126) ẍihab'$_1$ no7 oj$_2$ tu7$_3$
[rather]$_1$ [I had] a wire$_2$ in$_3$ my bottom$_4$ they say that said$_1$ that$_3$ coyote$_2$

(127) yapni$_1$ no7$_2$ yiñ$_3$ no7 conejo$_4$ tu7$_5$ (128) ay$_1$ hombres$_2$ cow$_3$ mach$_4$
as he$_2$ arrived$_1$ where$_3$ that$_5$ rabbit$_4$ [was] ah$_1$ man!$_2$ really$_3$ let's not$_4$

chi jal$_5$ huntu7$_6$ b'ela$_7$ (129) tinañ$_1$ lañan stañiloj$_2$ hun$_3$ coñob'$_4$ jalañ$_5$
talk about$_5$ that$_6$ see!$_7$ right now$_1$ this$_6$ one$_3$ village$_4$ under us$_5$ will be

ti7$_6$ la$_7$ (131) machmi$_1$ cha tzab'canoj$_2$ ninoj$_3$ ch'en$_4$
dying out$_2$ see!$_7$ would not$_1$ you$_2$ maybe$_1$ stay and grab$_1$ it$_4$ a little$_3$

(132) cat$_1$ hin to$_2$ hin saynoj$_3$ cab'oj$_4$ cu te7$_5$ (133) ta$_1$
and then$_1$ I will go$_2$ to look for$_3$ a couple of$_4$ big sticks for us$_5$ if$_1$

mach$_2$ xin$_3$ tañcanoj$_4$ hun$_5$ coñob$_6$ ti7$_7$ (134) ẍihab'$_1$ no7 conejo$_2$ tu7$_3$
not$_2$ then$_3$ this$_7$ one$_5$ village$_6$ is finished$_4$ they say that said$_1$ that$_3$ rabbit$_2$

(135) c'aynacantoj$_1$ yu$_2$ no7 oj$_3$ (136) c'ultic'a$_1$ xin$_2$ ẍihab'pax$_3$
it was lost$_1$ on$_2$ the coyote$_3$ all right$_1$ then$_2$ they say that added$_3$

no7 oj$_4$ (137) yocpaxtoj$_1$ no7$_2$ yalañ$_3$ hun$_4$ ch'en ch'en$_5$ tu7$_6$
the coyote$_4$ and he$_2$ got in also$_1$ under$_3$ that$_6$ one$_4$ rock$_5$

(138) niẍtejal$_1$ xin$_2$ stopaxcan$_3$ no7 conejo$_4$ (139) ab'$_1$ cow$_2$ hunay$_3$
a little later$_1$ then$_2$ the rabbit$_4$ was gone again$_3$ they say that$_1$ that$_6$

aycanic'oj$_4$ no7 oj$_5$ tu7$_6$ xin$_7$ la$_8$ (140) lahwitu7$_1$ xin$_2$
coyote$_5$ stayed put$_4$ for a long$_2$ while$_3$ then$_7$ see!$_8$ later$_1$ then$_2$ he$_4$ ended up

siquicaniloj$_3$ no7$_4$ xin$_0$ (141) tañoj ab'caniloj$_1$ hun$_2$ coñob$_3$ ti7$_4$
tired$_3$ would that$_1$ this$_4$ one$_2$ village$_3$ end up destroyed$_1$

(142) yila7$_1$ mach$_2$ woc$_3$ yiŋ$_4$ haŋ$_0$
so what!$_1$ I$_3$ don't$_2$ care$_3$ about it$_4$

(143) x̌ihab'$_1$ no7$_2$ sb'ejniloj$_3$ sb'a$_4$ no7$_5$ yalni$_6$ la$_7$
they say that$_1$ he$_2$ said$_1$ [as] he$_5$ threw himself$_4$ out$_3$ as he said it$_6$ see!$_7$

(144) ta7an$_1$ ab'$_2$ hunel$_3$ staŋi$_4$ ch'en ch'en$_5$
but in fact$_1$ [as] they say$_2$ the rock$_5$ stood$_4$ by itself$_3$

(145) ab'$_1$ ŋach'en$_2$ ch'en$_3$
they say that$_1$ it$_3$ [was] a cave$_2$

(146) nix̌tejal$_1$ xin$_2$ stopax$_3$ no7 oj$_4$ tu7$_5$
a little later$_1$ then$_2$ that$_5$ coyote$_4$ was on his way again$_3$

(147) ab$_1$ ayxaytoj$_2$ no7 conejo$_3$ sti7$_4$ hune7$_5$ ha7 ha7$_6$
they say that$_1$ the rabbit$_3$ was already down there$_2$ by the edge$_4$ of a body$_5$ of water$_6$

(148) yapni$_1$ no7 oj$_2$ tu7$_3$ xin$_4$
and that$_3$ coyote$_2$ arrived$_1$ then$_4$

(149) wal$_1$ tinaŋ$_2$ wux̌taj$_3$ cow$_4$ chach taŋcaniloj$_5$
well$_1$ now$_2$ my brother$_3$ for sure$_4$ you are finished once and for all$_5$

(150) cow$_1$ quin ha wa7canoj engañar$_2$ haŋ$_0$
you have tricked me$_2$ too much$_1$

(151) x̌ihab'pax$_1$ no7 oj$_2$ tu7$_3$
they say that said$_1$ that$_3$ coyote$_2$

(152) machoj$_1$ hombres$_2$ c'aynatoj$_3$ hun tu7$_4$
no$_1$ man!$_2$ forget$_3$ that$_4$

(153) tinaŋ$_1$ la$_2$ sak'al$_3$ hune7$_4$ queso$_5$ ahaytoj$_6$ yul$_7$ ha7 ha7$_8$ ti7$_9$ la$_{10}$
now$_1$ look$_2$ how delicious$_3$ [is] this$_9$ one$_4$ cheese$_5$ [that is] down there$_6$ in$_7$ the water$_8$ see!$_{10}$

(154) ab'$_1$ tato$_2$ chi lahwotoj$_3$ ha7$_4$ juc'ni$_5$ la$_6$
they say that$_1$ if$_2$ it(water)$_4$ is finished$_3$ [by] our drinking it$_5$ see!$_6$

(155) catxin$_1$ stzujchahoj$_2$ ju$_3$ cat$_4$ culonitoj$_5$
and then$_1$ it is reached$_2$ by us$_3$ and then$_4$ we eat it up$_5$

(156) x̌ihab'$_1$ no7 conejo$_2$ tu7$_3$
they say that said$_1$ that$_3$ rabbit$_2$

(157) cow$_1$ yel$_2$ cha wala$_3$ queso$_4$
very$_1$ true$_2$ [what] you say$_3$ [that it is] cheese$_4$

(158) x̌ihab'paxoj$_1$ no7 oj$_2$ tu7$_3$
they say that$_1$ that$_3$ coyote$_2$ said also$_1$

(159) queso$_1$ xin$_2$ ilc'anab'$_3$ jilni$_4$ la$_5$
[it is] cheese$_1$ of course$_2$ look$_3$ [how] we see it$_4$ see!$_5$

(160) x̌ihab'$_1$ no7 conejo$_2$ tu7$_3$
they say that said$_1$ that$_3$ rabbit$_2$

(161) ta7an$_1$ ab'$_2$ yechel$_3$ luna$_4$ chi jilaytoj$_5$ yul$_6$ ha7$_7$ tu7$_8$
in fact$_1$ they say that$_2$ [it is] the reflection$_3$ of the moon$_4$ [that] we see down there$_5$ in$_6$ that$_8$ water$_7$

(162) wal$_1$ tinaŋ$_2$ ila7xa$_3$
well$_1$ now$_2$ look already at$_3$

ha7$_4$ ch'aytoj$_5$ wu$_6$ han$_0$ la$_7$ (163) x̌ihab'$_1$ no7 conejo$_2$
the water$_4$ [that] has gone down$_5$ by my doing$_6$ see!$_7$ they say that said$_1$ that$_3$

tu7$_3$ (164) c'ultic'a$_1$ xin$_2$ x̌ihab'$_3$ no7 oj$_4$ tu7$_5$ (165) ab'$_1$
rabbit$_2$ all right$_1$ then$_2$ they say that said$_3$ that$_5$ coyote$_4$ they say

yocpax$_2$ no7$_3$ yuc'nuj$_4$ ha7$_5$ (166) ab'$_1$ cow$_2$ uc'uj$_3$ ha'$_4$
that$_1$ he$_3$ started also$_2$ to drink$_4$ it(water)$_5$ they say that$_1$ a lot of$_2$

chucanoj$_5$ no7$_6$ (167) ab'$_1$ cow$_2$ chi spotxcantoj$_3$ no7$_4$ ha7$_5$
drinking$_3$ water$_4$ he$_6$ does for good$_5$ they say that$_1$ he$_4$ gulped$_3$ a lot$_2$ of it$_5$

(168) wal$_1$ no7 conejo$_2$ ta7an$_3$ mach$_4$ chuc'$_5$ no7$_6$ ha7$_7$ (169) ab'$_1$ haxa$_2$
while$_1$ the rabbit$_2$ for sure$_3$ he$_6$ does not$_4$ drink$_5$ it$_7$ they say that$_1$

sliñcha$_3$ no7$_4$ yu$_5$ ha7 ha7$_6$ tu7$_7$ (170) ab'$_1$ yelpaxcanoj$_2$
when$_2$ he(coyote)$_4$ explodes$_3$ because of$_5$ that$_7$ water$_6$ they say that$_1$ that$_4$

no7 conejo$_3$ tu7$_4$ (171) ab'$_1$ cow$_2$ chi txib'canoj$_3$ no7$_4$ yiñ$_5$
rabbit$_3$ ends up running again$_2$ they say that$_1$ he(rabbit)$_4$ laughs$_3$ a lot$_2$ at$_5$

no7$_6$
him(coyote)$_6$

(172) nix̌tejal$_1$ xin$_2$ stocanoj$_3$ no7$_4$ xin$_5$ (173) ab'$_1$
a little later$_1$ then$_2$ he(rabbit)$_4$ was on his way$_3$ then$_5$ they say that$_1$

ayxapaxatoj$_2$ no7$_3$ swi7$_4$ hune7$_5$ map$_6$ (174) yapnipaxoj$_1$ no7 oj$_2$
he$_3$ was already again up$_2$ on top of$_4$ a$_5$ coyol tree$_6$ and arrived again$_1$ that$_3$

tu7$_3$ (175) wal$_1$ tinañ$_2$ wux̌taj$_3$ cow$_4$ chach tañiloj$_5$ (176) x̌ihab'$_1$
coyote$_2$ well$_1$ now$_2$ my brother$_3$ you are finished$_5$ for good$_4$ they say

no7 oj$_2$ tu7$_3$ tet$_4$ no7 conejo$_5$ tu7$_6$ (177) machoj$_1$ hombres$_2$ tinañ$_3$ la$_4$
that$_1$ that$_3$ coyote$_2$ said$_1$ to$_4$ that$_6$ rabbit$_5$ no$_1$ man!$_2$ now$_3$ see$_4$ let's$_5$ eat$_6$

ac'anab'$_5$ cu loni$_6$ hunk'ahan$_7$ nix̌tej$_8$ chin lo$_9$ ti7$_{10}$ han$_0$ la$_{11}$ (178) x̌ihab'$_1$
a few of$_7$ these$_{10}$ little things$_8$ [that] I am eating$_9$ see!$_{11}$ they say

no7 conejo$_2$ tu7 (179) a...$_1$ jab'e$_2$ (180) x̌ihab' pax$_1$
that said$_1$ that$_3$ rabbit$_2$ ah$_1$ let's taste them$_2$ they say that said

no7 oj$_2$ tu7$_3$ (181) machoj$_1$ ac'anab'$_2$ cu loni$_3$ (182) x̌ihab'$_1$
also$_1$ that$_3$ coyote$_2$ no$_1$ let's$_2$ eat them$_3$ they say that$_1$

no7$_2$ (183) slonitoj$_1$ no7$_2$ sb'ak'$_3$ te7 map$_4$ xin$_5$ (184) ay$_1$
he(rabbit)$_2$ said$_1$ and he$_2$ ate up$_1$ the seed$_3$ of the coyol$_4$ then$_5$ ah$_1$

an'$_2$ cow$_3$ sak'al$_4$ cu loni$_5$ (185) tzet$_1$ cha lo$_2$ ti7$_3$
taste$_2$ how$_3$ delicious$_4$ [they are] for us to eat$_5$ what$_1$ are you eating$_2$

cho7$_4$ (186) ẍihab'$_1$ no7 oj$_2$ tu7$_3$ (187) mat$_1$ ha wohtajoj$_2$
here$_3$ he you!$_4$ they say that said$_1$ that$_3$ coyote$_2$ don't$_1$ you know$_2$

hach$_3$ ti7$_4$ hombres$_5$ (188) cow$_1$ sub'utajcanoj$_2$ hune7$_3$ ti7$_4$ (189) hin b'ak'$_1$
you$_3$ here$_4$ man!$_5$ this$_4$ one$_3$ [is] very$_1$ easy indeed$_2$ my seeds

ma hin chaqu'iltij$_2$ han$_0$ ha7$_3$ chin lo$_4$ ti7$_5$ han$_0$
[testicles]$_1$ [that] I have pounded out$_2$ that is what$_3$ I am eating$_4$ here$_5$

(190) ẍihab'paxoj$_1$ no7$_2$ (191) lek'ti7al$_1$ cha wal$_2$ hayach$_3$ ti7$_4$
they say that$_1$ he$_2$ said also$_1$ lies$_1$ you are saying$_2$ you$_3$ here$_4$

(192) chac'c'anabiltij$_1$ ha wet$_2$ cat$_3$ ha loni$_4$ (193) ẍihab'$_1$ no7 conejo$_2$
pound$_1$ yours$_2$ out$_1$ and then$_3$ eat them$_4$ they say that said$_1$ that$_3$

tu7$_3$ (194) cow$_1$ yel$_2$ cha wala$_3$ (195) ho7$_1$ cow$_2$ yeli$_3$
rabbit$_2$ [is it] really$_1$ true$_2$ what you say$_3$ yes$_1$ very$_2$ true$_3$

(196) ay$_1$ hin ch'en$_2$ b'ay$_3$ ma hin chac'$_4$ han$_0$ la$_5$ (197) ẍihab'$_1$
I$_2$ have$_1$ a rock$_2$ with which$_3$ I pounded$_4$ see!$_5$ they say that$_1$ he$_2$

no7$_2$ (198) niẍtejal$_1$ xin$_2$ (199) ta$_1$ hactu7$_2$ chaltu7$_3$
said$_1$ a little later$_1$ then$_2$ if$_1$ that is$_2$ how it is$_3$ I will pound

chin chac'analtij$_4$ (200) ẍihab'$_1$ no7 oj$_2$ tu7$_3$ xin$_4$ (201) ab'$_1$
them out then$_4$ they say that said$_1$ that$_3$ coyote$_2$ then$_4$ they

schac'niltij$_2$ no7$_3$ sb'ak'$_4$ xin$_5$ (202) ab'$_1$ hactu7$_2$ yu$_3$
say that$_1$ he$_3$ pounded out$_2$ his testicles$_4$ then$_5$ they say that$_1$ that is how$_2$

scamcaniloj$_4$ no7 oj$_5$ tu7$_6$ (203) ya7nicanoj ganar$_1$ no7 conejo$_2$
that$_6$ coyote$_5$ did$_3$ finally die$_4$ and that$_3$ rabbit$_2$ finally won$_1$

Free Translation

(0) The Rabbit and the Coyote

(1) So this is what happened to a small rabbit. (2) Since he is very smart as we know, (3) they say that he used to go by all the time to nibble on the watermelons of an old woman. (4) And so one day they say that she goes over to give a present to the priest, see! (5) "Father! Here is a watermelon for you, see," (6) they say that she said. (7) "Ah! Good, thank you very much," (8) they say that the priest said. (9) But then apparently when he broke it open (10) it turned out to be rotten inside (11) because the rabbit had already taken a bite out of it, they say. (12) So the priest called back the old woman: (13) "What is this? Are you fooling me? (14) Look! the watermelon you gave me is already all rotten inside!" (15) They say that the priest complained. (16) "Ah! But, Father, it is really not my fault! (17) Really, I did not have anything to do with it. (18) It is because there is a small animal that keeps eating the inside of my watermelons; (19) he is always eating the inside (20) and I don't get anything out of them," (21) they say that she said. (22) "Ah

well! We will kill it then! (23) We will put down a trap," (24) they say that the priest said. (25) "Oh good, thank you very much!" (26) they say that she said. (27) "But bring some wax!" (28) they say that the priest continued. (29) "Good! All right!" (30) they say that she said. (31) So she brought him some wax, (32) and as the story goes, the priest shaped it like a cross, (33) after which he said, (34) "On its very path, that's where you should put it down," (35) they say that the priest said. (36) "All right!" she said, (37) as she took with her the cross. (38) So she went to set it down on the path of the rabbit.

(39) And here comes the little rabbit. (40) There he is, standing in front of the cross and looking at it: (41) "Move out of my way, he you!" (42) they say that he said, (43) but it did not move, apparently. (44) "Get moving, out of my way, (45) or else I'll hit you!" (46) That's how he talked to it, they say. (47) But no one moved. (48) "Get out! (49) or I'll hit you with this hand (50) and who knows where I'll send you!" (51) they say that he kept on. (52) Still no one moved. (53) So he hits it with his hand and the hand stays stuck, (54) since the thing is made of wax. (55) They say that after that he went on: (56) "Let go of my hand! (57) or else you'll get it with my other hand (58) and who knows where that will send you!" (59) they say that the rabbit yelled. (60) And he hits it with his other hand which stays stuck too, apparently. (61)"Let go of my hand! (62) or else I'll hit you with my foot, too!" (63) they say that the rabbit said. (64) "And then, who knows where you'll end up!" (65) they say that he added. (66) And the story goes that he hits it with his foot (67) and that the foot stays stuck, too, (68) and that he hits it with the other foot then. (69) That is how both his feet and hands stayed stuck actually, (70) and how he could not get out any more.

(71) That is when the old woman arrived, (72) while the rabbit was still in the trap (73) since he was immobilized in the cross made of wax. (74) "Well! So you are the one who is giving me all that trouble. (75) Look how small you are and how much trouble you give me! (76) You spoiled so many of my watermelons!" (77) they say that the old woman said. (78) "I am going to bring you some chocolate!" (79) This is apparently what she said, see!

(80) So the rabbit stayed by himself, (81) and that is when the coyote happened by. (82) "He you! What are you doing?" (83) they say that the coyote said. (84) "Oh nothing! I am waiting for my piece of chocolate," (85) they say that the rabbit said. (86) "What kind of chocolate?" (87) "Ah, who knows what kind of chocolate! (88) Maybe it is a very tasty one! (89) But what makes me sad about it is that maybe I won't be able to finish it because I am very small," (92) they say that the rabbit said. (93) "Ah! And even if it is really tasty?" (94) they say that the coyote asked. (95) "Even if it is tasty, I might not be able to finish it myself," (96) they say that the rabbit replied. (97) "He man! Why don't you take my place! (98) That way you can have it all to yourself (99) since you are so big!" (100) they say that the rabbit said to the coyote. (101) "All right, I'll get in," (102) they say that the coyote answered. (103) So the coyote helped the rabbit out (104) and put himself in the cross made of wax.

(105) That is when the old woman arrived. (106) "Ah, miserable! How vicious you are! (107) Once I came (108) and you were very small (109) and this time I come and you are already very big! (110) Have some chocolate!" (111) they say that she said, see! (112) But apparently what it was was a hot wire (113) that she pushed in the rear end of the coyote, (114) and all that was left for the poor little coyote to do was to take off crying, (115) while the rabbit, of course, (116) they say that he had gotten far away already, laughing all the way.

(117) A little later as the coyote was walking, (118) he arrived at a rock. (119) And the story goes that the rabbit was under that rock, very stiff from holding it on his back (120) when the coyote arrived. (121) "Well now, you are finished! (122) All you did was trick me. (123) 'Chocolate,' you said! That's why I stayed (124) when in fact I got hit (125) or rather, I had a wire pushed into my rear end," (126) they say that the coyote said (127) when he stumbled into the rabbit. (128) "He man! Let's not talk about that now, (129) while it will be the end of this village under here, see, (130) if we don't hold on to this rock. (131) Maybe, in fact, you could grab it for a while, (132) while I go and look for a couple of sticks; (133) otherwise this village is finished." (134) They say that the rabbit argued.

(135) The coyote did not think much: (136) "All right, then!" he said back (137) and he put himself under the rock. (138) Just after that the rabbit disappeared. (139) The coyote stayed quite a while, they say, (140) but then he got tired. (141) "May the end come to this village, (142) I don't really care about it!" (143) they say that he said as he freed himself, see! (144) But what happened was that the rock stood by itself (145) because it was, in fact, a cave.

(146) A little later the coyote was on his way again. (147) The story goes that the rabbit was down by the edge of the water (148) when the coyote arrived. (149) "Well, brother, this time your end is near; (150) you tricked me too much." (151) They say that the coyote said, (152) "No, man! Forget that! (153) Instead now look at this delicious cheese down there at the bottom of this water. (154) Apparently if we drank up all the water (155) we could reach it and eat it," (156) they say that the rabbit said. (157) "Is it really true what you say, that this is a cheese?" (158) the coyote added. (159) "Of course it is a cheese!" (160) the rabbit said. (161) But in fact it was only the reflection of the moon that one could see down there in the water. (162) "Well, look how I have made the water come down already," (163) they say that the rabbit said. (164) "All right then!" the coyote said, (165) and apparently he started drinking the water too. (166) They say that he sure drank a lot of water, (167) that he swallowed a lot of it; (168) while the rabbit, he certainly did not drink any. (169) And as the coyote was exploding from so much water (170) they say that the rabbit ran away again, (171) laughing all he could at the coyote.

(172) A little later, the rabbit was on his way again (173) and this time he was perched on top of a coyol tree (174) when the coyote arrived. (175) "Well now, brother, you are finished for good," (175) they say that the coyote said to the rabbit. (176) "No, man! See here? Let's eat some of these little things that I am eating," (178) they say that the rabbit suggested. (179) "Ah! Let's taste them!" (180) they say that the coyote said. (181) "No! Let's eat them!" (182) they say that the rabbit insisted. (183) And he ate the seeds of the coyol. (184) "Ah! taste how delicious they are!" (185) "He you! What are you eating here?" (186) the coyote asked. (187) "Come on man! Don't you know? (188) This is really easy indeed. (189) The seeds of my testicles that I have pounded out, that's what I am eating here," (190) they say that the rabbit answered. (191) "Liar! You are kidding me." (192) "Pound yours out and eat them!" (193) they say that the rabbit insisted. (194) "Are you really saying the truth?" (195) "Yes, only the truth. (196) See the rock with which I pounded them? (197) the rabbit said.

(198) A little while later: (199) "If that's what it is then, I will pound mine out too," (200) they say that the coyote announced. (201) And so the story goes that he pounded out his testicles (202) and that is how the coyote finally met his death, (203) and that the rabbit finally won.

Grammatical Notes

The Jacaltec language has been described by Day (1973) and Craig (1977). Two complementary grammatical sketches can also be found preceding the Jacaltec texts edited by Day (1976) and Craig (1976) in the first issue of IJAL-NATS Mayan Issue I.

1. Transcription System

The text is written in the official Spanish-based Guatemalan orthography which is familiar to literate Jacaltec speakers.

The phonemic inventory of Jacaltec in both the Guatemalan orthography and the corresponding phonetic notation where they differ is presented in the diagrams below:

vowels:				
	i			u
		e	o	
		a		

consonants:

p	t		c/qu [k]		7 [ʔ]
b' [p']	t'		c/qu' [k']	k' [q']	
b	d		g		
	tz [¢]	ch [č]			
	tz' [¢']	ch' [č']			
		tx [č̣]			
		tx' [č̣']			
f	s	x̌ [š]	j [x]		h
		x [ṣ̌]			
m	n		ñ [ŋ]		
	l				
	r				
w		y			

b , d , g are found in Spanish loan words only.

Word initial glottal stops are not marked. Glottalized consonants take an apostrophe C' while glottal stops are represented as 7.

Subscript $_0$ in the Jacaltec text means that the word has no translation in English. Parenthesized English words have no morphological correspondence in Jacaltec.

Stress occurs on the first syllable of a stem, and on the last syllable of a phrase except in questions and exclamations.

Spanish loan words keep their original lexical stress. They may acquire a stem initial stress but never take a phrase final stress.

2. Noun Classifiers

Jacaltec has a set of noun classifiers which classify most of the concrete world. Examples found in the text are: no7 'animal' as in (0.1) no7 conejo 'rabbit', (0.3) no7 oj 'coyote', (18.4) no7 nok' 'animal', (27.4) no7 ixcab' 'bee wax'; te7 'wood, plant' as in (3.6) te7 sandiya 'watermelon', (173.6) te7 map 'coyol tree or fruit'; ix 'woman, non-kin' as in (3.8) ix ixmam 'old woman'; ya7 'respected, older person' as in (4.10) ya7 palc 'priest'; ch'en 'rock, glass, metal' as in (112.3) ch'en alambra 'wire', (118.5) ch'en ch'en 'rock', (145.2) ch'en ñach'en 'cave'; ha7 'water' as in (147.6) ha7 ha7 'water'.

Noun classifiers function as pronouns for the nouns they classify, as in (9.4-5-6) spohnitoj ya7 te7 'he(respected person) broke it(fruit) open'.

3. Verbal Inflections

3.1 Aspect marking

ch(i) is the incompletive marker as in (3.1) chi b'eyc'oj 'goes by'; (17.4) chi wute 'I do it', (27.2) cha witij 'you bring'.

The San Marcos dialect of Jacaltec further distinguishes in the completive aspect between recent past and remote past. Thus, recent past is indicated by ma as in: (11.2) ma xa slotij 'had already just eaten; (13.4) ma hin ha wa7 engañar 'you have just fooled me'. Remote past is indicated by x- as in: (31.1) xinitoj 'brought', (38.1) xto 'went'.

3.2 Person Markers

Both the subject and the object inflect on the verb. In independent and main clauses, the assignment of person markers follows an ergative pattern of case assignment. Subjects of transitive verbs inflect with an ergative marker, while subjects of intransitive verbs and objects of transitive verbs inflect with an absolutive marker.

The ergative set (E)

with vowel initial stems is:

1 sg	w-	1 pl	j-
2	ha w-	2	he y-
3	y-	3	y-

with consonant initial stems is:

1 sg	hin	1 pl	cu
2	ha	2	he
3	s-	3	s-

The absolutive set (A) is:

1 sg	(h)in	1 pl	(h)oñ
2	(h)ach	2	(h)ex
3	Ø	3	Ø

Examples found in the text are:

(13.4) ma hin ha wa7 engañar
asp A1 E2-give
'you just fooled me'

(17.4) chi-Ø-w-ute
asp-A3-E1-do
'I do it'

(18.6) chi-Ø-b'ey-c'oj
asp-A3-goes-pass by
'he goes by'

(48.2) ch-ach eli
asp-A2 go out
'you go out'

(2.4-5) listocanoj Ø no7
smart A3 N.cl.(he,animal)
'he is smart'

(99.3-4) nimejal hach
big A2
'you are big'

The ergative is also the possessive marker as in: (5.4) ha sandiya 'your watermelon'; (125.4) hin yutz 'my rear end' and the marker of objects of preposition as in (7.4) ta wet 'to you'; (10.3-4) yul te7 '(its) inside of it'; (129.5) jalaн 'under us'. Furthermore, all subjects of aspectless embedded clauses are marked ergative as shown in:

(39.2-3-4) haxa y-apni no7
when E3-arrive he
'when he arrived'

3.3 Directionals

Most verbs of movement and action may take directional enclitics. The inventory of directionals found in the text is:

tij 'toward here' (3, 11, 19, 27, 78, etc....)
toj 'toward there' (9, 18, 20, 31, 37, etc....)
c! (oj) 'to the side, passing by' (3, 72, 84, 107, 139, etc.,..)
c (oj) 'in, against' (19, 50, 64, 104, 113, etc....)
il (oj) 'out, away from' (3, 19, 103, 121, 129, etc....)
ay (oj) 'down' (23, 38, 147, 161)
pax 'again, back' (62, 65, 67, 137, 138, etc....)
can (oj) 'once and for all, be left' (53, 67, 69, 75, 76, etc....)

4. Narrative Style

Characteristic of the narrative style of the text is the frequent use of some sentence particles and of coordinated sentences.

The sentence particles are: ab' 'they say' an uninflected form (1, 3, 4, 9, etc....) and the compound xihab' 'they say that X said' which takes the incompletive marker x found in the Jacaltenango dialect of Jacaltec (6, 8, 15, 21, etc....), xin 'then' (4, 9, 20, 25, etc....), la 'see!' an exclamatory expression (4, 5, 9, 79, etc....).

Except for the sentences coordinated with the conjunction i7 'and' (2, 4, 14), all the instances of coordination express or imply a time sequence. Sequential coordination is made explicit with the post sequentive conjunction cat 'and then' (132, 155, 192) and the presequentive conjunction lahwi 'and after' (33, 140). However, in the majority of cases, it is implicit in the use of aspectless verbs alone (37, 53, 68, 103, 104, 118, 137, etc....).

Aspectless verbs are characterized by their lack of aspect marker, their ergative inflection for all subjects, and a suffix -n(i) if they are transitive, as in:

(37.1-2) Ø-y-i-ni-toj ix
A3-E3-carry-suff-away N.cl/she
'and she took it'

(137.1-2) y-oc-pax-toj no7
E3-enter-also-away N cl/he
'and he got in there too'

5. Miscellaneous Morphemes:

han is a clause final particle which signals the presence of a first person in the clause. It is not necessarily an emphatic particle and has no correspondence in English (13, 14, 16, 17, etc....).

oj is an irrealis suffix which is found in non-specific NPs (4.9, 20.3, 23.2), in negation (16.6, 17.2), and with directionals (2.4, 3.2). The vowel o is subject to vowel harmony.

6. Spanish Loan Words

Spanish loan words are numerous in Mayan languages. The ones found in the text represent examples of noun, adjective, conjunction, and verb borrowing.

Compare the older borrowings exhibiting phonological adaptation: (4.10) pale < padre 'priest', (7.3) tiyox̌ < Dios 'God' to the most recent ones, with minimal or no adaptation: (0.1) conejo 'rabbit', (3.6) sandiya < sandia 'watermelon', (78.4) chocolate 'chocolate', (23.2) trampa 'trap, trick', (112-3) alambra < alambre 'wire', (153.5) queso 'cheese', (161.4) luna 'moon'.

The vocative forms and the interjective adjectives are: (5.1) padre 'Father', (97.1) hombres 'man!' (borrowed in the plural), (2.4) listo 'smart', (106.2) jodidos 'cursed' (borrowed in the plural), (106.4) mañoso 'vicious'.

Verbs are borrowed in the infinitive form and used in a verbal compound with the verb a'a 'to give' in an auxiliary function:

(13.4) ma hin ha <u>wa7</u> engañar engañar 'to fool'.

REFERENCES

ABBEY, EDWARD. 1968. Desert solitaire. New York: McGraw Hill.

AOKI, HARUO. 1970. Nez Perce grammar. (UCPL, 62.) Berkeley and Los Angeles.

BARCLAY, LILLIAN ELIZABETH. 1938. The coyote: animal and folk-character. Coyote wisdom, ed. by J. Frank Dobie et al. (Texas Folklore Society publications, 14), 36-103. Austin: Texas Folklore Society.

BARRETT, SAMUEL. 1908. The ethno-geography of the Pomo and neighboring Indians. (UCPAAE, 6.) Berkeley.

———. 1933. Pomo myths. Bulletin of the Public Museum, City of Milwaukee, vol. 15.

———. 1952. Material aspects of Pomo culture. Bulletin of the Public Museum, City of Milwaukee, vol. 20.

BENEDICT, RUTH. 1926. Serrano tales. Journal of American Folklore 30.1-17.

BRIGHT, WILLIAM. 1954. The travels of Coyote, a Karok myth. Kroeber Anthro. Soc. Papers 11.1-16. [Reprinted as 'Karok Coyote stories' in The American Indian reader: Literature, ed. by J. Henry, 79-91 (San Francisco: Indian Historian Press, 1973).]

———. 1957. The Karok language. (UCPL, 13.) Berkeley and Los Angeles.

———. 1972. Coyote lays down the law. Language in American Indian Education, Winter 1972, pp. 96-8. Salt Lake City: University of Utah.

———. 1978. Coyote steals fire: a Karok myth. To appear in Northern California texts, ed. by Victor Golla and Shirley Silver (IJAL Native American Texts Series).

BUNZEL, RUTH L. 1932a. Zuni origin myths. Bureau of American Ethnology, Annual Reports, 47.545-610.

———. 1932b. Zuni ritual poetry. Bureau of American Ethnology, Annual Reports, 47.611-836.

———. 1933. Zuni texts. (Publications of the American Ethnological Society, 15.) New York: Columbia University Press.

BURGESS, DON. 1970. Tarahumara phonology. Studies in language and linguistics 1969-1970, pp. 45-66. El Paso: University of Texas.

———. MSa. A grammatical sketch of Western Tarahumara. To appear in Uto-Aztecan grammatical sketches II, ed. by R. Langacker.

———. MSb. Tarahumara folklore--a study in cultural secrecy. To appear in Secrecy--a cross-cultural perspective, ed. by S. Tefft.

CALLAGHAN, CATHERINE A. 1963. A grammar of the Lake Miwok language. (268 pages on microfilm).

———. 1965. Lake Miwok dictionary. (UCPL, 39.) Berkeley and Los Angeles.

CARLSON, BARRY F. 1972. A grammar of Spokane: a Salish language of Eastern Washington. Ph.D. dissertation in Linguistics, University of Hawaii. (Also University of Hawaii Working Papers in Linguistics 4:4, June 1972.)

CHUNG, SANDRA. 1976. Compound tense markers in Tolkapaya. In Redden (ed.) 1976:119-28.

CRAIG, COLETTE G. 1976. A Jacaltec comedia. In Furbee-Losee (ed.), pp. 105-22.

———. 1977. The structure of Jacaltec. Austin: University of Texas Press.

CRAWFORD, JAMES M. 1976a. The Cocopa auxiliary verb ya· <u>be located, happen</u>. In Redden (ed.) 1976:18-28.

CRAWFORD, JUDITH G. 1976. The reduction of idú: <u>be</u> in Mohave. In Redden (ed.) 1976:45-54.

CROOK, DONALD E. 1976. Yuman *<u>t</u>. In Redden (ed.) 1976:35:44.

DAY, CHRISTOPHER. 1973. The Jacaltec language. (Language science monographs, 12.) Bloomington: Indiana University.

———. 1976. Someone else's dog: a Jacaltec story. In Furbee-Losee (ed.),pp.98-104.

DEMETRACOPOULOU, DOROTHY, and CORA DU BOIS. 1932. A study of Wintu mythology. Journal of American Folklore 45.375-500.

DOBIE, J. FRANK. 1949. The voice of the coyote. Boston: Little, Brown & Co. [Reprinted, Bison Books: Lincoln, University of Nebraska Press, 1961.]

DOZIER, EDWARD P. 1951. Resistance to acculturation and assimilation in an Indian pueblo. American Anthropologist 53.56-66.

———. 1953. Tewa II: verb structure. IJAL 19.118-27.

———. 1954. The Hopi-Tewa of Arizona. (UCPAAE, 44:3.) Berkeley and Los Angeles.

———. 1955. Kinship and linguistic change among the Arizona Tewa. IJAL 21.242-57.

DU BOIS, CORA. 1935. Wintu ethnography. (UCPAAE, 36:1.) Berkeley.

———, and DOROTHY DEMETRACOPOULOU [LEE]. 1931. Wintu myths. (UCPAAE, 28:5.) Berkeley.

EGGAN, FRED. 1950. Social organization of the western pueblos. Chicago: University of Chicago Press.

ENGLAND, NORA. 1975. Mam grammar in outline. University of Florida dissertation.

FARRAND, LIVINGSTON. 1917. Sahaptin tales. Memoirs of the American Folklore Society 11.135-79.

FEWKES, JESSE WALTER. 1899. The winter solstice altars at Hano. American Anthropologist n.s. 1.251-76.

FREELAND, L. S. 1947. Western Miwok texts with linguistic sketch. IJAL 13.31-46.

FURBEE-LOSEE, LOUANNA (ed.) 1976. Mayan texts I. (IJAL Native American Texts Series, 1:1.) Chicago: University of Chicago Press.

GIFFORD, EDWARD W. 1922. California kinship terminologies. (UCPAAE, 18:1.) Berkeley.

GILL, DON. 1970. The coyote and the sequential occupants of the Los Angeles Basin. AA 72.821-6.

GLOVER, BONNIE. 1977. Tolkapaya demonstratives. MS.

GOLDSCHMIDT, WALTER. 1951. Nomlaki ethnography. (UCPAAE, 42:4.) Berkeley and Los Angeles.

HALPERN, A. M. 1946-47. Yuma I-VI. IJAL 12.25-33, 147-51, 204-12; 13.18-30, 92-107, 147-66.

———. 1976. Kukumat became sick--a Yuma text. In Langdon (ed.), 5-25.

HARDY, HEATHER. 1977a. The development of the Pai vowel system. MS.

———. 1977b. Temporality, conditionality, counterfactuality, and contrast in Tolkapaya Yavapai. MS.

———, and LYNN GORDON. 1977. Paper presented at the Second Hokan/Yuman Workshop, Salt Lake City.

HARRINGTON, JOHN P. 1910. A brief description of the Tewa language. American Anthropologist n.s. 7.497-504.

———. 1947. Three Tewa texts. IJAL 13.112-8.

HILL, KENNETH C. 1967. A grammar of the Serrano language. Los Angeles: University of California dissertation.

———. 1969. Some implications of Serrano phonology. Papers from the 9th Regional Meeting, Chicago Linguistic Society, 357-65.

HINTON, LEANNE. 1976. The tar baby story: a Diegueño text. In Langdon (ed.), 101-6.

———, and MARGARET LANGDON. 1976. Pronominal prefixes in La Huerta Diegueño. Hokan studies: papers from the 1st Conference on Hokan Languages, ed. by Margaret Langdon and Shirley Silver, 113-27. The Hague: Mouton.

JACOBS, MELVILLE. 1929. Northwest Sahaptin texts, 1. (University of Washington publications in anthropology, 4:2.) Seattle.

———. 1931. A sketch of Northern Sahaptin grammar. (University of Washington publications in anthropology, 4:2.) Seattle.

———. 1934. Northwest Sahaptin texts. (Columbia University contributions to anthropology, 19:1.) New York.

———. 1937. Northwest Sahaptin texts. (Columbia University contributions to anthropology, 19:2.) New York.

KENDALL, MARTHA B. 1972. Selected problems in Yavapai syntax. Bloomington: Indiana University dissertation.

———. 1974. Relative clause formation and topicalization in Yavapai. IJAL 40.89-101.

———. 1975. The /-k/, /-m/ problem in Yavapai syntax. IJAL 41.1-9.

———. 1976. Selected problems in Yavapai syntax: the Verde Valley dialect. New York: Garland.

———. 1977. Fission and fusion in Yuman languages. MS.

———, and EMILY-SUE SLOANE. 1976. Skara kʔa·mca: the lofty wanderer. In Langdon (ed.), 63-83.

KRIENDLER, JACK. 1977. Approaches to relative clauses in Tolkapaya Yavapai. UCLA Master's thesis.

KROEBER, A. L. 1917. California kinship systems. (UCPAAE, 12:9.) Berkeley.

———. 1925. Handbook of the Indians of California. (Bureau of American Ethnology, Bulletin 78.) Washington, DC: Government Printing Office. [Reprinted by California Book Company, Berkeley, 1967; and by Dover Books, New York, 1977.]

KROSKRITY, PAUL V. 1976. The ethnohistorical significance of Arizona Tewa <u>hen-ki-khyaw</u> (war dance songs). Presented at the 75th Annual Meeting of the American Anthropological Association.

———. 1977. Aspects of Arizona Tewa language structure and language use. Bloomington: Indiana University dissertation.

———. 1978. On the lexical integrity of Arizona Tewa /-dí/: a principled choice between homophony and polysemy. IJAL (to appear).

LANGDON, MARGARET. 1974. Auxiliary verb constructions in Yuman languages. Paper presented to the American Anthropological Association, Mexico City.

——— (ed.) 1976. Yuman texts. (IJAL Native American Texts Series, 1:3.) Chicago: University of Chicago Press.

———, and PAMELA MUNRO. 1975. Subject and (switch) reference in Yuman. Paper presented to the Linguistic Society of America, San Francisco.

LEVI-STRAUSS, CLAUDE. 1971. L'homme nu. Paris: Plon.

LEYDET, FRANÇOIS. 1977. The coyote: defiant songdog of the West. San Francisco: Chronicle Books.

LOUNSBURY, FLOYD G. 1964. A formal account of the Crow- and Omaha-type kinship terminologies. Explorations in cultural anthropology: essays in honor of George Peter Murdock, ed. by Ward H. Goodenough, 351-93. McGraw-Hill: New York.

LUMHOLTZ, CARL. 1902. Unknown Mexico, I. New York: Scribner's.

MCKERN, W. C. 1922. Functional families of the Patwin. (UCPAAE, 13:7.) Berkeley.

MCLENDON, SALLY. 1975. A grammar of Eastern Pomo. (UCPL, 74.) Berkeley and Los Angeles.

———. 1977a. Cultural presuppositions and discourse analysis: patterns of presupposition and assertion of information in Eastern Pomo and Russian narration. Georgetown University Round Table on Languages and Linguistics, 1977: Linguistics and Anthropology, ed. by Muriel Saville-Troike.

———. 1977b. Ethnographic and historical sketch of the Eastern Pomo and their neighbors the Southeastern Pomo. (University of California Archaeological Research Facility, Contributions, 37.) Berkeley.

———. 1977c. Bear kills her own daughter-in-law, Deer. In Northern California texts, edited by Victor Golla and Shirley Silver. (IJAL Native American Texts Series.)

———. MS. A sketch of Eastern Pomo. To appear in the Handbook of North American Indians, Language volume, edited by Ives Goddard. Washington, DC: Smithsonian Institution.

———, and MICHAEL J. LOWY. 1978. Eastern Pomo and Southeastern Pomo. To appear in the Handbook of North American Indians, vol. 8, California, edited by R. F. Heizer. Washington, DC: Smithsonian Institution.

MARES TRIAS, ALBINO. 1975. Jena ra'icha ralámuli alué 'ya muchígame chiquime níliga. Aquí relata la gente de antes lo que pasaba en su tiempo. México: Instituto Lingüístico de Verano.

MATTINA, ANTHONY. 1973. Colville grammatical structure. Ph.D. dissertation in linguistics, University of Hawaii. (Also University of Hawaii Working Papers in Linguistics 5:4, April 1973.)

MERRIAM, C. HART. 1910. The dawn of the world: myths and weird tales told by the Mewan Indians of California. Cleveland: Arthur H. Clark Co.

MILLER, WICK R. 1967. Uto-Aztecan cognate sets. (UCPL, 48.) Berkeley and Los Angeles.

MORVILLO, ANTHONY. 1891. Grammatica linguae Numipu. Desmet: Indian Boys' Press.

———. 1895. A dictionary of the Nez Perce language. Part I, English-Nez Perce. St. Ignatius Mission, Montana: St. Ignatius Mission Press.

MUÑOZ, MAURILIO. 1965. Leyendas tarahumaras. Mexico: Instituto Nacional Indigenista.

MUNRO, PAMELA. 1976. Subject copying, predicate raising, and auxiliarization: the Mojave evidence. IJAL 42.99-112.

———. 1976. Topics in Mojave syntax. New York: Garland.

———. 1977a. From existential to copula: the history of Yuman BE. Mechanisms of syntactic change, ed. by Charles N. Li, 445-90. Austin:University of Texas Press.

———. 1977b. The Yuman *n Prefix. In Redden (ed.) 1977:52-9.

———, and NELLIE BROWN. 1976. A Mojave dictionary. Typescript.

NEWMAN, STANLEY. 1958. Zuni dictionary. (Indiana University Research Center in Anthropology, Folklore,and Linguistics, Publication 6.) Bloomington.

———. 1964. Comparison of Zuni and California Penutian. IJAL 30.1-13.

———. 1965. Zuni grammar. (University of New Mexico Publications in Anthropology, 14.) Albuquerque.

NEZ PERCE TRIBE OF IDAHO. 1972. Nu mee poom tit wah tit (Nez Perce legends). [N.p.]

———. 1973. Noon nee me poo (We, the Nez Perces). [N.p.]

ORNSTEIN, JACOB. 1976. Sociolinguistic constraints on lexical borrowing in Tarahumara: explorations in 'langue' and 'parole' and 'existential bilingualism--an approximation'. Anthropological Linguistics 18.70-93.

PARSONS, ELSIE CLEWS. 1926. The ceremonial calendar of the Tewa of Arizona. American Anthropologist 28.209-29.

PHILLIPS, EMILY M. 1930. Red Dawn. The Washington Farmer (June 12ff.)

PHINNEY, ARCHIE. 1934. Nez Perce texts. (Columbia University contributions to anthropology, 25.) New York.

PITKIN, HARVEY. 1963. Wintu grammar. Berkeley: University of California dissertation.

———. 1977a. Wintu grammar (revised). Submitted to UCPL.

———. 1977b. Wintu dictionary. Submitted to UCPL.

———. 1978. Coyote and Bullhead. In Northern California texts, edited by Victor Golla and Shirley Silver. (IJAL Native American Texts Series).

RADIN, PAUL. 1932. Patwin texts. Unpublished manuscript. American Philosophical Society Library.

———. 1956. The trickster: a study in American Indian mythology. New York: Pantheon. [Reprinted, New York: Schocken Books, 1972.]

RAY, VERNE F. 1939. Cultural relations in the Plateau of northwestern America. (Publications of the Frederick Webb Hodge Anniversary Publications Fund, 3.) Los Angeles: Southwest Museum.

———. 1942. Plateau. UC Anthropological Records 8.99-262.

REDDEN, JAMES E. 1976. (ed.) Proceedings of the 1st Yuman Languages Workshop. (University Museum Studies, 7.) Carbondale: Southern Illinois University.

——— (ed.) 1977. Proceedings of the 1976 Hokan/Yuman Workshop. (University Museum Studies, 11.) Carbondale: Southern Illinois University.

REED, ERIK K. 1943. The origins of Hano Pueblo. El Palacio 50.73-76.

RIGSBY, BRUCE. 1975. Sahaptin grammar. To appear in the Languages volume of the new Handbook of North American Indians. Washington, DC: Smithsonian Institution.

RYDEN, HOPE. 1975. God's dog. New York: Coward, McCann & Geoghegan.

SCHLICHTER, ALICE. 1977. Wintu dictionary. MS. Department of Linguistics, University of California, Berkeley.

SHATERIAN, ALAN. MS. Yavapai phonology, with lexicon.

SHIPLEY, WILLIAM. 1963. Maidu texts and dictionary. (UCPL, 33.) Berkeley and Los Angeles.

SLATER, CAROL E. 1977. The semantics of switch-reference in K^{w}itsa:n. Proceedings of the 3rd Annual Meeting of the Berkeley Linguistic Society, ed. by K. Whistler et al., pp. 24-36.

SMITH-STARK, THOM. 1976. Jilotepequeño Pocomam texts. In Furbee-Losee (ed.), 72-87.

SNYDER, GARY. 1977. The incredible survival of Coyote. In his The old ways: six essays, 67-93. San Francisco: City Lights.

SPEIRS, ANNA. 1974. Classificatory verb stems in Tewa. Studies in Linguistics 24.45-64.

SPEIRS, RANDALL H. 1966. Some aspects of the structure of Rio Grande Tewa. Buffalo: SUNY dissertation.

———. 1972. Number in Tewa. Studies in linguistics in honor of George L. Trager, ed. by M. E. Smith, 479-87. The Hague: Mouton.

SPINDEN, HERBERT JOSEPH. 1908a. The Nez Perce Indians. Memoirs of the American Anthropological Association 2.165-274.

———. 1908b. Myths of the Nez Perce Indians. Journal of American Folklore 21.13-23, 149-58.

STEVENSON, MATILDA COXE. 1904. The Zuni Indians. (Bureau of American Ethnology, Annual Report 23.) Washington, DC.

TEDLOCK, DENNIS. 1971. On the translation of style in oral narrative. Journal of American Folklore 84.114-33.

———. 1972. Finding the center: narrative poetry of the Zuni Indians. New York: Dial.

———. 1976. From prayer to reprimand. Language in religious practice, ed. by W. J. Samarin, 72-83. Rowley, MA: Newbury House.

———. 1977. Toward an oral poetics. New Literary History 8.507-19.

TEIT, JAMES A. 1928. The Middle Columbia Salish. University of Washington publications in anthropology 2.85-128.

TOELKEN, BARRE. 1969. The pretty languages of Yellowman: genre, mode, and texture in Navaho Coyote narratives. Genre 2.211-35.

VOGT, HANS. 1940. The Kalispel language. Oslo: Det Norske Videnskaps-Akademi.

VAN WORMER, JOE. 1964. The world of the coyote. Philadelphia: Lippincott.

WALKER, DEWARD E., JR. 1968. Conflict and schism in Nez Perce acculturation. Pullman: Washington State University Press.

WHISTLER, KENNETH W. 1978. Deer and Bear children: A Patwin text. To appear in Northern California texts, ed. by Shirley Silver and Victor Golla (IJAL Native American Texts Series).

YAMADA, JENI. 1977. Tolkapaya passives: a second preliminary look. MS.

YEGERLEHNER, JOHN F. 1957. Phonology and morphology of Hopi-Tewa. Bloomington: Indiana University dissertation.

———. 1959a. Arizona Tewa I: phonemes. IJAL 25.1-7.

———. 1959b. Arizona Tewa II: person markers. IJAL 25.75-81.